cram

International Propaganda

INTERNATIONAL PROPAGANDA

Its Legal and Diplomatic Control

L. JOHN MARTIN

University of Minnesota Press, Minneapolis

))

Acknowledgments

F OR permission to quote passages from the books, articles, and periodicals named below, I am indebted to the following copyright holders: Appleton-Century-Crofts, Inc., New York: Charles G. Fenwick, *International Law*, 3rd edition, 1948. *American Journal of International Law*, Washington, D.C.: Charles G. Fenwick, "Intervention: Individual and Collective," October 1945; Charles G. Fenwick, "Intervention by Way of Propaganda," October 1941; Lawrence Preuss, "International Responsibility for Hostile Propaganda against Foreign States," October 1934; Vernon B. VanDyke, "Responsibility of States for International Propaganda," January 1940. Butterworth and Company, Ltd., London: *Halsbury's Laws of England: Being a Complete Statement of the Whole Law of England*, 2nd edition by Viscount Hailsham, 1931. Carnegie Endowment for International Peace: Telford Taylor, "Nuremberg Trials, War Crimes and International Law," *International Conciliation*, No. 450, 1949. Clarendon Press, Oxford: J. L. Brierly, *The Law of Nations: An Introduction to the International Law of Peace*, 4th edition, 1949. The Foundation Press, Brooklyn: Edwin Dickinson, *Cases and Materials on International Law*, 1950. Georgetown University Press, Washington, D.C.: Leonard Shapiro, *Soviet Treaty Series*, Vol. 1, 1950. Harvard University Press, Cambridge: Louis L. Jaffe, *Judicial Aspects of Foreign Relations: In Particular of the Recognition of Foreign Powers*, 1933. Hollis and Carter, Ltd., London: Bronislaw Kusnierz, *Stalin and the Poles: An Indictment of the Soviet Leaders*, 1949. Little, Brown and Company, Boston: Charles Cheyney Hyde, *International Law, Chiefly as Interpreted and Applied by the United States*, 1945. Longmans, Green and Co., London: Oppenheim's *International Law*, 5th and 7th editions

v

by H. Lauterpacht, 1935, 1937, 1948, 1952. The Macmillan Company, New York: Philip C. Jessup, *A Modern Law of Nations — An Introduction*, 1950. New York University Press, New York: Clyde Eagleton, *The Responsibility of States in International Law*, 1928. The Open Road Press, Inc., Mays Landing, New Jersey: Theodore Schroeder, *Where Speech Is Not Free — in the U.S.A.: An Appeal to the Record*, 1944. *Recueil des Cours de l'Academie de Droit International*, The Hague: John B. Whitton, "Propaganda and International Law," 1948. *Reporter* magazine, New York: Arthur Mayer, "A Movie Exhibitor Looks at Censorship," March 2, 1954. Stevens and Sons, Ltd., London: Hans Kelsen, *The Law of the United Nations*, 1950. Time, Inc., New York: "Russia — Nice Old Gentleman," *Time*, December 1, 1941. UNESCO, Paris: Fernand Terrou and Lucien Solal, *Legislation for Press, Film and Radio*, 1951 (distributed in the United States through UNESCO Publications Center, 801 Third Avenue, New York 22). University of North Carolina Press, Chapel Hill: Ruth E. McMurry and Muna Lee, *The Cultural Approach, Another Way in International Relations*, 1947. West Publishing Company, St. Paul: Manley O. Hudson, *Cases and Other Materials on International Law*, 1936.

Contents

	INTRODUCTION	3
1	HISTORICAL BACKGROUND	5
2	DEFINITION OF PROPAGANDA	10
3	PROPAGANDA AGENCIES	21
4	THE TEACHINGS OF THE PUBLICISTS	55
5	CONTROL BY INTERNATIONAL AGREEMENT	62
6	CONTROL BY MUNICIPAL LAW	109
7	EXTRATERRITORIAL CONTROL OF PROPAGANDA	164
8	CONTROL BY DIPLOMACY	172
9	INTERNATIONAL PROPAGANDA IN RETROSPECT AND PROSPECT	199
	NOTES	211
	INDEX	257

International Propaganda

Introduction

PROPAGANDA is a term that has become so commonplace, hardly a day passes that it is not mentioned in the newspapers or tossed about in conversation. Its meaning ranges from "something somebody is trying to 'put across' on a person" to "a systematic attempt to influence opinion or attitude in the interest of some cause." It is in a sense closer to the latter definition that legislators tend to use the word. Yet even the legislator, as well as the social scientist, cannot avoid the connotations of the former definition. The politician has an uneasy feeling about using the word to describe the activities of his own group; he discredits the activities of his opponents by calling these activities propaganda.

While its definition is hazy, propaganda is nonetheless potent. The United States would not plan to spend an estimated $100,000,000 in 1958 on international propaganda if it did not believe so. The Soviet Union spends an even greater amount, and there is hardly a state so poor that it does not earmark some funds to be used in an attempt to influence foreign opinions and attitudes in its favor. Most governments also encourage their citizens to engage in private propaganda aimed at promoting the good of the nation.

Besides putting all this money into international propaganda, states have gone out of the way to sign treaties, especially since World War I, making important concessions to other states in exchange for a vague freedom from propaganda. Legislative bodies have drafted hundreds of statutes in an attempt to keep propaganda in check. Diplomats have cajoled, pleaded, threatened, and bargained to ward off the propaganda activities of other states. Publicists have argued vigorously on whether international propaganda, public or private, is admissible in international law.

3

In other words, the world is convinced today that propaganda is no mere talk. Propaganda is something that can be implanted in the minds of people, and is sufficiently potent to win battles without a fight — or to start a fight, if that is its aim. Propaganda can be dangerous for certain states at certain times, because it introduces controversy where no controversy exists, thus weakening controls. Obedience to authority is assured only where singlemindedness exists. Propaganda can cast doubts into the minds of people. It can also be used to promote international goodwill. And many international agreements have been signed, and resolutions adopted, calling upon the signatories to conduct various types of propaganda to this end.

While books and articles have been written on international propaganda and its control, few have examined the term closely enough. Furthermore, the art of international propaganda has been refined in recent years and the attitude toward it has changed, especially since World War II; so that a fresh look at the activity and its control is significant at this time.

An account of legal and diplomatic maneuvers in the attempt to control international propaganda — especially when they are so numerous and monotonously repetitive — is not always fascinating reading. But justice cannot be done to the topic without bringing out the very frequency of certain attempts. Wherever possible, similar legal provisions after a first mention have been put into notes at the end of the book.

The history of international propaganda activities is examined briefly to give the topic perspective, and the propaganda agencies of the United States, Britain, and the Soviet Union — the most active states in the field — are described to show the scope of such activities in the world today. The definition of propaganda has received extensive treatment; it is a decisive factor in the conclusion reached in this book — that international propaganda has little chance of being controlled or adjudicated at the international level. One exception is made, however. Should we ever be involved in another international war, it is almost certain that propaganda cases will come before a war crimes tribunal for adjudication.

At present, international propaganda is controllable and controlled by domestic courts, under the municipal laws of states. While the chapter on the municipal control of propaganda by no means covers all the domestic legislation on the subject, a broad enough selection of the laws of the various states has been included to show how well governments have fortified themselves against the darts of international propaganda.

1

Historical Background

IT DOESN'T make much difference who first invented the term "propaganda." Suffice it to say that it has long had bad connotations. Etymologists trace the term to Pope Gregory XV. It was he who founded the *Sacre Congregatio De Propaganda Fide* in 1622 to do missionary work abroad. Already in the early nineteenth century the term had acquired its present-day derogatory connotations. W. T. Brande's *Dictionary of Science, Literature and Art*, published in 1842, says of propaganda: "Derived from this celebrated society, the name propaganda is applied in political language as a term of reproach to secret associations for the spread of opinions and principles which are viewed by most governments with horror and aversion." It should be remembered that it is some time before a lexicographer takes note of popular usage.[1]

International propaganda activities, on the other hand, are as old as history itself. One reads of the success of Joshua's propaganda in the Old Testament, and how he convinced the Gibeonites that their land had been promised to the Israelites by Jehovah. Fighting under these circumstances, the Gibeonites decided, was useless. On the other hand, Sennacherib's propaganda was unsuccessful with the Israelites, and when the intelligence officers of his ill-fated army "cried with a loud voice in the Jews' speech unto the people of Jerusalem, that were on the wall, to affright them, and to trouble them; that they might take the city," they did not meet with much success.

History provides many another example of both successful and unsuccessful propaganda. Propaganda was not recognized as a powerful force and was largely ignored, however, until about the time of the French

Revolution. Among the first international incidents connected with propaganda was the one that arose out of the wartime activities of the French revolutionary soldiers. These were sent into battle armed with slogans of *Guerre aux châteaux, paix aux chaumières*! It was Robespierre's contention that France was fighting to liberate the entire universe. To assist the men in the field, the French National Assembly promised to help all nations ready to fight for their liberty, and it charged the executive power to advise French generals to assist "all citizens who have been, or shall in the future be, persecuted in the cause of freedom." [2]

The international incident was caused by Britain's reaction to this unusual activity on the part of the French. King George III spoke of the designs abroad "to destroy our happy Constitution" and "to overturn all order and all government." He told Parliament, "I cannot but view with serious disquietude the increasing indications that attempts are being made to create disorder in foreign lands with no regard for the rights of neutral states, but aiming at conquests and self-aggrandizement." [3]

The French were by no means certain that they were doing the right thing. They tried to explain away their propaganda, comparing it to Cromwell's similar activities and saying that this was only a reprisal against the illegal intervention of the allies. [4] However, they felt guilty enough to repeal the November Decree on April 13, 1793; and Britain was told that France would disavow any agent in a friendly country who sought to provoke a revolt against the established order, for this would be a violation of international law. [5] As a matter of fact, in its constitution of June 1793, France declared expressly that it had no intention of interfering with the government of any other nation. [6]

This was the beginning of world consciousness of international propaganda. Other incidents followed; but it was not until World War I that systematic propaganda was actually engaged in. It was then discovered that total war could be fought only by attacking the minds as well as the bodies of men. Without the invention and universal use of wireless communication, this would have been impossible. But by a not unusual historical coincidence, the Germans found that they were cut off from the rest of the world at the beginning of the war because the Allies controlled the cables. They were therefore forced to turn to wireless communication, and by 1915 amateurs and agents abroad were receiving daily news bulletins from Germany.

The Allies, too, saw the power of wireless communication, and they broadcast Wilson's Fourteen Points all over the world. Later the Bolsheviks used radio for revolutionary purposes. They sent revolutionary messages to all the world, and their broadcasts during the Brest-Litovsk peace negotiations were an attempt to bring pressure to bear on the German leaders. The propaganda activities of Béla Kun, the Hungarian Communist leader, after World War I worried Austria and Switzerland to such an extent that they protested vigorously. Kun was addressing his propaganda broadcasts to proletarians all over the world.

It is significant that systematic propaganda came with democracy and with technical improvements in communication. It was bred in the school of revolution and came into its own about the same time as the studies of sociology, economics, and social psychology. Appealing to the common people in the days of the old diplomacy would have been considered extremely vulgar, as Harold Nicolson has put it.[7] It was the dictatorships that first organized propaganda in peacetime. Dictatorships are generally born of a revolution of the masses, who then immediately turn over the rights they have fought for to a despot. At times, the dictator, whose greed for power is seldom satisfied, attempts to spread out in search of *Lebensraum*. To do this he appeals to the masses of neighboring states, because he knows that the thought of a leader, a guardian, or a father, has strong popular appeal. Occasionally his propaganda is intended to vindicate him by explaining himself to the world.

It is not surprising, therefore, that the credit for the development of international propaganda as an instrument of foreign policy in peacetime is generally given to Lenin and Hitler. But it was Lenin and Trotsky who originated the idea of broadcasting to foreign peoples over the heads of their governments. The time was ripe for this, and they addressed themselves to a highly receptive audience. The problem of ethnic minorities had become acute following the peace treaties and the shifting of boundaries. Territorial changes were often accomplished without regard for the linguistic or national backgrounds of the population. It is not surprising, therefore, that a new feature was introduced into international radio propaganda — that of attempting to reach whole population groups by appealing to them in their own languages. To the great chagrin of the nations concerned, Soviet Russia began to broadcast in German, English, Polish, and other foreign languages from its powerful Moscow stations. Either the official protests of Finland, Estonia, Poland, Germany, Britain, the United States, and others went unheeded, or Russia merely claimed that the broadcasts were destined for the national minorities within the Soviet Union itself. At the same time Bukharin, a member of the Central Executive Committee, the Politburo, the Communist party, and the Comintern, announced in his program of 1918: "The program of the Communist Party is the program not only of liberating the proletariat of one country; it is the program of liberating the proletariat of the world, for such is the program of the 'International Revolution'." [8]

Not that the Soviet government acknowledged its propaganda activities officially. A correspondent of an American newspaper was told that Russia was not engaged in fostering Communist propaganda abroad, and if anything of this sort was being done, the Comintern was responsible.[9] Later the German government used the National Socialist party as its scapegoat, and the Chinese used the Kuomintang.

It was at this time that the United States decided it could not recognize the Bolshevik government in Russia until that government had given assurances that it would concede the obligations of diplomatic intercourse to include "abstention from hostile propaganda by one country in the territory of the other." [10]

By the middle of the 1920s propaganda by most countries in most other countries had become quite commonplace. The *Völkischer Beobachter* of January 31, 1934, alleged that Poland's budget provided four million francs annually for propaganda in France. Berlin and Paris both used propaganda in the controversy over the Ruhr, and Germany and Poland used it when the Upper Silesian question arose. In 1926 Moscow and Bucharest engaged in radio warfare over Bessarabia. In Latin America radio was brought in to help in the quarrel over boundaries. Since diplomatic protests and the international conferences that attempted to regulate propaganda were ineffectual, other nations began to adopt the same tactics. Short wave was first used by the countries possessing colonies, and in this the Netherlands was the pioneer in 1927. During the French Colonial Exposition in 1931, France began to broadcast to its colonies in the French language and in the languages spoken in those territories. The BBC's Empire Service in English was inaugurated in 1932, and Germany began to broadcast to *Auslandsdeutsche* in 1933. France initiated its foreign-language programs in 1936, addressing itself in German ostensibly to the Alsatians but actually, it is thought, to the whole German people. Italy had started broadcasting in Italian to its nationals in South America as early as 1935. By 1937, however, it was broadcasting in eighteen languages. The broadcasts included programs in Arabic to the Near East. The Anglo-Italian Accord of 1938 was signed after Britain had protested to Italy about its Arabic broadcasts, and the agreement provided, among other things, that Italy would refrain from attempting to undermine the British position in this area through its propaganda. In 1938 too, Britain began broadcasting in foreign languages through the BBC, addressing the Germans and Italians directly. At the outbreak of the war in 1939, the BBC had programs in sixteen languages in its Empire, Arab, Latin American, and European services.

The United States was obviously at a disadvantage in the realm of international propaganda. Since its radio facilities were largely privately owned, it could not as a government enter into the race. The haphazard and often detrimental efforts of private United States citizens to "sell" their country or, more often, their products were no match for the government-organized and subsidized propaganda of certain other states. Furthermore, the tradition of free speech and nonmeddling on the part of the government in communications activities made many suspicious when the government finally entered the race, somewhat belatedly, in 1939. Even then the United States limited its activities to the Western Hemisphere.

On the other hand, it must be remembered that the United States is in the enviable position of being practically immune to foreign radio propaganda owing to the bad reception on the North American continent of European, Asiatic, African, Australian, and even South American broadcasts. As a result, there is hardly any market for short-wave radios; and the United States, not having the regulating problems that other states have, is not so interested in the control of international propaganda as is Europe — that veritable Babel of the air. In the early days of radio this was true of other countries as well. In the 1920s, for instance, when Moscow began broadcasting in English, strong protests were voiced in the British Parliament. It was soon discovered, however, that only the most expensive British receivers were able to pick up the signals, and the broadcasts ceased to be taken seriously.

2

Definition of Propaganda

THE term propaganda is susceptible of so many definitions that it is hard to make it the subject of a law. Yet in combating foreign propaganda, or propaganda of any kind, legislators have to decide exactly what it is that they are legislating about. Hence a definition of propaganda must be attempted before a study of laws relating to it can be profitably made.

General Definition

Not only lexicographers and lawyers, but also sociologists, psychologists, social psychologists, political scientists, and journalists have attempted to define propaganda at various times. Of twenty-six different definitions examined,[1] all agree that propaganda is the art of influencing, manipulating, controlling, promoting, changing, inducing, or securing the acceptance of opinions, attitudes, action, or behavior. Norman John Powell defines propaganda with these two elements and nothing else: propaganda is the "spreading of ideas or attitudes that influence opinions or behavior or both," he writes. Other writers have said that the attempt must be systematic, organized, deliberate, or intentional. Among these are William Albig, Charles Bird, Leonard W. Doob (in *Propaganda*), Knight Dunlap, Violet Edwards, Edgar H. Henderson, E. Pendelton Herring, and Quincy Wright. Harold D. Lasswell and Dorothy Blumenstock add that the issue with which propaganda concerns itself must be controversial. David B. Truman concurs.

The medium through which propaganda is made is not always specified. In the *Encyclopedia of the Social Sciences*, Lasswell says it is made through "representations" which, he continues, "may take spoken, writ-

10

ten, pictorial or musical form." A year later he wrote in *Propaganda and Promotional Activities*: "Not bombs nor bread, but words, pictures, songs, parades, and many similar devices are the typical means of making propaganda." In *World Revolutionary Propaganda* Lasswell says that "Propaganda is the manipulation of symbols . . ." Bird, too, speaks of symbols as the medium. He also adds suggestion, as the means by which propaganda is conveyed. Suggestion is the term used by Doob (in *Propaganda*) and Wright, while Henderson calls it persuasion-techniques. Truman limits the means to "words and word substitutes."

Some of the experts say there must be some interested individual or group conducting the propaganda. Among these are Albig, Doob, Herring, Alfred McClung Lee, and J. L. Woodward. Doob's early definition is "Propaganda is a systematic attempt by an interested individual (or individuals) to control the attitudes of groups of individuals through the use of suggestion and, consequently, to control their actions." John G. Hargrave may have been thinking of the same thing: "Propaganda is the putting forward of, and the insistence upon, a particular point of view"; and so, perhaps, was Violet Edwards, writing for the Institute for Propaganda Analysis: "Propaganda is expression of opinion or action by individuals or groups deliberately designed to influence opinions or actions of other individuals or groups to predetermined ends." The latter definition, however, does not go quite so far as to state whose the predetermined ends are.

Then there is another group of writers, comprising especially social psychologists, who define propaganda as containing something hidden or deceitful. F. E. Lumley's definition is often quoted: "Propaganda is promotion which is veiled in one way or another as to 1) its origin or sources, 2) interests involved, 3) the methods employed, 4) the content spread, and 5) the results accruing to the victims — any one, any two, any three, any four, or all five." Others agreeing with him are Albig, Kimball Young, and O. W. Riegel. F. C. Bartlett, B. H. Liddell Hart, and Henderson follow somewhat similar lines of thought. They exclude from their definition of propaganda promotion that permits the recipient to make a search for reasons. Henderson, for instance, defines propaganda as the "process which deliberately attempts through persuasion-techniques to secure from the propagandee, before he can deliberate freely, the responses desired by the propagandist."

A more recent definition by Doob might perhaps be included here. He says (in *Public Opinion and Propaganda*) that "Propaganda can be called the attempt to affect the personalities and to control the behavior of individuals towards ends considered unscientific or of doubtful value in a society at a particular time."

Funk and Wagnall's *New Standard Dictionary of the English Language* defines propaganda as "2. . . . any institution or systematic scheme for propagating a doctrine or system . . . 3. Effort directed systematically toward the gaining of support for an opinion or course of action." *Webster's Collegiate Dictionary* (fifth edition) defines propaganda as "2. any organized or concerted group, effort, or movement to spread particular doctrines, information, etc. 3. a. a doctrine or ideas, spread through propaganda (sense 2). b. a plan for the propagation of a doctrine or system of principles." The dictionary definition is important because in a court of law it would certainly be taken into consideration. "The time honored rule of construction as announced by the courts from an early day, is that words are to be given their usual and generally accepted meaning," said the court in *U.S. v. Hautau.*[2]

In popular usage propaganda is organized, systematic, deliberate, or intentional, as witness dictionary definitions. As far as international propaganda is concerned, it is highly probable that in most cases the impact of any nonsystematic activity of this nature would be minimal. Such activity would hardly be the subject of litigation. Hence propaganda is here defined as something deliberate and organized.

A definition might be "propaganda is a systematic attempt through mass communications to influence the thinking and thereby the behavior of people in the interest of some in-group."

It is important to name the means by which propaganda is conducted, because attitudes and behavior can also be influenced through threats of violence or by direct compulsion; the promise of a reward will affect a person's decisions. The term "mass communications" seems to cover all the necessary human mental relationships. The activity must be conducted in the interest of some in-group, and, as it is generally used and will be used in the context of this book, must deal with public affairs.

To say that propaganda must concern itself with controversial topics would be tautological. Controversy can exist only when there are two sides to a question. If the interests of an in-group are promoted, then obviously there must be two sides to the question; otherwise the interests of the in-group would be similar to those of the out-group, that is, universal, and there would be no propaganda.

12

The writers who believe that propaganda must contain deceitful or unscientific information apparently confuse simple definition with the methods used. It is probably demonstrable that propaganda can be more effective in many cases when the recipient is given no time to reason things out for himself. It may also be helpful if the source, methods, content, interests involved, or results accruing to the recipient can be kept secret. But this has nothing to do with the definition of propaganda.

If only deceitful or unscientifically presented material is propaganda, then open and logical statements intended to influence behavior in the interest of some in-group cannot be so named. This means that, if the arguments used are frank and sound, advocating the overthrow of a foreign government, for instance, or urging a state to go to war, is not propaganda. Even aside from these extremes, such a narrow definition would not include most of the activities of a modern propaganda agency.

In any case, the receiving state usually labels even bona fide information as deceitful and untrue. Stevan Dedijer, Yugoslav delegate to the United Nations Sub-Commission on Freedom of Information and the Press, showed this clearly when he said: "I join the words 'information' and 'propaganda' because Mr. Binder pointedly separated them. And today in the cold war that is impossible. Today there is no neutral news and no neutral information." [3] It is legitimate, therefore, to label truthful information as propaganda when it is disseminated to promote the interests of some in-group.

Legal Definition

The fifth columnist does not openly advocate insurrection, as a general rule. His methods are far more subtle. "The legislation which speaks in terms of advocacy of violent overthrow falls patently wide of the mark," says Herbert Wechsler. He continues, "It represents an uncritical acceptance of a formula devised . . . when revolutionaries operated by declaring rather than disguising their principles . . ." [4] The trouble is that laws that are too broad are oppressive to law-abiding citizens; if too narrow, they do not sufficiently restrict the wily subversive.

An example of a broad definition of propaganda is the Spanish Decree of December 23, 1944 (as amended by the law of July 17, 1946). Article 251 reads: "Any person carrying on propaganda of any kind whatsoever, whether inside or outside Spain, for any of the following purposes shall be liable to minor imprisonment and a fine. . . . Propaganda shall be deemed to include the printing of any type of books, leaflets, handbills, newspapers and any other kind of typographical or other publication, as well as their distribution or possession for distribution, speeches, radio broadcasting, and any other process assisting publicity. . . ." [5] A narrower definition of propaganda is to be found in an amendment to the U.S. Foreign Agents Registration Act of 1938: "Sec. 1(j) The term 'political propaganda' includes any oral, visual, graphic, written, pictorial or other communication or expression by any person (1) which is reasonably adapted to or which the person disseminating the same believes will, or which he intends to, prevail upon, indoctrinate, convert, induce, or in any other way influence a recipient or any section of the public within the United States with reference to the political or public interests, policies or relations of a government of a foreign country or a foreign political party or with reference to the foreign policies of the United States or promote in the United States, racial, religious or social dissensions, or (2) which advocates, advises, instigates or promotes any racial, social, political, or religious disorder, civil riot or other conflict involving the use of force or violence in any other American republic or the overthrow of any government or political subdivision of any other American republic by any means involving the use of force or violence. As used in this section 1 (j) the term 'disseminating' includes transmitting or causing to be transmitted in the United States mails or by any other means or instrumentality of interstate or foreign commerce or offering or causing to be offered in the United States mails." [6] The Spanish definition is broad because it equates propaganda with publicity. The United States definition is narrower because of the qualifying words and phrases used which limit the term to certain activities.

Propaganda never stands alone as the subject of a law. Generally there are two, sometimes three elements in such laws. First, there is the verbal phrase, which may be "to engage in or make propaganda"; or neutral verbs, to "disseminate," "assert," and "exhibit," or weighted verbs, to "advocate," "attack" or "incite." [7] But no law anywhere says that it is wrong or right merely to engage in propaganda or to disseminate ideas. All laws dealing with the subject go on to qualify propaganda or ideas. Weighted verbs are followed by objects specifying the type of activity that is wrong or right. Most common among these activities are defaming an individual or a group of individuals, causing a breach of the peace, spreading subversive doctrine, and treason.[8] The third element that often enters into the law is an adverbial phrase which specifies the agency through which the propaganda is carried out.[9]

Even the most narrowly defined law lends itself to difficulties in interpretation. The dictionary definition of the verbal element in these laws has occasionally been used in the courts of the United States. ". . . To advocate means 'to plead in favor of, to defend by argument before a tribunal or the public, to support, vindicate or recommend publicly.' *Webster's International Dictionary*," the judge quoted in an internal revenue case. He found that this "does not express an educational purpose, although it may be educational in some degree to those who listen to or read the theories urged." He did not attempt to define "educational purpose." "It has for its purpose the dissemination of controversial propaganda," he continued, "which means a plan for the publication of a doctrine or system of principles." The judge then elaborated upon the difference between propaganda and education by pointing to the selfish motive in the former: "This we do not regard as exclusively educational within the meaning of the statute, but on the contrary it tends, we think, to accomplish the purpose of the person proposing it. . . ." [10]

United States courts have defended the acceptance of the common definition of English words in daily use. A New Jersey court rejected the argument "that since the legislature alone has the power to define what shall constitute a crime it cannot delegate this power to a jury. It is claimed that the legislature has practically delegated its power, in this respect, by leaving to the jury to determine what is meant by 'advocate, encourage, justify, praise or incite,' etc. This contention is palpably unsound [the court continues] . . . There is no organic law or rule of sound public policy that requires the legislature to define the meaning of English words in common and daily use." [11] The trouble arises when there is no definition that is universally acceptable. Emotive words such as "communism" have created problems. In *U.S. v. Hautau* [12] the judge worried it out in the following words: "The time honored rule of construction as announced by the courts from an early day, is that words are to be given their usual and generally accepted meaning. In endeavoring to ascertain whether there is now any unity of thought bearing on the word Communist, I have made inquiries of men of reasonable intelligence." He asked them whether those who believed in government ownership of irrigation projects and dams were Communists. Some told him yes, others said no, and still others said to a certain extent. "It is my own view [the judge continued] that the word has the vagueness and uncertainty in it which Chase expounds in his book, [*The Tyranny of Words*, pp. 10–11] and that the minds of men do not meet in a general acceptation of its import. Therefore, the defendant in this indictment is found in a position of doubt as to what the charge against him is and can not be called on to defend himself."

Other courts have considered propaganda to be the "subject for expert testimony." [13] In *U.S. v. German-American Vocational League, Inc.*, the circuit court of appeals pointed out that "the question of the expert's competency was for the Trial Court." It continues: "The District Judge properly left the weight of Davidson's testimony to the jury, saying in his charge: 'There was expert testimony given in the course of the trial which the court allowed and it was subject to cross-examination. Simply because that testimony was allowed does not mean that it is binding on you. It is evidence which you may consider and to which you will give that degree of importance and weight which you think it merits'." [14] In evaluating the expert's testimony, both jury and bench are influenced by current sentiment, as the judge admitted in *U.S. v. Pelley*, "The character of every act depends upon the circumstances in which it is done . . . When a nation is at war many things that might be said in time of peace are such a hindrance to its efforts that their utterance will not be endured so long as men fight and that no Court could regard them as protected by any constitutional right." [15]

International Propaganda

International propaganda is addressed to people at large, or to a regional, national, racial, religious, or professional group. A crossing of international boundaries — either real or imagined — is understood. That is, international propaganda takes place when the citizen or government of one state transmits propaganda to the citizens of another state, regardless of the territory in which the propaganda originates. Similarly, international propaganda takes place when the propaganda originates in the territory of one state and is received in the territory of another state, regardless of the citizenship of the person or persons issuing the propaganda. International propaganda may be open or covert. It involves appealing to the masses, as opposed to governments, and it can therefore be termed an attempt at world democracy. Carried to its logical conclusion, national sovereignty together with the idea of the community of sovereign states is inconsistent with international propaganda. However, the idea of international democracy has become fashionable since World War II, as witness the opening words of the Preamble of the United Nations Charter: "We the Peoples of the United Nations . . ." while the Covenant of the League of Nations began: "The High Contracting Parties . . ." Lasswell writes "Propaganda . . . assists in making a fiction of the national state and in fabricating new control areas which follow activity areas, intersecting old control areas in every direction. Thus propaganda on an international scale is one important medium for transmitting those pressures which are tending to burst the bonds of the traditional social order." [16] In a world that has become so small that people have come to think only in terms of total wars and total cold wars, there is much to be said for Lasswell's statement that "propaganda is an instrument of total policy, together with diplomacy, economic arrangements and armed forces. Political propaganda is the management of mass communications for power purposes. . . . The aim is to economize the material cost of world dominance." [17]

The content and methods of propaganda are extremely varied. Propaganda may either advocate a line of action, vilify some person or group, or extol some person or group. Generally the propagandist attempts to extol himself or his group, and in so doing often tries to debase or debunk someone else. Since World War I, and more especially during and since World War II, the vilification of other states or their nationals has been widely condoned as an inevitable concomitant of international propaganda.

News is the most important tool of the propagandist. The successful propagandist combines favorable with unfavorable news, playing down the latter and making it seem of no consequence, while playing up the former. The favorite accusation of the opposition is that the propagandist has been using the "big lie." Said President Harry Truman to the American Society of Newspaper Editors: "Deceit, distortion and lies are systematically used by the Communists as a matter of deliberate policy. This propaganda can be overcome by truth — plain, simple, unvarnished truth — presented by newspapers, radio and other sources that the people trust." [18]

It must be remembered, of course, that the propagandist has a choice of truths. Furthermore, he is on firmer ground when he is telling the truth than when he's telling direct lies. Not that lies will deter people who are determined to believe what they want to believe. But if a propagandist is caught lying by the other side, his lies may be used as a powerful weapon against him. Generally it is a matter of minor importance that is picked

17

up by the opposition, disproved with a great deal of fanfare, and tendered as an important example of the propagandist's statements.

Sometimes a combination of propaganda and other methods of promotion is used for better effect. W. Phillips Davison, for instance, tells of the long struggle between Bolivia and Paraguay over the Chaco district. In 1927 Paraguay issued a stamp with a map on it that showed the district as part of Paraguay. Bolivia, in turn, put out a similar stamp with the words *Chaco Boliviano* printed across the disputed territory. Both sides later issued new stamps. The Paraguayan set had printed on it: "The Chaco has always been Paraguayan, is now and always will be!" [19]

Edward W. Barrett, former assistant secretary of state for public affairs, suggests that the ideal propaganda is "the propaganda of action." As an example he mentions the Berlin airlift which was an action taken by the United States and then fully publicized by the Voice of America, the United States Information Service, and newsreels. As a corollary, "Our *actions* must be in line with our words," Ralph K. White points out. He calls the "propaganda of the deed more potent than the propaganda of the word." This is carrying things a little too far. If "propaganda" were seen in deeds, there would be no end to the inclusiveness of the term. White explains what he means in the following sentence: "The propaganda of the word is effective in direct proportion to the deeds which it is able to publicize." [20] It is the publicizing, of course, that makes propaganda.

Experiments have shown that people evaluate information according to their prior attitudes. "Predispositions account for all or most . . . disbelief," says Powell, while the truth or falsehood of a statement is discounted.[21] The "initial German propaganda triumphs [in World War II]," writes H. G. Nicholas in *Chambers's Encyclopaedia*, "turned out to be largely by-products of the successes of their armed forces." [22] As long as the Germans were successful in their military campaigns, Allied propaganda cannot have had too great an effect on them, because they were predisposed to disbelieve any foreign propaganda.

In international propaganda it is not sufficient to tell the recipient of propaganda the advantages of one's cause. People have been conditioned to listen to such gratuitous information with skepticism if not with outright incredulity. At best it makes them resentful of the propagandist's good luck; or else they cannot see any advantages in his cause at all. There must be active dissatisfaction on the part of the listener with his government: not with its form or make-up — that in itself cannot move a man, there being very few with discriminating feelings about governmental forms — but with the government's achievements.

Naturally all countries claim that they, and they alone, tell the whole, pure, and unadulterated truth. The Polish vice-premier, discussing the American and the Polish press, charged that "the main difference between the two countries' press . . . was that the Polish press almost 100 per cent presents the picture in America in true colors while the American press misrepresented the facts about the situation in Poland." [23]

It is naïve to believe that any country, in fact, accepts the news emanating from another country as nonpropagandistic, and it must have been a rude shock to American authorities when the Austrian government asked for the return of their broadcasting facilities. The American news broadcasts, according to the Austrians, were considered in Austria as propaganda, just as the Russian broadcasts were.[24]

The propagandist is not generally interested in educating his public. As a matter of fact, a completely different process is involved in propaganda. Lack of information on international affairs is no barrier. Any interpretation that is necessary is made by the propagandist himself. The propagandist does not attempt to inform; he attempts to move his public. Prior attitudes can be exploited.

For instance, people knew very little about Japan before World War II. If we can take the *World Book Encyclopedia* as evidence for what they did know, the Japanese were regarded in the United States as "fun-loving, laughter-loving people — quaint as the characters in Gilbert and Sullivan's *The Mikado*." [25] Or take the attitude of people toward Japan in World War I, when Japan was on the side of the Allies. A caption under a picture in a national magazine showing a handful of neatly dressed German officers followed by three or four armed soldiers and a herd of prisoners less clearly seen, says: "Germans captured in Kiao-Chau, China, being changed from one internment camp to another. Japan has cared well for the prisoners taken from the land once held by the Huns, land which they hoped to make the center of a great empire." [26] But then memories are short.

Riegel suggests that international propaganda is generally unsuccessful if it attempts to change attitudes toward countries whose political relations have already been crystallized. He gives France and Germany as an example, "where propaganda, except when it is a propaganda of intimidation or provocation, is seldom effective against a deeprooted heritage of hatred and fear." He also mentions Canada and the United States, "where a tradition of harmony and mutual interest has prevented propaganda from assuming dangerous proportions." [27] Yet there are exceptions. The Western attitude toward the Soviet Union before 1939, and especially between 1939 and 1941, was anything but cordial. It can safely be said that the hostile attitude between Russians and the West had crystallized. In December 1941, however, even before the United States had officially entered the war, *Time* magazine wrote: "Dictator Joseph Stalin, who disposed of his Russian opposition simply by shooting it, was once widely regarded in the democracies as a sort of unwashed Genghis Khan with blood dripping from his fingertips. But as his armies have provided the principal opposition to Adolf Hitler, Dictator Stalin has come to seem increasingly benign to his new democratic friends. Last week United Press Correspondent Wallace Carroll, just out of Russia, reported that one U.S. official, after being guest at a Kremlin dinner celebrating the completion of aid-to-Russia arrangements, described the Dictator as a 'nice old gentleman'." [28]

Regardless of what the feeling was among the leaders themselves, the peoples were made to see the better side of each other, at least for the duration of the short honeymoon. Other examples may be found in the West's attitude toward Yugoslavia and its brand of communism, the changing attitude in the United States toward Spain, the switch from age-long enmity between France and England to one of close cooperation in two wars.

3

Propaganda Agencies

To UNDERSTAND the context in which international propaganda is being waged and controlled today, it is necessary to examine the facilities through which most countries in the world carry on propaganda programs. Private individuals, governments, and nongovernmental organizations carry on much "commercial propaganda," but for the purposes of this book, only propaganda in the realm of public affairs will be discussed. It is in that area that most attempts to control propaganda have been made, and it is the area which is most likely to demand urgent attention in the future.

Almost all states carry on a certain amount of propaganda through their consular and diplomatic agents abroad. This is often done through newsletters, in which news from or about the country or its citizens preponderates. The newsletters are prepared by a press attaché, an information officer, or some other diplomatic or consular official. Some embassies and consulates hand out printed or mimeographed brochures, pamphlets, or books about their country to interested inquirers. Some of these are specially written and published for such circulation; others are reprints of favorable articles, magazines containing favorable articles, or books and pamphlets written about the country and published commercially but distributed free by the embassies or consulates because of the friendly attitudes expressed in them toward the country in question. Documentary films, photographs, newspapers, and periodicals of the state are also used. Speaking engagements are arranged for visiting nationals; libraries and reference rooms are sometimes maintained. All these are the propaganda activities of consulates and embassies.

Many states engage in propaganda through a government department, bureau, or ministry — often the ministry of education or of propaganda. They invite students or scholars from abroad to study in their country. They arrange guided tours for foreign opinion leaders, often paying all their expenses. They send ambassadors of good will abroad. They organize international conventions and appeals, and they encourage correspondence between their nationals and recent emigrants or the nationals of other states. Most states or their nationals own radio transmitters with which they broadcast abroad. Radio is probably the most universal medium of international propaganda. The radio stations that engage in international propaganda are largely government-owned and operated, though some are semiofficial, and others are privately owned or operated.

News agencies, whether government or privately owned or semiofficial are an effective means of propaganda and are often exploited for this purpose. Colleges and universities may carry on unofficial propaganda for their country, as may clubs and other organizations. Businessmen who invest abroad find it profitable to follow up their investments with propaganda campaigns designed to extol their own countries.

The United States, Great Britain, and the Soviet Union conduct the most elaborate propaganda activities and spend most money on international propaganda. For these reasons, and also because these three are the major powers in the world today, their propaganda agencies have been selected for closer study.

Propaganda Activities of the United States

Before World War II the United States government conducted little international propaganda. Following the Buenos Aires Convention of 1936, at which twenty-one American republics met "for the promotion of inter-cultural relations," and provided for the exchange of two graduate students every year and a professor every two years between all signatory governments, President Roosevelt set up in 1938 an Inter-Departmental Committee on Cooperation with the American Republics (renamed in 1944 the Inter-Departmental Committee on Scientific and Cultural Cooperation), as well as a division of cultural relations within the Department of State.

The function of this inter-departmental committee was to coordinate the work of the various government departments in the field of cultural relations so as to develop a program with other American republics. The chairman of the committee was a representative of the State Department. Both the committee and the Division of Cultural Relations were interested solely in the Western Hemisphere, and their creation was motivated by Axis activities in the hemisphere.

In January 1942 the President allocated money from his emergency fund to extend the program to the Far East by giving China technical assistance, exchanging professors, and giving Chinese students travel grants for study in the United States. In July 1943 a further allocation from the emergency fund made it possible to include the Near East in the program.

In the meantime, in June 1942, the Office of War Information was established under Elmer Davis. It was the first United States venture in the field of international propaganda on a world-wide basis, and it taught American military and political leaders the importance of psychological warfare. Under the OWI the first official Voice of America was established broadcasting over eleven short-wave stations. Information offices were set up in every possible country. Collectively these were known as the United States Information Service, and their activities covered the making and distributing of documentary films, the translation of books, radio broadcasts, photo displays, libraries, talks before leadership groups, exchange of persons programs, news releases, press photographs, magazine articles, posters, film strips, and pamphlets.

Other agencies were added during the course of the war. On January 15, 1944, Departmental Order 1218 of the State Department created a motion picture and radio division responsible for liaison between the State Department, the Office of War Information, the Coordinator of Inter-American Affairs, the War Department, and the Office of Censorship on matters relating to international propaganda through the medium of motion pictures and radio. That same year the Division of Science, Education, and Art, which was soon renamed the Division of Cultural Cooperation, was set up, and in December 1944 it absorbed the Inter-Departmental Committee on Scientific and Cultural Cooperation.

Under President Truman's Executive Order 9608 of August 31, 1945, an interim international information service in the Department of State replaced the following agencies: the Office of War Information; the Office of Inter-American Affairs; the Special Assistant to the Secretary for Press Relations, who prepared and issued a daily radio bulletin for Foreign Service officers; the Division of International Information of the Office of Public Affairs; the Division of Cultural Cooperation; and the Secretariat of the Inter-Departmental Committee. William Benton was made assistant secretary of state for public affairs and was ordered to cut the wartime program "to the bone." At the same time the President declared that "the nature of present-day foreign relations makes it essential for the United States to maintain informational activities abroad as an integral part of the conduct of our foreign affairs." He directed the new agency to see "that other people receive a full and fair picture of American life and of the aims and policies of the United States government."

When the Office of International Information and Cultural Affairs (the OIC) was established on January 1, 1946, Benton cut the overseas news service by 80 per cent, dropped the OWI's radiophotography system, slashed radio programing, eliminated wartime magazines such as *Victory*, *En Guardia*, *Voir*, *Photo Review* (leaving only the Russian-language *Amerika*), and reduced personnel from 11,000 to 3,000.

The new office consisted of five area divisions (Europe, the Near East and Africa, the Far East, the American republics, and the occupied areas), and five operational divisions (libraries and institutes, exchange of persons, press and publications, radio, and motion pictures). It was a modest office. "This government will not attempt to outstrip the extensive and growing information programs of other nations," President Truman said in his declaration of August 31, 1945.

On August 1 of the following year the Fulbright Act provided for a student exchange program using the foreign currencies derived from the sale of war surplus equipment abroad. The entire program came under the assistant secretary of state for public affairs through the Office of International Information and Cultural Affairs, renamed in the fall of 1947 the Office of International Information and Cultural Exchange.

On May 15, 1947, the House of Representatives passed a bill of budget cuts which eliminated altogether the State Department's information program. The State Department immediately sent General Eisenhower, General Marshall (then secretary of state), and Lt. Gen. Walter Bedell Smith (then United States ambassador to Russia) to testify before a House foreign affairs subcommittee under the chairmanship of Representative Karl Mundt. Their reports in favor of a counterpropaganda program by the State Department induced Congressman Mundt to introduce a measure in Congress aimed at permitting the department to continue its information activities.

In the fall of that year, a joint congressional foreign affairs subcommittee led by Senator H. Alexander Smith and Representative Mundt went on a tour of United States Information Service centers in twenty-two countries to examine the effect of American propaganda abroad. Their discovery that anti-American propaganda activity was even stronger in some countries than the propaganda put out by the United States resulted in the passage of the Smith-Mundt Act on January 27, 1948. Its official name was the United States Information and Education Act of 1948, and its function was "to promote the better understanding of the United States among the peoples of the world and to strengthen cooperative international relations."

The propaganda activities of the State Department now had permanent legislative status. George V. Allen took over from William Benton, and the program was split between the Office of International Information, which took charge of the mass media functions — radio, press and publications, and motion pictures — and the Office of Educational Exchange, which became responsible for the exchange of persons and the support of libraries and institutes. The U.S. Advisory Commission on International Information and the U.S. Advisory Commission on Educational Exchange, comprising leading private citizens, were set up to advise their respective offices.

The United States planned to promote a better understanding of itself in other countries and increase mutual understanding under the Smith-Mundt Act through "(1) an information service to disseminate abroad information about the United States, its people, and policies promulgated by the Congress, the President, the Secretary of State and other responsible officials of government having to do with matters affecting foreign affairs." The law also authorized an elaboration of the Fulbright Act of 1946 which it did not, however, replace.

The educational exchange program was to be on a reciprocal basis between the United States and other countries, and it was to involve students, trainees, teachers, guest instructors, professors, and leaders in fields of specialized knowledge or skill.

Besides the interchange of persons, the secretary of state was also empowered to exchange books, periodicals, documents, and other educational material, as well as to translate them. He could render assistance to schools, libraries, and community centers abroad, provided they were founded and sponsored by citizens of the United States. A United States citizen could accept an office from a foreign government if this would help him in performing his duties under the act; but he was not to take an oath of allegiance to a foreign government.

Whenever and wherever possible, an existing private agency or its facilities were to be used, and, in general, "the Secretary shall reduce" the government's "information activities whenever corresponding private information dissemination is found to be adequate," the act stated. The program was to come as much from the people as possible. The secretary could "accept reimbursement from any . . . private source in a foreign country, or from state or local governmental institutions or private sources in the United States, for all or part of the expenses of any portion of the program undertaken hereunder." And section 1005 of the act reads: "It is the intent of Congress that the Secretary shall encourage participation in carrying out the purposes of this Act by the maximum number of different private agencies in each field consistent with the present or potential market for their services in each country."

These latter provisions were to satisfy the many private agencies and individuals who had been worried about government competition in, or even entry into, the field of communication. In 1946 the Associated Press and the United Press had refused to sell their news services to the government, and they were backed by such leaders in the field of communications as Dean Carl W. Ackerman of the Columbia University School of Journalism. Later that year the State Department contemplated handing the Voice of America over to a government-financed agency run by private citizens. The Smith-Mundt Act specifically stated that "nothing in this Act shall be construed to give the Department a monopoly in the production or sponsorship on the air of shortwave broadcasts and programs, or a monopoly in any other medium of information."

On April 19, 1950, President Truman, in an address before the American Society of Newspaper Editors, launched his "campaign of truth," with the words: "Everywhere that the propaganda of Communist totalitarianism is spread, we must meet it and overcome it with honest information about freedom and democracy. . . . We must pool our efforts with those of the other free peoples in a sustained, intensified program to promote the cause of freedom against the propaganda of slavery. We must make ourselves heard around the world in a great campaign of truth." [1]

Following the outbreak of the Korean War, a classified executive order of the President dated September 13, 1950, sent to American missions all over the world made the Campaign of Truth the official program. It changed the emphasis from one of promoting mutual understanding and presenting the world with a "full and fair picture" of the United States to "a more dynamic psychological weapon to meet the growing threat of Communism." It directed the State Department to take the offensive against Communist propaganda "by exposing its lies and listing its incon‑ sistencies . . . [and] by subjecting it to ridicule." [2]

Later in 1950 a Psychological Operations Coordinating Committee was set up, the function of which was to assist the secretary of state in making recommendations in regard to psychological operations requiring inter‑ departmental action. Meeting under the chairmanship of the assistant secretary of state for public affairs, it included representatives from the Department of Defense, the Joint Chiefs of Staff, the Mutual Security Administration, and the Central Intelligence Agency.

Not to be confused with this committee is the Psychological Strategy Board, which was established by a presidential directive of June 20, 1951, and which is headed by a director appointed by the President. Its regular members are the undersecretary of state, the deputy secretary of defense, and the director of the Central Intelligence Agency; and it "carries on strategic psychological planning intended to influence opinions, attitudes and behavior abroad in support of national objectives." [3]

In January 1952 the information program underwent a major admin‑ istrative reorganization. A relatively autonomous unit within the State Department, called the International Information Administration, was established to carry out the information program of the department. How‑ land Sargeant replaced Edward W. Barrett, who had been assistant sec‑ retary of state for public affairs since February 1950. Barrett's functions had been limited to the alignment of information policy with existing foreign policy. The responsibility of Dr. Wilson Compton, who was made administrator of the new International Information Administration, was broadened to include the formulation of information policy; the assistant secretary of state for public affairs then became liaison man between the Department of State and the IIA.

Among the first ideas that President Eisenhower presented to Con‑ gress following his election was a reorganization plan for the United States' information program. Known as Reorganization Plan 8 of 1953, it provided for the establishment of an independent agency to be called the United States Information Agency. The plan was adopted by Con‑ gress and became effective on August 1, 1953. The new agency took over the function of the International Information Agency of administering the United States Information and Educational Exchange Act of 1948. Executive Order 10477 of August 1, 1953, also empowered the director of the USIA to exercise certain authority available by law to the secretary of state and the director of the Foreign Operations Administration. (The FOA was later abolished by Executive Order 10610 of May 9, 1955.)

Theodore C. Streibert was appointed first director of the USIA. Writing to President Eisenhower on October 27, 1953, Streibert said the approach of the USIA would be "harder hitting than [the] previous more diffuse approaches," but that it would avoid "a propagandistic tone." On November 15, 1956, Arthur Larson assumed the directorship just before the beginning of President Eisenhower's second term. George V. Allen, returning to international information activities, replaced Larson on October 16, 1957.

In his letter accepting Streibert's resignation, President Eisenhower wrote: "You and your colleagues have developed the United States Information Agency into a strong arm of our country in our struggle for world freedom. It has now been firmly established. It presents the truth about the United States and our foreign policy factually to all the world which is free to hear its voice, and many behind the curtain who are not free have managed to hear it also. The pioneering work which you have done has proved the validity of our concept in creating the Agency three years ago." [4]

Today the United States Information Agency conducts its activities through several media operations departments as well as through its information programs in the field.

The Voice of America, its radio outlet, in 1956 broadcast in forty-three languages to Europe, Latin America, the Near East, South Asia, Africa, and the Far East. It also has a program of music directed to Europe, which has an audience response of an average of 1,000 letters a month. The broadcasts in foreign languages range from 30 minutes daily in Greek and in certain Indian and Pakistani languages to 23 hours and 15 minutes daily in Russian.

The USIA supplied more than 460 television programs to 150 stations in the free world in the first half of 1956, and estimates that some 40 million persons saw them. The programs included news and special events, adaptations of American shows, and some original productions. It prepares a current events documentary on the United States for exhibition abroad to supplement commercially distributed newsreels. It also helps foreign governments develop closed circuit television for educational purposes.

USIA's International Press Service prints leaflets, pamphlets, and posters, and sends daily news bulletins overseas. These bulletins include the complete texts of major policy statements by the President, his cabinet members, and other top government officials. The International Press Service also provides foreign newspapers with cartoons, photographs, and other pictorial material. It publishes magazines, such as *America Illustrated* which is distributed through newsstands in the Soviet Union, and it gives away a booklet called *Facts about the United States* in English, Spanish, German, Portuguese, Arabic, Danish, Greek, Serbo-Croatian, French, and Dutch.

Through its information center service, the USIA distributes American books abroad, "especially in areas where Red propaganda and Communist books are most plentiful." It stimulates the publication of popular editions of American books, such as the *Classics of Democracy* series, which it makes available in underdeveloped areas at 10 or 15 cents per copy. The USIA also supports the translation of American nonfiction works. It has helped American publishers sell millions of dollars' worth of American books to countries with a dollar shortage by making possible the conversion of foreign currencies into dollars. The art exhibits sponsored by the USIA have been especially popular abroad.

Its posts abroad have made a number of documentary and feature films as well as newsreels. The USIA also has produced a number of documentary films in the United States for world-wide distribution. From time to time it acquires motion pictures from private organizations for use overseas both in cinemas and on television.

The Office of Private Cooperation of the USIA encourages private individuals and organizations in the United States to supplement the work of the government's official overseas information program by helping to convey the American message abroad. It has planned a "people-to-people" program inspired by President Eisenhower to function through American business firms and opinion leaders.

The USIA operates Radio in American Sector — better known as RIAS — which is beamed from Berlin and Hof, Germany, into the Soviet Zone, to Poland and Czechoslovakia, and, on a 20,000-watt short-wave transmitter, to the Balkans. Although RIAS is run by the USIA, it has a large amount of autonomy. It broadcasts news summaries including tips about Communist informers, also forums and good entertainment.[5] About sixteen hours are original programs; the rest are relays from the Voice of America.

Set up by the United States Army as a 1,000-watt station in 1946 when the Russians refused to let their Western Allies share the facilities of Radio Berlin, RIAS began to build stronger stations when the Russian-controlled Radio Berlin jammed its small transmitters. Today its powerful 300,000-watt transmitter has been referred to as one of the West's best weapons in the Cold War.

On a much more modest scale, other government departments carry on international propaganda. The Office of Information and Education of the Department of Defense has a foreign information program of its own. The Armed Forces Radio, which broadcasts short-wave programs from New York and Los Angeles over Voice of America transmitters, and over Armed Forces Network stations in Germany, is intended for American servicemen. But the Department of Defense estimates that 90 per cent of its listeners are the local inhabitants of the countries to which these broadcasts are beamed. A number of publications, which "find their way eventually into other hands" than the United States military personnel abroad for whom they are intended, are put out by the Defense Department. They include discussions of current events, weekly newspapers, and guides to foreign countries. Educational motion pictures, while not intended for local populations, might also be mentioned here, because they are often designed to improve relations between United States personnel and the inhabitants of the host country.[6]

Several nongovernmental organizations in the United States carry on systematic international propaganda. The majority of them were set up after World War II.[7] President Eisenhower has encouraged nongovernmental propaganda through his "people-to-people" program.

The Institute of International Education is a private agency that sponsors educational exchanges between the United States and other countries. More than $700,000 of its $1¼ million budget come from private sources, including the Ford, Carnegie, Rockefeller, and other foundations. The remainder comes from the government as reimbursement for the institute's help in supervising certain government-sponsored educational exchanges and aid to the Department of Defense in the education of Ryukyans.

The Common Council for American Unity, sponsored by prominent Americans, conducted a "letters from America" campaign to help Americans make their letters to families and friends abroad more effective messages in the Campaign of Truth. The council has been working with immigrants since World War I, trying to help them assimilate. The General Federation of Women's Clubs donated community-type receiving sets to overseas communities. In addition to these, more than one hundred business firms, some twenty nonprofit organizations, numerous schools and colleges, cities, and trade organizations are playing their part in promoting good will toward the United States.

Four private organizations that engage in international broadcasting are of special interest. They are the World Wide Broadcasting System, Inc., which operates station WRUL; the Free Europe Committee, with its Radio Free Europe; the Committee for a Free Asia, with Radio Free Asia; and the American Committee for Liberation from Bolshevism, Inc., broadcasting over Radio Liberation.

The World Wide Broadcasting System was founded almost twenty-five years ago, and is, according to its founder and president, Walter S. Lemmon, the only existing private broadcasting company actively engaged in "private enterprise international broadcasting." It broadcasts over WRUL, located near Boston, Massachusetts, using five short-wave transmitters. Regular commercial sponsors are found for its broadcasts which go out in twenty-four languages. The station claims that it has received listener mail from at least fifty-eight countries. Among the sponsors have been the Gillette Safety Razor Company, Philco, Reynolds Metals, Remington Rand, and some religious organizations. The Voice of America has leased the station's transmitting equipment for some of its broadcasts, and the government has made $100,000 available to the company for developing a program of English lessons for Spanish-speaking Latin Americans. Arrangements have been made by the company with more than forty Latin American stations, with Radio Luxembourg, and with the South African Broadcasting System to have some of its programs rebroadcast on the local wave lengths. In the opinion of the company's president, "broadcasting to our friends is really just a phase of international public relations, speaking somewhat as a business man. It is not psychological warfare, nor is it propaganda *per se*. Like other public relations activities, it is a matter of making friends and cultivating the interests of our allies." [8]

The Free Europe Committee is by far the most extensive and best known of the private American propaganda organizations. Founded in 1949 by a group of private American citizens, the National Committee for a Free Europe, through the Crusade for Freedom led by General Lucius D. Clay, raised $3½ million for its operation. Radio Free Europe was organized by the committee in December 1949. It started broadcasting to Poland and Hungary on July 4, 1950, and to Czechoslovakia and Romania on July 14; transmissions to Bulgaria and Albania were added later.

Radio Free Europe's aim is to conduct "psychological warfare" against the Communist regimes of the satellite states. "Its broadcasting policy," said its former director, Robert Lang, "is primarily designed to encourage the enslaved people of the captive countries in their hope of ultimately regaining their national freedom as well as individual liberty." Furthermore, "Radio Free Europe does not speak as an instrument of and for the people of the United States — it is not the Voice of America, but that of Free Hungary, of Free Czechoslovakia, of Free Poland, Free Bulgaria, Romania and Albania." [9]

The nerve center of RFE is in Munich, Germany, where its administrative, news-gathering, programing, and engineering headquarters are located. Since May 1951 it has had a 135,000-watt medium-wave transmitter in Holzkirchen near Munich; it also has twenty-nine short-wave transmitters at Biblis (near Mannheim), Germany, and Lisbon, Portugal. By means of these transmitters, RFE is on the air over nine short wave lengths and one medium wave length for more than fifteen hundred hours a week. General policy directives and about 10 per cent of the programing come from the New York headquarters of the committee. John Scott, roving editor of *Time* magazine, reporting on a visit to RFE, writes: "Radio Free Europe's radio operations are indeed impressive. When I was in Berlin a few weeks ago Radio Free Europe had more employees on its news gathering staff there than the Associated Press, *Time*, Inc., and the *New York Times* put together. Its archives, research and evaluation departments are not only larger and more thorough than that of any publication I know of, but are also larger and more effective than those of any except half a dozen governments." [10]

As a private, foreign organization in Germany, RFE is subject to German domestic law. However, its operations are governed by a special contractual agreement signed with the Federal Republic of Germany. Until the end of the occupation, its personnel were granted certain special priviileges by the United States government, such as the use of Army PXs, service stations, and the Army post office; and the German government still permits them to travel at reduced rates on the railways.

Besides its broadcasting activities, the Free Europe Committee, which includes the Free Europe Press and the Free Europe Exile Relations Division, issues publications and operates the Free Europe University in Exile. Among the committee's most publicized activities has been the dispatch of balloon-borne leaflets called "Winds of Freedom" into Czechoslovakia, Poland, and Hungary. These operations ceased in late 1956. The Free Europe Committee ascribes its success to the radical idea of excluding exile politics from the propaganda activities of the organization.

The Committee for a Free Asia, Inc., was founded in 1951 by American citizens to fill "the gaps of truthful, factual information available to countries of Asia either facing or already under Communist domination." In September of the same year, Radio Free Asia began operations under the committee with a ninety-minute daily program to China in Mandarin, Cantonese, and English. The broadcasts, which originate in San Francisco, are relayed from Manila. The activities of the Committee for a Free Asia, reconstituted as the Asia Foundation in 1955, were on a much more modest scale than those of the Free Europe Committee. Students were its primary concern, because they were the most accessible in the majority of Asiatic countries.

The American Committee for Liberation from Bolshevism, Inc., was organized on February 8, 1951, and incorporated under the laws of the state of Delaware. Its declared aims are to "(1) aid the world-wide Russian and Soviet national minorities' emigration in its effort to sustain the spirit of liberty among the peoples of the USSR, and work toward their liberation from Soviet tyranny. (2) Preserve and sustain the historic cultures of Russia and the national minorities. (3) Aid the united emigration in hastening understanding of the worst within the USSR."

After eighteen months of quarrels and disappointments, the Coordinating Center of Anti-Bolshevist Struggle was formed in October 1952, representing several parties and national minorities, which was to formulate policies for the voice of the committee — Radio Liberation. The president of the committee, Vice Admiral Leslie C. Stevens, USN (Ret.), however, considered that a far more important function of the center should be "to train the Soviet political emigrés to work together democratically." [11] In

September 1954 Howland Sargeant was named to succeed Admiral Stevens as president.

Radio Liberation broadcasts on nine transmitters located in central Germany, from studios in Munich. Six of the transmitters broadcast fifteen-minute programs in Russian, while the three remaining transmitters are used to broadcast the same programs in minority languages such as Armenian, Azerbaijani, Georgian, North Caucasian, and Turkestani. About 40 per cent of the scripts originate in New York; 30 per cent come from the Munich staff, and 30 per cent from outside contributors. No music is broadcast. Programs are addressed to the peoples, as opposed to the government of the Soviet Union. Radio Liberation does not always agree with official United States foreign policy.

These are by no means all the private American agencies engaged in systematic propaganda abroad. But they are the ones that have received widest and most consistent publicity, and they are, no doubt, the most effective.

Propaganda Activities of Great Britain

Britain, like the United States, and unlike the Soviet Union, did not recognize the value of international propaganda in the conduct of peacetime foreign affairs until the late 1930s. The British attitude is summed up very well in the words of the late Ernest Bevin, then British foreign secretary: "The right way to deal with things," he told the House of Commons as late as 1945, "is to deal with them and not to carry out propaganda wars of nerves." Lord MacDonald, representing the United Kingdom at the United Nations, told the General Assembly that in his belief the BBC was interested only in spreading the truth. That, of course, is what all nations will claim for their information programs.

The British government engaged in wartime propaganda from the opening weeks of World War I. Until February 1918 British propaganda was carried on by the various ministries interested in spreading a point of view, and by Wellington House, "an adjunct of the Foreign Office." In December 1916 a department of information, directly responsible to the Prime Minister and with access to the War Cabinet, was set up and put in charge of all British propaganda. In February 1918, when the war was nearing its end, a Ministry of Information under Lord Beaverbrook replaced the Department of Information. Its function was to engage in publicity work in neutral and Allied countries and in the British dominions. Propaganda work in enemy countries was the task of a committee under Lord North-cliffe at Crewe House.

After the war, the Ministry of Information and Northcliffe's Department for Enemy Propaganda were abolished, and propaganda in Britain was neglected until late 1934 when the British Council was set up. It was not until February 1938, however, that growing world tension caused Parliament to think about counterpropaganda. The House of Commons then passed a motion which read: "Having regard to the increasing activity of certain foreign governments in the field of propaganda, political and cultural, by means of the press, broadcasting and films, this House being of the opinion that the evil effects of state propaganda of a tendentious or misleading character can best be countered not by retaliation, but by the widespread dissemination of straightforward information and news based upon an enlightened and honest public policy, urges the Government to give the full weight of its moral and financial support to schemes to further the wider and more effective presentation of British news, views, and culture abroad." [12]

A modest beginning in foreign-language broadcasting had already been made when Parliament passed this motion. But it was decided to expand Britain's foreign-language broadcasts.

With the outbreak of another war, propaganda lost any stigma it might have had, or at least was accepted as a necessity. The Ministry of Information continued its activities throughout World War II. Soon after the war — on March 31, 1946 — the Ministry of Information was abolished, and the British propaganda system was decentralized, although Herbert Morrison, the lord president of the council, was put in charge of all home and foreign publicity on behalf of the Cabinet. "It is important that a true, adequate picture of British policy, institutions and way of life should be presented overseas" was the British government's point of view. Certain information services had "an important and permanent part in the machinery of government under modern conditions." [13]

Today British international propaganda is the concern of a number of ministries, government departments, and two independent public corporations. These are the Foreign Office, the Commonwealth Relations Office, the Colonial Office, the Economic Information Unit (Treasury) and the Board of Trade (which deal with economic publicity), the Central Office of Information, the British Broadcasting Corporation, and the British Council. The first and the last two are easily the most important. Acting as a broad coordinating and reviewing board is the Overseas Information Services (Official) Committee.

The Foreign Office has primary responsibility for foreign publicity, and its information policy department works with the various regional offices to formulate policy and overseas information. The Information Service Department of the Foreign Office is responsible for the British information agencies overseas, the Cultural Relations Department for the British Council and UNESCO activities, and the News Department for the foreign and domestic press in the United Kingdom.

In May 1942 the Ministry of Information had established the British Information Services "in response to widespread demands in the United States for a source of authoritative information about all things British." BIS absorbed the British Library of Information, which had been founded in 1920, and the British Press Service, founded in 1940. With the abolition of the Ministry of Information, the British Information Services became the responsibility of the Foreign Office.

With the many budget cuts that British overseas information has suffered, some information personnel have had to go; but the work has been continued by other officers. The BIS has become so thoroughly integrated with diplomatic missions to which it is attached that many foreign service career officers are rotated among information, commercial, and diplomatic assignments, senior BIS officers frequently holding diplomatic rank. The British Information Services works through a reference division, a press and radio division, a film division, and a general division. The general division arranges speaking engagements and exhibitions, and is responsible for the publications of the BIS in each country. Through these four divisions, the BIS serves the head of the British mission by advising him on matters relating to local public opinion. At the same time, the BIS staff keeps in touch with local opinion leaders, supplying them with information on British affairs by means of bulletins and pamphlets and through the BIS libraries, reading rooms, and information centers.

The BIS does its best to promote the sale of British books, periodicals, and newspapers, and of British films. It helps the BBC by advertising its programs, securing local relays, sponsoring local broadcasts, and reporting on listener reaction. It shows British documentary films, arranges exhibitions, lectures, and tours for visiting dignitaries, and assists British correspondents locally, and foreign correspondents who plan to visit the British Isles. Finally, it distributes news releases and background stories to the local press. These stories are more in the nature of feature-type time copy than spot news.

In the United States, where there is no British Council program, the BIS does the work of both — it deals with political matters and current policies, which is its usual function, and with the British Council's cultural and educational duties. This distinction between the purposes of the two agencies has often been made.

In the Middle East the British Foreign Office has long been suspected of subsidizing local journalists. In Turkey the BIS operated the Anatolian Agency, which distributed editorials and comments from the British press every day. In Cyprus the Foreign Office owns and controls the Near East Arab Broadcasting Corporation, which broadcasts in Arabic to the Middle Eastern states.

Through the British Information Services, the Foreign Office has arrangements for the circulation of newsreels in a number of countries. These are often dubbed in the appropriate languages.

When Britain started its BBC Empire Service in 1932 — five years later than another colonial power, the Netherlands — it spoke in English, primarily to British dominions and colonies all over the world. These programs had other audiences, however, among British communities in foreign countries and English-speaking foreign listeners. The BBC later launched its foreign-language programs to "counteract the increasing activity of certain foreign governments in the field of propaganda," but on a very modest scale. The Latin American programs begun in March 1938, for instance, were mainly in English, except for some news programs in Spanish and Portuguese.

The war years saw a rapid increase both in the number of languages and in the program hours of the BBC Empire Service. Friendly nations helped by relaying the BBC's broadcasts. By the fall of 1940, eighty-eight stations in the United States and a number of Canadian stations, were relaying BBC news. The Mutual Broadcasting System was giving rebroadcasts of the news from London. At the peak of the BBC's wartime operation in 1944, it was broadcasting 109 hours and 35 minutes daily in thirty-nine languages.

On March 24, 1946, hardly more than a year after the end of World War II, the BBC "found it necessary" to begin regular broadcasts in the Russian language because of a "Soviet press and radio campaign against Britain." There were three daily programs of news and opinion of thirty minutes each beamed to Russia on four transmitters. The United States had broadcast in Russian before this time, and the Soviet Union had objected to the Russian-language programs. Britain informed the Soviet Union of the projected broadcasts "as a matter of courtesy," but did not ask for the Soviet government's consent. The schedules of the broadcasts were published in Britain's Russian-language weekly, *British Ally*, in Moscow. By September 1946 the BBC was broadcasting on thirty-one transmitters in forty-six languages, 616 hours and 25 minutes weekly.

The British Broadcasting Corporation is a public corporation governed by a charter that was first granted on January 1, 1927, for a ten-year period and has been renewed every ten years. The current charter of the BBC, which came into effect July 1, 1952, says that the corporation will "carry on as public services" over stations established in the British Isles and under a license granted by the postmaster general, broadcasts "of matter which may for the time being be permitted by . . . such licence for reception by the public in Our United Kingdom of Great Britain and Northern Ireland, the Channel Islands and the Isle of Man, in Our Dominions beyond the seas and the territories under Our protection, and in other countries and places and by persons on the seas. . . ." It can also "establish and work stations in countries or places without" the British Isles for broadcasting "such matter as may . . . be permitted by . . . such consent, for reception in such countries or places as may be therein designated. . . ." This is "subject to the prior consent in writing . . . of Our Postmaster General . . . and to the acquisition . . . of any requisite licences. . . ." The BBC is authorized "to collect news and information in any part of the world and in any manner that may be thought fit and to establish and subscribe to news-agencies. . . ." This is in contradistinction to the original license granted in 1922 to the private company, antecedent of the BBC, which forbade the broadcasting of news except "such as they may obtain from one or more of the following news agencies, viz.: Reuters, Ltd., Press Association, Ltd., Central News, Ltd., Exchange Telegraph Company, Ltd., or from any other news agency approved by the Postmaster General." [14] The charter further provides that "the Corporation shall send efficiently on every day (including Sundays)," during hours prescribed by the postmaster general after consultation with the corporation, "programmes of broadcast matter for reception in the British Islands or by persons on the seas," known as the Home Services, and "programmes of broadcast matter for reception in His Majesty's Dominions beyond the seas and territories under His Majesty's protection and foreign countries," known as "the External Services."

The scope of the External Services is set forth in Article 4(5) of the "Licence and Agreement between His Majesty's Postmaster General and the British Broadcasting Corporation." This says that the corporation is to consult about its programs in the External Services with the postmaster general, the lords commissioners of the Treasury, the Admiralty, the Air Ministry, the Colonial Office, the Commonwealth Relations Office, the Foreign Office, and the War Office. The corporation is also instructed to "obtain and accept from them such information regarding conditions in, and the policies of His Majesty's Government towards, the countries so prescribed and other countries as will enable the Corporation to plan and prepare its overseas programmes in the national interest."

The overseas services of the BBC fall into two categories: the European Service and Overseas (non-European) Services. The General Overseas Service in the non-European programs is directed to English-speaking people. The Regional Overseas Services are both in English and in the languages of the area concerned. The Transcription Service is a separate department which provides foreign stations with BBC programs, either in script or recorded form, for local broadcast.

For purposes of international law, the BBC, despite its charter and its separate legal entity as a corporation, is an agency of the British government. But even if it were not one, most of its overseas listeners would believe it to be. Joseph B. Phillips, former U.S. deputy assistant secretary for public affairs, said on the basis of evidence collected by American observers: "I do not think that the audience makes any distinction between the BBC as an independent corporation and the BBC speaking for the British government." [15] The External Services of the BBC are paid for by a grant-in-aid from the government.

The BBC has representatives in many countries who serve both as correspondents and in helping to sell the BBC services locally. They arrange for relays of BBC programs, such as the ones over the All-India Radio, buy advertising space in the press to publicize the BBC programs, and buy time on the air. The BBC publicizes its programs in its numerous English and foreign-language publications, which bring in a large advertising revenue.

A comparison of the BBC's performance with that of the Voice of America may be pertinent. Robert J. Francis, former acting director, International Broadcasting Service (which operates the Voice of America), says: "The British Broadcasting Corp. apparently is better liked in the free world than the Voice, although the Voice runs a close second to BBC. In the Iron Curtain we are better liked than the BBC. We are not as objective. We are a little more hard hitting than the BBC, and they, you see, like us for that reason behind the Iron Curtain." He emphasized this by naming East Germany, Czechoslovakia, Hungary, and border countries such as West Germany and Greece, as the countries that prefer the Voice of America. France, India, and Latin America are the countries in which the BBC has larger audiences. The Voice, he said, receives four times as much audience mail, and is attacked three times as much by press and radio in Iron Curtain countries.[16]

In a study of the Hungarian uprising based on 1,000 personal interviews with Hungarian refugees in Austria, Elmo C. Wilson's International Research Associates, Inc., a private organization, found that 67 per cent of the respondents had listened to the BBC during 1956, as against 82 per cent who had listened to the Voice of America. In the same period, 3 per cent had listened to RIAS, 3 per cent to the American Forces Network, 96 per cent to Radio Free Europe, 5 per cent to Radio Moscow, and 13 per cent to the Vatican Radio. Listeners to foreign broadcasts were then asked whether they thought these were generally reliable or not reliable. Ninety-one per cent thought the BBC news programs were generally reliable, as against 85 per cent who thought the Voice of America news programs were generally reliable. The figure for RIAS was 87 per cent, for the American Forces Network 77 per cent, Radio Free Europe 69 per cent, and the Vatican Radio 79 per cent. Understandably, 95 per cent held that Radio Moscow's broadcasts were generally unreliable, the remaining 5 per cent coming under the "don't know" category.[17]

The British Council is a semiofficial, independent corporation, functioning under a royal charter. Soon after World War I it was suggested to the British ambassador in Cairo that something be done by the British government to promote the study of the English language in Egypt. It was pointed out that the French had a head start, and that Egyptian opinion leaders had adopted French culture, French customs, and the French language. The British ambassador, so the story goes, merely shrugged his shoulders and said: "French is good enough for the natives."

Things had changed by 1934, and in November of that year the British Council for Relations with Other Countries was established on the advice of the Foreign Office. Its function was to teach and interpret the British way of life abroad. "No country today can expect to be understood by others if it remains aloof and passive," the London *Times* wrote. "Some form of national publicity, if wisely directed, with the Government, education and industry in a working partnership, can do much to provide a fruitful ground of policy." [18]

The distinctive cultural and educational mission of the British Council appealed to the British people and government. In 1941, when the possibility of placing the council under the wartime Ministry of Information was discussed, the idea was rejected. "In the work of the British Council is to be found, in my judgment, the form of propaganda or publicity to which no one can take exception," said the Earl Winterton in Parliament.[19]

The royal charter of incorporation was granted in 1940. Under its terms the council exists for the "purpose of promoting a wider knowledge of our United Kingdom of Great Britain and Northern Ireland and the English language abroad, and developing closer cultural relations between [them] . . . and other countries, for the purpose of benefiting the British Commonwealth of Nations." [20]

The charter provides for an executive committee which appoints a chairman and a vice-chairman or vice-chairmen, as well as a director-general. These offices "shall be previously approved by His Majesty's Principal Secretary of State for Foreign Affairs," and, according to the British Council report of 1940–1941, "the chairman . . . holds office for such a period as the Secretary of State approves." The executive committee consists of "not less than 15 and not more than 30 members," according to Article 4 of the charter, and must be British subjects. Nine of these members are nominated by members of the government and appointed by the government. The services of these members are voluntary and unpaid. The British Council itself comprises more than two hundred members, but power is vested in the executive committee, which meets monthly. The council meets annually. To assist the executive committee, advisory committees and panels are selected from among distinguished experts in various fields of endeavor.

The British Council's activities were directed at the start to those areas "where hostile propaganda was the strongest." These were mainly Latin America, the Mediterranean, and the Balkans. Some well-known British institutes already existed. One, in Florence, had been founded by a group of British residents in 1918. The institute was given financial aid by the

British government, and it was incorporated by royal charter in 1923. In 1927 a similar British institute was founded in Paris, and in 1928 an Argentine Association of English Culture was formed in Buenos Aires. When the British Council was launched in 1934, it at first supported these existing institutes, as well as those in Montevideo, Lima, Rio de Janeiro, São Paulo, Santiago, the Anglo-Egyptian Union in Cairo, and the Sino-British Cultural Association in Nanking. Where needed it set up further centers. Later it took them all over.

During World War II, activities of the council developed especially in the neutral countries of South America, in Mexico, Spain, Portugal, Sweden, China, the Middle East, and in Britain itself among the many from abroad who found a temporary home there. In May 1945, the government reported that the council operated in 38 countries and had "some activities in 21 others" not counting the liberated areas of Europe.

Soon after the war, the Foreign Office set up a cultural relations department, which was to be responsible for British Council policy and expenditures. At the same time the council extended its activities to the dominions, and in June 1946, offices were established in Australia and New Zealand. The council had had offices in some of the Mediterranean colonies and Aden even before the war. After the war its activities were extended to East and West Africa, Southeast Asia, and the West Indies. The staff of the British Council is recruited by the council itself, with the advice of the government departments concerned. They are not civil servants.

The British Council helps cultivate an appreciation for the British way of life through

1. The formation of new or the encouragement of existing British cultural centres abroad. These are the British Institutes.

2. The encouragement of new or existing Anglophil Societies abroad. These Societies, varying greatly in size, are combinations of persons interested in Great Britain. They spring from the soil of the country in which they are situated and are controlled by, and the property of, the citizens of that country.

3. The encouragement, and if need be the formation, of British schools abroad.

4. The encouragement of English studies in foreign schools and universities.

5. The encouragement throughout these institutions and elsewhere of the knowledge of the English language.

6. To bring students, whether undergraduate or post-graduate, from

countries overseas to undertake courses of education, study, or industrial training in the United Kingdom.

7. To spread among the widest public abroad a knowledge of those things which it is the Council's business to make known, through the medium of a Press service, films, the distribution of literature, exhibitions, lectures, concerts, and theatrical performances.[21]

Other functions include the exchange of professors and lecturers; "facilitating contacts between British citizens and those of other countries both at home and abroad"; disseminating information about British law, government, science, drama, art, music, literature, philosophy; supplying British Institutes and foreign users with films, books, periodicals, pamphlets, and photographs on British, cultural, scientific, and educational subjects; and helping foreign countries find and select technical advisers, professors, lecturers, scientists, and technicians.

Some of the methods developed by the British Council are time-honored, others are new. In the latter category is the book export scheme. A monthly book list of selected British publications is sent to reputable booksellers abroad. They are favored with a special arrangement, whereby any books not sold by them within six months are bought back by the council for disposal as it sees fit. The exhibitions of books, photographs, periodicals, and displays illustrating various aspects of British life and work have been especially rich.

Besides a regular newsreel called "British News," which is produced from the weekly materials of five British newsreel companies, the council also commissions the filming of documentaries, and shows and distributes them. The British Council institutes and centers abroad have large student memberships. The council helps select British students for scholarships in other countries and subsidizes university professorships in foreign universities. British lecturers are hired to tour foreign countries for the council. The council also arranges the exchange of scientific and other learned journals between the United Kingdom, the Commonwealth, and foreign states. It arranges for the translation of English prose and verse, and medical and other scientific texts. All translations are done in the countries concerned, as is the publishing itself. The council approves the translations, pays for them, and often assists the publisher with small subsidies. The council also publishes a number of brochures, mostly in English, under various titles such as *British Life and Thought*, *Science in Britain*, and *Supplements to British Book News*. In Britain the council has cooperated in the formation of national centers such as the Belgian Institute in London and the Scottish-French House in Edinburgh.

Most of the support of the council comes from the British government and only small amounts are received through voluntary subscriptions and donations. "It will be clear, therefore," the 1940–1941 report of the British Council said, "that the Council's work must be carried on under the supervision of the Foreign Office." Some of the council's revenue is derived from dues and charges for services rendered.

From 1940 to 1945, the government grant-in-aid was made entirely through the Foreign Office vote. Since 1945 the Colonial Office has paid for its share of the council's expenses, and since 1947–1948, the Commonwealth Relations Office grant has provided the money spent in commonwealth countries. About one third of the council's expenditures are in the colonies and the Commonwealth.

Because of its nonpolitical, purely cultural activities, the British Council has acquired a reputation for being an independent, "unofficial" body. The London *Spectator* speaks of the advantage of its not being a "part of the government." [22] Yet three secretaries of state — for foreign affairs, for the colonies, and for commonwealth relations — are responsible to Parliament for the work of the council in their special spheres of interest.

The strength of the council, its success as a propaganda agency, has been that its sphere of activity is expressly limited to cultural matters, as distinct from political. This has made it appear to be independent of the government, which, of its very nature, is political. Being divorced from the government in the minds of many people, it is, to them, nonpropagandistic. Radio Free Europe, which is independent to a far greater degree, on the other hand, has the stigma of politics, hence government connections. The difference is that Radio Free Europe wants to make its mark in a hurry — today — the British Council can wait.

Other British propaganda activities may be summarized briefly. The Colonial Office has only two regional information offices of its own, in East and West Africa. Other publicity is done by the public relations officers of the colonial governments themselves. The Commonwealth Relations Office has information offices attached to the high commissioner's offices in Canada, Australia, New Zealand, South Africa, India, Pakistan, and Ireland. The Treasury and the Board of Trade engage in overseas publicity through regular information officers, commercial-diplomatic officers, and, in the Commonwealth, through trade commissioners. The

Board of Trade has an economic information unit which briefs government officials addressing overseas audiences, gives foreign correspondents in England economic information, and is generally responsible for guiding other departments of the government in economic matters.

With the exception of the BBC, and for certain things the British Council, all agencies of the British government are required to obtain their material for any type of publicity from the Central Office of Information. The COI was established on March 31, 1946, as a nonministerial department to replace the Ministry of Information, which came to an end on that date. Since then ministers have been responsible for their own publicity. The overseas services, which had been under the Ministry of Information, became the responsibility of the Foreign Office. The functions of the COI are to act as the central agency for the preparation of publicity material required by government departments; to organize publicity on home matters of interdepartmental scope; to provide a daily service of comment and background information for press officers and other British representatives overseas; to provide a regional publicity organization in Britain for the use of government departments; and to provide a central agency for issuing government news.[23]

The COI edits and publishes a magazine called *Today*, in English and Swahili. It is distributed in the colonies, and to a lesser extent in Greece, Turkey, Poland, India, Pakistan, Burma, and the Middle East and Pacific areas. It also produces international reviews in the local languages in Paris, Milan, Utrecht, Helsinki, Athens, Hamburg, and Munich, known variously as *Echo, Eco del Mondo, Internationale Echo, Parhaat, Eklogi,* and *Neue Auslese.*

There is no nongovernmental agency engaged in systematic propaganda for Britain or the Commonwealth that is equivalent to the Free Europe Committee in the United States. But private special interest groups exist and the English-Speaking Union is typical of them.

The English-Speaking Union of the British Commonwealth is similar in purpose to, but legally and financially distinct from, the English-Speaking Union of the United States. Its objective is "to draw together in the bond of comradeship English-speaking peoples of the world," and British and United States citizens are eligible for membership. Besides having headquarters in the United States and the United Kingdom, it has branches in Australia, Bermuda, Canada, England, India, Malta, and New Zealand.

The programs of the union include lectures, discussions, debates, lunch-

45

eons, teas, and dinners. A magazine, the *English-Speaking World*, is published by the union eight times a year and sent to members. Fellowships and scholarships are awarded by the union to British college students and public school (i.e., private school) boys for study in the United States. American boys of high school age are also sent to the United Kingdom to study in British public schools. An interchange of teachers is arranged, and libraries are maintained at headquarters and at the various branches.[24]

Propaganda Activities of the USSR

Organized propaganda is more complex in the Soviet Union than in any other country. Many of communism's battles are fought with ideological weapons, and among these propaganda is the most important. Because the nature of Communist doctrine requires the participation of the masses, and because international propaganda is most effective when it is addressed to the masses, propaganda became a natural weapon in the Communist arsenal.

In most cases the aims of Communist propaganda and the propaganda of the Soviet Union are identical. However, in the present study, Soviet propaganda and Communist propaganda will have to be separated. Propaganda activities of the government itself will have to be examined; secondly, it will be necessary to look into private propaganda carried on by Soviet citizens; thirdly, there are the Communist propaganda activities of non-Soviet nationals within their own countries. As it has often been pointed out, one might show that there is little difference between these three types of propaganda. Within the Soviet Union, censorship and strict control make impossible the expression of facts or opinions that are inimical to the government. Furthermore, only the most loyal Communist party members are allowed to engage in public enlightenment. Abroad, the party maintains "a pattern of similar behavior" through the reading of Communist literature. Strict controls are, of course, more difficult to exercise abroad. As far as the legal responsibility for propaganda is concerned, there is a difference between propaganda conducted at home and abroad.

Since 1939 the propaganda activities of the Soviet Union have been controlled by Agitprop — the Department of Propaganda and Agitation of the Communist Party Central Committee. It is assisted by the All-Union Committee on Radio Information and the Ministry of Cinematography. Policy is, of course, made by the Presidium of the Communist party, which since 1953 has been the name of the former Politburo.

Agitprop is divided into fifteen sectors, each responsible for a different medium or type of propaganda activity, with a special administration for international affairs.[25]

The Soviet Foreign Office in Moscow and the diplomatic corps abroad also engage in international propaganda. The Foreign Office is said to have a large staff in its psychological warfare department. In foreign countries the ambassador himself often directs the propaganda activities and is assisted by the press attaché, several Russian specialists, and a number of Communists among the local population who work either openly or covertly for the embassy.

Russia's international radio propaganda is prepared by the psychological warfare department of the Foreign Office, known as the Administration of Central Broadcasting or the Foreign Broadcasting Sector. The department is divided into language units, and people from the language area concerned, under the supervision of a Russian, work in each unit. The number of languages used has varied from time to time and there are no reliable figures for any one period, but in 1954 USIA listed 39.[26]

Of some sixty-eight nations engaged in international propaganda by radio, providing a total of more than 7,000 broadcast hours a week, Russia was first in 1952 with almost 700 hours. In 1953, for instance, the Soviet Union broadcast 78 hours a week to the United States, while Voice of America broadcasts to Russia in ten different languages totaled 52½ hours.[27] Following an initial drop in the number of hours it broadcast abroad immediately after World War II, the Soviet Union has been steadily increasing its output since 1946. There are no reliable figures available for the number of transmitters used by the Soviet Union in its foreign broadcasts. The Stalin transmitter in the Ural Mountains, one of the world's most powerful, is known to be used for this purpose. Furthermore, it is estimated that there are 250 sky-wave (i.e. short-wave) jammers and about 1,000 ground-wave (i.e. medium-wave) jammers in use in the USSR today.[28] These are regular transmitters that could conceivably be used for broadcasting programs abroad.

The International Book Publishing Corporation, a branch of the Soviet Ministry of Foreign Trade, distributes books for the Soviet Union. It has representatives in twenty-four countries. Books are also published locally under the sponsorship of Soviet diplomatic personnel. Both political books and general works of fiction and nonfiction are distributed. It is believed that both in Europe and in Latin America the Soviet Union is spending substantially more on the distribution of books than is the United States. The Moscow Foreign Language Publishing House was organized in 1946 under the directorship of Boris Suchov, head of the Foreign Section of the State Literary Publishers, known as OGIZ. Its function is to coordinate all foreign-language translations of Russian works.

Soviet literature is an important source of revenue for some local branches of the Communist party. They are rarely given direct subsidies by the Soviet government. Instead they are given free literature, which they can either give away or sell. This produces added incentive to the local parties to distribute as much of the literature as possible. Official and unofficial book agencies of the USSR in various countries, especially the branches of the International Book Publishing Corporation mentioned above, are another outlet.[29]

None of the prewar periodical publications of the Soviet Union remain, at least in name. Most of them were stopped during the war; the rest ceased publication by 1950. Newspapers have been discontinued, and more popular, richly illustrated weeklies, biweeklies, and monthlies have taken their place. In underdeveloped countries, where both the economic and educational levels are low, Russia spends more money on these periodicals, as well as on simply-written brochures, than on books. The majority of the monthly publications stress Soviet achievements, rather than world revolution. In this category is the monthly *Soviet Union* which is published in Russian, Korean, English, Chinese, German, French, and Spanish. *VOKS Bulletin* is another monthly publication devoted to cultural relations with foreign countries. *Soviet Literature* is produced by the Soviet Writers Publishing House in Russian, English, French, German, Spanish, and Polish; and the bimonthly *Soviet Woman* appears in English, Chinese, French, German, Spanish, and Russian.

Two political journals published by the Soviet trade unions require special mention. The older one is the weekly *New Times*, which was started as the *War and the Working Classes* in June 1943. Its aim, according to an editorial, is to afford "wide Soviet public circles an opportunity to express their opinions on all vital questions of international life." It is published in English, French, German, Czech, Romanian, Spanish, Russian, Polish, and Swedish. The English-language biweekly *News*, on the other hand, was started in July 1951 to create "a closer understanding between the peoples of the Soviet Union and the Anglo-Saxon world."

The Communist press in countries outside Russia is supplied with news by Sovinformburo, a war-born agency attached to the Council of Ministers. Tass, the Telegraphic Agency of the Soviet Union, has a virtual monopoly on the gathering and dissemination of all Russian news abroad. It has correspondents in most countries, but none in Latin America. It is the major source of international news for about one third of the people of the world. Photographic material is supplied by Sovfoto, a branch of Tass. By Russia's own admission, Tass is an agency of the Soviet government.[30]

The Sovfilm Movie Distributing Agency provides news and features through its foreign branch Sovexportfilm to those countries that will admit them. It is handicapped, however, by a relatively small film industry in Russia.

Government, church, and civil opposition outside the USSR often makes it impossible for Sovfilm to distribute its films. In some countries, as for instance in India, the Soviet embassy rents a theater for perhaps a year, showing its films with a measure of diplomatic immunity. It often runs a film for as long as a month. Soviet films naturally find their widest circulation in the satellite countries of Eastern Europe and in China. But Russian films have had a steady, though since 1946, declining market in the United States, Britain, and Western Europe. Soviet films are also bought on a small scale in the Latin American countries, Japan, Finland, and Israel.

The Soviet exchange programs are very similar to the work of the British Council and unlike the American system. This is true only of its overt administrative characteristics, of course, since, like most other things in the Soviet Union, the participants in the Soviet exchange programs are under constant and close government supervision. The Moscow *Literary Gazette* has referred to the program as "the best propaganda," and a senior official of the program has said that visitors who go to Russia under government auspices return to their homes as "sympathetic supporters of the USSR."

The principal agency in charge of the Soviet cultural exchange program is VOKS — the All-Union Society for Cultural Relations with Foreign Countries. VOKS was founded in 1925, ostensibly a "public" society rather than a branch of the government, and it is headed by a public figure. The state travel bureau, Intourist, helps supervise visitors from abroad. They generally come in delegations rather than as individuals, and as many as five hundred persons have been known to come in one delegation. VOKS works with interest groups, such as sports, youth, women, the arts, and trade unions, often playing up racial and religious ties. With each

49

group of non-Communists comes a number of party members and fellow travelers.

VOKS not only arranges tours for visitors from abroad, but it also sends Russian delegations to foreign countries, especially to help in the celebration of Communist holidays and anniversaries. Soviet artists, musicians, ballet dancers are also sent as cultural emissaries, as are professors who go to teach at universities in satellite countries. In exchange, students and technicians from satellite areas go to Russia for their studies.

VOKS' headquarters in Russia are in Moscow and Leningrad, where the staff is divided into sections of regional experts. Each cultural activity is headed by a committee of outstanding Russian leaders in that field, who advise on programs and help entertain visitors.

Besides its cultural exchange program, VOKS also maintains sections that distribute all kinds of literature, including clippings, newsletters, bulletins, and books. VOKS describes Soviet life through a series of chronicles. Among these are *Pedagogical Chronicle, Medical Chronicle, Sciences in the U.S.S.R., Agriculture, Soviet Architecture, Music Chronicle, Chronicle of Soviet Fine Arts, Chronicle of Soviet Chess,* and *Chronicle of the Soviet Theatre.* Each is prepared by the corresponding section of VOKS. VOKS has also arranged for the shipment of a large number of Soviet works to foreign libraries, including the Library of Congress.

VOKS is not the only agency that invites visitors from abroad to the Soviet Union. They may come on the invitation of the Central Council of the Trade Unions of the USSR, the Soviet Women's Anti-Fascist Committee, the Soviet Anti-Fascist Youth Committee, or the Soviet Peace Committee. These agencies work through Soviet friendship societies, Slavic committees, and Russian Orthodox churches all over the world.

Soviet friendship societies are small committees that have been set up in many countries to help Russia approach those who are less receptive to outright Communist propaganda. While their number has declined in the Western world, they are still a very influential factor in the underdeveloped areas of Asia and, of course, within the Soviet orbit itself.

The Slavic Committee of the USSR encourages pan-Slav movements and the formation of Slavic committees among immigrants. After a preliminary all-Slav meeting in Moscow in August 1941, a permanent body, known as the All-Slav Committee, was set up. It appealed to "brother oppressed Slavs" to form a united front against Nazi Germany. Since then pan-Slavic groups have been organized in the United States, New Zealand,

Great Britain, Yugoslavia, Bulgaria, Czechoslovakia, and South America. Mouthpiece of these movements is *Slavyane* (The Slavs), a monthly magazine. Special broadcasts are also directed each week to immigrants of Slavic extraction, and Communist propaganda is sent to them through the mails. The better educated persons are enticed into private study circles. This was discovered by the Canadian government when the Canadian atomic spy ring was being investigated in 1946.

Russia often uses the Western press for propaganda purposes. This it can do because it has almost complete monopoly on the news emanating from the Soviet Union. Hence it can introduce its special point of view in the news stories about itself. Similarly, Communist members of Western legislatures can use franking and other privileges and the legislative forum to disseminate Soviet-inspired, Communist propaganda.

Another method that has been used by the Soviet Union to spread Soviet propaganda under the guise of Communist propaganda has been through the camouflage of peace propaganda. The World Peace Council, directed by Moscow, has launched such world-wide peace offensives as the Stockholm Peace Petition. In the United States it has worked through the Partisans of Peace and the American Peace Crusade.

The Russian Orthodox Church has been used to make contacts for the Soviet Union abroad through missions, conventions, and donations.

Soviet propaganda has also been performed through the international organization known as the Comintern, and later through the Cominform. The Third International — Communist International (Comintern) — was set up in March 1919 in Moscow. "The ultimate aim of the Communist International," according to its program adopted at the Sixth World Congress of the Comintern on September 1, 1928, was "to replace world capitalist economy by a world system of communism."

Early in the history of the Comintern, Russia denied any responsibility for its activities. Russia, said a Soviet official in an interview with an American newspaperman, was not engaged in fostering Communist propaganda abroad. If there was anything of that nature, it was being done by the Comintern. In reply to the charges of the British government that a letter written by M. Zinoviev, president of the Presidium of the Executive Committee of the Communist International, had ordered "violence, sedition [and] subversion of the [British] army and navy," Christian Rakovsky, the Soviet chargé d'affaires in London, wrote: "I am instructed by my Government to reiterate the declarations repeatedly made as to the complete political and administrative independence of the Communist International from the government of the U.S.S.R. My Government has never undertaken, and cannot undertake, to refuse the right of asylum to the Communist International, or to any other working-class organization. Still less can it undertake to exercise pressure upon them." The British replied that "No one who understands the Constitution and relationships of the Communist International would doubt its intimate connection and contact with the Soviet government." [31]

As a concession to its allies, Russia dissolved the Comintern during World War II. In an announcement of May 22, 1943, the Presidium of the Executive Committee of the Comintern said that "long before the war, it became more and more clear that, with increasing complications in internal and international relations of various countries, any sort of international center would encounter insuperable obstacles in solving the problems facing the movement in each separate country." The Communist party of the United States had already withdrawn from the Comintern in November 1940. The Presidium had now decided to "make a rule avoiding interference in the internal organizational affairs of the communist parties" elsewhere.[32]

Had the Comintern really been dissolved? People were skeptical. On October 5, 1947, after a meeting in Warsaw of Communist party delegates from Bulgaria, Hungary, France, Czechoslovakia, Italy, Poland, Romania, Yugoslavia, and the Soviet Union, it was announced that a Communist information bureau to be known as Cominform was to be set up with headquarters in Belgrade. The bureau was to have a fortnightly (later weekly) organ — *For a Lasting Peace, For a People's Democracy* — to be published in French and Russian and, if possible, in other languages. The number of languages at the peak of its activities was eighteen, including all the leading European languages, Arabic, Chinese, Korean, and Japanese.

The task of the information bureau was "to organize and exchange experience and, in case of necessity, coordinate the activity of communist parties on foundations of mutual agreement." More explicitly, a manifesto that accompanied the resolution said that "the anti-imperialistic democratic camp has to close its ranks and draw up and agree on a common platform to work out its tactics against the chief forces of the imperialist camp, against American imperialism, against its English and French allies, against the Right-Wing Socialists, above all, in England and France." [33]

On April 17, 1956, bowing, it is believed, to the demands of Yugoslav Premier Tito, the Cominform was abolished. The dissolution was announced simultaneously in Moscow and the satellite capitals. The reason given was "in view of the modification in the international situation in the past two years the office as constituted in 1947 has exhausted its usefulness." Thus, for the second time, an international propaganda medium for the dissemination of Marxist-Leninist doctrine was officially set aside when such action seemed to serve the best interests of the Soviet Union.

While both the Comintern and the Cominform were international organizations purportedly dedicated to the furtherance of world communism, their Russian originators were interested in nothing but the aggrandizement of the USSR. Communism was a mere camouflage in the name of which Russia was recruiting the assistance of nationals of all countries to further Russia's own nationalistic aims. The program adopted by the Sixth World Congress of the Comintern in 1928, for instance, says in part: "In view of the fact that the U.S.S.R. is the only fatherland of the international proletariat, the principal bulwark of its achievements and the most important factor for its international emancipation, the international proletariat must on its part facilitate the success of the work of socialist construction in the U.S.S.R. and defend her against the attacks of the capitalist powers by all means in its power." And again, "in the event of the imperialist States declaring war upon and attacking the U.S.S.R., the international proletariat must retaliate by organizing bold and determined mass action and struggle for the overthrow of the imperialist governments with the slogan of: Dictatorship of the proletariat and alliance with the U.S.S.R." [34]

In September 1950 the Cominform journal called, in an editorial, for a "militant offensive of Marxist-Leninist propaganda intimately linked with revolutionary practice" among Communists on both sides of the Iron Curtain. One of its objectives was "to develop love and loyalty for the Soviet Union." [35]

As the "fatherland of the international proletariat," the Soviet Union has the backing and active assistance of all the satellite countries in its propaganda activities. Russian broadcasts are relayed by the satellite radio stations. Thus, 38.5 per cent of Lithuania's Radio Vilnius' programs were rebroadcasts from Radio Moscow, according to the calculations of Radio Free Europe.[36] On December 31, 1954, it was estimated that Russia's European satellites broadcast 812 hours a week to foreign countries, as against the USSR's 623 hours. At the same time Communist China did

88 hours a week of international broadcasting. Besides official Communist radio activities, the Communists sponsor such clandestine stations as Radio España Independiente, Radio Free Greece, and Radio Free Japan.[37] More than 3,100,000 copies of 265 Soviet textbooks were printed in Communist China over a period of one year, according to Radio Peking.[38] This type of cooperation often means that Soviet propaganda is carried not only to the peoples of the cooperating state, but also beyond the latter's borders to nationals and others speaking the same language.

Conclusion

How effective are these propaganda programs? An evaluation is difficult, because the effectiveness varies not only from place to place and from time to time, but from campaign to campaign.

There is no doubt, however, that the Soviet Union spends the most on its propaganda activities. The United States is next, followed by Great Britain. But while an audience can be bought, it is doubtful whether such an audience gives its heart as well as its ear.

Soviet propaganda is most successful in those areas where the foundation has been laid not by the Soviet Union itself, but by years of Western colonialism. Where nationalism and the desire for self-determination have outdistanced in their speed and fervor Western willingness to withdraw and hand over the reins of government to the people, those are the areas that listen most willingly to Soviet propaganda. No matter how good Western counterpropaganda is in such countries, or how poor the Soviet efforts, the predisposition of the people is to accept the Communist line.

In other words, it depends on the product propaganda tries to sell. United States propaganda has been successful to the extent and so long as United States deeds have remained acceptable. In one respect Britain has had a little more success than most countries. Britain, through the British Council, has sold culture to those people, at those social levels, that were willing to buy it and ask for no more. And when the British way of life began to appeal to those who could afford the luxury of culture, they would visit the United Kingdom to get more.

The United States and the Soviet Union are trying this road to successful propaganda, too. It is the quickest, possibly the only road to effectiveness in propaganda, since, once a person has invested in an expensive foreign education, he has everything to gain by backing the country that gave it to him.

4

The Teachings of the Publicists

I T IS fairly obvious from a brief examination of its history, definition, and agencies that international propaganda has become so broad in scope, intensive in action, and powerful in its potential that the feasibility of its control will have to be studied. No control of international propaganda has yet been effected by any particular rule of international law that may have crystallized over the years. Yet there are plenty of the *elements that make up international law* on the topic. These elements or evidences must be examined for any possible rule of international law that is likely to develop.

International law is a generic term that has been used since the seventeenth century and is based on the common consent of nations. Whether a rule of international law exists on a specific issue must always be verified and proved in much the same way that a mathematician must prove his theorems. This is done either by an international lawyer in his writings or by some international tribunal when the question is put to it. The International Court of Justice under Article 38 of its statute is enjoined to verify the existence of a rule of international law by examining: "a. international conventions, whether general or particular, establishing rules expressly recognized by the contesting states; b. international custom, as evidence of a general practice accepted as law; c. the general principles of law recognized by civilized nations; d. subject to the provisions of Article 59 [which says that "The decision of the Court has no binding force except between the parties and in respect of that particular case"], judicial decisions and the teachings of the most highly qualified publicists of the various nations, as subsidiary means for the determination of rules of law."

The following chapters present and examine these indicators of the rules of international law on the subject of international propaganda. And, while the writings of publicists are, for the International Court of Justice, only a "subsidiary means for the determination of the rules of law," the court may very well follow similar lines of reasoning as those expounded in this book to arrive at a decision, should it ever be faced with a case involving international propaganda.

Events of the past few decades indicate that several of the elements of international law on the subject of international propaganda are extremely abundant. The propaganda of Soviet Russia, of international communism, of the Nazi and Fascist states could not go unnoticed by the countries at which it was directed. There resulted a proliferation of bilateral and multilateral agreements with regard to propaganda, especially in the 1920s and to a lesser extent in the 1930s. The Roosevelt-Litvinov exchange of notes in 1933, whereby the United States recognized the Soviet Union, dwelt very emphatically on the question of propaganda. The preoccupation of both the League of Nations and the United Nations with the problem has made headline news over and over again. The domestic laws of probably every state in the world have been altered or broadened to provide for the control of various forms of international propaganda since World War I, and more especially since World War II.

The question is, what rule of international law on the subject of international propaganda has emerged, or is likely to emerge, from the international activity revolving around propaganda?

While the teachings of the "most highly qualified publicists" form only a subsidiary means for the determination of international law, it is wise to study them first. From their writings one can gain a general picture of the field; and their arguments have carried so much weight with jurists that the whole course of international law has been modified. In general, their opinions are based, as are the opinions of jurists, on the interpretation of existing international conventions, international custom, the general principles of law, and previous judicial decisions. Hence these texts are more than statements of opinions based on subjective evaluations, they are compilations of the best available evidences. Such compilations cannot be ignored by the researcher.

Since jurists and students of international law rely on them, and because the rules of international law are continuously changing and developing, there is a need for monographs on all aspects of international law that are brought up-to-date every few years. The need is especially great in the realm of international propaganda, since it is through propaganda that many of our international conflicts of the future will be decided. Psychological warfare, the war of words, the battle for men's minds — these are the methods of the present and of the future. Unfortunately, most writers on legal and diplomatic considerations of international propaganda today are so strongly influenced by the reasoning of the publicists of the past that their arguments have failed to keep up with the realities of propaganda.

Propaganda is a relatively new concept to occupy the minds of international lawyers and publicists. But in 1758 Emer de Vattel wrote: "It is in violation of the law of nations to call on subjects to revolt when they are actually obeying their sovereign although complaining of misrule. . . . No power would fail to regard other than as a grievous injury any attempt of a foreign nation by means of agents, to stir up its subjects to revolt." [1] Vattel started what might be called a fashion, and since no cases of international propaganda have ever come before an international tribunal, his has remained almost the last word on the topic. The majority of writers since his day have, with possibly a little more sophistication, agreed that governments must refrain from spreading propaganda hostile to other governments. In 1875 William O. Manning even went so far as to suggest that a state had the right to go to war "great as that evil is, rather than submit to that total ruin of the community which must result from the forcible provocation of anarchy." [2] Among other writers who have asserted that states may not engage in propaganda that is harmful or hostile to other states are, in chronological order, F. F. Martens, Paul L. E. Pradier-Fodéré, Carlos Calvo, Alphonse Rivier, Antoine Pillet, Heinrich Triepel, Henry Wager Halleck, James M. Spaight, John Westlake, P. Quincy Wright, Ellery C. Stowell, Paul Fauchille, Robert Redslob, William E. Hall, Scipione Gemma, H. Lauterpacht, A. Verdross, Lawrence Preuss, L. Oppenheim, Vernon Van Dyke, C. C. Hyde, and John B. Whitton.[3]

Certain writers have departed somewhat from the Vattel formula. Paul Fauchille wrote that not only is it wrong for states to engage in propaganda hostile to other states, but they may not even establish governments with principles based on hostility toward other nations. He modified his statement, however, by saying that such action would not, as a rule, justify intervention by other states. Fauchille probably based his assertion on what Sir Robert Phillimore wrote in 1854.[4] Such concepts must have gone out the window with the recognition by the United States of the Soviet Union in November 1933, or even earlier. In the 1920s and 1930s it was fashionable for certain states to claim that it was not they but a political party within their territory that was engaged in propaganda activities. Several writers noted this side-stepping of responsibility and suggested that the state is responsible for the propaganda activities of parties or organizations that are in actual control in the state.[5]

We have considered only the propaganda activities of states themselves or of parties in power within the states. What about hostile propaganda engaged in by individuals? Responsibility may be assigned for two different things: The state may be responsible for failing to prevent the deed, and also for failing to punish the culprit. Publicists disagree on whether the state is responsible for the hostile propaganda activities of individual private residents. Some contend with Vattel that the state is responsible for such activities. They include David Dudley Field, Johann Kaspar Bluntschli, Pradier-Fodéré, Rivier, Calvo, Richard Kleen, Franz von Liszt, Fauchille, Redslob, A. Cavaglieri, Karl Mannzen, and Hyde.[6]

In Hyde's words, "It should be clear that when a State itself undertakes in fact to control particular agencies or instrumentalities within its limits it cannot well avoid responsibility for such of their activities as are subversive of the political independence of a foreign State." [7]

Clyde Eagleton might have been added to the list of those who say that states are responsible for propaganda activities of individuals within their borders. He writes: "The state owes at all times a duty to protect other states against injurious acts by individuals from within its jurisdiction." [8] His position is less clear, however, a few pages later, when he says that "the state . . . is, with the occasional exception of acts of individuals directed against foreign governments, not responsible for acts of individuals except when it has failed in its duties of intervention and punishment, of restraint and redress." [9] This may, of course, be a roundabout way of saying that a state is responsible both for failing to prevent the deed and for failing to punish the culprit.

In 1937 Stowell wrote that states are required to see to it that individuals show due respect to foreign symbols and heads of state. In 1921, however, he had written that "it is not customary for the great civilized states to make acts of propaganda a ground of complaint, provided that none but private citizens participate in them and that the acts, however hostile in sentiment, are confined to demonstrations such as parades, mass meetings, etc." [10] Triepel makes states responsible only for that private propaganda which is directed against the "protected rights" of a state; although earlier he had been among those who said that all hostile propaganda of individuals is the responsibility of the state from which it is conducted.[11]

Jan de Louter, who says that every state must see that no danger originating within its territory affects any other state, contradicts himself a few pages later. Here he categorically denies that the state can, under any circumstance, be made responsible for the acts or words of its subjects simply because the individuals happen to use its territory from which to express opinions in public which the state neither directly nor indirectly originated.[12] Another writer, William E. Hall, appears to distinguish between words and deeds. Hall says that a state must not lend shelter to individuals preparing armed attacks against a foreign state; but he does not mention individuals conducting hostile propaganda campaigns.[13]

Zellweger writes that the state is responsible for hostile statements in its press directed against foreign governments or states if it in some way controls, either through censorship or through outright ownership, its organs of communication. Does Zellweger mean to exonerate the state that does not practice censorship or own the press? Or is such a state less to blame for the harmful propaganda activities of individuals? Zellweger fails to say. At the same time he says that "no customary international law can develop regarding the responsibility of states for private propaganda because of the divergent attitudes of France and Germany, on the one hand, and Britain and the United States on the other." [14]

Dionisio Anzilotti points to the fact that in their protests against the propaganda activities of individuals directed against them from foreign territories, the complaining states often speak of the connivance of the foreign state with the propagandists. He adds that it is not the act of the individual so much as the attitude of the state harboring him which may constitute a delict in international law.[15]

Oppenheim's arguments are worth quoting in full. He agrees that "International Law imposes the duty upon every State as far as possible to prevent its own subjects, and such foreign subjects as live within its territory, from committing injurious acts against other States." But he also writes: "The duty of a State to prevent the commission within its territory of acts injurious to foreign States does not imply any obligation to suppress all such conduct on the part of private persons as is inimical to or critical of the regime or policy of a foreign State. Thus there is no duty to suppress revolutionary propaganda on the part of private persons directed against a foreign Government. So long as International Law provides no remedy against abuses of governmental power, international society cannot be regarded as an institution for the mutual insurance of established Governments." [16]

Oppenheim distinguishes between deeds and words: "For it is the duty of every State to prevent individuals living on its territory from endangering the safety of another State by organising hostile expeditions or by preparing common crimes against its Head, members of its government or its property." On the other hand, he writes: ". . . it is doubtful whether a State is bound to prevent its subjects from such acts as violate the dignity of foreign States, and to punish them for acts of that kind which it could not prevent." And, he says, there are words and "words": "In any case a State must prevent and punish such acts only as really violate the dignity of a foreign State. Mere criticism of policy, historical verdicts concerning the attitude of States and their rulers, utterances of moral indignation condemning immoral acts of foreign Governments and their monarchs, need neither be suppressed nor punished." [17]

On the other hand, at least one writer in the nineteenth century and a few of no mean stature in the twentieth century have said quite clearly that states are not responsible for the propaganda activities of individuals within their territories even though they are responsible for the activities of the governments. In 1854 Sir Robert Phillimore, who so violently opposed the establishment of governments "avowing a principle of hostility to the existing governments of all other nations," also wrote that states are not, however, responsible for the propaganda activities of private individuals within their territories.[18] Twentieth-century writers who have said the same thing are Gemma, Maurice Bourquin, Lauterpacht, Edwin D. Dickinson, Verdross, Preuss, and Van Dyke.[19]

Except for two, all publicists appear to agree on one thing: hostile propaganda is an international crime if it is conducted by governments themselves. The two who disagree are Jean Radulesco and H. Donnedieu de Vabres.[20] Radulesco argued in 1932 that as far as war propaganda is concerned, we must make aggressive war an international crime before we can make war propaganda a crime in international law. As for the dissemination of false news endangering peace, only three states have made this a crime in their municipal laws, and we were not ready for international law on the subject. Both these activities are far more easily controlled on a national basis.[21] De Vabres admitted that war propaganda, false news, and chauvinistic propaganda are a danger to international peace, but said that the problem of punishing a state or an individual for infractions is too great to make them a delict in international law. Better methods exist for fighting international propaganda.[22]

This is how the publicists stand on the question of international propaganda in international law. Some hold definite views, others dot their statements with qualifications. A few have noted changes in the international propaganda activities of individuals and states, but have failed to make a full study of these activities. They continue to look to the past for guidance.

This is not meant in any way to minimize the standards of scholarship or the impartiality of the writers of texts and monographs on the subject. It merely suggests that a new look at the activities of international propaganda is long overdue. It is not enough to examine the usual sources of international law, viz., international conventions, international custom, general principles of law as recognized by civilized nations, and judicial decisions. A closer look at some of the treaties or national statutes that use the term propaganda or a synonym, immediately indicates that the drafters had no clear idea of what they were writing about.

We must, therefore, examine the existing international conventions, general and particular, on the question of propaganda. Chapters 6 and 7 will consider the general principles of law recognized by civilized nations, and Chapter 8 discusses international custom relating to propaganda as evidence of a general practice accepted as law. Since no judicial decisions by international tribunals on an international propaganda question have ever been made, certain analogous cases will be discussed in the final chapter.

5

Control by International Agreement

W HILE custom is the oldest and what has often been referred to as the original source of international law, treaties, especially of late, have become the most important source. It is necessary for an understanding of the role of treaties in the control of international propaganda to examine their function in international law. Writers speak of "general" and "particular" international law, according to whether the treaties that create it are made by a large number of states or only a few. All treaties have lawmaking properties in that, as in a private contract, they prescribe the rules for the future conduct of the signatory parties. However, only the parties to the treaty are governed by this "law." For if international law had provided for the obligation created by the treaty, there would have been no reason to sign it.

On the other hand, as Charles G. Fenwick has pointed out, a series of bilateral agreements such as the extradition treaties become after a time "practically equivalent to a source of international law." [1] In the same way, general treaties which are the result of conventions signed by a majority of states including the leading powers have the tendency to become universally accepted. The question that may be asked is whether these treaties, particular or general, have lawmaking properties because they have been adopted universally, or whether, on the contrary, they were adopted universally because it was found that custom had created a rule of international conduct that all or most nations found expedient to observe. The answer is probably that both these premises are true to a large extent. In other words, not only do treaties derive their power from custom because a customary rule of international law says that treaties are binding, but the ones that are lawmaking and the lawmaking part of the others are themselves based on what has become customary or considered to be morally right.

The International Court of Justice, under Article 38 of its statute, applies to the disputes submitted to it as its first criterion, "international conventions, whether general or particular, establishing rules expressly recognized by the contesting states." In other words, the International Court of Justice is not expected by its statute to apply treaties to any but the states parties to the treaties. The rule *pacta tertiis nec nocent nec prosunt* has prevailed, if not to the present day, at least until World War II. "As a treaty only creates legal rights and duties between the contracting parties, 'in the case of doubt, no rights can be deduced from it in favour of third States'," writes Schwarzenberger.[2]

It would appear on the surface that the behavior of nations since World War II has pointed toward the universalization of general treaties, the drawing in of nations not parties to certain treaties, and the application of majority decisions to the entire membership of international organizations. In the trial of the Nazi war criminals, arguments were put forward supporting the view that the Kellogg-Briand Pact of 1928, renouncing war as an instrument of national policy, created law that was binding on both signatories and nonsignatories.[3] In other words, it was suggested that there was sufficient evidence to show that international customary law had been created by the large number of international undertakings outlawing war since before the turn of the century, and more especially in the interwar period. The theory that these treaties merely affirmed already existing natural law, and were therefore "morally binding on all nations apart from any treaty" has been put forward.[4] Others believe it is just as possible that the war crimes tribunals merely applied the law of their charters, and that no new standards of international conduct need necessarily have been set up.[5]

The argument of some publicists that Article 2(6) of the United Nations Charter is a departure from the rule of *pacta tertiis nec nocent nec prosunt* has been rejected by other writers. Article 2(6) reads: "The Organization shall ensure that states which are not Members of the United Nations act in accordance with these Principles so far as may be necessary for the maintenance of international peace and security," and it has been suggested that this does not put nonmembers of the United Nations under any obligation. It merely warns them that, under certain circumstances, the United Nations would take concerted action to force them to comply with its principles.[6]

Treaties bind states only, as a rule, and not their subjects. While states can, if they wish, pass on certain rights and duties in international law directly to their subjects, the latter derive these rights and duties from their states, not from the treaties, according to the Permanent Court of Arbitration in the North Atlantic Fisheries case. In other words, the right belongs to the state, which may, if it so desires, pass it through its municipal laws to its subjects. Since World War II, however, the tendency appears to be, especially in connection with the trial of war criminals, to place the responsibility for the observance of treaty obligations directly on the shoulders of individuals. Quoting *ex parte* Quirin (1942) 317 U.S. 1, the International Military Tribunal held that "international law imposes duties and liabilities upon individuals as well as upon states." It continued: "Crimes against international law are committed by men, not by abstract entities, and only by punishing individuals who commit such crimes can the provisions of international law be enforced." [7]

Of course, the case against the spy in *ex parte* Quirin rested not on his breach of international law but on his breach of the municipal law of the United States. Similarly, in the Nuremberg trials, the jurisdiction claimed by the Allied powers with respect to war crimes might simply be interpreted to have been based on either the protective principle, i.e., by reference to the national interest injured, or on the universality principle, i.e., by reference to the custody of the person committing the offense. In the latter case the concept of piracy *jure gentium* is being broadened to include war crimes. That the rules of international law were not consciously taken into consideration in some of these instances is borne out in a prisoner of war case tried in an Australian military court at Rabaul. "The defence had submitted," said the court, "that the provisions of the Geneva Convention did not apply to the accused as Japan was not a signatory of the Convention. The Judge Advocate, however, advised the Court that that was immaterial, 'as the law applied in this court is that of England as embodied in Australian law'." [8]

Applying these principles to international propaganda, it would therefore seem that if there exists a large body of treaties, whether general or particular, controlling such activities, this would be an important source of international law governing propaganda among nations. While this international behavior would not necessarily affect third parties, there is evidence that in the event of war the victors might give them universal application. And lastly, it is highly probable that punishment would be meted out to the individual if any punishment is found to be necessary.

In the municipal courts of most states, treaties that involve changes in the municipal law of the state do not override the law of the land unless they have been implemented by the lawmaking body. The United States, Mexico, and Paraguay alone recognize the paramountcy of treaties over the state laws and constitutions.[9] In regard to the federal statutes, the United States law is that "a treaty may supersede a prior act of Congress, and an act of Congress may supersede a prior treaty." [10]

The fact that some countries require legislation to implement a treaty and that legislation is not forthcoming in no way absolves a state from its responsibilities in regard to that treaty. In the case of the Danzig Railway officials (1928), the Permanent Court of International Justice held that Poland could not derive any rights on the basis of "the non-fulfilment of an obligation imposed upon her by an international engagement," viz., making the necessary changes in its national law to implement a treaty.[11] In the case relative to the exchange of Greek and Turkish populations, the Permanent Court of International Justice held that it was "self-evident" that "a State which has contracted valid international obligations is bound to make in its legislation such modifications as may be necessary to insure the fulfillment of the obligations undertaken." [12]

This is the way international tribunals have handled conflicts between treaties and the municipal laws of nations. But this does not mean that all states have changed their behavior to remain "within the law." In June 1948, for instance, when the Soviet government protested against an alleged violation by the Netherlands of the anti-warmongering resolution of the United Nations General Assembly, the reply of the Netherlands was merely that the article in question appearing in a Dutch newspaper did not violate any Dutch law. The British practice has been to refrain from ratifying a treaty until the necessary implementing legislation is passed or until it is certain that the legislation will be passed.

A state cannot plead that a provision in its constitution, which was there at the time the treaty was signed, is in conflict with the provisions of the international agreement, hence making it impossible for the state to carry out its obligation. Nor, a fortiori, can it justify its evasion on the passage of ordinary legislation, either before or after the signing of the treaty, for then it could by such action free itself of its treaty obligations.

For the same reason, a state cannot claim that it has no power to enforce a treaty. Britain pointed this out to the Soviet Union in very direct language in its note of October 24, 1924, when Russia refused to assume responsibility for the propaganda activities of the Comintern: "His Majesty's Government mean that these undertakings shall be carried out both in the letter and in the spirit and it cannot accept the contention that whilst the Soviet Government undertakes obligations, a political body, as powerful as itself, is to be allowed to conduct a propaganda and support it with money, which is in direct violation of the official agreement. The Soviet Government either has or has not the power to make such agreements. If it has the power it is its duty to carry them out and see that the other parties are not deceived. If it has not this power and if responsibilities which belong to the State in other countries are in Russia in the keeping of private and irresponsible bodies the Soviet Government ought not to make agreements which it knows it cannot carry out." [13]

The signing of a treaty by a state makes an inroad on the sovereignty of that state in almost all cases. Even if there is no *quid pro quo*, the state accepts certain rights or duties which it is bound to retain, whether it likes to or not, during the lifetime of the treaty. Whatever the force that keeps the state from breaking the treaty, as long as an international agreement is being observed, one might say that a power tantamount to a supranational government is functioning. Many of our international needs can be and have been satisfied only by mutual relinquishment of certain domestic sovereign rights.

In controlling international propaganda, however, the question is not whether the legislation exists. There are plenty of enabling municipal laws in most states, as will be seen below, to prevent what one might term harmful international propaganda. The question is whether the will exists to eliminate such propaganda. If the desire does exist, the propaganda may be expunged either legally or by executive action extralegally, according to the custom of the state concerned. But the decision as to what is and what is not propaganda must remain highly flexible and arbitrary. No treaty or law has ever successfully attempted to define propaganda or the propaganda type of activity which gave rise to its drafting.

General Treaties Limiting International Propaganda

Little attention was given to the problem of international propaganda before the turn of the century. At the first World Press Conference in

Chicago in 1893, the subject of avoiding international misunderstandings and the role of the press to this end was broached. This, of course, was a nongovernmental agency which could do no more than recommend action by governments. But nongovernmental agencies have played a leading role in urging the control of international propaganda, both as pressure groups and in laying the groundwork for action by governmental bodies. Another nongovernmental organization interested in the problem was the Inter-Parliamentary Union — a group representing members of all national parliaments — which in 1914 prepared a draft resolution recommending that the powers "establish, by means of their legislation, efficacious penal sanctions, in order to prevent the wilful propagation, by means of the public press, of false or sophisticated news capable of compromising peaceful relations between states." [14]

At the twenty-third Inter-Parliamentary Conference in Washington and Ottawa in October 1925, the problem of propaganda dangerous to peace was discussed, and a resolution condemning the dissemination of false news liable to disrupt world peace adopted. The 1932 conference of the union, meeting in Geneva, urged its members to introduce legislation by April 13, 1933, at the latest, for the punishment of "persons inciting the country to war by writing, speech or any other form of publicity, or who, either by deliberately disseminating false news or false documents, or by fraudulent machinations, have disturbed international relations or increased the tension between certain countries." [15]

A group of press experts met under League auspices in Geneva in August 1927 and adopted a resolution expressing the desire that "newspapers and news agencies of the world should deem it their duty to take stringent measures to avoid the publication or distribution" of news that was biased, exaggerated, deliberately distorted, or obviously inaccurate, and which was "calculated to cause undesirable misunderstanding among nations and suspicions detrimental to international peace." [16]

The International Federation of Journalists, comprising twenty-nine journalistic societies, decided at its meeting in October 1930 to create a tribunal of honor which could pass on the worthiness of newspapermen guilty of publishing untrue or biased information to exercise their profession. Journalists from sixteen states were represented, as well as the League Secretariat and the International Labor Organization. The tribunal of honor was set up at The Hague on October 12, 1931.

A conference of governmental press bureaus and representatives of the press was called by the Danish government. It met from January 11 to 14, 1932, in Copenhagen with thirty-four government press departments, the League Secretariat, and a number of independent news agencies represented. The group endorsed the tribunal of honor set up by the International Federation of Journalists the previous October, and adopted a resolution to the effect that the international press had full rights to its liberty and circulated only such news as it believed in good faith to be true; that the "campaign against the dissemination of inaccurate news is one of the necessities of international life," but that the most effective antidote to inaccuracy is "the rapid spread of accurate and abundant information through the agency of the Press Bureaus." [17] The United States and Soviet representatives refused to endorse the tribunal of honor. The American position was that it recognized only two duties. One was to its public, the other was to operate under the laws of the country in which it functioned. "We can see no need, so far as we are concerned, for any other agency to deal with matters which already fall within existing jurisdictions," they said.[18] The tribunal was resurrected by the International Organization of Journalists meeting in Brussels in February 1948. There it adopted a unanimous resolution calling upon the United Nations Sub-Commission on Freedom of Information and the Press to consider the preparation of a code of ethics for newspapers and reporters and the setting up, in cooperation with the International Organization of Journalists, of a court of honor. This time the United States, which was represented at the conference, endorsed the resolution; the Soviet Union was not represented.

The dissemination of false news was also attacked by another international press conference meeting under League auspices in Madrid in November 1933, and by the twentieth Congress of the International Union of Press Associations, which met in Antwerp in June 1934 and was attended by representatives from twenty-four countries. The World Peace Congress, with a membership in many European countries and in the United States, expressed at its twenty-eighth conference, held in Brussels in July 1931, the hope that legislation would be passed by its members' nations outlawing incitement to war by word, pen, or other and similar means. And again at its 1932 meeting in Vienna, it adopted a resolution directed against war propaganda and the dissemination of inaccurate news likely to harm international understanding.

The International Bureau for the Unification of Criminal Law, representing fourteen governments,[19] adopted a resolution in 1930 recommending punishment, under the municipal law of each state, of individuals who conduct propaganda favoring war. The resolution included the following statements: "(a) Propaganda in Favour of Wars of Aggression: Any person or persons conducting propaganda in public in favour of wars of aggression shall be punishable with (punishment to be inserted). The penalty defined . . . shall be applied only provided such penalty exists in the law of the country against which the propaganda in favour of war was being conducted." [20]

The League of Nations itself gave active consideration to the problems of international propaganda. Although the League Covenant does not expressly discuss propaganda, Article 10 provides that "the members of the League undertake to respect and preserve as against external aggression the territorial integrity and existing political independence of all Members of the League. . . ." In 1922 the Supreme Council of the League adopted a resolution at Cannes declaring: "Nations can claim no right to dictate to each other regarding the principles on which they are to regulate their system of ownership, internal economy, and government. It is for every nation to choose for itself the system which it prefers in this respect." [21] In theory this affected the rights of nations to a limited extent in their official propaganda activities, but the resolution is so broad in scope that it was not necessarily limiting in practice.

The problems raised by Lenin's technique of appealing to peoples over the heads of their governments disturbed the members of the League continuously. Already in 1926 the dangers to international peace inherent in propaganda by radio were brought up and discussed in the League of Nations. On April 25, 1931, the Swedish government sent the secretary-general of the League a note pointing out the need for curbing false information. Sweden suggested that the Special Committee Appointed to Frame a Draft General Convention to Improve the Means of Preventing War should say in Article 4(a) of the convention: "[The High Contracting Parties] undertake to endeavour, so far as their national laws permit, to suppress all verbal or written propaganda designed to prevent a peaceful settlement of the crisis." The General Convention to Improve the Means of Preventing War adopted in May did, in fact, urge the Assembly to take up the problem of war propaganda, "recognising that aggressive propaganda against a foreign Power may, in certain circumstances, constitute a veritable threat to the peace of the world . . ." [22]

On September 23, 1931, and February 13, 1932, Poland sent memoranda to the League urging that when it took up the matter of war propaganda and the publication of false news, it should recommend that "severe measures [be] taken to deal with any person attempting to undermine the moral bases of world peace by a propaganda of hatred. A suitable modification of national legislation would only be the logical complement of international agreements now in force." Since national laws did not take into account "the new necessities arising out of the development of international relations," states should be urged to consider adjusting their national laws regarding the press, education, broadcasting, the films, and the stage.[23]

Following the assassination of King Alexander I of Yugoslavia and French Foreign Minister Louis Barthou, the Council of the League resolved on December 10, 1934, "That it is the duty of every state neither to encourage nor tolerate on its territory any terrorist activity with a political purpose; that every State must do all in its power to prevent and repress acts of this nature and must for this purpose lend its assistance to governments which request it." [24] Obviously this applies to propaganda of a terrorist nature.

The legal committee of the Conference for the Reduction and Limitation of Armaments proposed that a clause be included in its draft convention which would outlaw "Direct public propaganda urging the State to be the first to commit, contrary to its international understandings, any one of the following acts: (a) declaration of war upon another state; (b) invasion by its armed forces, even without declaration of war, of the territory of another state; (c) attack by its land, naval or air forces, even without declaration of war, upon the territory, vessels or aircraft of another state; (d) naval blockade of the coasts or parts of another state; (e) assistance given to armed bands, organised in its territory, which have invaded the territory of another state, or refusal, in spite of the request of the invaded state, to take in its own territory all possible steps to deprive the aforesaid bands of all assistance or protection." It also suggested that states be called upon to ban "(4) The dissemination of false news, reports or of documents forged, falsified or inaccurately attributed to third parties, whenever such dissemination has a disturbing effect upon international relations and is carried out in bad faith. (5) Causing prejudice to a foreign state by maliciously attributing to it acts which are manifestly untrue and thus exposing it to public resentment or contempt." [25]

70

It should be noted that in section (4) only false statements are mentioned, that this is modified by the terms "carried out in bad faith" and "maliciously," and that the whole clause is further modified by the rider that the dissemination must have a "disturbing effect upon international relations."

Despite all the draft conventions, memoranda, and proposed resolutions that were considered by the League, nothing that directly mentioned propaganda was ever passed in the form of a resolution either by the League Assembly or the League Council. The League's virtue lay rather in the encouragement it gave to private international and national organizations [26] and to the conventions concluded under its auspices.

Like the League Covenant, the Charter of the United Nations has no specific reference to international propaganda as a threat to peace. Some have read into Article 2(4) of the Charter condemnation of certain types of propaganda, especially propaganda that may be labeled a "threat of force." [27] However, like the League, the United Nations took up the matter of international propaganda early in its career. The Soviet Union submitted a draft resolution to the General Assembly at its second session in 1947 on measures to be taken against war propaganda. The Yugoslav delegation also submitted one on the prevention of propaganda harmful to foreign states and to international understanding. [28]

Soviet delegate Vishinsky argued that the Charter itself made it obligatory to punish warmongers by making one of its purposes the maintenance of international peace and security and the development of friendship among nations. Yugoslavia wanted the resolution to provide for the punishment of publishers of false news and reports liable to aggravate international relations. United Kingdom delegate Mackenzie remarked that the Soviet proposal "omitted any reference to such important questions as censorship, freedom to travel, arbitrary expulsion and the withholding of news from the people of a country." [29]

The governments of Australia, Canada, France, and Venezuela submitted resolutions to replace the Soviet resolution on warmongering, and several amendments and joint resolutions were also offered. Finally, on October 27, 1947, the Political and Security Committee of the General Assembly completed a draft resolution condemning war propaganda adopted by a vote of 56 to 0, Haiti being absent. On November 3, this resolution was placed before the General Assembly and was adopted unanimously. [30] It read:

71

Whereas in the Charter of the United Nations the peoples express their determination to save succeeding generations from the scourge of war, which twice in our lifetime has brought untold sorrow to mankind, and to practice tolerance and live together in peace with one another as good neighbours, and

Whereas the Charter also calls for the promotion of universal respect for, and observance of, fundamental freedoms which include freedom of expression, all Members having pledged themselves in Article 56 to take joint and separate action for such observance of fundamental freedoms,

The General Assembly

1. *Condemns* all forms of propaganda, in whatsoever country conducted, which is [*sic*] either designed or likely to provoke or encourage any threat to the peace, breach of the peace, or act of aggression;

2. *Requests* the Government of each Member to take appropriate steps within its constitutional limits:

(a) To promote, by all means of publicity and propaganda available to them, friendly relations among nations based upon the Purposes and Principles of the Charter;

(b) To encourage the dissemination of all information designed to give expression to the undoubted desire of all peoples for peace;

3. *Directs* that this resolution be communicated to the forthcoming Conference on Freedom of Information.[31]

The resolution left up to each member state the definition of "propaganda designed or likely to provoke a threat to the peace," and "propaganda designed to promote friendly relations among nations." No action on the part of the United Nations was envisioned by the resolution, unless, of course, a state's propaganda activities resulted in a dispute, and the Security Council decided to establish that the dispute was "in fact likely to endanger the maintenance of international peace and security" (Article 37 of the Charter). But the Security Council is extremely unlikely to take such a responsibility, especially when a great power is involved, because of the veto and because all states today are engaged in international propaganda.

The vote on the Yugoslav resolution, which was later replaced by one submitted by France, was unanimous; but this text was even more circumspect, in that it invited members "to study measures as might with advantage be taken on the national plane to combat, within the limits of constitutional procedures, the diffusion of false or distorted reports likely to injure friendly relations between States."[32] Like the resolution on warmongering, this one was brought to the notice of the Sub-Commission on Freedom of Information and of the Press by the General Assembly.[33]

A Polish proposal at a subsequent UNESCO meeting that legal action be taken against warmongering was rejected, and a French compromise resolution against warmongering was unanimously adopted, condemning the idea that war was inevitable.[34]

At a plenary meeting on November 17, 1950, the General Assembly reaffirmed its resolutions condemning propaganda against peace.[35] Condemnation of war propaganda and the dissemination of false information likely to endanger international peace was as far as the United States was prepared to go. The British draft convention on freedom of information, for instance, which was one of three draft conventions approved by a majority of the members of the Sub-Commission on Freedom of Information and of the Press, did not get the American vote. The draft convention subscribed to the concept of freedom of information, but as a freedom subject to penalties, liabilities, and restrictions under the law for its abuse. It also included a clause which read: "The systematic diffusion of deliberately false or distorted reports which undermine friendly relations between peoples or States" is subject to penalty. Similarly, the United States rejected the Polish suggestion that the French draft convention on the right of official denial should include a guarantee for the enforcement of a state's obligations. The United States delegate said that the best his country could do is to make official denials of reports submitted by states available to the press, which the latter could choose to publish or not. Finally, by way of compromise, it was agreed that if proper publicity was not given to official denials they could be submitted to the secretary-general of the United Nations, who would give them appropriate publicity.[36] Neither of the draft conventions has yet been adopted by the General Assembly.

At its one hundred and twenty-third meeting, on November 21, 1947, the General Assembly instructed the International Law Commission of the United Nations to prepare a draft declaration on the rights and duties of states. This the commission did, and the resulting draft declaration was adopted by the commission by 11 votes to 2. Vladimir M. Koretsky and Manley O. Hudson voted against it.[37] Article 3 of the declaration reads: "Every State has the duty to refrain from intervention in the internal or external affairs of any other State." Article 4 reads: "Every State has the duty to refrain from fomenting civil strife in the territory of another State, and to prevent the organization within its territory of activities calculated to foment such civil strife." [38] The draft declaration was sub-

73

mitted to the General Assembly, which on December 7, 1951, resolved to postpone its consideration for the time being. The Assembly also urged member states to comment on the draft declaration and requested the secretary-general to publish the comments and suggestions.[39]

It is doubtful whether any states can be held by any resolutions of the United Nations. While the United Nations Charter is "nothing more nor less" than a multilateral treaty [40] which is binding upon the member states where the language is definite,[41] "the fact that the Charter, as a treaty, refers to a matter is in itself not a sufficient reason for the assumption that the Charter imposes obligations with respect to this matter upon the contracting parties." [42] As Chief Justice Gibson of the California Supreme Court pointed out in *Sei Fujii v. State*, ". . . although the member nations have obligated themselves to cooperate with the international organization in promoting respect for and observance of, human rights, it is plain that it was contemplated that future legislative action by the several nations would be required to accomplish the declared objectives and there is nothing to indicate that these provisions were intended to become rules of law for the courts of this country upon ratification of the charter." [43]

Nor is the United Nations a superstate with legislative powers. Hence, the resolutions of the General Assembly, which may only "recommend measures" (Article 14 of the Charter), cannot compel action by member states. As to the Security Council, Article 25 ("The Members . . . agree to accept and carry out the decisions of the Security Council . . ."), when read in conjunction with Article 39 ("The Security Council shall . . . decide what measures shall be taken . . . to maintain or restore international peace and security"), may be considered to be binding.[44] Subsidiary agreements, conventions, declarations, or the like are not binding, unless the language is definite and the state is a signatory.[45] When a state is not a signatory, especially if the state is a powerful one and the treaty is recent and has not yet found universal acceptance, no responsibility will devolve upon it.[46]

Besides the work of the nongovernmental organizations, the League of Nations, and the United Nations, a number of agreements have been signed on a regional basis affecting the dissemination of international propaganda. The treaty between Spain, France, and Britain of December 18, 1923, regarding propaganda activities in Tangier would fit under the heading of particular agreements, too; but it is mentioned here because the provisions are extended to other countries. Article 10 of the treaty said: "Any agitation, propaganda or conspiracy against the established order in the French or Spanish zones of Morocco is forbidden from the zone of Tangier. Similar agitation against any foreign state is also forbidden." A similar agreement was signed by Spain, France, Great Britain, and Italy regarding the zone of Tangier on July 25, 1928.[47]

The Franco-Italian treaty of January 7, 1935, should also be mentioned. Although it was signed only by France and Italy, it was an expression of general sentiment about international propaganda, and an invitation to all states to join with the signatories in condemning intervention in the internal affairs of other states. The two states said: "Having examined the situation in Europe, and especially in Austria, they firmly recommend to all states that, within the framework of the League of Nations, they should conclude a convention containing especially a mutual pledge not to intervene in one another's internal affairs. They should also pledge to one another not to sustain or aid any agitation or propaganda or attempt at intervention that is aimed at the territorial integrity, or that aims to change by force the political or social regime of a contracting state. The way should be left open for the individual states to make bilateral agreements to this effect with the concurrence of the League of Nations."[48]

Several of the conferences held in the Western Hemisphere adopted resolutions on propaganda and activities likely to disturb international understanding. The Pan American convention signed at Montevideo in December 1933 stated in Article 8: "No state has the right to intervene in the internal or external affairs of another,"[49] which may be interpreted to include intervention by means of propaganda. The meeting of foreign ministers in Panama, September 23 to October 3, 1939, produced a resolution to safeguard American republics against the "unlawful activities undertaken by individuals, whether nationals or aliens, residing therein, with the purpose of benefiting any foreign belligerent state." To prevent "foreign ideologies inspired by diametrically opposite principles" from encroaching upon the neutrality of the American republics, Resolution 11 exhorts the signatories to prohibit, "in accordance with their internal legislation, the inhabitants of their territories from engaging in activities capable of affecting the neutral status of the American Republics."[50]

At the second meeting of foreign ministers in Havana in July 1940, the resolutions of the first meeting were elaborated. Resolution 2 urged the American governments to prevent diplomats and consular agents in their territory from engaging in political activity that might endanger the American democratic tradition. Resolution 3 was aimed at the "activities directed, assisted or abetted by foreign governments, or foreign groups or individuals, which tend to subvert the domestic institutions, or to foment disorder in their international political life, or to modify by pressure, propaganda, threats or in any other manner" the sovereign rights of Americans to choose their own governments. And Resolution 7 prohibits the "diffusion of doctrines tending to place in jeopardy the common inter-American democratic ideal or to threaten the security and neutrality of the American Republics." [51]

Following World War II, the Inter-American Treaty of Reciprocal Assistance and Final Act of the Inter-American Conference for the Maintenance of Continental Peace and Security was signed on September 2, 1947, at Rio de Janeiro. Article 6 of this treaty provides for mutual consultation among the seventeen signatory American states in case of "aggression which is not an armed attack," or any "situation that might endanger the peace of America." [52] The Charter of the Organization of American States signed at Bogotá on April 30, 1948, and which came into force on December 13, 1951, includes the following clauses: "Article 15. No State or group of States has the right to intervene, directly or indirectly, for any reason whatever, in the internal or external affairs of any other State. The foregoing principle prohibits not only armed force but also any other form of interference or attempted threat against the personality of the State or against its political, economic and cultural elements." And Article 16 reads: "No State may use or encourage the use of coercive measures of an economic or political character in order to force the sovereign will of another State and obtain from it advantages of any kind." Of the 21 signatories, 15 have ratified the treaty, including the United States. But the United States has the following reservation: "That the Senate give its advice and consent to ratification of the Charter with the reservation that none of its provisions shall be considered as enlarging the powers of the Federal Government of the United States or limiting the powers of the several states of the Federal Union with respect to any matters recognized under the Constitution as being within the reserved powers of the several States." [53]

The fifteen signatories of the European Convention for the Protection of Human Rights and Fundamental Freedoms signed in Rome and Paris in November 1950, agreed that freedom of expression "may be subject to such formalities, conditions, restrictions or penalties as are prescribed by law" (Article 10(2)); that in time of war "or other public emergency threatening the life of the nation" they may tighten the law "to the extent strictly required by the exigencies of the situation" (Article 15(1)); and that the signatories may impose any restrictions they like on the political activity of aliens (Article 16).[54]

The control of international propaganda via telegraph and cable communication should be mentioned. This type of communication has always been subject to national censorship. The international conference at St. Petersburg in 1875 which, with modifications, is still in force gave all states complete right to control the information that flowed through their cables. So did subsequent conferences at London, Paris, Berlin, Budapest, and Lisbon.[55] The International Telecommunication Convention signed at Atlantic City on October 2, 1947, includes the following provisions: "Article 29.1. Members and Associate Members reserve the right to stop the transmission of any private telegram which may appear dangerous to the security of the state or contrary to their laws, to public order or to decency, provided that they immediately notify the office of origin of the stoppage of any such telegram or any part thereof, except when such notification may appear dangerous to the security of the state." Article 29(2) permits a state to cut off private telephone or telegraph communications if they appear dangerous to the security of the state. Under Article 30 a state may suspend its international communication service generally, for certain relations or for certain types of correspondence.[56] The International Telecommunication Union held a plenipotentiary conference in Buenos Aires from October to December 1952, but no radical changes were made in the Atlantic City convention.

Much attention has been given to the control of radio propaganda ever since it became apparent in the early twenties that listening to radio broadcasts was to become universal. This was one way in which governments and individuals could appeal directly to the peoples of other nations, and it was difficult to stop them. If the powers of government inhere in the people themselves, and if people could so easily be swayed by the spoken word, then it was obvious that a mass medium such as radio could be exploited to great advantage by directing it to the people.

On December 17, 1903, the Wright brothers succeeded in making their first flight in a mechanically propelled, heavier-than-air machine. It was not, of course, the first feat of aeronautics. Balloons and other lighter-than-air and unpropelled craft had previously traversed the atmosphere. But this was incontrovertibly the birth of air communications. Yet two years earlier Paul Fauchille had already written his *Le Domaine Aérien* in which he propounded his thesis of "freedom of the air." This was adopted in 1906 by the Institute of International Law when it proclaimed that the air was free and that states had "only the rights necessary for their preservation." [57] World War I threw new light on the possibilities of aircraft and changed the general attitude toward them. At the Paris Convention on Aerial Navigation in 1919 it was established that "each State has complete and exclusive jurisdiction over the air space above its territory." [58]

An airplane flying over the territory of an unwilling state can be forced down or harassed. A radio broadcast cannot or, at least, could not at the time. But because radio came into universal use later than did the airplane, and more especially because it came at a time when sovereignty over the air space above a state's territory had become a necessity, the first reaction of international lawyers was to say with C. C. Hyde: "It is doubtless the right of a State to control the passage of Hertzian waves through the air space over its territory." [59] This appears to have been the general attitude until the early 1930s. Wrote Lauterpacht: "The principle of exclusive sovereignty in the air space for the subjacent State, which has received general approval in connection with aerial navigation, enables that State to prohibit the disturbance of the air space over its territory by means of Hertzian waves caused for the purpose of wireless communication and emanating from a foreign force. Neither the Washington Convention of November 25, 1927, nor the General Radio Communication Regulations attached to the International Telecommunication Convention of Madrid of December 9, 1932, nor the European Broadcasting Convention of Lucerne of June 19, 1933, derogate from that principle." [60]

This sovereignty of the air could be interpreted differently, however. In 1929 the United States, Canada, Cuba, and Newfoundland signed an agreement regarding high frequencies which said that "the sovereign right of all nations to the use of every radio channel is recognized." [61] The sovereignties are mutually exclusive. True, regulative conditions were being put into international agreements. The Inter-American Radiocommunications Convention signed at Havana in 1937 repeated the permissive statement above in its Article 11, and added, "The American Governments, upon the sole condition that no interference will be caused to the services of another country, may assign any frequency and any type of wave to any radio station under their authority." [62]

The International Radiotelegraph Conference held in Madrid in 1932, and later the International Telecommunication Conference at Cairo in 1938, while maintaining "the principle of the right of nations to make assignments of any frequency" they desired, set the condition that no interference should result with the signals of other states. "However, if frequencies to be used are capable of causing interference, the nations agree to assign frequencies to services in accordance with the table of allocations." [63]

By 1947 the air was so full of radio traffic that traffic regulations were taken for granted. Thus the International Telecommunication Conference meeting in Atlantic City that year begins the Preamble of the convention with: "While fully recognizing the sovereign right of each country to regulate its telecommunication," and says in Article 42 that "Members and Associate Members recognize that it is desirable to limit the number of frequencies and the spectrum space used to the minimum essential to provide in a satisfactory manner the necessary services." [64]

The North American Regional Broadcasting Agreement signed at Havana on December 13, 1937, by the United States, Canada, Cuba, Mexico, the Dominican Republic, and Haiti put it this way: "The Governments recognize, however, that until technical developments reach a state permitting the elimination of radio interference of international character, a regional arrangement between them is necessary in order to promote standardization and to minimize interference." [65]

The attitude, therefore, has changed from a claim of sovereignty by a subjacent state over its atmosphere to a claim of the sovereign right of a state to send Hertzian waves into the four corners of the earth, limited only by the state's own sovereign will as expressed in treaties.

The question of propaganda by broadcasting came before the League of Nations as early as 1926. It was brought to the attention of the Council by the International Broadcasting Union,[66] which on March 25 and July 6, 1926, adopted resolutions to eliminate broadcasts prejudicial to good international relations.[67] The International Broadcasting Union stressed that "national transmissions should not contain, in the political, religious, economic, intellectual, and artistic fields, any attack on the spirit of cooperation and international good will, which are unquestionable necessities for the international development of broadcasting." The League's Advisory and Technical Committee for Communication and Transit placed the matter on the agenda of a later session.[68]

The matter was fully discussed by the Assembly in 1928, and a Romanian delegate, V. Pella, pleaded strongly for an international convention to repress hostile propaganda. The Sixth Committee did, in fact, adopt a report calling the attention of governments to "broadcasting inspired by a spirit antagonistic to that of the League." Again in 1928 the International Broadcasting Union notified the League that certain inadmissible types of propaganda had been carried on by broadcasting, and in May 1929 told the League that it was desirable "that broadcasting should not be hampered by being utilized for purposes of undesirable propaganda, to the detriment of its development as a means of promoting mutual understanding between peoples." [69]

The International Broadcasting Union itself worked among its members, when incidents occurred, trying to bring them together by making them sign bilateral and multilateral agreements of noninterference and abstention from hostile propaganda. But while some governments were meticulous in forbidding the broadcasting of matter that might give offense to nearby nations, others disseminated propaganda in the guise of internal broadcasts, sometimes even using the languages of neighboring states, ostensibly addressing themselves to their own foreign-language minorities.

Probably the most important agreement signed with the express purpose of curbing undesirable international propaganda by radio was the International Convention Concerning the Use of Broadcasting in the Cause of Peace. In 1931 the Sixth Committee of the League Assembly approved a study to be made by the Committee on Intellectual Cooperation — an agency of the League — on the use of international broadcasting in the cause of peace and for the promotion of international understanding. In September 1933 the League authorized the Committee on Intellectual Cooperation to prepare a draft convention on propaganda and a preliminary draft international agreement for the use of broadcasting in the cause of peace.[70]

The International Convention Concerning the Use of Broadcasting in the Cause of Peace which developed out of this was attended by delegations from twenty-eight countries (not including the United States). The meeting was held in Geneva, and the convention was signed on September 23, 1936. It came into force on April 2, 1938, after receipt by the secretary-general of the League of the sixth ratification, in compliance with Article 11 of the convention.[71] To date it has been ratified by 13 states [72] and acceded to by 9 others.[73] So far 15 states have failed to ratify it.[74]

Articles 1 to 4 of the convention contain the repressive clauses aimed at broadcasting that might incite peoples or states to war, and at the use of inaccurate statements likely to create international misunderstanding. Under Article 6 the parties pledge themselves to control radio stations within their jurisdiction so that they will abide by the provisions of the convention. The full text of these articles is:

Article 1. The high contracting parties mutually undertake to prohibit and, if occasion arises, to stop without delay the broadcasting within their respective territories of any transmission which to the detriment of good international understanding is of such a character as to incite the population of any territory to acts incompatible with the internal order or the security of a territory of a high contracting party.

Article 2. The high contracting parties mutually undertake to ensure that transmissions from stations within their respective territories shall not constitute an incitement either to war against another high contracting party or to acts likely to lead thereto.

Article 3. The high contracting parties mutually undertake to prohibit and, if occasion arises, to stop without delay within their respective territories any transmission likely to harm good international understanding by statements the incorrectness of which is or ought to be known to the persons responsible for the broadcast.

They further mutually undertake to ensure that any transmission likely to harm good international understanding by incorrect statements shall be rectified at the earliest possible moment by the most effective means, even if the incorrectness has become apparent only after the broadcast has taken place.

Article 4. The high contracting parties mutually undertake to ensure, especially in time of crisis, that stations within their respective territories shall broadcast information concerning international relations, the accuracy of which shall have been verified — and that by all means within their power — by the persons responsible for broadcasting the information.

Article 6. In order to give full effect to the obligations assumed under the preceding articles, the high contracting parties mutually undertake to issue, for the guidance of governmental broadcasting services, appropriate instructions and regulations, and to secure their application by these services.

With the same end in view, the high contracting parties mutually undertake to include appropriate clauses for the guidance of any autonomous broadcasting organizations, either in the constitutive charter of a national institution, or in the conditions imposed upon a concessionary company, or in the rules applicable to other private concerns, and to take the necessary measures to ensure the application of these clauses.

Britain, India, and Spain had urged Drafting Committee II of the Conference on the International Convention to say something about the dangers of broadcasting in foreign languages. But the committee was against this, since it "would be no obstacle to the carrying on by a country of provocative propaganda among the populations and, more particularly, the minorities of the same language in another country." The committee also felt that "the mere fact that the transmission is broadcast in a language other than that of the country of origin does not imply that it is intended, for provocative ends, for listeners in another country." [75]

Belgium, Spain, and Russia signed with reservations.[76] Significantly, none of these states has ratified the convention. Articles 8 to 15 entrust various functions to the League of Nations. Since, however, nothing has been done to transfer these functions to the United Nations, the provisions of accession under Articles 10 and 12, of denunciation under Article 13, application to dependent territories under Article 14, and revision under Article 15, are at present not applicable.[77]

The major weakness of the convention is that it does not define a transmission "which to the detriment of good international understanding is of such character as to incite the population of any territory to acts incompatible with . . . internal order or . . . security. . . ." It does not say what constitutes "an incitement . . . to war," or how states can determine the accuracy of the millions of statements made on radio stations each year. There are several other weaknesses. In modern psychological warfare, truth is the weapon more often than not. It is through the choice of the truth that states deliver their most stinging darts. Many disputes are bound to arise when states feel they have the law on their side. And should these come to arbitration, the treaty prescribes no penalties for infringements. What, therefore, does a state stand to gain through litigation? Finally, as Finland pointed out at the Conference on the International Convention, "it is extremely probable that the signatory States would be among those which, even without being committed by such a convention, do not adopt, in the matter of broadcasting, an attitude contrary to the proposed stipulation." [78]

In the Western Hemisphere a number of multilateral agreements have been signed which specifically mention the dangerous potentialities of propaganda by short wave. At the seventh International Conference of American States held at Montevideo on December 28, 1933, there was signed the Convention on Rights and Duties of States which included a reference to intervention in the internal or external affairs of a state.[79]

More explicit was the South American Regional Agreement on Radio Communications signed at Buenos Aires on April 10, 1935. In Article 7 the signatories "pledge . . . to control the sources and accuracy of information broadcast, avoid defamatory emissions, and abstain from participation in the political and social tendencies operating in other adhering states." Adherence to this agreement and to the Geneva International Convention Concerning the Use of Broadcasting in the Cause of Peace was pledged in Resolution XIV of the Inter-American Conference for the Maintenance of Peace, held at Buenos Aires from December 1 to 23, 1936. Resolution XV at the same conference warned the signatories to avoid broadcasts that were likely to disturb international relations or offend foreign listeners. However, the United States delegate abstained from voting on Resolution XIV, and voted for Resolution XV only subject to the limitations of the internal legislation of the United States.[80]

The following year the South American Regional Agreement on Radio Communications was signed at Rio de Janeiro on June 6, 1937.[81] It was revised by the South American Radio Communications Agreement signed at Santiago on January 17, 1940; but Article 2 of each agreement remains the same: "Article 2. *Transmissions of an International Character.* The administrations of the signatory countries shall take the necessary steps: (1) To ensure that during the dissemination of information of an international political nature relating to the signatory countries, and particularly during the dissemination of merely political news, the origin of such information shall be accurately given, and to ensure that no such information the source of which is not absolutely certain or the publication of which has not been duly authorized may be disseminated; (2) To ensure that the dissemination of news or of commentaries which might disturb the good relations between States, offend national sentiment of other countries or injure the work of the organization and consolidation of peace, as well as all which might offend the officially designated authorities of States, shall be avoided; (3) To ensure their propagation through broadcasting ideas which might threaten the sovereignty and integrity of States shall be avoided."[82]

For the duration of World War II, the International Convention Concerning the Use of Broadcasting in the Cause of Peace and the South American Regional Convention on Radiocommunications were renounced by the Inter-American Neutrality Committee in Rio de Janeiro on June 22, 1940. The preamble to the recommendations on telecommunications read in part: ". . . these stipulations were designed for a time of peace and it does not appear that they can have a strict application with respect to the duties of the neutral state in time of war; and for this reason, each State should decide to what extent the application of these principles is in accord with the duties of neutrality." Both Articles 5 and 6 of the recommendations of the Neutrality Committee prohibited the dissemination of "information of a military character of propaganda relative to the hostilities which in the judgment of the neutral State is contrary to neutrality." [83]

One of the major problems in international broadcasting being the allocation of frequencies, thirty-one nations met in 1939 at Montreux, Switzerland, to redistribute the available broadcasting channels. But the agreement came to naught when war broke out, and the states continued to adhere to the old allocations. In October 1947, seventy-eight nations met in Atlantic City to draft the International Communication Convention mentioned above. This adopted a world-wide frequency allocation table, extending the previous (Cairo) table devised in 1938 from 30,000 kilocycles to 10,500,000 kilocycles. The following year, a High Frequency Broadcasting Conference met in Mexico City from October 22, 1948, to April 9, 1949. Sixty-nine countries were represented. The task of this conference was almost impossible. Before World War II fewer than twenty countries had engaged in high frequency broadcasting. By 1947 some seventy-seven states were actually broadcasting in the high frequency bands or preparing to do so. The requirements submitted were about three times the space available in the high frequency range, and this meant that the assignments were fewer than the requests. Although only sixty-nine countries were represented at the conference, the plan called for allocations to eighty-five states and territories. The United States was ninth in the number of frequencies allotted, and it refused to sign the agreement. So did the Soviet Union, some of its satellites, and Liberia, Chile, and Guatemala. Altogether fifty states signed the final agreement.[84]

The following year another International High Frequency Radio Conference met in Florence during April and May. An attempt was made to allocate new short wave lengths, and forty-nine nations attended. But before the conference was over, Russia and its satellites had walked out, refusing even to share the expenses of the conference.[85] The United States had not attended the Florence conference. Since the United States neither signed nor approved the Mexico City agreement, it cannot be bound by it. Nor can the United States be bound by the European Broadcasting Convention, which it refused to sign at Copenhagen in September 1948. The convention allocated medium and long waves to the thirty-three countries in the European region.[86] The result was that the United States could, and did, use frequencies in Europe that had not been allocated to it. The European Broadcasting Convention was to come into force on March 15, 1950. On March 13 the United States announced that the sixteen frequencies being used by it in Germany were insufficient and that it was assigning itself another fourteen, "to maintain its position in the propaganda aspects of the 'cold war'." The Copenhagen agreement had assigned three frequencies to the American Zone and only eight to all West Germany. The United States took over the additional frequencies, although American officials in Europe were embarrassed.[87]

International propaganda over the radio can be made ineffectual, and can thus be controlled, by the receiving state through jamming. This became a well-developed science only after World War II. The Russians began to interfere with the Russian-language broadcasts of the United States in February 1948; and on April 24, 1949, they started using more than 1,000 broadcasting stations, it was estimated, to jam both American and British services beamed to Russia and its satellites. Even the United Nations broadcasts were jammed, and Hernán Santa Cruz, the Chilean delegate to the United Nations, in a discussion of radio jamming, mentioned that he had listened in to the Security Council's deliberations on Korea when he was in Geneva and could hear only Jacob Malik. The rest had been jammed. The United States protested to the Soviet government and the International Telecommunication Union on May 2, 1949. That organization forwarded the United States protest to Russia the following day, and no more was heard of it.[88]

The Yugoslav delegate, Ratko Pleić, also complained of the interference with radio broadcasts on November 18, 1950. He said that Russia, with its advanced technology, had developed an entire system of interference with foreign radio signals. Russian jamming transmitters cost more than "the entire international broadcasting system of the United States," the American delegate suggested. Pleić asserted that under existing international treaties states were bound to refrain from interfering with foreign broadcasts. Besides violating international obligations, interference, he said, threatened to destroy the entire radiocommunications system.[89]

Pleić was right. Every radio convention since the Berlin Conference of 1906 mentions the elimination of interference and its prevention as far as possible.[90] Article 44 of the International Telecommunication Convention signed in Atlantic City in 1947, states that "1. All stations, whatever their purpose, must be established and operated in such a manner as not to result in harmful interference to the radio services or communications of other Members or Associate Members or of recognized private operating agencies, or of other duly authorized operating agencies which carry on radio service. . . . 3. Further, the Members and Associate Members recognize the desirability of taking all practicable steps to prevent the operation of electrical apparatus and installations of all kinds from causing harmful interference to the radio services or communications mentioned in paragraph 1 of this Article."[91]

The United Nations and its committees have on three different occasions — all in 1950 — condemned jamming. The UN Sub-Commission on Freedom of Information and the Press, in May 1950, adopted a resolution of the United States condemning the USSR for "deliberately interfering with the reception by the people of the U.S.S.R. of certain radio signals originating beyond the territory of the U.S.S.R.," by a vote of 8 to 0, with 3 abstentions. The Economic and Social Council, meeting in Geneva for its eleventh session the following August, similarly condemned jamming, as did the General Assembly on December 14, 1950, by a vote of 49 to 5.[92]

The Russians countered that they were merely trying to protect their citizens and nullify the psychological warfare being waged by the United States and Great Britain. Jerzy Michalowski, the Polish delegate, added that "each country had . . . the sovereign right to defend itself against this form of aggression, just as it had the right to prevent opium smuggling, the sale of pornographic literature or the traffic in persons. . . . To drag the United Nations in as a defender of such radio broadcasts was one of the most cynical acts ever recorded in the annals of international relations." He accused the Voice of America, the BBC, Radio Free Europe,

Radiodifusion Française in Paris, and Radio Nacional in Madrid of disseminating slander and lies.[93]

The USSR either abstained from voting or voted against all three resolutions of the United Nations condemning jamming. Furthermore, the resolutions had no provisions which might have forced a state to comply. Article 44 of the International Telecommunication Convention of 1947, for instance, is binding on Russia, a signatory, and the language is definite. Yet the United States protests to both Russia and the ITU in Geneva were ineffective. In June 1949 the *New York Times* reported that 101 British and United States transmitters had failed to get through the Soviet jamming which, according to Assistant Secretary of State Allen, was 70 to 75 per cent effective. The Russians could follow any change in wave length within 12 seconds, Allen reported. One method used to overcome jamming is to "cuddle up" to a station and broadcast on a wave length close to it. This method is as illegal as is the jamming that has made it necessary.[94]

It is a moot point whether the Russians could justify in an international court their argument of self-defense in disregarding Article 44 of the Atlantic City convention. Fenwick quotes Heffter, Bluntschli, and Treitschke as having defended the right of a state to repudiate treaties that conflict with the "rights and welfare" of the people.[95] But these writers are among a very small minority. *Pacta sunt servanda* is the principle on which the majority of states insist, i.e., treaties are to be observed. The "rights and welfare" of the people should have been taken into consideration by all parties before the treaty was ratified. Russia might argue that a new and unforeseen element had crept in, and that the treaty was subject to the *clausula rebus sic stantibus*. But there does not appear to be any evidence of changing circumstances in this case. International propaganda is not a postwar innovation, nor is the United States the only country that engages in it.

A case might have been worked out if the United States had first been guilty of a breach of the Atlantic City convention. "The innocent party may, at its own option, abrogate a treaty between it and a party committing a breach thereof."[96] But no mention is made of psychological warfare in the International Telecommunication Convention, thereby possibly making the United States broadcasts illegal. The United States contravened Article 42 of the Atlantic City convention when it began to use "intruder" tactics, i.e., "cuddling up" to a Russian radio frequency, in that it did not "limit the number of frequencies and the spectrum space used to the minimum essential to provide in a satisfactory manner the necessary services." But this happened only after Soviet jamming had been going on for many months.

Although Russia was the first to ignore the treaty, and United States' representations to the Soviet government, the International Telecommunication Union, and the United Nations were fruitless, the United States still had no right to take retaliatory action. It could have declared the treaty void with respect to the USSR. This declaration was not made.[97]

The transmitting of propaganda by airplanes, balloons, dirigibles, rockets, and other airborne vehicles has been tried on numerous occasions.[98] Radio Free Europe has launched freedom balloons carrying propaganda leaflets to countries behind the Iron Curtain. In wartime, propaganda materials have been fired behind the enemy lines by cannon and dropped from airplanes. As to such practices in wartime, a commission of jurists, meeting at The Hague in 1923, wrote that incidents in World War I had shown the desirability for a "distinct rule on the question whether the dropping of leaflets for propaganda purposes was a legitimate means of warfare." Because some states had penalized airmen who were captured in the act of dropping leaflets, Article 21 of "Rules of Aerial Warfare" drawn up by the commission provides that "The use of aircraft for the purpose of disseminating propaganda shall not be treated as an illegitimate means of warfare. Members of the crews of such aircraft must not be deprived of their rights as prisoners of war on the charge that they have committed such an act." The commission of jurists explained that this activity "is not limited to dropping leaflets, as aircraft can disseminate propaganda by other means, such, for instance, as emitting trails of smoke in the form of words in the sky." They excluded propaganda inciting to murder or assassination.[99]

The activities of aircraft are controlled by the Convention on International Civil Aviation adopted at Chicago on December 7, 1944. Article 1 of this convention states that "The Contracting States recognize that every State has complete and exclusive sovereignty over the airspace above its territory." And Article 3(c) reads: "No state aircraft of a contracting State shall fly over the territory of another State or land thereon without authorization by special agreement or otherwise, and in accordance with the terms thereof." Under Article 4 "Each contracting State agrees not to use civil aviation for any purpose inconsistent with the aims of this Convention." The aims of the convention are set out in the preamble, and include the statement that the convention is designed to "help to create and preserve friendship and understanding among the nations and peoples of the world . . . to avoid friction and to promote that cooperation between nations and peoples upon which the peace of the world depends." [100] This excludes the dropping of propaganda materials from aircraft, whether state owned or privately owned, without the acquiescence of the receiving state.

A passenger may not drop propaganda materials from an airplane, since Article 35 prohibits the carrying of munitions of war or implements of war, and "Each State shall determine by regulations what constitutes munitions of war or implements of war for the purposes of this Article." [101] Furthermore, Article 35(b) states that "Each contracting State reserves the right, for reasons of public order and safety, to regulate or prohibit the carriage in or above its territory of articles other than those enumerated in paragraph (a)." Annex 2 to the convention has a clause on "Dropping Objects," which, if broadly interpreted, would place the onus of responsibility on the pilot if a passenger or member of the crew were to drop propaganda materials from the air.[102]

The use of other airborne vehicles, such as balloons, rockets, projectiles of all kinds, or dirigibles is prohibited under Article 8: "No aircraft capable of being flown without a pilot shall be flown without a pilot over the territory of a contracting State without special authorization by that State and in accordance with the terms of such authorization." The Soviet Union is not a party to the convention. Only Poland and Czechoslovakia of the countries in the Soviet sphere are members of the International Civil Aviation Organization.

Particular Treaties Limiting International Propaganda

Various bilateral and multilateral treaties have been signed by states designed to curb their own propaganda activities or the dissemination of propaganda by individuals within their jurisdiction. While examples of such treaties were not numerous prior to World War I, they did exist. Britain and Denmark signed an agreement in the middle of the seventeenth century pledging the parties to refrain from harboring "the enemies or rebels of the other." [103] More directly concerned with propaganda activities of individuals was the treaty signed by France and Russia in 1801, which included the following language: "Article 3. The two contracting parties, wishing in so far as it is in their power to contribute to the tranquillity of their respective governments, mutually oblige themselves not to permit any of their subjects to carry on any correspondence whatever, direct or indirect, with the internal enemies of the existing government of the two states to propagate their principles contrary to their respective constitutions, or to incite disorders." Restrictive of government propaganda was a treaty between Austria-Hungary and Serbia signed in 1881.[104]

Far more numerous were the agreements signed between World War I and World War II aimed at curbing the propaganda activities of states and their subjects. Among these treaties the ones signed by the Soviet Union are the most numerous. A very large number of treaties merely provided that the contracting parties would "refrain from any agitation or propaganda against the Government or the public and military institutions of the other Party. In so far as this obligation devolves upon Russia, it holds good also for the territories occupied by the powers of the Quadruple Alliance." [105] This was the wording of Article 2 of the peace treaty of Brest-Litovsk, signed by the RSFSR and the Central Powers on March 3, 1918. In the same treaty (Article 6) Russia promised to put an end to propaganda activities directed against the Ukrainian People's Republic and against the public institutions of Finland. In other words, the parties agreed to refrain from engaging in official propaganda activities through the agency of some government department or a government official. This included, in some treaties, a pledge not to send agitators into the territory of the other party to stir up strife.[106]

Similar treaties, pertaining to the dissemination of propaganda by official sources were signed by the RSFSR with the United Kingdom on March 16, 1921,[107] Poland on March 18, 1921,[108] Norway on September 2, 1921,[109] Italy on December 26, 1921,[110] and Czechoslovakia on June 5, 1922.[111]

In the exchange of notes between the United Kingdom and the USSR regarding *de jure* recognition of the Soviet Union signed in Moscow on February 1 and in London on February 8, 1924, the parties pledged themselves to abstain from interfering with each other's internal affairs and from conducting propaganda against each other's institutions and government.[112] Article 4 of a treaty signed by the USSR with Persia on October 1, 1927, forbids the officials of one party to engage in propaganda against the government of the other party in the latter's territory.[113] In an exchange of notes of the same date, the Persian minister in Moscow informed the Soviet government "that all political propaganda and agitation among the local population and workmen, and all interference in the internal political, religious and social affairs of Persia by Soviet citizens employed by the Company . . . are strictly forbidden." [114] Afghanistan signed a treaty with Russia on June 24, 1931.[115] This treaty refers to armed or unarmed interference in the internal affairs of the other party. France signed a similar treaty on November 29, 1932,[116] as did Czechoslovakia and Romania on June 9, 1934,[117] and Bulgaria on July 23, 1934.[118]

In addition to these treaties, which were formulated in fairly general terms, a number of agreements were signed by Russia limiting the activities of members of delegations engaged in the exchange of prisoners of war. Article 14 of the treaty signed by the RSFSR and the Ukrainian SSR with Austria on December 7, 1921, is typical, and reads: "The delegations of the Contracting Parties (diplomatic officials through this treaty) and the persons employed by them shall, in carrying out their work, strictly confine themselves to the duties devolving upon them in accordance with the present Agreement. In particular, they shall be required to refrain from any kind of agitation or propaganda against the Government or the state organizations of the country in which they are temporarily resident." [119]

The treaties or the exchanges of notes conferring recognition on the Soviet Union had, in a number of cases, a special clause in which the parties pledged themselves to refrain from encouraging or assisting groups or individuals desirous of conducting propaganda activities outside the borders of the state. Such clauses were included in the agreement between Russia and the United Kingdom of March 16, 1921; [120] Poland, signed on March 18, 1921; [121] Italy of December 26, 1921; [122] the exchange of notes of May 29, 1923, between the Soviet government and Britain;[123] the Russo-Japanese treaty of January 20, 1925;[124] the Anglo-Soviet protocol signed in London on October 3, 1929, and the exchange of notes that followed on December 21, 1929;[125] and the Roosevelt-Litvinov exchange of notes of November 16, 1933, in which the United States recognized the Soviet Union.[126]

Article 15 of the treaty of February 26, 1921, between Persia and the RSFSR should, perhaps, be mentioned separately. This was a treaty of friendship signed in Moscow and ratified on February 26 of the following year. In it Russia promises to cease its "religious missionary propaganda."

The article reads in full: "The Soviet Government of Russia is ready, in view of the principles which it has declared with respect to the freedom of religious ideas, to stop religious missionary propaganda in the Islamic countries, the secret aim of which was political influence among the masses and to help the vicious Tsarist intrigues." [127] The treaty is unique. It will be noted that the Soviet abstention applies to all Islamic countries and not to Persia alone.

A series of treaties signed by the Soviet Union with contiguous states since World War II is noteworthy. The words agitation and propaganda are not mentioned in any of them; but the tenor remains the same. Typical of all these agreements is the Russo-Polish Treaty of Friendship, Mutual Assistance, and Post-War Cooperation signed in Moscow on April 21, 1945. Article 2 reads in part: "The High Contracting Parties will strengthen friendly cooperation between both countries in accordance with the principles of mutual respect for their independence and sovereignty and also of non-intervention in internal affairs of the other State." [128]

Besides these agreements signed by Russia controlling the propaganda activities of the contracting parties, there were other treaties in which the signatories pledged themselves to control the activities of private organizations or groups within their territories which were hostile to the other party to the agreement. In Article 7(5) of the treaty between Russia and Estonia of February 2, 1920, for instance, the parties agreed to "forbid the formation, and the presence in their territory, of any organizations or groups whatsoever claiming to govern all or any part of the territory of the other contracting party, and the presence of representatives or officials of organizations or groups whose object is to overthrow the Government of the other party to the treaty." [129]

Other states among themselves have seldom signed treaties controlling propaganda activities. However, such agreements are not altogether lacking. The treaty between Saudi Arabia and Iraq of April 2, 1936, prohibited the use of subversive propaganda by the parties.[130] In July 1936, Germany agreed with Austria not to interfere in the other's internal affairs either directly or indirectly.[131] The treaty signed by Yugoslavia and Italy on March 25, 1937, pledged the signatories not to assist groups active in the dissemination of propaganda against the other party.[132] On July 8, 1937, Afghanistan, Iraq, Iran, and Turkey signed a treaty of non-aggression, Article 1 of which reads: "The High Contracting Parties undertake to pursue a policy of complete abstention from any interference in each other's internal affairs." The Gentlemen's Agreement signed by Italy and Great Britain on April 16, 1938, included the following clause: "The two Governments welcome the opportunity afforded by the present occasion to place on record their agreement that any attempt by either of them to employ the methods of publicity or propaganda at its disposal in order to injure the interests of the other would be inconsistent with the good relations which it is the object of the present Agreement to establish and maintain between the two Governments and the peoples of their respective countries." [133] Article 5 of the treaty of nonaggression between the United Kingdom and Thailand pledges the parties to refrain from intervening in each other's internal affairs and to "abstain from any action calculated to give rise to or assist any agitation, propaganda or attempted intervention against the integrity" of the territories of the other party.[134]

In April 1948 India and Pakistan signed an agreement regarding the cooperation of the press. In it both governments promise to "ensure that their respective organizations handling publicity, including publicity through radio and the film, refrain from and control" propaganda against the other dominion, or news "likely to inflame, or cause fear or alarm to, the population or a section of the population in either Dominion." [135] One might also add the Treaty of Friendship and Neighborly Relations between Iraq and Turkey of March 29, 1946, in which "Each of the High Contracting Parties undertakes to respect their territorial integrity and their common frontiers as defined and delimited in the Treaty concluded in 1926." [136]

In all the agreements quoted above, the propaganda referred to is official propaganda carried on by an agency of the government of a contracting party. Two more articles of the treaty between Iraq and Turkey of March 29, 1946, deserve separate mention. The first, Article 23, deals with propaganda of an official nature, but is unique in its provisions. It reads: "The authorities of both Parties shall abstain from any correspondence or any relations with nationals of the other State who are at the time in the latter's territory." The other article provides for an exchange of information regarding "harmful and subversive propaganda." It reads: "Article 10. The High Contracting Parties undertake to exchange any information in their possession with regard to harmful and subversive propaganda contrary to the laws and likely to compromise the other Party's security and to arouse a spirit of rebellion." [137]

This article is perhaps more closely allied with the next series of treaties signed by states other than the Soviet Union, treaties that deal with the control of propaganda activities of private organizations or individuals. The Political Agreement between Austria and Czechoslovakia signed on December 16, 1921, is an example of this type of treaty. Article 4 reads: "Both States undertake not to tolerate on their territories any political or military organization directed against the integrity and security of the other contracting party. . . ." [138]

Article 7 of the July 1937 treaty between Afghanistan, Iraq, Iran, and Turkey provides that "Each of the High Contracting Parties undertakes to prevent, within his respective frontiers, the formation [of] . . . associations or organizations to subvert the established institutions, or disturb the order or security of any part, whether situated on the frontier or elsewhere, of the territory of any Party, or to change the constitutional system of such other Party." The treaty between Greece and Turkey of April 27, 1938, has similar provisions. [139] During World War II, Britain, acting for the Sheikh of Kuwait, signed a treaty with Saudi Arabia, promising to make every effort to prevent the use of each other's territories "as a base for any unlawful act," leaving the interpretation of the term up to the individual governments. [140] Egypt and Yemen agreed on September 27, 1945, "to take all measures to prevent the commission on its territory of any act against peace and tranquillity within the territory of the other party." [141] Under the treaty of April 14, 1947, the heads of state of both Iraq and Transjordan undertook, in case of the outbreak of disturbances, "(2) To prevent his subjects from taking part in the disturbances or disorders or from helping or encouraging the insurgents; and (3) To prevent any kind of help being given to the insurgents either directly from his own territory or otherwise." [142] The agreement between India and Pakistan of April 1948, mentioned above, included the following provisions:

1. Any propaganda for the amalgamation of Pakistan and India or of portions thereof including East Bengal on the one hand and West Bengal or Assam or Cooch Behar or Tripura on the other, shall be discouraged.
N.B. The word "propaganda" shall be taken as including any organization which might be set up for the purpose.

2. (i) Both Governments recognize that the wholehearted cooperation of the Press is essential for creating a better atmosphere and therefore agree that every effort should be made, in consultation with the representatives of the Press, wherever possible, to ensure that the Press in each Dominion does not:
    (a) Indulge in propaganda against the other Dominion;

(b) Publish exaggerated versions of news of a character likely to inflame, or cause fear or alarm to, the population or a section of the population in either Dominion;

(c) Publish material likely to be construed as advocating a declaration of war by one Dominion against the other Dominion or suggesting the inevitability of war between two Dominions.[143]

The treaty of October 6, 1948, between Lebanon and Greece includes a clause permitting one party to expel the nationals of the other "if they have become guilty of subversive activities or activities detrimental to public order . . . or . . . tranquillity." [144] And Article 20 of the Treaty of Friendship, Commerce, and Navigation between the United States and Ireland, signed on January 21, 1950, says that "the present treaty does not accord any rights to engage in political activities." [145]

During the celebration in 1931 of the tenth anniversary of the plebiscite in Upper Silesia, radio stations in Germany and Poland gave vent to their feelings in a number of broadcasts that were extremely uncomplimentary to the other state. This led to protests and the intervention of the International Broadcasting Union, which soon arranged a settlement. An agreement was signed on March 31, 1931, which is noteworthy because the signatories were not the foreign offices of Germany and Poland but the Reichsrundfunkgesellschaft and the Polskie Radio.[146]

Germany and Italy signed a cultural agreement in November 1938 in which each agreed to prohibit the publication of works biased against the other state and the writings of emigrants from the other state. This treaty is remarkable in that it permits one party to decide what publications are to be forbidden in the territory of the other — a sort of censorship from abroad.[147] Another treaty that refers especially to newspapers was the "Press-Non-Attack-Pact" between Poland and Lithuania of November 1938. It provided that neither party would permit its press to make propaganda that was unfavorable to the other.[148]

An unusual agreement affecting word-of-mouth propaganda across national frontiers that was signed by Norway and the USSR in Oslo on December 29, 1949, set up a commission in Article 19.B, whose duty it was "To investigate and in due course settle frontier disputes and incidents, for example . . . 3. Use of insulting expressions or behavior against the other Party across the frontier . . . 13. Conversation or any other form of communication across the frontier between unauthorized public officers or private persons." [149] While the word propaganda is not specifically used here, it is easy to see how this treaty can be restrictive of propaganda activities across the frontier between Norway and Russia.

General Treaties Permissive of International Propaganda

While the limitation of international propaganda has been the subject of many treaties, a number of nations have been equally concerned with the freedom to say anything to anyone anywhere. Whether freedom of expression and the existence of treaties prohibiting international propaganda are contradictions is a moot point. Some aver that one might as well say that there is no freedom of the road because there are traffic regulations. Others see in efforts to curb propaganda the first step toward the muzzling of the media of communication. To make freedom of expression possible, certain other freedoms are necessary. There is the freedom to enter a foreign state; to gather the news; to take or send information out of the state; to buy or obtain the facilities; to sell, give, or impart the information to the public; and for that public to buy or receive the information. All these are concomitants of the freedom of speech and of the press.

Some have been concerned about the lack of benevolent propaganda. Treaties have been signed that positively enjoin states and organizations to disseminate propaganda of a specific nature — generally the type that would tend to promote international good will and understanding. This does not entitle them to carry on propaganda indiscriminately. The positive treaties referred to describe and delimit the type of propaganda, publicity, or information that may be disseminated under the treaty. It is almost universally left up to the contracting parties to decide what specific items of intelligence would bring about the effect described as desirable by the treaty.

The preoccupation of the first World Press Conference, held in Chicago in 1893, with the role of the press in dispelling international misunderstanding has already been mentioned. In 1919 American journalists made an effort to have a provision for freedom of the press written into the Treaty of Versailles. They were unsuccessful; but the Western powers were more conscious of freedom of speech following World War II. The defeated countries were forced to pledge to all persons under their jurisdiction freedom of expression, press, and publication under the peace treaties signed by them with the Allied and Associated Powers in Paris on February 10, 1947.[150]

The Treaty of Economic, Social, and Cultural Collaboration and Collective Self-Defence, known as the Brussels Pact, which was signed by Belgium, France, Luxembourg, the Netherlands, and the United Kingdom on March 17, 1948, included the following: "Article 3: The High Contracting Parties will make every effort in common to lead their peoples towards a better understanding of the principles which form the basis of their common civilization and to promote cultural exchanges by conventions between themselves and by other means." [151]

The statute of the Council of Europe signed in London on May 5, 1949, says the aim of the members is the "maintenance and further realization of human rights and fundamental freedoms." [152] The following September, the Consultative Assembly of the council adopted a recommendation that went further. Article 2 read: "In this Convention, the Member States shall undertake to ensure to all persons residing within their territories . . . (6) Freedom of opinion and expression, in accordance with article 19 of the United Nations Declaration [of Human Rights]." And the Convention for the Protection of Human Rights and Fundamental Freedoms signed by the Council of Europe on November 4, 1950, says in Article 10: "(1) Everyone has the right to freedom of expression. This right shall include freedom to hold opinions and to receive and impart information and ideas without interference by public authority and regardless of frontiers. This article shall not prevent States from requiring the licensing of broadcasting, television or cinema enterprises." [153]

Despite the limitations inherent in the last sentence of this article and in one or two other articles of the convention quoted elsewhere, it appears to have been the sincere intention of the signatories to grant their subjects the widest possible freedom of expression that is consistent with the duties and responsibilities that accompany such freedom, and with national security in times of crisis.[154]

The Universal Declaration of Human Rights was adopted by the General Assembly of the United Nations on December 10, 1948. Article 19 reads: "Everyone has the right to freedom of opinion and expression; this right includes freedom to hold opinions without interference and to seek, receive and impart information and ideas through any media and regardless of frontiers." [155] The declaration, however, is no more than a recommendation. As Kelsen has pointed out, the General Assembly merely proclaims it "as a common standard of achievement for all peoples and all nations." [156] And it is lacking in another feature, one equally lacking in many of the resolutions of the United Nations and most international provisions relating to the freedom of expression. No provisions are made for international legal remedies in case of violation of these freedoms.

Other treaties that are filled with similar good intentions and weaknesses are the Constitution of UNESCO, which provides for freedom of information in Article 1, and the Constitution of the ILO, as amended in May 1944, which provides for freedom of expression in Annex I(b). Resolution 424(V) of the United Nations General Assembly, adopted on December 14, 1950, also calls upon members to refrain from interfering "with the right of their peoples to freedom of information." [157]

The Inter-American Conference on Problems of War and Peace, meeting in Mexico City in 1945, recommended very emphatically that freedom of expression and free access to the truth be granted to all as "an essential condition to the development of an active and vigilant public opinion." It saw as a fundamental lesson of World War II "that there can be no freedom, peace or security where men are not assured of free access to the truth through the various media of public information." [158] It therefore recommended in section 4 "That the American Republics, having accepted the principle of free access to information for all, make every effort to the end that when a juridical order in the world is assured, there may be established the principle of free transmission and reception of information, oral and written, published in books or by the press, broadcast by radio or disseminated by any other means, under proper responsibility and without need of previous censorship. . . ." The first step, therefore, is the achievement of that "juridical order."

Since one of the important prerequisites for the dissemination of benevolent propaganda, or, if it is more acceptable, to freedom of expression, is the ingress and egress of newsgatherers and of the news itself, the United Nations has passed several resolutions to abolish obstacles to freedom of movement. Resolution 290(IV) of the General Assembly adopted on December 1, 1949, called on all nations "to remove the barriers which deny to peoples the free exchange of information and ideas essential to international understanding and peace." This resolution was reaffirmed on November 17, 1950, at which time, by a vote of 49 to 0, with 7 abstentions, the General Assembly condemned any measures that tended to prevent peoples from acquiring information about international events and about the activities of the United Nations. [159]

For the reasons mentioned above, the Social Committee of the United

Nations General Assembly approved by a vote of 28 to 8 (the Soviet bloc being opposed) a proviso that "outgoing news dispatches shall not be censored, edited or delayed except in situations relating directly to the protection or national defense of a country." [160] Similarly, the first World Convention on the International Transmission of News and the Right of Correction made the following recommendation to the United Nations General Assembly, which was approved by 33 votes to 6, with 11 abstentions: "Article 8. Each contracting state shall permit all news dispatches of correspondents and information agencies of other contracting states to enter its territory and reach information agencies operating therein on conditions which are not less favorable than those accorded to any correspondent or information agency of any other contracting or non-contracting state." [161] This is obviously not a far-reaching agreement; yet 17 states saw fit to withhold their approval.

In the same vein, the Conference on Freedom of Information of the United Nations condemned the arbitrary expulsion of foreign correspondents. The stand was approved by 17 votes to 2, with 5 abstentions, among them the Soviet Union.[162]

The United Nations Educational, Scientific, and Cultural Organization has worked as hard as any group to bring about international understanding through the dissemination of cultural and scientific information about all peoples. Article I.1 of the UNESCO Constitution states that "The purpose of the Organization is to contribute to peace and security by promoting collaboration among the nations through education, science and culture. . . ." This it proposes to do "through all means of mass communication" (Article I.2 (a)). The Arab League attempts to achieve an exchange of cultural and scientific information by organizing visits for journalists, broadcasters, and other mass media practitioners.[163]

An injunction that is more specifically aimed at the dissemination of "good" propaganda — propaganda intended to promote international understanding and good will — is Resolution 110(II) of the United Nations General Assembly. This was unanimously adopted on November 3, 1947, and it "2. *Requests* the Government of each Member to take appropriate steps within its constitutional limits: (a) To promote, by all means of publicity and propaganda available to them, friendly relations among nations based upon the Purposes and Principles of the Charter; (b) To encourage the dissemination of all information designed to give expression to the undoubted desire of all peoples for peace." [164]

The Charter of the Organization of American States prepared at the ninth International Conference of American States at Bogotá and signed on April 29, 1948, called on the signatories to promote cultural development cooperatively (Article 4), proclaimed the fundamental rights of all (Article 5), and pledged that "With due consideration for the national character of each State, the Member States undertake to facilitate free cultural interchange by every medium of expression." [165]

Articles 2 and 13 of the Pact of the League of Arab States are similar in purpose. Article 2(c) states the purpose of the league to be the drawing of members closer together through cooperation in cultural matters.[166] And Article 13 reads: "The States of the Arab League will work for acquainting their sons with the social, cultural, economic, and political conditions in all Arab countries, by means of broadcasts, the stage, cinema and press or by any other means." [167]

More specific in content is the information to be disseminated under the UNESCO Resolution of June 17, 1950. It invites member states to teach children about the Universal Declaration of Human Rights, the United Nations, and its specialized agencies.[168]

The International Broadcasting Union was much concerned with broadcasts that would be conducive to the promotion of good international relations. Resolutions stating this were adopted on March 25, 1926, and July 6, 1926. In May 1929 the International Broadcasting Union informed the League of Nations that it was desirable "that broadcasting should not be hampered by being utilized for purposes of undesirable propaganda, to the detriment of its development as a means of promoting mutual understanding between peoples." [169] This is a roundabout way of saying that broadcasting can be used for both desirable and undesirable propaganda, and that it should concentrate on the former.

The International Convention Concerning the Use of Broadcasting in the Cause of Peace signed in 1936 was devoted mainly to the negative aspects of propaganda. But in Article 5 the signatories undertook to place at one another's disposal "items calculated to promote a better knowledge of the civilization and the conditions of life of [their] . . . own country as well as of the essential features of the development of . . . [their] relations with other peoples and of . . . [their] contribution to the organization of peace." [170]

A number of the regional conferences held in the Western Hemisphere have concerned themselves with the problem of the dissemination of information likely to improve relations among American states. The seventh International Conference of American States held at Montevideo in December 1933 made recommendations for the positive use of radio to promote mutual understanding.[171] In December 1936 the Inter-American Conference for the Maintenance of Peace adopted three resolutions concerning broadcasting and peace at Buenos Aires. Resolution XXI — the third resolution — recommended the establishment of the Pan American Radio Hour. Program materials for this broadcast were to be provided by each of the governments' diplomatic and consular officials in the capitals of the member states, and these materials were to "emphasize important governmental measures and events and anniversaries of historical importance." [172] Local political affairs and subversive propaganda were not to be permitted, however.

Article 3 of the South American Regional Agreement on Radio Communications signed at Rio de Janeiro on June 6, 1937, dealt with positive steps to be taken by each party toward the improvement of international relations through broadcasting.[173] The first of several inter-American radio conferences, held in December 1937 at Havana, included a clause on "Cultural Broadcasting." It reads: "Article 19. The contracting governments shall take the necessary measures in order to facilitate and promote the re-transmission and exchange of international cultural, educational and historical programs of the countries of the American continent by their respective broadcasting stations." [174]

The subcommittee on freedom of information of the third Inter-American Radio Conference held at Rio de Janeiro in September 1945 unanimously adopted a resolution calling for the freest circulation of news throughout the Western Hemisphere. This was later approved by the plenary session of the conference. It also discussed the setting up of an Inter-American Association for Radio Broadcasting, which was done the following September. Its objectives were "to establish principles of freedom and responsibility within the radio broadcasting industry, so as to promote peace and continental solidarity and a better understanding among peoples." It was the intention of the association to protect the right of free expression of thought by radio, and the right of all freely to listen to the broadcasts of national and foreign stations. In 1950, at its meeting in São Paulo, the association agreed to set aside time for the broadcasting of news from and about the United Nations.[175]

Particular Treaties Permissive of International Propaganda

Bilateral and multilateral agreements between states designed to encourage the dissemination of propaganda of certain types were not numerous before World War II. The idea underlying the treaties that have been signed in recent years has been that propaganda is a powerful weapon for good as well as for evil. It is in the interest of international peace and amity to encourage the type of propaganda that is conducive to the improvement of relations among nations. In many of the treaties the methods or means, though not the content, are specified.

A few treaties — all signed before World War II — contradict the principle that if propaganda is allowed it should be used in the interest of promoting international good will. Two were signed by Greece and Serbia in 1867 and 1868 in which the signatories agreed to spread certain types of propaganda in neighboring Turkish territory that were not exactly in the interest of international understanding. Two other treaties might be mentioned, both of them understandably secret. One was the Convention Concerning Poland allegedly signed at Brest-Litovsk on December 22, 1917, by Germany and the RSFSR, Article 3 of which read: "The Council of Commissars of the People has the right to remain in touch with the democratic, revolutionary centers existing in Poland, in order to propagate revolutionary ideas by sending into Poland agitators inscribed in the lists of the German information bureaus at Petrograd and also at Warsaw." The other was a treaty of recognition, mutual assistance, and cooperation allegedly signed by Lenin and Liebknecht, president of the so-called German Soviet Republic, on January 5, 1919. The terms of this alleged secret treaty are summarized by Leonard Shapiro: "By the terms of the treaty Lenin undertook to: 1. Recognize Liebknecht as President of the German Soviet Republic. 2. Furnish important funds for Spartacist propaganda. 3. Place specially trained agents at the disposal of the Spartacists. . . . Liebknecht pledged himself to . . . 2. Observe faithfully and put into practice all the teachings of Lenin's doctrine."[176]

But to return to bilateral treaties encouraging "good propaganda," an agreement was signed by the Reichsrundfunkgesellschaft and the Polskie Radio on March 31, 1931. One of the clauses of this agreement reserved for each signatory "the right to carry on a certain amount of positive propaganda in regard to its national activities." This positive propaganda would be of a cultural and commercial nature.[177]

During World War II and immediately thereafter, Brazil signed a series of treaties with its neighbors and with Canada in which the parties agreed to promote mutual understanding through various means. The Agreement on Cultural Exchanges signed with Paraguay at Rio de Janeiro on June 14, 1941, spoke of the exchange of university professors (Article 1), the opening of national centers in each other's territory (Article 2), and the awarding of scholarships for exchange students (Article 3). The Cultural Agreement with Chile signed at Santiago on November 18, 1941, included the same provisions in Articles 1 to 3, but added the translation of each other's classics (Article 4), assistance to cultural institutes already established (Article 5), the exchange of books (Article 6), and the exchange of cultural information through the communications media (Article 7). Similar treaties were signed by Brazil with Venezuela on October 22, 1942, the Dominican Republic on December 9, 1942, Ecuador on May 24, 1944, and again with the Dominican Republic on April 9, 1945, which dealt with the exchange of books and publications omitted in the earlier treaty. An exchange of notes by Brazil and Canada on May 24, 1944, constituting a cultural agreement, spoke of the "desirability of promoting a greater mutual knowledge and wider comprehension of the respective peoples, their cultures, traditions, and institutions. . . ." This promotion was to be achieved through the exchange of publications, through exhibitions, lectures, radio programs, and films.[178]

Another series of agreements was being signed by China at about the same time. All these agreements included the following clauses:

The nationals of each of the High Contracting Parties in the territory of the other shall enjoy the full protection of the laws and regulations of the country, as regards their persons and property.

They shall have the right to travel, reside, work and engage in industries and trade in all the localities where the nationals of any other country might do the same, subject, however, to the laws and regulations of the country.

They shall have the liberty to establish schools for the education of their children, and shall enjoy the liberty of assembly and association, of publication, of worship and religion, in accordance with the laws and regulations of the country.

With regard to this article, the laws and regulations of each of the High Contracting Parties shall not establish discriminatory provisions against the nationals of the other.[179]

Belgium has signed a number of cultural agreements with European states. The one with France, for instance, signed on February 22, 1946, provides for the exchange of professors and teachers (Article 4) as well as students (Article 5). The parties agree to open cultural institutes (Article 6), to provide scholarships for the study of each other's cultures (Article 7), and to work through youth organizations (Article 10). After stating that they would organize concerts, lectures, exhibitions, and broadcasts, and exchange films, books, and periodicals to promote a better understanding of each other's cultures, Article 11 reads: "The Contracting Parties consider it desirable that, subject only to any measures of public security which may be adopted, books, newspapers and periodicals published in one of the two countries shall be admitted freely into the territory of the other without incurring duty . . . with regard to broadcasting, the administrative authorities concerned shall endeavour to secure the reciprocal concession of broadcast programmes intended to make French culture known in Belgium and Belgian culture known in France." [180]

In other words, certain types of propaganda are found to be desirable by these states, subject only to public security. France and Belgium are friendly states, and the point at which public security might be adversely affected would not be reached as soon as between two states that are potential enemies. One might say that the reaction to propaganda can be measured on a continuum. At one extremity lies the state of affairs in which everything that is said may be interpreted to be unfriendly. At the other extremity is the situation in which everything said may be taken to be friendly. Obviously, these extremities can only be approached. But it immediately becomes clear that in actual experience the impact of what is said depends not so much on what is said, as on the degree of friendship between the states involved. The fact of the friendship between France and Belgium is pointed up in Article 13 of the agreement, which mentions a common cause: "The Contracting Parties shall consult together with a view to the protection of their common cultural interests abroad."

Other cultural agreements were signed by Belgium with the Netherlands on May 16, 1946,[181] Czechoslovakia on March 6, 1947,[182] Norway on February 20, 1948,[183] and Italy on November 29, 1948.[184]

The United Kingdom, too, signed a convention for the promotion of mutual understanding and intellectual, artistic, and scientific activities with Czechoslovakia on June 16, 1947. In it the two states pledged to work through the university, cultural institutes, student and teacher exchanges, scholarships, learned societies, youth organizations, through exchanges of all kinds, and through the promotion of public cultural activities. This treaty was renounced by Czechoslovakia on May 12, 1950. Great Britain also signed a cultural treaty with Norway on February 19, 1948, similar to that signed by Norway with Belgium. Agreements to promote each other's cultures and for the exchange of publications and publicity were signed by France with the Netherlands on November 19, 1946, Poland on February 19, 1947, and Austria, in addition to the one with Belgium mentioned above.[185]

Since World War II, the eastern European countries in the Soviet sphere of influence have signed a series of bilateral treaties among themselves designed to promote benevolent propaganda in each other's territories. Like the treaties signed by Western states, these speak of scientific and cultural exchanges. They aim at facilitating relations between their press systems, thereby promoting better understanding in each other's territory. Treaties signed by states with Slavic populations also have clauses such as the following: "The High Contracting Parties will endeavour to remove the harmful consequences to learning and culture of German-Fascist and any other fascist propaganda against the Federal People's Republic of . . ."[186] Similar cultural agreements were signed by Yugoslavia and Poland on March 16, 1946, Yugoslavia and Czechoslovakia on April 27, 1947, Czechoslovakia and Bulgaria on June 20, 1947, Yugoslavia and Romania on June 26, 1947, Poland and Bulgaria on June 28, 1947, Poland and Czechoslovakia on July 4, 1947, Yugoslavia and Albania on July 9, 1947, Czechoslovakia and Romania on September 5, 1947, Yugoslavia and Hungary on October 15, 1947, Poland and Hungary on January 31, 1948, and Poland and Romania on February 27, 1948.[187] Treaties of assistance and friendship, in addition to the cultural treaties mentioned above, were signed by Yugoslavia with Hungary on December 8, 1947, and with Romania on December 19, 1947, in which Yugoslavia, at least, expected the other parties to encourage their press to write positively about its achievements. Poland and Romania also signed a supplementary treaty on January 26, 1949, in which they agree that "the best guarantee of friendship and cooperation is to be found in the common road toward socialism."[188] The Soviet Union has signed treaties with its satellites in all of which "the High Contracting Parties declare that they will act in a spirit of friendship and cooperation for the further development and strengthening of the economic and cultural ties between the two States. . . ."[189]

In some of its postwar treaties, the United States has included a clause on freedom of information and access to news sources. The Treaty of Friendship, Commerce, and Navigation between the United States of America and the Italian republic of February 2, 1948, includes the following language: "Article XI(2). The High Contracting Parties declare their adherence to the principles of freedom of the press and of free interchange of information. To this end, nationals, corporations and associations of either High Contracting Party shall have the right, within the territories of the other High Contracting Party, to engage in such activities as writing, reporting and gathering of information for dissemination to the public, and shall enjoy freedom of transmission of material to be used abroad for publication by the press, radio, motion pictures, and other means. The nationals, corporations and associations of either High Contracting Party shall enjoy freedom of publication in the territories of the other High Contracting Party, in accordance with the applicable laws and regulations, upon the same terms as nationals, corporations or associations of such other High Contracting Parties. The term 'information,' as used in this paragraph, shall include all forms of written communications, printed matter, motion pictures, recordings and photographs." Speaking of the treaty, Senator Thomas of Utah said: "I think this treaty marks the beginning of what may be called a new era in treaty making in the United States. It is a treaty which was promised in the peace treaty with Italy, and it carries out the broad provisions of the peace treaty, such as the guaranty of freedom of worship, freedom of information, and so forth. Those matters are new." [190]

The agreement was a great concession on the part of Italy. In a propaganda war between two states, where everything is permitted and admitted, and in which neither state can fall back upon its sovereign right to exclude or to control anything it sees fit, it is highly probable that the state that can provide the highest financial backing for its propaganda campaign will win. Such a situation does not exist, of course, as no state will sign away its birthright of sovereignty — at any rate, not yet. But a great deal depends upon the degree of friendship between the signatories, and the amount of pressure that the stronger state can bring to bear upon the weaker.

A similar treaty of friendship, commerce, and navigation was signed by the United States with Ireland on January 21, 1950. Article 1 of this treaty reads in part: "Nationals of either Party, within the territories of the other Party, shall be permitted . . . (e) to gather and to transmit material for dissemination to the public abroad, and otherwise to communicate with other persons inside and outside such territories by mail, telegraph and other means open to general public use . . . subject to . . . measures . . . necessary to maintain public order and . . . to protect the public health, morals and safety." [191]

Treaties of a slightly different nature, but still permissive of propaganda are the agreements signed by Greece and Lebanon, and by the Netherlands and Indonesia. The former, signed at Beirut on October 6, 1948, includes a clause permitting the parties to carry on educational activities in each other's territories "in accordance with the laws and regulations of the country." [192] The latter, signed at The Hague on November 2, 1949, states: "Article 7: Everyone has the right to freedom of thought, conscience and religion. This right includes freedom to change his religion or belief and freedom, either alone or in community with others and in public or private, to manifest his religion or belief in teaching, practice, worship and observance of the commandments and prescriptions and by educating the children in the faith or belief of their parents. Article 8: Everyone has the right to freedom of opinion and expression." [193]

An agreement signed by the United States and West Germany on June 11, 1952, is peculiar in that it permits the use of the territory of one state by another for the launching of propaganda into a third state. Under this agreement the Federal Republic of Germany permits the government of the United States to operate radio transmitters on its territory. These transmitters are the Voice of America station in Munich and the RIAS station in Hof, a zonal border transmitter for the United States broadcasting station in Berlin. The agreement was signed by Chancellor Adenauer and acting United States High Commissioner Samuel Reber, and it was reached "only after very difficult negotiations, which for a time threatened to affect the Bonn peace contract with the Western Allies," according to the *New York Times*. It was signed for an indefinite period, and it may be terminated on one year's notice after it has been in effect for five years.[194]

Conclusion

The preoccupation of governmental and nongovernmental organizations and of states with the problems raised by international propaganda since the turn of the century, and more especially since World War I, is incontrovertible. The world suddenly became aware of this new force that could be used to capture men's minds and, through their minds, their physical being, their strength, and their property. One can see in many resolutions adopted by official and unofficial organizations the desire to control international propaganda and to channel it in the interest of world peace and understanding. This desire is no new thing. Man has witnessed attempts to control every new weapon of offense from the bow and arrow to the H-bomb. Some weapons, such as poison gas, nations have managed to control; others have passed into their armories and become commonplace. Propaganda is likely to develop into the latter type of weapon.

Propaganda has many of the properties of gunpowder. Used sporadically by individuals and turned on game, gunpowder is relatively harmless to society. It is through the concerted use of gunpowder either by individuals or by states that the force becomes a menace. Hence, the majority of treaties and international agreements ban the use of propaganda or any of its means or methods by states and organized groups for aggressive or offensive purposes. The desire to ban such propaganda, however, is modified by the knowledge that one must control one's own propaganda as a *quid pro quo*. Of course, most states will claim that any propaganda they may engage in is absolutely harmless to others and merely attempts to tell the world the truth. In other words, it is purely defensive propaganda. But it must be remembered there are two ways in which one can defeat an enemy. One can attack him with verbal darts, or one can inflate oneself and one's friends until the enemy, by comparison, is completely deflated.

The majority of particular treaties signed in the interwar period were between the Soviet Union and one or more other states. Russia was the most highly feared menace of the day, and an attempt was made to control its activities. This shows a desire to create an obligation in a special case only, that is, where no general law previously existed. The existence of a large number of these treaties, therefore, does not in any way create a new principle of customary international law. Rather is it a sign that states could normally live unmoved by one another's propaganda, and that special legislation was necessary only when one particular state turned out to be a maverick especially to be feared. It is significant perhaps that after World War II, when the international propaganda activities of the majority of states were increased and regular propaganda programs became the accepted thing, no further bilateral treaties were signed to outlaw harmful international propaganda.

6

Control by Municipal Law

THE International Court of Justice and other international tribunals recognize "the general principles of law recognized by civilized nations" as a source of international law. Both public and private international law often need to be ascertained in the municipal courts of individual nations, and the resulting judicial decision is usually accepted as a general principle of international law, at least for that state.[1] It is not uncommon, however, for the decision of a court in one state, on a rule of international law, to influence courts in other countries.

Since municipal courts are far more active than international tribunals, it is not surprising that practically every type of case involving international law has received some judicial attention in municipal courts. These decisions contribute to international law by being evidence of a state's attitude or practice; and when a sufficient amount of evidence in a large enough number of states can be adduced to show that certain practices are recognized, those practices become a general principle of international law.

The acceptance of generally recognized principles is an important element in the evolution of international law. In the Eastern Extension, Australasia & China Telegraph Co., Ltd. case, the U.S.–Great Britain Claims Arbitration Tribunal held: "International law, as well as domestic law, may not contain, and generally does not contain, express rules decisive of particular cases; but the function of jurisprudence is to resolve the conflict of opposing rights and interests by applying, in default of any specific provision of law, the corollaries of general principles, and so to find . . . the solution of the problem. This is the method of jurisprudence; it is the method by which the law has been gradually evolved in every country resulting in the definition and settlement of legal relations as well between States as between private individuals." [2]

The general principles of law recognized by civilized nations are considered by many authorities to be only a subsidiary source of international law.[3] One writer even doubts whether "they can ever come into play." He argues that "They form, almost necessarily, limitations of State sovereignty, and the principle of the independence of States is a rule of international customary law which belongs to a higher order than the general principles of law within the hierarchy of the sources of international law." [4] This may be true of municipal courts, but there is sufficient evidence that both arbitral tribunals and the Permanent Court of International Justice have considered these general principles of law in their decisions. There is no reason to believe that the International Court of Justice would not do the same.

It appears from a closer study of cases and the writings of publicists that general principles of law are recognized in two ways by civilized nations. The first is through the statements of municipal courts that a generally recognized rule of international law — customary law — does in fact exist. It is not enough merely to affirm that a certain action or behavior is in keeping with international law. The rule of international law must at least have been accepted in an earlier case by the courts of the state — this is especially true where the principle of *stare decisis* is recognized. Or else the rule must be one that is "of such a nature, and . . . so widely and generally accepted, that it can hardly be supposed that any civilized state would repudiate it." [5]

The second way that civilized nations recognize the general principles of law is through their statutes and constitutions. At times they do this consciously, either by incorporating in their statutes a universally recognized principle of international law,[6] or by including a clause in their constitutions or basic laws to the effect that international law forms a part of the law of the land.[7] It may also be said — and some writers, such as the adherents of the monistic doctrine, have said it — wherever there is a consensus of states, as articulated in their laws, that certain rights or duties exist, the consensus is merely a manifestation of an existing international rule. Let us assume that international law is contrary to the national law of these states. There would then be a constant conflict of duties, which is intolerable. "The state which disclaims the authority of international law places herself outside the circle of civilized nations," said Sir Henry Sumner Maine,[8] and that would be tantamount to a goodly proportion of states being outside the comity of nations.

One might look at it from a different point of view. International law, in a sense, merely summarizes the rights and duties that governments claim and recognize for themselves and others. The Harvard Research Committee argues, therefore, that in searching for the general principles of law recognized by civilized nations in their work of codifying international law, "The work of codification becomes, in one aspect at least, a search for the greatest common denominator of national law and practice with respect to a matter of international concern." [9]

It may, therefore, be reasoned that a principle which is to be found in a large number of the legal systems of the civilized world must be so reasonable that its inclusion in national statutes, as well as in world law, is to be taken for granted. Searching for a consensus of states is especially important where lacunae exist in the rules of international law. Both in Europe and in the United States draft conventions have been prepared to fill these gaps, largely through the examination of municipal laws and practice. General signature of these conventions would serve to establish them more definitely as the law of nations.

There are numerous judicial precedents for examining the practice of states, their statutory laws and their constitutions to discover what a rule of international law ought to be. In the case of The Hoop, tried by the British High Court of Admiralty, the court examined the laws of Holland, France, and Spain to discover whether there appeared to be any consensus on a certain rule of law. The court found there was, and argued that "it may . . . without rashness be affirmed to have been a general principle of law in most of the countries of Europe." [10] The court laid stress on the fact that a certain rule appeared "in the law of almost every country" in its effort to discover what was the "universal principle of law."

In the Trail Smelter arbitration case, the Arbitral Tribunal of the United States and Canada based its argument on an analogy between itself and the Supreme Court of the United States dealing with controversies between the states of the Union. "Where no contrary rule prevails in international law and no reason for rejecting such precedents can be adduced from the limitations of sovereignty inherent in the Constitution of the United States," the tribunal stated, the findings of the United States Supreme Court could "legitimately be taken as a guide in this field of international law." [11] The umpire in *Italy (Gentini) v. Venezuela* examined the practice of nations to bear out his statement that prescription is "a principle well recognized in international law." [12] The Tribunal of the Permanent Court of Arbitration, in considering a claim for interest-damages, used the analogy of "the general principles of public and private law in this matter." It found that "All private legislation of the States forming the European concert admits, as did formerly the Roman law," that there was the obligation to pay at least interest for delayed payments.[13]

In the *S.S. Lotus* case, the Permanent Court of International Justice asserted that "The territoriality of criminal law . . . is not an absolute principle of international law and by no means coincides with territorial sovereignty," by first finding "that in all systems of law the principle of the territorial character of criminal law is fundamental," and that "it is equally true that all or nearly all these systems of law extend their action to offences committed outside the territory of the State which adopts them, and they do so in ways which vary from State to State." Later the Court talks in this vein: "For if it were found, for example, that, according to the practice of States . . ." and so forth. A clear indication that the Court was willing to let itself be influenced by the general practice.[14]

As a rule states do not defy through their statutes the recognized duties of international law. And if states are careful to write statutes that do not contradict international law, the corollary would hold, that the laws of a state are a good indication of what the law of nations actually is. The courts, both national and international, do, in fact, accept this corollary, as has been shown above. The only thing they look for is a sufficiently broad consensus. Ultimately all states recognize international law to be superior to their domestic law.

It is appropriate at this point to re-examine the meaning of propaganda before considering the controls that are set upon it by municipal law, or, more broadly, "the general principles of law recognized by civilized nations." Propaganda is a composite term. It belongs to the genus of communication and is distinguishable from other forms of communication by its purpose, and possibly its method. While its purpose is always to promote the interests of those using it, its effect need not always redound to the disadvantage of those at whom the propaganda is aimed. On the other hand, the effects of propaganda may be highly detrimental to the latter, either in fact or because there are those who believe it is to their detriment.

No case involving international propaganda has ever come before an international tribunal. This fact may mean one or both of two things. The problem may not yet have arisen. The dispatch of propaganda across national frontiers of the type that cannot be satisfactorily controlled by domestic legislation is a relatively new phenomenon. Or else international propaganda is not a breach of international law, (a) because of the difficulty of defining and delimiting it, and the fact that it includes both acceptable and unacceptable behavior, (b) because, as between two states, there is such a potentially vast difference in the interpretation of what is acceptable — what is acceptable in one state being unacceptable in another — or (c) because states do not want it to be, preferring to be free to carry on propaganda activities.

Propaganda, unlike some other types of activities subject to legislation, has never been satisfactorily defined for legal purposes. Standing by itself it encompasses such varied activities that some of them have been commended while others have been condemned. Hence any existing laws must determine what may or may not be done, through what medium and for what purpose, rather than control propaganda in general. The word propaganda need not even appear in the legislation. It is sufficient that words or materials that may be verbalized are used in a conscious attempt with some self-seeking motive to influence the opinions, attitude, or behavior of individuals or groups. But since law concerns itself with the rights and duties of citizens and noncitizens, and since it is not an indictable offense in any country to improve and promote oneself unless one thereby infringes upon the rights of others, any laws controlling propaganda must specify the type, and the extent to which the rights of others have been endangered or reduced.

Municipal laws can control the originator, the relayer, or the recipient of propaganda. They may be aimed at propaganda originating within the state or abroad. They may apply to citizens or aliens. They may inhibit propaganda directed at the state's internal structure, institutions, or officials, its security, laws, or citizens; or else they may forbid propaganda aimed at other states, their institutions, laws, officials, citizens, or security. Finally, municipal laws may attempt to control propaganda designed to precipitate international conflict.

Two points must be examined. The first is the controls to which states subject international propaganda through their internal laws. The second is the degree of consensus among states that might exist for the control of any of the component parts of propaganda, so that it may be possible to arrive at the general principles of international law. International propaganda, it should be remembered, need not go beyond the borders of a state. It may be propaganda by a citizen and directed against some foreign state, or propaganda by an alien directed against the state in which he is resident. The only requisite is that two or more states be involved.

While states have always attempted to protect themselves in one way or another against attacks on their dignity, or on the dignity or person of their officials and citizens, laws that give adequate protection against the clever techniques of modern propaganda are a comparatively recent thing. Nevertheless, these laws have proliferated so rapidly that there is hardly a state today that cannot feel fairly secure, within its borders, from the darts of undesirable propaganda.

However, the more secure a state feels and the more developed and orderly its government, the more liberal its laws are apt to be. Small and insecure states acquire maximum protection by giving minimum liberty. Most states also manipulate internal attitudes and opinions sufficiently to counteract any propaganda that may get by them to the people. The climate of opinion is such in the vast majority of free states that even if foreign propaganda antagonistic to the government circulated freely, it would be rejected by all but a handful of the population. In this the government in power in a state has a great advantage over any outside groups or powers. Not only can it shut out undesirable propaganda, but it can get there first and more tellingly with counterpropaganda.

Permissive Provisions of Municipal Law

Since propaganda is a type of communication, a permissive rule of law affecting it might say: "You may say, write, express, or communicate anything you like." Even in an anarchist state there can be no total freedom of speech or of the press. If nature's bounties had been evenly distributed, if it never rained on one man's field but that it rained on the fields of others, if power, profit, and ascendancy held no attractions, if love, patience, and tolerance were the heritage of all, it might be conceivable that freedom of expression could exist without overt control. But the anarchist paradise would exist only because the controls would be self-imposed instead of being prescribed from above. Freedom of speech and of the press can exist only where there is confidence, security, and stability. They cannot be absolute. They must be balanced against responsibility toward other individuals, groups, the state, and, generally, other states. Inevitably and universally they are also balanced against responsibility to the loci of power and to vested interests. Hence any laws or bills of rights that offer freedom of expression, of speech, of the press, or of opinion as a heritage to all people, either do so with tongue in cheek or by making them subject to a number of conditions and qualifications.

Yet these freedoms have come to mean so much to people in all countries of the world since the nineteenth century that of ninety-seven more or less independent states in the world with constitutions or bills of rights, only two make no provisions for freedom of the press and freedom of speech. These two are San Marino and Saudi Arabia. Nine states had no fundamental law or bill of rights of any kind at the time of writing. They are Andorra, Bhutan, Israel, Kuwait, Morocco, Musqat, Oman, Qatar, Tunisia, and Yemen. Only the Vatican City's press provision is negative. It reads "Article 8. The public exercise of printing, lithography, photography, and other mechanical or chemical reproduction of characters, designs, or figures is forbidden without the authorization of the Governor. It is forbidden to affix or offer to the public even gratuitously, announcements, writings, printed matter, books, engravings, lithographs, photographs, statues, of any kind without the authorization of the Governor." [15]

At the other extreme are the completely permissive provisions of such constitutions as that of Albania. Article 20 of this constitution reads: "Freedom of speech, freedom of the press, freedom of association, freedom of organization, freedom of assembly and freedom of public demonstration shall be guaranteed to all citizens." Equally permissive constitutions are those of the Republic of China (Article 11), the People's Republic of China (Article 87), Ethiopia (Article 41), Hungary (Article 55), Indonesia (Article 19), Japan (Articles 19 and 21), Democratic People's Republic of Korea (Article 13), the Philippines (Article 3, section 1(8)), the United States of America (Amendment 1), and the Democratic Republic of Vietnam (North) (Article 10). All other independent states with constitutional provisions for freedom of speech and of the press qualify these freedoms by saying under what circumstances they either do or do not exist or may be withdrawn.

The majority of states have a simple clause which modifies the freedom by making it subject to law, public order, and morality. An example is Article 17 of the Constitution of Burma: "There shall be liberty for the exercise of the following rights subject to law, public order and morality: (i) the right of citizens to express freely their convictions and opinions. . . ." Another form that this occasionally takes is that in the Constitution of Austria. Article 13 reads: "Everyone has the right to express his opinion freely, within the limits established by law, in speech, in writing, in print or in pictorial form." Other states that qualify their freedom of the press or speech provisions in this way are Afghanistan (Article 23), Argentina (Article 14), Bolivia (Article 6), Cuba (Article 33),[16] Czechoslovakia (Section 18), the Dominican Republic (Article 6), Ecuador (Article 187), Egypt (Articles 44 and 45), Finland (Article 10), the Democratic Republic of Germany (Article 9), Greece (Section 14), India (Article 13), Iran (Article 20), Ireland (Article 40.6(1)), Italy (Article 21), Iraq (Article 12), Jordan (Article 15), the Republic of Korea (Article 13), Laos (Preamble), Lebanon (Article 13), Liechtenstein (Article 40), Mexico (Articles 6 and 7), Nepal (Section 16), Norway (Article 100), Pakistan (Section 8), Panama (Article 38), Paraguay (Article 19), Peru (Article 63), Portugal (Article 8), Sudan (Article 7), Switzerland (Article 55), Thailand (Section 26), Turkey (Articles 70 and 77), and Venezuela (Article 35).

Other states qualify the freedom in a slightly different way. They say that freedom of expression may be suppressed if offenses are committed in the use of the freedom. Occasionally the freedom is modified by a statement that liability remains for the abuse of the freedom. An example is Article 14 of the Constitution of Belgium: ". . . free expression of opinion in all matters [is] guaranteed with the reservation of power to suppress offenses committed in the use of these liberties." Or Article 141 of the Constitution of Brazil: "Section 5: The manifestation of thought is free and shall not depend upon censorship . . . and each person shall be responsible in the cases and in the form in which the law may establish, for any abuses he may commit." Similar provisions are to be found in the constitutions of Cambodia (Article 9), Chile (Article 10), Colombia (Article 42), Costa Rica (Article 29), Denmark (Article 77), France (Article 11),[17] Federal Republic of Germany (West) (Article 5), Guatemala (Article 57), Haiti (Article 19), Honduras (Article 59), Iceland (Article 72), Liberia (Article 1, section 15), Libya (Article 22),[18] Luxembourg (Article 24), Monaco (Article 10), the Netherlands (Article 7), Nicaragua (Article 113), El Salvador (Article 158), Sweden (Article 87), Syria (Article 14),[19] and Uruguay (Article 29).

Seven states restrict the freedom in other ways than by making it subject to suppression for abuses under the law or subject to law, public order, or morality. The states are Bulgaria, the Mongolian People's Republic, Poland, Romania, Spain, the USSR, and Yugoslavia. The Spanish provision, for example, is in Article 12: "All Spaniards may freely express their ideas as long as they do not advocate the overthrow of the fundamental principles of government."

Paraguay further restricts its freedom of the press by specifying in Article 19 that "All inhabitants of the Republic enjoy the . . . rights to publish their ideas freely in the press without previous censorship provided they refer to matters of general interest."

A large number of states provide against undermining the authority or foundation of the state, the fundamental principles of government, or the political and social order. They are Brazil, Colombia, Cuba, the Dominican Republic, Ireland, India, Pakistan, Portugal, and Spain. Article 55 of the Swiss Federal Constitution says in part: "The Confederation may also prescribe penalties in order to suppress abuses directed against itself or its authorities."

For the protection of the people, Bulgaria, for example, provides in Article 71 of its Constitution, ". . . every preaching of racial, national or religious hatred is punishable by law." Brazil says the same thing in Article 141, section 5, as do Czechoslovakia (Section 37(2)), the Democratic Republic of Germany (Article 6), Paraguay (Article 35), and Poland (Article 69(2)).

King and Crown are protected by Section 14 of the Greek Constitution and Section 35 of the Constitution of Thailand. And the courts and the laws are protected in Section 8 of the Constitution of the Islamic Republic of Pakistan. In Portugal, under Article 89.2, the National Assembly may suspend from office any deputy who expresses opinions contrary to the existence of Portugal as an independent state, or who in any way advocates the violent overthrow of the social and political order.

A number of states, for one reason or another, fear the force of public opinion and of nationalism. Article 40.6(1), paragraph 2 of the Constitution of Ireland, for instance, makes the following point: "The education of public opinion being, however, a matter of such import to the common good, the state shall endeavor to insure that organs of public opinion . . . while preserving their rightful liberty of expression, including criticism of government policy, shall not be used to undermine public order or morality or the authority of the state." Similarly Article 22 of the Portuguese Constitution: "Public opinion is a fundamental element of the political

117

life and administration of the country; it shall be the duty of the state to protect it against all those influences which distort it from the truth, justice, good administration and the common weal."

A number of Iron Curtain countries fear a resurgence of nationalism and stipulate in their constitutions that such demonstrations are forbidden. Thus Article 81 of the Constitution of Romania reads: ". . . any manifestation of chauvinism, race hatred, national hatred, or nationalistic chauvinistic propaganda, is punishable by law." Similar provisions are to be found in the constitutions of Bulgaria (Article 71), Czechoslovakia (Article 37(2)), and the Mongolian People's Republic (Article 79), which refers to "imperialistic chauvinism," apparently the special problem of the people of Mongolia. East Germany, on the other hand, has a special fear of boycotts. Hence, Article 6, states: "Incitements to boycott democratic institutions or organizations . . . shall be crimes within the meaning of the criminal code."

Some states are worried that the activities or statements of their citizens might involve them in wars. Brazil is one of these, and Article 141, section 5 of its Constitution, therefore, states that "propaganda for war . . . shall not be tolerated." War propaganda is outlawed under Article 6 of the Constitution of the Democratic Republic of Germany. Cambodia puts it differently. Article 9 reads: "Every Cambodian . . . may express, disseminate, and defend any opinion through the press or by any other means provided that he does not thereby . . . endanger the peace." Article 6 of the Mexican Political Constitution has a similar provision. Section 8 of the Constitution of Pakistan imposes restrictions on freedom of the press in the interest of "friendly relations with foreign states." Bulgaria looks at the problem negatively, and says in Article 87 that ". . . the law forbids and punishes the formation of and participation in . . . organizations which openly or secretly . . . *facilitate imperialist aggression.*"

One way to ensure full control of the informational activities within the state is to specify that only citizens may own or publish a newspaper, or to grant freedom of speech and of the press specifically only to citizens. Not all these provisions are as definite as Article 23 of the Constitution of Afghanistan which reads: "The right of publishing the news belongs only to the Government and to Afghan subjects." Article 160 of the Constitution of Brazil states that "the principal responsibility of [journalistic concerns] as well as their intellectual and administrative orientation, shall be the exclusive prerogative of Brazilians." The Colombian Constitution says in Article 11 that "foreigners shall enjoy in Colombia the same civil rights as are conceded to Colombians. But the law may, for reasons of public order, subject to special conditions or deny the exercise of specified civil rights by foreigners." And Article 42 of the same constitution states: "No newspaper enterprise may, without the permission of the government, receive subsidy from other governments or from foreign companies." Greece, too, says (Section 14): "Only Greek citizens in full possession of their political rights are allowed to publish newspapers." But other constitutions like the Constitution of the Hashemite Kingdom of the Jordan merely name the citizens of the state as the grantees of freedom of the press: "Every Jordanian is free to express his opinion verbally, in writing, and pictorially, and in other forms of expression within the limits of the law" (Article 15 (1)). Similar provisions are contained in the constitutions of Iraq (Article 12), Democratic People's Republic of Korea (Article 13), Laos (Preamble), Pakistan (Section 8), Portugal (Article 8), Sweden (Article 86), Syria (Article 14(1)), Turkey (Article 70), and the Democratic Republic of Vietnam (North) (Article 10).[20]

Paraguay forbids anonymity in printing (Article 31), and the constitutions of Brazil (Article 141, section 5) and Portugal (Article 8, paragraph 2) require that periodicals publish a correction or explanation free of charge whenever a citizen is "libeled or abused in a periodical publication." Portugal also requires the press to publish any government notices sent to it (Article 23).

Bolivia (Article 12), Bulgaria (Article 45), and the Philippines (Article 32(1)) penalize public officials who attempt to restrain freedom of speech or the rights of citizens. So does the state of Bavaria within the Federal Republic of Germany (Article 111(2)).[21] And the constitutions of Guatemala (Article 57), Ireland (Article 40. 6(1) (i)), and Switzerland (Article 55) ensure the right of publications to criticize public officials without fear of punishment.

Freedom of speech is useless without its concomitant, freedom to acquire information. In many states this is taken for granted. The Federal Republic of Germany, having suffered from restriction of this right under the Nazi regime, has written the freedom into its postwar constitution and into the constitutions of almost every one of its states.[22]

It is fashionable for governments to pretend that they permit complete freedom of the press, of speech, and of opinion. But they are either fooling themselves or are attempting to fool the public. Pakistan wrote to the United Nations Secretariat in reply to a questionnaire that "There are absolutely no restrictions in this respect if the expression of opinion, etc., does not break the moral, social and any other law of the country and is not likely to endanger the public safety or the security of the country." [23] These qualifications that restrict what is termed "absolute freedom of opinion and expression of thought" may mean much or little according to the ideology of the state imposing them.

Repressive Provisions of Municipal Law

One of the basic problems in the consideration of freedom is whether it should go so far as to permit the repression of freedom itself. Some states specifically stop at that point. But granted that freedom to express opinions is and should be restricted at this or some other point, the question remains what should this limit be? The clear and present danger formula of Justice Oliver Wendell Holmes is a good one for a state's internal and even external relationships, viewed from the vantage point of the state itself. Within the national ideology, if one can speak of such a thing, there is a range of possible behavior beyond the bounds of which freedom cannot go. But when it comes to international relations the task of setting boundaries on free speech becomes extremely difficult, if not altogether impossible. There are several reasons for this, one being that what is looked upon as education by one state may be considered propaganda of the worst nature by another. But a major consideration is often forgotten by the protagonists of international freedom of information. The clear and present danger test is one that may be applied in a highly organized state, a state that can wait almost to the point where the delinquent can be apprehended in *flagrante delicto*. The weaker, the less organized a state, the earlier it must clamp down upon activities that may possibly lead to contraventions of the law. The United States and Great Britain are good examples of highly organized, strong states with stable traditions. They can count on their citizens to remain law-abiding to a much greater extent than can almost any other state in the world. This is a sign of strength. Russia's repressive laws are an outward sign of an inward weakness. The international scene is governed by the same principles. When potential international delinquencies can be forcefully arrested at the danger point, international freedom of opinion will come closer to realization. In the meantime informational anarchy reigns because the international community has failed to realize this inexorable truth.

It is in the light of this that the municipal laws governing international propaganda must be viewed. Such a law existing in a strong state, balanced against a constitutional guarantee of freedom of speech — which most constitutions appear to have — would be more liberally interpreted than would the same law in a weak and unstable state. The former could wait to the point where words begin to burgeon forth in action; the latter would have to nip them in the bud.

Propaganda is repressed or controlled through the municipal laws of states in many ways. Through their laws states protect (1) themselves, (2) their officials, (3) their citizens and noncitizen residents, and (4) other states and their officials. The repressive measures include protection against (5) unrest and breaches of the law, (6) parties and doctrines that might cause such unrest, (7) international implications and complications, including involvement in wars, and (8) comfort and assistance to foreign powers, especially if these powers are considered to be enemies. But merely to say that propaganda with a specific purpose or having certain predetermined results is forbidden often is insufficient security for the state. Hence, most states double their security by also controlling (9) the media themselves, (10) the contents, and (11) the reception of communications or propaganda. Finally, (12) they also attempt to control the disseminator or the potential disseminator.

PROPAGANDA AGAINST THE STATE

Since governments are most jealous of their own integrity and stability, a large number of laws have been written banning propaganda aimed at their demise by violence. An example of this type of law is Article 251 of the Decree of December 23, 1944, of Spain. This reads: "Any person carrying on propaganda of any kind whatsoever, whether inside or outside Spain, for any of the following purposes shall be liable to minor imprisonment and a fine ranging from 10,000 to 100,000 pesetas: 1. To subvert by violence or to destroy the political, social, economic or legal structure of the state. . . ." Another example is section 2(2) of the Alien Registration Act of 1940 in the United States. This makes it unlawful for any person "with the intent to cause the overthrow or destruction of any government in the United States, to print, publish, edit, issue, circulate, sell, distribute or publicly display any written or printed matter ad-

121

vocating, advising, or teaching the duty, necessity, desirability or propriety of overthrowing or destroying any government in the United States by force or violence." [24] Even incitement to hostile measures against the state or to disaffection is prohibited by some states. An example is Article 124A of the Indian Penal Code of 1868, as amended, which reads: "Whoever by words, either spoken or written, or by signs, or by visible representation or otherwise, brings or attempts to bring into hatred or contempt, or excites or attempts to excite disaffection towards the government established by law in India shall be punished with transportation for life, or any shorter term, to which a fine may be added."

These laws refer to what might be termed the cause. The effect is covered by such laws as Article 58 of the Austrian Penal Code of May 27, 1852, as amended, which reads: "A person is guilty of the crime of high treason when he does anything to (c) . . . tend to produce or aggravate danger to the security of the state from without or from within. . . ." The neighboring state of Switzerland says in its Federal Act Amending the Swiss Penal Code, October 5, 1950, Article 272(2), that inciting "others to acts that are liable to compromise the internal or external security of the confederation . . ." is regarded as "particularly serious."

Not only offenses against the state, but also those committed by inciting people against the government are banned by a large number of penal codes. "Those who pose as a government, those who have formed organizations or groups with the object of provoking disturbance and revolt," are to be punished under Article 1 of the Korean Revised National Security Law of December 23, 1949. And Article 3 imposes a maximum punishment of ten years in prison for discussing, instigating, or propagating means of implementing such objectives. Of a similar nature are such statutory provisions as Article 26 of Peru's Law of Internal Security, Decree-Law No. 11049 of July 1, 1949, which reads: "It shall be prohibited to use the cinema and radio for purposes of sectarian or subversive propaganda or to use posters, advertisements, inscriptions, paintings or drawings for such purposes." Belgium, Portugal, and the West Bengal province of India have legislation permitting them to control "subversive opinion." India forbids propaganda undermining the authority and foundation of the state. Loss of citizenship is the price that Nicaragua asks for political or racial propaganda contrary to the sovereignty and democratic government of the state. The right to teach does not absolve Germans, in both the Western and the Soviet zones, from loyalty to the constitution. Hence, propaganda through the medium of education must not be directed against the basic law of the state. Hungary prohibits incitement against the democratic convictions of its citizens. Spain and Turkey forbid propaganda destroying or weakening national feeling.

An interesting contrast is Article 79 of the Constitution of the Mongolian People's Republic, which states that "the manifestation of imperialistic chauvinism, discrimination and propaganda on nationalistic grounds are punishable by law."

The principal object of the press is the defense of national interests, according to Article 187, section 11, of the Constitution of Ecuador. The publication of propaganda contrary to the national interests is prohibited by a number of states. Pakistan, for instance, in Article 9(2) of the law entitled Fundamental Rights of the Citizens of Pakistan and Matters Relating to Minorities adopted October 6, 1950, says that the state may restrict and regulate freedom of speech in the public interests.

Propaganda likely to injure the national honor and dignity of the state is prohibited under the laws of Hungary and Portugal. Statements contrary to the independence and the integrity of the state are prohibited by the Czech Constitution. Naturalized citizens are liable to lose their citizenship in Ceylon and Chile for any offenses against the state "or other offenses." Even citizens by birth can lose their nationality in Czechoslovakia by dwelling abroad and "undertaking any form of activity hostile to the state or which may prejudice its interests." For carrying on propaganda harmful to the state Spanish and Swiss citizens may be punished. West Bengal province of India simply prohibits the dissemination of any "prejudicial report," while Argentina has a penalty for "disrespect in the press."

Propaganda can often be couched in insulting terms. When the insult is directed against the sovereign, the head of state, the flag, or some national emblem, a number of states have legal provisions for the punishment of the offender. "Insults against the person of the sovereign are prohibited," under Article 18 of the Afghanistan Act Concerning the Press of December 31, 1950. Chile's Act Regarding Permanent Defense of Democracy, No. 8987 of September 3, 1948, says in Article 3 "An offense against public order, punishable by the maximum degree of minor imprisonment, penal servitude, forced residence or deportation and a fine of 3,000 to 20,000 pesos, is committed by persons who (1) publicly insult the name, flag, or emblem of the nation; or, in like manner, commit the offenses of calumny, defamation, offering violence or threats against the President of the Republic or the Ministers of the State, whether in connection with their public duties or not." Liechtenstein and the Saar make it a crime to hold up the state organs or authorities to ridicule.

Public officials may not abuse their office and compromise the interests or dignity of the state under Articles 131, 163, and 164 of the Spanish Penal Code. They may not engage in political propaganda under Article 57 of the Constitution of Uruguay. In Colombia, Thailand, and the United States, government funds may not be used for official propaganda purposes.[25]

PROPAGANDA AGAINST THE PUBLIC OFFICIALS OF A STATE

Insults and abuse directed against a state minister or public official in carrying out his duties are prohibited by the laws of a few states. An example is Article 4(6) of Sweden's Constitutional Act Relating to the Freedom of the Press of April 5, 1949, which reads: "Libel or other defamatory acts against a person who holds or has held an official position or other office to which an official responsibility attaches, or a person who by order of the Crown enjoys protection as an official, provided that the defamation is committed with respect to his office," is punishable by law. Sweden, as does Spain, also prohibits agitation intended to prevent the authorities from carrying out their duty. Turkey outlaws propaganda jeopardizing the confidence of the public in the government.

Propaganda likely to incite the public to the murder of public officials is specifically forbidden by the laws of a number of states. The Swiss Criminal Code includes provisions to curb propaganda advocating the infliction of severe bodily harm and the deprivation of liberty. The United States has legislation against advocating the "assassination of any officer of any . . . government" within the United States. The Democratic Republic of Germany states in Article 6 of its Constitution that "incitement . . . to murder Democratic politicians . . . [is a crime] under the Penal Code." And the United States and Great Britain forbid incitement to mutiny.[26]

PROPAGANDA AGAINST THE PEOPLE

Propaganda against groups, organizations, racial, linguistic, religious, or national entities is covered by another series of laws. One type of law that is the most frequent is that which prohibits incitement to hatred of a race, religion, or nationality. Article 21(4) of the Constitution of Burma, for instance, says that "the abuse of religion for political purposes is forbidden; and any act which is intended or is likely to promote feelings of hatred, enmity or discord between racial or religious communities or sects is contrary to this Constitution and may be punishable by law." Several state statutes in the United States have similar provisions. Israel alone has incorporated the United Nations Convention on the Prevention and Punishment of Genocide into its municipal laws. The act in question makes genocide and incitement thereto a punishable offense. Agitation to commit acts of hatred in general is a crime in Great Britain and the United States, as well as in other countries.

A few states refer specifically to incitement to boycott. Examples are the Democratic Republic of Germany and Switzerland. "Any person who slanders other peoples or races, incites to hatred against them or advocates a boycott against them, for the purpose of disturbing friendly relations between [them] . . . shall be liable to imprisonment, and in serious cases to hard labor," says Article 1 of the Defense of Peace Act of December 15, 1950, of the Democratic Republic of Germany. Spain forbids agitation to destroy or deprive a political or social class of its property. It is prohibited to insult another's convictions under the laws of the Belgian Congo, the Sudan, and Yugoslavia.

Propaganda directed against religions is prohibited under several constitutions, and by Great Britain under the British Act of Uniformity of 1548, 1558, and 1662. Uttering or publishing of seditious words against the established religion in Britain, against the Lord's Supper, or the Book of Common Prayer, or causing "the Minister in any parish church, etc., to use any other form of prayer is a misdemeanor." [27] The constitutions of some states forbid propaganda through religions. This, for instance, is a possible interpretation of "religious liberty and freedom of public worship, as well as free expression of opinion in all matters, are guaranteed with the reservation of power to suppress offenses committed in the use of these liberties," in Article 14 of the Belgian Constitution. Mexico, in addition to its constitutional provision with regard to religious propaganda, also outlaws the radio "transmission of matters of a political or religious nature." The Swiss Federal Constitution gives very broad powers to the government for the control of the activities of religious orders, especially the Society of Jesus, which is specifically mentioned. Article 51 reads: "Neither the Society of Jesus nor any allied society shall be suffered in any part of Switzerland and all participation of their members either in church or school is prohibited. This prohibition may also be extended by Federal Law to other religious orders whose action is dangerous to the state or tends to destroy the peace between the various confessions." Article 52 prohibits the establishment of new orders or monasteries.[28]

PROPAGANDA AGAINST FOREIGN STATES AND THEIR OFFICIALS

States, through their municipal laws, protect not only themselves but also other states, their rulers, and public officials. In a study conducted under the auspices of UNESCO, Fernand Terrou and Lucien Solal found that "every country penalizes insults to heads of states, foreign ambassadors and foreign diplomatic agents. This is a rule of international courtesy and a part of the law of nations." [29] Vernon B. Van Dyke made a study of the laws of fifty-one states and found in 1940 that while thirty-seven of them were willing to protect resident foreign diplomats from libel and the rest probably gave diplomatic representatives the same protection granted to private individuals, no more than twenty-eight gave legal protection to foreign sovereigns and heads of state, and three protected sovereigns only. The others made no statutory mention of the subject. Van Dyke concludes that "protection of resident foreign diplomats from libel is so generally afforded by municipal law as to indicate a response to a requirement of international law." [30] This is corroborated by C. C. Hyde: "Respect for the State which he represents demands that a minister shall at all times enjoy the right to fulfill his diplomatic function without hindrance or molestation. To that end it is essential that his person be afforded complete protection. This principle, for which deference has been expressed in varying forms, is solidly entrenched in the law of nations. . . . A foreign minister is entitled to the same degree of protection for his reputation as for his person, and for like reasons. Hence it behooves the State to which he is accredited to shield him from insults as well as personal violence, and to prosecute with vigor him who attempts to defame him." [31] In *Frend et al. v. U.S.*[32] the U.S. Court of Appeals of the District of Columbia held a similar view: "The law of nations requires every government to take all reasonable precautions to prevent doing of things which would intimidate, coerce, harass, or bring into public disrepute any diplomatic or consular representative of a foreign government." [33]

Since Van Dyke's study other states have added legislation protecting foreign diplomats, heads of state, and heads of governments. He found that "only France and Italy appear willing to grant thorough protection" to heads of state. More recent legislation has added several other states to this list. Afghanistan protects sovereigns and presidents of friendly powers from insults "even in the absence of reciprocal arrangements," in its Act Concerning the Press of December 31, 1950, Article 19. Austria gives protection to heads of states "maintaining recognized international relations with the Austrian state," in its amended Penal Code of May 27, 1852, Article 494(a), while Nationalist China protects the heads of friendly nations in Article 116 of its Criminal Code. On terms of reciprocity, Colombia is willing to indict any person for "calumny or insult against the head of a foreign nation," under Article 46 of Act No. 29 Concerning Press Regulations of December 15, 1944, and Costa Rica gives full protection to the heads of friendly nations under its Police Code of August 21, 1941 (Article 87). In the absence of war, Cuba will punish anyone offending the head of a foreign state (Code of Social Defense of 1938, Article 162(b)), and the Dominican Republic prohibits "libel or slander against the heads and sovereigns of friendly nations," under Article 369 of its Penal Code, although not against "the memory of the late president of a foreign state." No public entertainment or radio broadcast in the Dominican Republic may "hold up to international scorn or defame friendly nations or nationals or foreign heads of states" (Act No. 5906 of July 5, 1949, Article 31). In Article 181 of its Penal Code of July 31, 1937, Egypt appears to give thorough protection to foreign sovereigns and heads of state from any verbal or pictorial provocation against their persons, and France protects them from public insults (Act Concerning the Freedom of the Press of July 29, 1881, Articles 36, 60(1)). Only section 103a, protecting the symbols of foreign states, and section 104, protecting foreign ambassadors and consular officials from insults, remain in the German Criminal Code in connection with the protection of foreign states and their officials. Greece prohibits "insulting, ridiculing or slandering a foreign government," and Iran forbids "attacks against the sovereigns of friendly states."[34] Guatemala grants foreign governments reciprocal protection, and Italy provides it for foreign sovereigns and heads of state.

Van Dyke's statement that Japan grants protection to foreign sovereigns and presidents only when these are within the Japanese jurisdiction is apparently no longer true. Article 90 of the Japanese Criminal Code has since been deleted. However, under Chapter 34 of the same code, which deals with "Crimes against Reputation," an addition of October 6, 1947, reads: "Article 232 *(Complaint)* The crimes provided in this Chapter shall be prosecuted only on complaint. When the person who may make a complaint . . . is a sovereign or president of a foreign power, a representative of the country concerned shall make it on his behalf." This does not seem to limit complaints to crimes committed within Japanese jurisdiction.

Full protection is granted to any head of state by the Principality of Liechtenstein, and Mexico will punish a person guilty of abuse, defamation, or slander of a foreign government if information is laid. The Netherlands will punish "any wilful insult to a reigning prince or other head of a friendly State," [35] and New Zealand condemns anyone "who, without lawful justification, publishes any libel tending to degrade, revile, or expose to hatred and contempt in the estimation of the people of any foreign State any prince or person exercising sovereign authority over any such State." Norway and Sweden punish libels directed against the heads of foreign states, the Saar against the "chief of state of a foreign country." Switzerland categorically prohibits public insults to a "foreign State in the person of its head, [or] its government." "Entertainments constituting an insult to any foreign nation, its sovereign or its government" are forbidden in Switzerland under Executive Regulation of the Cinemas and Theaters Act, May 2, 1949, Article 39(c).

Several old British cases point to a protection of foreign sovereigns and heads of state. In *King v. Peltier*, an 1803 case, the court said ". . . any publication which tends to degrade, revile, and defame persons in considerable situations of power and dignity in foreign countries may be taken to be and treated as a libel, and particularly where it has a tendency to interrupt the pacific relations between the two countries." There is evidence, however, that, especially since World War II, the attitude has changed. The Uruguay Penal Code of December 4, 1933, says unequivocally (Article 138) that ". . . Any person who by direct action makes an attempt, within the national territory, on the life, person, liberty or honour of the Head of a foreign State, or of its diplomatic representatives, shall be liable to four to ten years' penal servitude, in the case of an attack on life, and in the other cases to two to six years' penal servitude. . . ." And the Vatican provides the same penalty for attacks on sovereigns, chiefs of state, and chiefs of government as the guilty person would have been awarded if he had been on the territory of the offended state.

Insulting any foreign official or member of a foreign parliament is forbidden in Iran, while Switzerland will punish excessive criticism of foreign ministers of state.[36] Britain's Offences Against the Person Act of 1861, section 4, which reads: "Whosoever shall . . . encourage . . . or endeavour to persuade . . . any person to murder any other person, whether he be a subject of His Majesty or not and whether he be within the King's dominions or not, shall be guilty of a misdemeanour," has been interpreted by the courts to protect foreign sovereigns from incitement to murder.[37]

Australia, Costa Rica, the Dominican Republic, and Yugoslavia forbid activities that may be offensive to any "friendly nation," and the Soviet Union, knowing no friendly nations that are not "toilers' states," added a provision to its Criminal Code in 1927 protecting "any other toilers' state" from counterrevolutionary activities. Several states do not specify that the nation must be friendly. Theodore Schroeder reports the case of Ludobico Comminita who was indicted in New Jersey for exhibiting a picture in his shop window "contriving and intending the peace of the State to disturb and to bring the Government of the Kingdom of Italy into great hatred and contempt and to incite and move the citizens of this State into hostility and hatred toward the said government of the Kingdom of Italy and the law and constitution thereof." [38]

Not all propaganda is defamatory of a state, its institutions, or its rulers and representatives. But some of it may be; and to the extent that it is, these laws would serve to curb it.

Other propaganda may be directed against the territorial integrity of foreign states. Such small and vulnerable countries as Switzerland, Cuba, and Liechtenstein are careful not to permit anyone, while on their territory, to violate the territorial sovereignty of another state. Liechtenstein, Switzerland, Belgium, and Israel for the same reason, provide for the punishment of anyone instigating rebellion and endangering the security of foreign states. Austria is willing to punish such acts on a basis of reciprocity, and Germany gave similar reciprocal protection in its criminal laws until the relevant statute was repealed early in 1946.

The larger states, however, are less willing to grant foreign states this protection. The USSR, it is true, protects its fellow "toiler states" "by virtue of the international solidarity of interests of all toilers." [39] But it is only self-interest that prompts Russia to provide this protection under Article 58(1) of its Criminal Code. The states under its hegemony are hard enough to keep in line without any gratuitous counterrevolutionary propaganda being carried on from Russia's own soil. Britain and the

United States are positive on this point: "Seditious libels are such as tend to disturb the government of this country. In my opinion a document published here which was calculated to disturb the government of some foreign country is not a seditious libel nor punishable as a libel." [40] Thus spoke a British judge early in the century. Lawrence Preuss pointed out that both Britain and the United States have followed the line expressed by Thomas F. Bayard, U.S. secretary of state, to the Spanish minister in 1885, in answer to Spain's protest over the use of United States territory as a base for hostile agitation against the Spanish authorities in Cuba. Bayard said: "The Executive of the U.S. has no authority to take cognizance of individual opinions and the manifestation thereof, even when taking the shape of revolutionary or seditious expressions directed against our own government: and it is no less incompetent to pass upon the subversive character of utterances alleged to contravene the laws of other lands." [41]

Even the Swiss courts have been known to find persons not guilty of instigating foreign nationals abroad to armed rebellion, because "international law does not prohibit seditious propaganda against foreign states." [42] On the other hand, the antianarchist laws of the United States would appear to protect foreign states as well. A New Jersey law, for instance, states that "Any person who shall, in public or private, by speech, writing, printing, or by any other mode or means advocate the subversion and destruction by force of any and all government, or attempt by speech, writing, printing, or in any other way whatsoever to incite or abet, promote, or encourage hostility or opposition to any and all government, shall be guilty of a high misdemeanor. . . ." [43]

The United States has also been known to convict Mexican revolutionaries for promoting revolutions across the border. Hence the United States has not been consistent in its attitude expressed by Secretary of State Bayard. Nor has Great Britain been consistent when it came to aliens using British territory as a base for hostile propaganda activities against foreign states. Prince Carol of Romania was asked to leave the United Kingdom in May 1928 for sending planes to Romania to drop handbills claiming his right to the throne of King Michael.[44] In wartime, the United States Neutrality Law of June 15, 1917, would bar the use of American territory as a base for aid to one of the belligerents. The Dominican Republic expressly enjoins upon aliens and refugees admitted into the country "(a) To take no hostile action against the lawful institutions, or those which the Republic recognizes, of the State of which he is a national, or of other States, and to take no part in any activity of this nature. (b) To make no public abusive or defamatory statement, accusation or imputation against those institutions or against the person of their office-holders or members." Finally, Switzerland, long the meeting place of international organizations and at the same time a traditionally neutral state, has incorporated into its laws a restriction upon any propaganda activities directed against such organizations or the representatives attending them.[45]

PROPAGANDA CAUSING UNREST AND BREACHES OF THE LAW

So far the laws have dealt with "who was hit." The next two sections answer the question "with what result?" One result that states study to avoid is alarm among the population created by the spreading of false or distorted information. "The distribution and sale of individual books, newspapers and other printed matter, shall be prohibited if they contain . . . (8) dissemination of false and alarmist reports . . ." says Article 11 of the Yugoslav Law on the Press of July 8, 1946. Many states have such laws, or laws that prohibit the publication of misleading or deceiving information. "Spread of thought by any of the methods of publicity covered by this law shall be deemed immoral when it . . . (c) publishes or disseminates false or distorted news of current events which might lead to a disturbance of the peace or order of the Republic or discredit the nation. Such news shall also be punishable when it causes a rise or fall in the prices of commodities unless it is derived from tables or news received from abroad through news agencies recognized in Guatemala," says Article 43 of the Guatemala Law on the Spread of Thought by Methods of Publicity of April 24, 1947. Article 22 of Panama's Decree No. 469 of February 20, 1950, is typical of many other such laws. It strictly forbids the transmission of "false news or news of a tendentious nature which may cause a disturbance of public tranquillity." The law refers specifically to amateur radio stations, but similar laws are applied generally in many other states. Almost all states have laws forbidding publications causing a breach of the peace. Britain's Public Order Act of 1936, section 5 reads: "Any person who in any public place or at any public meeting uses threatening, abusive or insulting words or behavior with intent to provoke a breach of the peace or whereby a breach of the peace is likely to be occasioned is guilty of an offense." In the United States the courts have held that "at common law a criminal prosecution for libel is warranted . . . when the necessary or natural effect of the alleged publication is to cause an injury to a person or persons of such a nature and extent as to render a breach of the peace imminent or probable." [46] In *State v. Gardner* the court held "the gist of the crime [of criminal libel] is not the injury to the reputation of the person libelled, but that the publication affects injuriously the peace and good order of society." [47] The Turkish provision is contained in the Law Concerning the Press, as amended on September 20, 1946 (Article 34): "I. Correspondents propagating false or entirely biased information or persons who knowingly publish or transmit such information shall be punished as follows: (a) if such information is liable to disturb the internal peace or to cause excitement among the public, the penalty shall be imprisonment from three months to one year and a fine of not less than 500 Turkish pounds."

Incitement to breaches of the law is also almost universally frowned upon. Section 136 of the Danish Penal Code of April 15, 1930, prohibits "public encouragement to crime or secession." Chile provides in Article 4 of its Act Regarding the Permanent Defense of Democracy, Act No. 8987 of September 3, 1948: "If a person incites another to the subversion of public order, or to revolt or rise against the established government, or if a person, for the same purposes, incites another to commit homicide, robbery or arson or . . . crimes or minor offenses referred to in . . . the Penal Code, he shall be guilty of an offense against the internal security of the state and against public order and shall be liable to . . . [among other things] deportation." Encouraging breaches of the law is considered so serious that many states have provided in their constitutions that freedom of the press be withheld from a person who has "incited others to disobedience to the laws," as Article 100 of the Norwegian Constitution puts it.

Hungary forbids the praising of war crimes, and Guatemala makes it a punishable offense to justify another's crime. Incitement to arson or murder through the mails is a crime in the United States; while one of its member states — Iowa — will punish any person who "shall advise, counsel, encourage the unlawful killing, within or without the state, of any human being, even where no such killing takes place." [48]

PROPAGANDA CAUSING INTERNATIONAL UNREST AND WAR

States worry not only about their internal peace, but also their external peace. Most countries have some laws to protect themselves against propaganda or any other activity of individuals or groups aimed at vitiating their foreign relations or security. India, proud of the traditions of Gandhi, guards its external security zealously. Section 3 of its Preventive Detention Act of 1950 says: "(1) the central government or the state government may — (a) if satisfied with respect to any person that with a view to preventing him from acting in any manner prejudicial to — (i) the defense of India, the relations of India with foreign powers, or the security of India, or (ii) the security of the state . . . make an order directing that such person may be detained." And Section 12 reads: "(1) Any person detained in any of the following classes of cases or under any of the following circumstances may be detained without obtaining the opinion of an advisory board for a period longer than three months, but not exceeding one year from the date of his detention, namely, where such a person has been detained with a view to preventing him from acting in any manner prejudicial to — (a) the defense of India, relations of India with foreign powers or the security of India; or (b) the security of a state or the maintenance of public order." Article 58(1) of the Criminal Code of the Soviet Union prohibits "activity directed toward the undermining or sabotage or weakening of the U.S.S.R. and its foreign security." Many states ban propaganda detrimental to their international relations. "If a publication contains statements or news which refer to Finland's relations with other states and which are of a nature that might endanger the external security of the state or other basic interests, it may be confiscated and, if the publication is a periodical, temporarily suspended," reads Article 1 of the Finnish Decree on the Press and Other Publications, No. 898 of December 29, 1946. Britain and the United States have similar provisions, and a Japanese law prohibits the broadcast of programs overseas which might "impair the maintenance of friendly relations among states." Iran prohibits "the lowering of [its] prestige . . . abroad whether or not followed by any effects," as do a few other states. The credit of the state is protected against propaganda by the laws of a number of European and American states. Romania does it through its Constitution (Article 96). And Paraguay punishes with loss of citizenship anyone who makes an "attempt against the independence and security of the state."

No state likes to be forced into a war. Hence, a number have had laws since the turn of the nineteenth century making it a crime for any citizen or alien to engage in activities that might provoke a war against the state, or to furnish grounds to some foreign state for a declaration of war. A more recent provision is that of the Spanish Decree of December 23, 1944, as amended by the Law of July 17, 1946. Article 127 reads: "Any person who, by any illegal or not duly authorized act, provokes or furnishes grounds for a declaration of war against Spain by another power, or who exposes Spaniards to molestation or reprisals against their persons or property, shall, if a public official, be punished by minor confinement, and if not, by major confinement."

Nor may anyone carry on propaganda urging a state to go to war against a foreign state under the laws of a fairly large group of nations. Many, especially former Axis powers, prohibit this in their constitutions. Thus Article 11 of the Italian Constitution reads: "Italy repudiates war as an instrument of aggression against the liberties of other peoples and as a means of settling international disputes. . . ." Article 9 of the Japanese Constitution reads: "Aspiring to an international peace based on justice and order, the Japanese people forever renounce war as a sovereign right of the nation and the threat or use of force as a means of settling international disputes." The preparation and plotting of a "private war" upon a foreign state, whatever that means, is banned by Article 93 of the Japanese Criminal Code, as amended in 1947: "A person who prepares or plots to wage war privately upon a foreign state shall be punished. . . ." The Peace Defense Law of the USSR of March 12, 1951, calls war propaganda "the most grave crime against humanity," and decrees "2. to bring to court persons guilty of war propaganda and to try them as having committed a most grave criminal offense." It should be noted that this decree applies to all persons wherever they may be and irrespective of the state against which they carry on their war propaganda. Is this the law under which the Soviet Union plans to try future "war criminals"? [49]

PROPAGANDA FAVORING PARTIES AND DOCTRINES

So long as the beneficiary of propaganda is *persona grata* with the state, it may not object to many types of propaganda. But there are certain individuals, groups, and states with whom the governments of some countries simply will not have anything to do. Nor will they let their citizens associate with them or give them aid or comfort. Political parties can be a thorn in the side of some states, and many of them have restrictions on the formation of parties with certain objectives, or the dissemination of propaganda in support of such parties. The most common type of law in this category is the one that prohibits publications or parties contrary to the constitutional system. At least thirty-five states have provisions that express much the same sentiment as Article 98 of the Constitution of Costa Rica: "All citizens have the right to form parties in order to take part in national politics. Nevertheless, the formation or operation of parties which, because of their ideological programs, methods of action or international connections, tend to destroy the foundations of the democratic organization of Costa Rica, or threaten the sovereignty of the country, shall be prohibited if the legislative assembly so decides by a vote of not less than two-third of its members after consulting the Supreme Electoral Tribunal." Article 58(10) of the USSR Criminal Code forbids counterrevolutionary propaganda, and the United States Hatch Act makes it illegal for federal employees on pain of dismissal to belong to an organization that "advocates the overthrow of our constitutional form of government of the United States."

"Publications . . . containing propaganda against national unity are prohibited," according to Article 14 of the Act Concerning the Press in Afghanistan. The national unity is also safeguarded against parties in Czechoslovakia, Peru, and Spain. Another form that such laws take is to outlaw associations undermining the government, or political or national unity. Article 9(a) of the Turkish Law Regarding the Formation of Associations of June 5, 1946, is an example.

Some states merely ban all propaganda favoring forbidden doctrines. The Israeli Criminal Code Ordinance, for example, refers to "unlawful associations" and defines them as any body of persons which by its "constitution or propaganda or otherwise, advocates, incites, or encourages the overthrow of the Constitution of Israel by revolution or sabotage." The Communist party and its propaganda are banned or, as for instance in the United States, placed under disabilities in a number of states. In *U.S.v. Dennis et al.*,[50] the United States Court of Appeals unanimously affirmed the convictions of eleven American Communist leaders under the Smith Act of 1940 "for conspiring to organize the Communist Party of the United States as a group to teach and advocate the overthrow of the government of the United States by force and violence." In 1950, the *New York Times* listed the following nations as having outlawed the Communist party: Greece, Turkey, Lebanon, Syria, Republic of Korea, Burma, Indonesia, Indochina, Malaya, Portugal, Spain, Bolivia, and Venezuela. Australia, Egypt, and Denmark were, according to the *New York Times*, considering similar action.[51] Since then Syria, at least, appears to have lifted the ban.

A number of countries in the Soviet sphere of influence, on the other hand, have outlawed Fascist propaganda and organizations. Fascism has also been barred by a few Western states. A Bulgarian act of July 23, 1949, bars persons who have shown Fascist or other antipopular tendencies from election as the people's representatives. The Nicaraguan Constitution of January 21, 1948, stated (Article 100) "the state does not recognize the legal existence of political parties of international organization, nor that of Communist and Fascist parties or parties of similar aims under other designations." Its Constitution of November 1, 1950, on the other hand, limits itself to the statement (Article 116) that "the state prohibits the formation and activities of any internationally organized political parties. . . ." The United States prohibits the employment of members of the Nazi Bund.

Anarchists and their propaganda are excluded by the laws of a few states, such as France which has an act for the repression of anarchist activity dating back to July 28, 1894. This provides that offenses "shall be tried before the correctional police tribunals when they are committed for purposes of anarchist propaganda." There are, also, antianarchist laws in a number of states in the United States. In the United Kingdom, on the other hand, "crimes committed by anarchists are not regarded as political offenses, as, in order to constitute an offense of a political character, there must be two or more parties in the State, each seeking to impose the government of their own choice on the other, and the act done must be committed not for private or personal reasons, but in pursuance of that object." [52]

PROPAGANDA FAVORING FOREIGN STATES

The political parties outlawed in the previous section are either nationally or internationally constituted. They may be privately organized as, for instance, anarchist parties generally are, if indeed one can speak of an anarchist "party." Or they may be prompted, subsidized, or directed by some foreign state. They may be nationalist or internationalist in their program, and it is their program, purportedly, rather than their entity that is taken exception to.

Another body of municipal laws is directed against propaganda, the beneficiary of which is some foreign state or states. The laws of several countries forbid relations with foreign persons or organizations to commit a crime or to influence the conduct of foreign relations. Chile's Act Regarding the Permanent Defense of Democracy of September 3, 1948, states in Article 2(5) that it is an offense to "maintain relations with foreign persons or associations, for the purpose of receiving instructions or assistance of whatever nature, with a view to committing" certain punishable acts. And, Article 266(a) of the Swiss Penal Code of October 5, 1950, reads: "1. Any person who, for the purpose of instigating or supporting foreign enterprises or designs directed against the security of Switzerland, enters into relations with a foreign state or with foreign parties or other organizations abroad, or with their agents, or who issues or disseminates false and misleading information, shall be liable to a term of imprisonment not exceeding five years." Supporting a foreign agent to commit a crime in the state — and the crime might include propaganda activities such as those mentioned above — is forbidden in certain other states. The Soviet Zone of Germany forbids propaganda to induce enlistment in a foreign military organization.

Another form that these legal provisions might take is exemplified by Article 3 of the Defense of the State Act of Liechtenstein (March 14, 1949): "If any person acting in the interest of a foreign authority, party or other organization to the detriment of the country or of its nationals or inhabitants conducts or sets up an information service regarding the political activities of persons or political associations, or if any person enrolls any other person for or gives assistance to such services, he shall be deemed to be guilty of an offense and shall be liable to close detention for a term not exceeding three years. . . ." The same sentiment is expressed by the laws of a number of other states that make it a crime to carry on propaganda favoring an enemy of the state. Thus Article 37 of the Constitution of Paraguay speaks of "one who joins its enemies," and Yugoslavia's Law on the Press of July 8, 1946, mentions (Article 11(6)) "condonation or encouragement of the activities of the enemies of the Federal People's Republic of Yugoslavia abroad." Article 58(1a) of the Soviet Criminal Code also imposes heavy punishment on anyone assisting the enemies of the state.[53]

TREASON

The crime of treason, recognized by most states, can prove to be a catchall. It could easily be applied to propaganda activities favoring the enemies of the state in time of war, but also in peacetime under some laws. The most common definition of treason is similar to that contained in the

Constitution of Argentina (Article 103), which says: "Treason against the Nation shall consist only in taking up arms against it or in adhering to its enemies, giving them aid and comfort. . . ." Giving aid and comfort to the enemy can be and has been interpreted to include the dissemination of propaganda in behalf of the enemy. In the case of U.S. v. Burgman, 87 F.S. 568 at 571, the court held that "Acting as a radio commentator, as the defendant did in this case, for the purpose of spreading and disseminating pro-enemy propaganda, constitutes treason." Of course, "intent to adhere to the enemy is required in treason" in the United States. "A citizen intellectually or emotionally may favor the enemy and harbor sympathies or convictions disloyal to this country's policy or interest, but so long as he commits no act of aid and comfort to the enemy, there is no treason." [54] The act here would be taken as evidence of intent. Unlike other types of crime in many countries, treason is a crime over which states will assume jurisdiction even when it is committed outside the state's territory.[55]

"Loose words, not relative to any act or design," are not treason in England. "But arguments and words of advice or persuasion, uttered in contemplation of some traitorous purpose actually on foot or intended, and in prosecution of it, and consulting together for such a purpose" are treason.[56] The propaganda activities of William Joyce, better known as Lord Haw-Haw, during World War II, were held to be treason.[57] And the United States Court of Appeals for the District of Columbia held that an American citizen who had "participated in a German propaganda program designed to convince Americans that the invasion of Europe by Allied forces during World War II would be a fiasco," would be prosecuted despite the constitutional guarantees of the First Amendment.[58]

Some states, however, especially those in the Soviet sphere of influence, will go further. "It is the duty of every citizen to be loyal to the Czechoslovak Republic," says Section 30(1) of the Czechoslovak Constitution, "to uphold the Constitution and the laws and in all his actions to be mindful of the interests of the State." Anyone who ignores this duty is guilty of treason. Article 91 of the Constitution of the Mongolian People's Republic is typical: "The defense of the motherland is the sacred duty of every citizen of the Mongol People's Republic. Treason to the motherland — the violation of the oath of allegiance, desertion to the enemy, impairment of the military power of the State, and espionage — is punishable as the most heinous of crimes." The provisions of this article would be applicable even in peacetime, especially as Iron Curtain countries do not hesitate to call Western states, with which they are technically at peace, "enemy" powers.[59] An example of a broad interpretation of treason in the Western Hemisphere is Article 37 of the Constitution of Paraguay: "One who joins its enemies, taking up arms or helping them, or who makes attempts of any kind against the independence and security of the Republic of Paraguay, commits treason against the Fatherland."

The Criminal Code of prewar Germany — both the pre-Hitlerian and the Hitlerian laws — listed a great number of crimes against the state under the heading of either high treason or treason. These crimes included everything from undertaking or advocating the alteration of the Constitution by force and "selling" the country to a foreign state (Articles 81(2), 81(3), 85) to publicly announcing "former state secrets" already known to the foreign government to which they are revealed (Article 90(b)). The laws relating to treason are contained in Articles 80 to 93 of the German Criminal Code, all repealed by Law No. 11 of January 30, 1946, of the Allied Control Council for Germany.[60]

CONTROL OF THE MEDIA

Despite these many and varied laws banning propaganda of certain types, most states still feel insecure both internally and externally. They therefore add a second type of insurance to protect themselves against abuses of freedom of speech and of the press. Perhaps, as a mitigating circumstance, it ought to be said that in some states these controls are imposed also to protect the people.

The second type of control referred to is the control of the media through which propaganda is liable to be spread. In a country that is truly free — a condition that so far has been nonexistent — these controls, whether of content or of media, would exist, but would be self-imposed. To the extent that people do not impose necessary restrictions upon themselves, or, to the extent that a state fears they will fail to impose them, or alternatively, to the extent that there is a lack of agreement on what is a "necessary restriction," controls are imposed by legislation. The restrictions to be discussed in this and the following sections are sometimes used in an attempt to surmount the dilemma of reconciling freedom with responsibility.

Most states attempt to control communications either through government ownership or varying forms and degrees of supervision of the media. Of all media, radio comes most often under government supervision and ownership. The number of newspapers that could be published is almost unlimited, and whatever limitation might exist would be governed by the demands of the consumer. The same is true of the film industry. The number of possible radio stations is strictly limited by nature and the speed with which scientific discovery can push its boundaries back.

The majority of states own the country's broadcasting facilities outright. Some others share them with commercial enterprises, while a few leave all broadcasting to privately owned and controlled stations. A distinction must be drawn between domestic broadcasting and international broadcasting. The latter is almost always a state enterprise.

Although the state may not own all or any of the radio stations in the country, it always has control over the air waves. The United States, for instance, sets out its claim in the following language: "It is the purpose of this Act, among other things, to maintain the control of the United States over all the channels of interstate and foreign radio transmission; and to provide for the use of such channels, but not the ownership thereof, by persons for limited periods of time, under licenses granted by Federal authority, and no such license shall be construed to create any right, beyond the terms, conditions, and periods of the license." [61] Even the state itself, in a sense, does not own the air waves. They are allocated to it by international agreements which regulate their use. Hence a claim such as that made by Colombia is only relatively true: "All frequencies capable of being used for radiocommunications belong to the State and only the National Government is empowered to dispose of, or allocate, them and to grant concessions for their use or exploitation." [62] The state has a prior claim, since the allocations are made to the states, which in turn pass them on to their citizens.

The daily and weekly press is more generally privately owned. There are a few exceptions, however. In Afghanistan the press is an organ of the government, because private enterprise has not yet been developed. In the Soviet Union, newspapers are owned by collective organizations and are controlled by the Communist party. The Central Committee of the Communist party appoints the editorial staff of the newspapers which are all under strict government control. This is not the same as state ownership, although the effect might be the same.

Some states own a wire service, which is the only newsgathering and distributing agency in the country. Toward the end of World War II, for instance, the French government saw that if there was to be a French news agency preparing news from the French point of view, it would have to be organized, controlled, and supported by the government. Agence France-Presse, therefore, became a government agency.[63] For similar reasons, that is, the inability of the country's press to support an agency of its own, Czechoslovakia established the Czechoslovak Press Bureau (CTK) in 1918. The agency has been a state undertaking since 1924. Its budget is supervised and approved by the Czechoslovak parliament. Slovakia has its own news agency — the Slovak News Agency (ZAS). The Iranian government owns and operates a news agency called PARS. The Soviet News Agency, Tass, is owned and operated by the Soviet government. The Romanian agency, Agerpress, the Polish agency, PAP, and the Yugoslav agency, Tanjug, are run on lines similar to Tass. Turkey owns 40 per cent of the stock of its Agence Anatolie.

Not every country has a film industry, although most have at least some form of newsreel enterprise. In the smaller states newsreels and documentaries are generally produced by the state, which has the major interest in seeing them prepared. Most of the countries in the Soviet sphere of influence have state-owned film industries. In addition, trade unions, political and cultural organizations, and educational establishments are permitted to produce their own films. In Poland the relevant law permitting the setting up of such undertakings is Article 4(2) of the Decree of November 13,1945. Poland acquired its film industry by nationalizing the existing private companies.[64] Both production and distribution of films are state monopolies in Czechoslovakia under the law of August 28, 1945, establishing the Czechoslovak Film Company. Hungary, under a decree of May 1948, set up a Hungarian Film Office in the prime minister's department which is responsible for the production, distribution, and exhibition of films through a number of national companies.

In an intermediate position, between complete government ownership and private enterprise, are the film undertakings in Italy, France, Denmark, and Spain, which either obtain government subsidies and protection against foreign competition or are partially government controlled.

Education is under the supervision of the state in most if not all countries of the world. Certain uniform standards have to be maintained which can be done only with the help of the state's powers of law enforcement. In the same sense the profession of medicine is under state supervision. But some states go further than others in controlling their schools. The Constitution of Albania, for instance, says (Article 28) that ". . . the schools belong to the State. Private schools can be opened only by special permission. All their activities are supervised by the State. . . ." Here the state says that the schools actually belong to it. As the tradition of church-affiliated schools dies hard, these and similar establishments have been permitted to function, but under the strict eye of the state. Other constitutions provide for the right of state inspection and control. Chile's Constitution says (Article 10(7)) that "Public education is preferentially an affair of the state. . . . There shall be a bureau of public education in whose charge will be the inspection of national instruction and its direction under the authority of the Government." The Argentine Constitution of 1949, on the other hand, says (Article 37) that "The responsibility for education and instruction rests upon the family and upon the private and official establishments which collaborate with the family. . . ." And the Jordanian Constitution says (Article 21) that "The communities shall have the right to establish and maintain their schools for the teaching of their own members," but the schools must "conform to the general requirements prescribed by the law." [65]

Many states that do not own their media, control them nevertheless by requiring them to register or to obtain a permit before they begin to operate. The registration requirement may be meaningless, or may actually be to the advantage of the media in that they can obtain certain tax, postal, and other privileges. On the other hand, registration can either mean or facilitate control. In the Soviet Union, for instance, the registration of all radio receiving sets made it possible for the government to call them in during World War II and thus "protect" the people from the "evil influences" of international propaganda.[66]

The Czech Constitution states (Section 21) that "2. Who shall be entitled and on what conditions, to publish periodical journals, in particular with regard to the principle that profit should not be the aim of such publication, shall be prescribed by Act. 3. The manner of the planned direction of the issue and distribution of non-periodical publications, in particular books, musical scores and reproductions of works of art, while maintaining the freedom of science and the arts and with a view to the protection of valuable works, shall be prescribed by Act." And the Czech Press Law of June 1947 implements the above provision by ruling that "Only political parties, public institutions and corporations of national importance are allowed to publish periodicals. The right to publish newspapers is denied to individuals and anonymous groups." [67]

In France no new paper may be published without previous authorization, and the same is true of certain other states. Many require registration, including the United Kingdom, New Zealand, Switzerland, Italy, Mexico, Uruguay, Turkey, and Sweden. In addition to registration, bond must be deposited before a newspaper can be published in Lebanon, the Union of South Africa, Egypt, and Colombia. Certain states, on the other hand, expressly forbid the demanding of a bond or caution money. Belgium put this into its Constitution by saying (Article 18) that ". . . no security shall be exacted of writers, publishers, or printers."

The Vatican does not permit the distribution of any type of literature without a permit. Professional hawkers of newspapers and periodicals must register with the government of Lebanon.

In the realm of public entertainment, most states require a permit for the presentation of public spectacles and censor them before the permit is granted.

Lebanon and Turkey require the registration of all associations, although the Lebanese law specifically states that this does not involve authorization.

As mentioned above, broadcasting stations in all countries require prior authorization. The United States, which is one of the few countries that has private companies engaging in international broadcasting, has a provision (section 301 (c) and (d)) in its Communications Act of 1934 requiring special permission to broadcast across state boundaries.[68]

While many constitutions provide for the freedom to meet peacefully in public places, the constitutions of Denmark and Luxembourg, to mention two countries with such provisions, go on to say that open-air meetings may be forbidden if they become a danger to the public peace.

An Iranian decree published on October 24, 1949, empowers the state to close all foreign institutes carrying on cultural and educational activities in the country.[69] And a Spanish law forbids the founding of "teaching establishments which are contrary to the law in their objects or methods."

"No newspaper enterprise may, without permission of the government, receive a subsidy from other governments or from foreign companies," reads a paragraph in Article 42 of the Constitution of Colombia. This is implemented by Decree No. 109 of January 24, 1945, Articles 1 and 4 of which prohibit the receipt of subsidies from foreign governments or companies by firms publishing periodicals or by broadcasting stations. Similar provisions are contained in the laws of other countries. In the United

States, for instance, section 310(a) of the Communications Act of 1934 forbids the issuance of a radio station license to an alien or to a foreign corporation or to a United States corporation that is financed by foreign capital or that has alien officers or directors.[70]

CONTROL OF THE CONTENT

It is not enough to make sure that the "right people" own the media of communications and that the owners have been told what they may not say. Many states feel that it is necessary to have a double check, and the most common double check is censorship.

Censorship is one of the most arbitrary, systematic controls of expression. It can be employed without reference to any law, the only criterion being the whim of the censor. The authoritarian state is likely to impose censorship to enable it to perpetuate its authority. The democratic state, which has a government that is accountable to the people, generally finds it harder to impose censorship except in times of great emergency. Wartime censorship is permissible in most states. In the realm of public entertainment, however, people appear to have a more kindly attitude toward censorship.

While there is no official censorship in the United States of films that leave this country, one publication points out that pressure is brought to bear on movie producers to prevent the export of certain types of films: "In addition to the Treasury Department, both the State Department and the Department of Commerce keep a watchful eye on proposed pictures. They realize the profound effect that American movies exert all over the world on our prestige and the appreciation of democratic institutions. They lack the legal authority to forbid the showing of an American picture abroad, but they can often bring sufficient pressure to bear on producers to make it inexpedient to export films which they regard as potentially harmful. As a practical consequence films so regarded will not knowingly be made in Hollywood, since approximately forty-four per cent of the revenue of American film companies and frequently all of their profits, if any, result from foreign distribution." [71]

Censorship may take the form it has in Spain, where all newspapers are required to submit copies to the government, or in South Africa, where the minister of defense and the postmaster general have said that the government could reject any telegrams destined for abroad of which it disapproved. In recent years censorship has been imposed for one reason or another in a number of states. Finland reimposed wartime censorship in 1947 after a news agency had sent some "false" news abroad. Guatemala imposed censorship on outgoing news to "prevent the spread of false information." Lebanon introduced censorship on outgoing news on the principle that "irrespective of truth, only news favorable to Lebanon can be sent to foreign publications." And Turkey liberalized its censorship by shifting its power to suspend newspapers from the press director to the courts.[72]

In a world censorship survey made by the Associated Press at the end of 1956, it was found that "the world had more censorship in 1956 than since the Korean War ended."[73] Associated Press correspondents reported that the following countries imposed more or less regular censorship on outgoing dispatches: the USSR, Spain, Egypt, Jordan (although censorship was lifted late in the year), Syria, Lebanon, Iraq, the states in southern Arabia, Israel, Iran, Indonesia, Burma, Afghanistan, Colombia, Paraguay, Venezuela, and Haiti. Countries that censored the domestic press were Spain, Portugal, the Democratic Republic of Germany, Algeria, Egypt, Jordan (later lifted), Syria, Lebanon, Iraq, the southern Arabian states, Israel, Cyprus, Communist China, Singapore, Malaya, Afghanistan, Venezuela, Nicaragua, and the Dominican Republic. In many countries, such as those in the Soviet orbit, newspapers practiced self-censorship, and in others, the strict enforcement of the repressive laws mentioned in other sections ensured a fairly careful self-censorship on the part of the press. Among the states where virtually no restraints existed, the Associated Press listed Canada and the Philippine Islands. The survey did not include several small countries "which rarely yield news of importance."

An effective way of controlling the content of communications' media is by denying access to certain types of information. The idea that the press, and hence the public, has a right to know what government is doing and that any information gathered by government officials in the course of their duty is public property, or that the activities of government officials in the performance of their duties are in the public domain, is a peculiarly American one. Yet not even the United States gives full access to the press, and many public officials act as though they were a law unto themselves. Of course, the situation is much worse in all other countries. By virtue of his office, the government official has autocratic powers of varying degrees elsewhere in the world.

The people's right to know, all over the world, merits a study of its own. Every country, however, has laws that regulate certain types of classified information. The Associated Press survey mentioned above showed that news at the source was controlled in some degree in the following states and territories: Yugoslavia, the USSR, Italy, the Netherlands, Belgium, Greece, Norway, Algeria, Israel, Cyprus, Hong Kong, and Mexico. The news agency also listed the Allied armed forces in Germany and Japan. No state likes to have its secrets broadcast to a potential enemy or even to friends, so it prohibits the disclosure of what it calls "state secrets." The major states, which, presumably, have more secrets of importance to conceal, threaten with severe punishment those who divulge secrets of the state. In Nazi Germany the law said that "Whoever undertakes to betray a state secret shall be punished by death." [74] Revealing state secrets was treason in Germany. In the Soviet Union, the disclosure of some types of secrets of the state is treason. Even if it is not treason, however, the Russian law lists many categories of information which may not be transmitted abroad.[75] In the United Kingdom, state secrets are protected by the Official Secrets Act of 1920,[76] and the United States makes it a crime to gather, transmit, or lose defense information, or to deliver such information to a foreign government.[77]

Another type of law provides for the punishment of anyone who relays information to a foreign power. This goes beyond secrets of the state. Thus when Czech employees of the Associated Press in Prague lost their accreditation, any news they sent out of the country would have been considered under this heading, they were told.[78] Turkey has a similar law. The United States will punish not only the disclosure of state secrets but also the receipt of classified information. It is obvious that such laws may be exploited to the detriment of the citizen, as, apparently, they have been in Czechoslovakia. The state is free to decide what shall be a state secret and can punish a person for handling what might otherwise be harmless information. In effect the state is controlling undesirable propaganda material.

Effective control over propaganda can be exercised by a state by insistence on conformity. In Estonia, for instance, newspapers were ordered to consider in their articles the "recommendations of the government based on the requirements of the Home and Foreign policy." [79] The Swiss government's directions to its radio news writers have a similar effect. They say: "In view of its considerable importance and immense influence, broadcasting should be used wisely and judiciously. It is, moreover, a national institution, and so to some extent, though not officially, represents our country abroad. Its news service should therefore conform to the national dignity and interests." [80]

It is in the realm of education, however, that the greatest conformity is demanded. Most states expect their educational institutions to be guided by the national spirit. Many have incorporated in their constitutions clauses to this effect. The Mexican Constitution, for instance, says in Article 3: "The education imparted by the state — federation, states, municipalities — shall be designed to develop harmoniously all the faculties of the human being and shall encourage in him at the same time love for the country and the consciousness of international solidarity in independence and justice. (I) . . . (a) It shall be democratic, considering democratic not only as a legal structure and a political regimen, but as a system of life founded on the constant economic, social and cultural improvement of the people; (b) it shall be national insofar as — without hostility or exclusiveness — it shall achieve the understanding of our problems, the utilization of our resources, the defense of our political independence, the assurance of our economic independence, and the continuity and augmentation of our culture; and (c) it shall contribute to better human relationships, not only by the elements which it contributes toward strengthening and at the same time inculcating, together with respect for the dignity of the person and the integrity of the family, the conviction of the general interest of society, but also by the care which it devotes to the ideals of fraternity and equality of rights of all men, avoiding privileges of race, sect, group, sex or person."

Some governments not only forbid the dissemination of certain types of information such as state secrets, excise them through censorship if they are included, and recommend the "correct" line to be taken, but they also protect themselves by legislation which permits them to make statements or present their side of an issue through the communications media. The media are forced to publish these communiqués. Certain states also protect the people against unfair, libelous, or otherwise injurious publications through what is known as the "right of reply." When a government has the power to force the publication or broadcast of official statements, it exercises a certain amount of influence over the propaganda effect of news and opinion in the country. The Australian Broadcasting Act, for instance, authorizes the postmaster general to require radio stations to broadcast anything he considers to be in the public interest. This applies not only to the state-owned radio stations, but also to commercial broadcasting stations, which may be required to include in their programs without charge "such items of general interest or utility as the Minister from time to time determines, provided that the requirements of the Minister shall not be such as to entail the broadcasting of matter for a period in excess of 30 minutes in any consecutive period of 12 hours." [81] This, and similar laws in numerous other states, give governments the right to have their communiqués broadcast over local radio stations. Under Article 23 of the Portuguese Constitution, the press "may not refuse to insert any official notice of normal dimension, on matters of national importance sent to it by the government."

The right of reply, which exists in some countries, makes it possible for anyone who feels slighted by what the papers say about him, or what is broadcast by a local radio station, to claim the right of answering the statement free of charge, if a court will uphold his claim. The right of reply by radio is covered by such laws as the Cuban Presidential Decree of August 3, 1950, which says: "(1). Any individual or corporate body referred to directly or indirectly in any radio broadcast in offensive terms, whether explicit or veiled, touching his reputation, or to whom acts have been attributed falsely or in a distorted form shall have the right to request the Ministry of Communications, through the Directorate of Radio, that the correction of such remarks shall be published by the broadcasting undertaking used for the transmission of the said version, the appropriate announcement being read either by the station's announcer or by the person concerned himself." The right of reply in the press is covered by such laws as the Act Concerning the Press of December 31, 1950, of Afghanistan: "Article 17: If a newspaper or magazine publishes criticism of a government official or of an employee of a non-governmental establishment or of a governmental or non-governmental administration relating to the performance of his or its functions, the reply made by that person or administration shall be published in the same type and in the same position in one of the three issues published after the date of receipt of the reply in the case of a newspaper, and in the next issue in the case of a magazine. If this provision is violated, a newspaper may be suspended for three months and a magazine for six months." [82] Of course, the right of reply is also permissive. And in countries where bad faith is automatically assumed in libel, it can be a potent safety valve.

CONTROL OF THE DISSEMINATORS

Control of the media and of their content can be very effective. But many states feel safer if they control the disseminators instead of, and more often in addition to, the media. The disseminator is more susceptible to apprehension and punishment. This is especially true if the disseminator is a citizen of the state. Aliens are often more slippery, and, of course, they cannot be trusted to follow an acceptable line. Furthermore, especially in the field of broadcasting, where the available frequencies are few, states are loath to allocate any of their precious facilities to foreigners. Thus by insisting on citizenship for newspaper owners and editors, for radio commentators and station owners, and for others engaged in communications, much can be done to control the propaganda that might find its impact on the population.

Article 23 of the Constitution of Afghanistan says that the publisher of a newspaper must be a citizen of Afghanistan. Owners and shareholders must be citizens under Article 160 of the Brazilian Constitution. China says that the publisher and the editor must be residents. In Colombia, the director, manager, or owner of a newspaper dealing with domestic politics must be a citizen and the greater part of the capital must be citizen owned under Article 13 of the Law of 1944. French law requires that the owner, partner, shareholder, or other persons with financial interests must hold French allegiance, and the Greek Constitution requires the publisher to be a Greek. Other forms that these laws take are to require citizenship of the responsible director (Italy), the director of the printing works (Poland), the responsible editor (the Saar), and the publisher, owner, manager, and editor (Switzerland). Sweden requires that the owner be a citizen, but the editor need only be a resident; and Article 7 of the Law on the Press of Yugoslavia states that "foreign nationals may be publishers or responsible editors of newspapers and periodicals only after being previously approved by the Federal Minister of Internal Affairs."

Some states which allow private ownership of radio stations specify that these owners must be citizens. Guatemala's Law on the Spread of Thought by Methods of Publicity of April 24, 1947, states (Article 36): "The director or legal representative of every broadcasting station and radio-magazine must be a Guatemalan within the meaning of Article 6 of the Constitution." This is required by the United States Communication Act of 1934, as well, and the law applies even to foreign diplomats.[83] Article 160 of the Brazilian Constitution reads: "The ownership of jour-

149

nalistic concerns, either political or simply for news, as well as radio broadcasting is forbidden to corporations having bearer shares and to foreigners. Neither the latter nor juridical persons, except the national political parties, may be shareholders of the corporations owning such concerns. The principal responsibility of them, as well as their intellectual and administrative orientation, shall be the exclusive prerogative of Brazilians."

Only citizens may distribute domestic or foreign books in Czechoslovakia; and in Sweden citizens have the right to sell, distribute, or otherwise circulate printed matter. No mention is made of aliens. The Mexican Constitution (Article 130) limits the practice of religious ministry of any denomination to Mexican citizens by birth.

Assignment of responsibility is necessary for effective control of the press, and it is another means for keeping an eye on the disseminator and his propaganda. There are two principal methods by which responsibility may be assigned. Some states ascribe the responsibility to only one person. This person may be the author, the editor, the publisher, the printer, or a responsible editor or director. Other states, including those states following the Anglo-Saxon legal system, either make all persons connected with the writing, publishing, printing, and distributing jointly responsible for contraventions of the law through the publication, or make two or more of the participants in the publication responsible.

Belgium is an example of a state where only one person is responsible for press offenses. But in common with a number of other states, it has adopted the "waterfall" system of responsibility to be sure to find someone to whom responsibility may be assigned. Article 18 of the Belgian Constitution says that "In case the writer is known and is a resident of Belgium, the publisher, printer, or distributor shall not be prosecuted." But if the author is not known or within the state's jurisdiction, the printer is made jointly responsible until the author is caught, according to the Belgian Press Decree of July 20, 1931. The "waterfall" of responsibility is clearly seen in Article 42 of the French Act Concerning the Freedom of the Press of July 29, 1881: "The following, in the order named, shall be liable as principals to the penalties enacted for the repression of crimes and offenses committed through the Press: (1) the managers or publishers, whatever their profession or description; (2) failing these, the authors; (3) failing the authors, the printers; (4) failing the printers, the sellers, distributors and billposters."

Iran makes the author and publisher responsible in Article 20 of its Constitution, but exonerates the latter "if the author is well known and resident in Iran." The Iranian Act Concerning the Press of February 1908, on the other hand, makes the managing editor responsible if the author is abroad. The editor is responsible in Denmark unless he denounces the author. The Luxembourg Constitution has provisions similar to Belgium's, and the authors, importers, and distributors may be punished for offenses committed in the foreign press under Article 17 of the Luxembourg Act of July 20, 1869. If the matter is reprinted in a Luxembourg newspaper, the printer and distributor are responsible, unless the person who ordered the printing is a citizen and resident of Luxembourg. Haiti has similar provisions. The author alone is responsible in Mexico unless the responsibility of others is demonstrated. Except in the case of "high treason, threats to the independence of the Confederation, diplomatic treason (Articles 265 to 267), support of foreign enterprises or designs directed against the security of Switzerland (Article 266a), espionage (Articles 272 to 274), infringements of the constitutional order (Article 275), subversive propaganda (Article 275a), illicit associations (Article 275b), and infringements of military security (Articles 276 and 277)," the Swiss Federal Act Amending the Swiss Penal Code dated October 5, 1950, states that the author is responsible unless he cannot be found or is not within Swiss jurisdiction, in which case the publisher, or, failing him, the printer is responsible.

A number of states require the newspaper to have a responsible editor or director who answers for everything that goes into the paper. Article 3 of Italy's Act No. 47 of February 8, 1948, says: "All newspapers or other periodicals must have a responsible director." Sweden's Constitutional Act Relating to the Freedom of the Press of April 5, 1949, merely says (Chapter V, Article 2): "A printed periodical shall have an editor." If the director of a newspaper is a member of parliament, and hence immune to prosecution, a codirector must be appointed in Mexico and Italy.

In other states responsibility for offenses in the press is held conjointly by the author and publisher and, occasionally, other collaborators on the newspaper, even if the author is known and in the country. The Political Constitution of Peru states (Article 63) that ". . . the responsibility appertains to the author and the publisher of the punishable publication, who shall be jointly responsible for the indemnification due to the injured person." In the Saar the responsible editor and the publisher are jointly responsible unless they name the author, who must be a person within the legal jurisdiction of the Saar, or must have been there at the time of publication if he is dead. The editor and publisher can also exonerate themselves if they can prove that the offense took place despite the employment of "all the necessary professional care."

The Soviet occupation authorities warned Austrian newsboys and dealers in 1948 that they would be responsible for any anti-Soviet articles in the newspapers they sold.[84] In the United States everyone engaged in the production of a newspaper is prima facie liable for its torts. The owner, printer, and carrier are all responsible. But the courts have been very liberal in interpreting this liability. The managing editor is held jointly liable if he has an active part in the formulation of policy,[85] but not if he is merely an agent of the owner. As the court put it: "He cannot be held liable without disregarding the settled rule of law by which no man is bound for the tortious act of another over whom he has not a master's power of control." The United Kingdom has much the same attitude as the United States on the question of liability. But the courts are more strict and the fines allowed are generally higher. The printer's assistant and the vendor have been held liable for the contents of news periodicals under British law.[86]

As far as radio stations are concerned, the little legislation on responsibility for radio broadcasts that is available does not show clearly where the responsibility lies. In Canada the licensee of a private station is the "trustee of the frequency," and is responsible for everything that goes on the air over his station. Under Act No. 5906 of July 5, 1949, of the Dominican Republic the management of the broadcasting station is not responsible for the content of paid programs or of news reports emanating from a government department or an authorized news agency (Articles 43 and 44). But the management (Article 41) is "answerable to the National Commission [on broadcasting] for any change made in the program without proper authorization of the Commission." This makes the management's position rather ambiguous.

The situation is similar in the United States. In *Kelly v. Hoffman*, a 1948 New Jersey case, the court held that "The defendant-respondent as a radio broadcasting company which leased its facilities is not liable for a defamatory statement during a radio broadcast by the person hired by the lessees and not in the employ of the radio broadcasting company, the words being carried to the radio listeners by its facilities, if it could not have prevented publication by the exercise of reasonable care." [87] This makes the broadcasting company not liable for a lessee's contraventions of the law.[88] On the other hand, there have been cases in which the court has held that the broadcasting company is liable for offenses committed by a lessee, regardless of whose fault it is, and even if the lessee broadcasts unscheduled material.[89]

Austria was in a rather different position from that of a normal station licensee when it announced that it could not assume responsibility for the news that was broadcast over one of its stations. The Russian-controlled station at Ravag would broadcast news that was often embarrassing to the Austrian government. It therefore issued an announcement "to avoid misunderstanding" stating that it was obliged, as the *New York Times* put it, to broadcast "news over whose selection and composition it has no influence . . . and for which Austria must decline all responsibility." Argentina has extended its law on radio broadcasting to the cable companies. These are made responsible for everything that is sent over their wires, even when the circuits are leased.[90]

Propaganda may be kept under control by forbidding anonymity in the publication of books, newspapers, and periodicals. Anonymity is forbidden in Brazil, Paraguay, and Sweden, for instance. In the United States all newspapers that want second-class mailing privileges must publish annually the names of their editors, managers, and owners. Peru requires annual publication of the names of all shareholders and the number of shares held by each. All Danish-language publications printed abroad and imported into Denmark must bear the name and city of the printer. And the United States requires that all information material distributed by foreign governments or private agencies indicate the source. If the organization is either a Communist-action or a Communist-front group, it must clearly label its literature: "Disseminated by . . . a Communist organization." In the case of a radio or television broadcast, the program must be preceded by: "The following program is sponsored by . . . a Communist organization." Many states in the United States require that political advertisements be signed with the names of the persons who pay for them.

A few countries have laws barring persons with certain types of background from publishing, editing, and, occasionally, working for a newspaper. A person convicted of treason or other crimes detrimental to the nation may not own or edit a newspaper in Denmark. In Turkey the owner of a newspaper must not have been convicted of "having been hostile to the country, to the fight for national liberation, the Republic or the 'Reform'." A newspaperman in Turkey may be disqualified from his profession for collaboration with the enemy during a war, for serving a foreign state either in a military or in a civilian capacity, or if he has been convicted of disseminating propaganda insulting to a foreign head of state or diplomatic representative.

In Argentina and Peru, foreign correspondents are kept under control by being forced to register with the ministry of interior in the latter state and the ministry of labor in the former. Czechoslovakia requires accreditation of all foreign correspondents.[91]

The United States has been especially zealous in requiring the registration of foreign agents, on the theory that once they are registered they are easier to control. The Foreign Agents Registration Act of 1938 requires all persons engaged in information service for a foreign government to register with the attorney general. The relevant section reads: "No person shall act as an agent of a foreign principal unless he has filed with the Attorney General a true and complete registration statement and supplements thereto as required by this section." The Voorhis Act of 1940 required four types of organizations to register with the attorney general. These were organizations subject to foreign control and engaging in political activity; organizations engaging in both civilian military activity and in political activity; organizations subject to foreign control engaging in civilian military activity; and organizations which aim to control or overthrow any government or subdivision thereof by the use of force, violence, military maneuvers, or threats. The more recent Act to Revise, Codify and Enact into Positive Law "Title 18 U.S.C." has the following provision: "Sec. 951. Whoever, other than a diplomatic or consular officer or attaché, acts in the United States as an agent of a foreign government without prior notification to the Secretary of State shall be fined . . . or imprisoned . . . or both." The Internal Security Act of 1950 requires the registration annually of all Communist-action and Communist-front organizations, and sets up a subversive activities control board to determine what organizations fall under these categories.

Aliens can be a problem for any country that is interested in controlling international activities within its borders. It was thought necessary to register all aliens in the United States so as to maintain a check on subversive activities. Most states require resident aliens to register. Even if aliens do not own or operate communications media, they can engage in propaganda activities of the type that states seek to control. Therefore, many states find ways and means of limiting their rights. Aliens may not claim more rights than citizens in a number of states. In Colombia, Liechtenstein, and Poland aliens are granted the same rights as those the nationals of the three states receive in the alien's state. The Constitution of Costa Rica (Article 19, paragraph 2) says that aliens may not seek diplomatic protection except as provided in international agreements. On the other hand, Burma's Constitution states in Article 26 that "Every citizen, whether within or beyond the territories of the Union, shall be entitled to claim the protection of the Union in his relations with foreign states." Free speech may be restricted for aliens in Belgium; and newsmen who are not citizens may be forbidden from working for local publications or the local radio in Argentina and Colombia. In Afghanistan, Cuba, and Panama, only certain specified subjects may be taught by aliens. The social sciences are generally excepted. Britain restricts the right of aliens to participate in the promotion of strikes before they have spent at least two years in the United Kingdom engaged in a specific industry.

Many states have laws excluding aliens who profess certain forbidden doctrines. An example is Chile's Act Regarding the Permanent Defense of Democracy, which excludes aliens who advocate the violent overthrow of the government. Ecuador has a similar provision. Once admitted, aliens may lose their right of residence if they intervene in local politics or spread forbidden doctrine, under the laws of several states. Aliens who are guilty of propaganda harmful to the state, who slander the state, or compromise its internal or external security, or who influence public opinion abroad against the state are subject to deportation in a number of states.[92]

CONTROL OF RECEPTION

The final point at which propaganda may be controlled is at the receiving end. If a state cannot legislate against propaganda that is harmful to specified interests, or produces certain results, or benefits unpopular causes or entities; if a state fails to achieve its purposes by controlling the media or the content, or by keeping an eye on the disseminator, it can make a final stab at controlling the reception of propaganda. One method is by restricting the importation of publications. A Czech ordinance (No. 72 of 1933) was invoked in February 1948 to ban twenty-seven foreign publications, including newspapers and magazines from the United States, Britain, and France. In 1950 Egypt banned the London *Daily Express* and the London *Daily Graphic* for reporting the romances of King Farouk. Another ban existed on *Time* magazine between July and November 1948. Anti-Soviet newspapers were forbidden entry into Finland in December 1946, and the Cominform organ *For a Lasting Peace, For a People's Democracy*, published in Bucharest, was banned by the French Ministry of Interior in 1951. Soviet-sponsored newspapers were excluded from the British Zone of occupied Germany in January 1949. Syrian newspapers were excluded from Jordan in September 1947, and the Sudan police confiscated copies of *Newsweek* and *Time* in January 1950, for reporting the Farouk romances.[93] The United States has from time to time excluded certain publications through its customs laws, which permit officials to refuse entry to any publications "advocating or urging of treason or insurrection against the United States, or forcible resistance to any law of the United States, or containing any threat to take the life of, or inflict bodily harm upon, any person in the United States." [94] Certain Soviet periodicals have been excluded under this law. In Iran, section 16 of the Act Concerning the Press of February 1908 states: "The introduction and publication of newspapers and publications printed abroad, in any language, may be prohibited in consideration of the proprietor and the country of origin. Whenever there are grounds for prohibiting a single issue, the decision of the Ministry of National Education shall suffice for its retention and confiscation, but a general prohibition must be considered by the Council of Ministers. Any person introducing or reproducing a newspaper or publication prohibited under the terms of this section will be liable to imprisonment for a term of not less than one month and not more than one year."

Israel stopped the importation of United States, Canadian, and French newspapers, but admitted Russian and British newspapers. The ban was actually on foreign exchange from the countries concerned, since dollars and French francs are hard currencies in Israel.[95] There is no reason to believe that Israel is interested in keeping its population from reading the publications of these countries; but it can easily be seen how foreign exchange control can be used to exclude undesirable publications.

Some states expressly say that foreign publications are free to enter the country. Yugoslavia, for instance, has a law stating that "Newspapers, books and other printed matter published abroad may be freely brought into and distributed in the Federal People's Republic of Yugoslavia without prior permission." On the surface this sounds very liberal. But this law (Article 15 of the Law on the Press of July 8, 1946) continues, "Domestic and foreign concerns and institutions which have been specifically authorized for the purpose by the Presidium of the Government of the Federal People's Republic of Yugoslavia shall be entitled to distribute foreign printed matter." In other words, the law is deceptive. For if only licensed distributors may distribute the publications, or, as it appears, even import them, the control lies in licensing the importer rather than in censoring the paper.

Another example is the control that inheres in the negative statement of the Afghanistan Act Concerning the Press of December 31, 1950. Article 33 reads: "Foreign books and printed matter may be freely imported and sold in the country, provided that they contain no propaganda directed against religion, national unity, or the Government, and that they are not contrary to the interests of Afghanistan." The control could not have been more explicit.

The Fezzan, Libya, reported to the Human Rights Division of the United Nations Secretariat that "although no papers are published in the Fezzan, those from Tripoli, Benghazi, Tunis and Cairo are free to enter." [96] The high degree of illiteracy in Libya makes it unnecessary to control newspapers from abroad. But the question of freedom remains. Is the state one that is likely to continue to admit foreign publications regardless of their content? Or does the state not trust its citizens? Poland is a good illustration of how this can work: "Restrictions on the importation of foreign periodicals, other than those of Communist origin, amount to a virtual ban. This may be seen from official statistics: e.g. in February, 1946, 29,800 copies of Soviet periodicals were imported into Poland, as compared with 200 British. While it is not forbidden to read papers and periodicals published in the Western democratic countries, their importation is nevertheless viewed unfavourably by the authorities. In a police State, such disapproval is tantamount to forbidding their circulation in the country." [97]

An example of how high duties can effectively control incoming propaganda may be seen in the film industry. Britain imposed a 75 per cent import tax on foreign motion pictures. Quincy Howe, president of the National Board of Review of Motion Pictures, pointed out that this raised the "whole question of free communications among free peoples." In

Britain's case it is doubtful that there was any thought of censorship; but the tax could easily be used for that purpose. The *New York Times* had pointed out earlier that fifty-six different types of barriers were operating against motion pictures alone.[98]

If the contents of the publications imported are unlawful — treasonous in Germany — the importer and his accomplices may be punished, in Denmark under section 5 of Act No. 147 Concerning the Use of the Press of April 13, 1938, in Sweden under Article 3, Chapter 13, of the Constitutional Act Relating to the Freedom of the Press of March 23, 1949. The relevant section in the German Criminal Code was section 83(4). This has now been repealed. In Sweden, if the person responsible for the importation of such propaganda is abroad, the literature may be impounded. For purposes of jurisdiction, both Sweden and Austria have laws which state that if the matter was published abroad, "the place of the offence is held to be that in which the matter was distributed." [99]

Some states are especially strict about publications in their own language. A Danish law says, "Everything printed in the Danish language in foreign countries and imported for commercial purposes or for public distribution in this country shall bear the name or style of the printer and the place of printing." Yugoslavia provides severe punishments for the infringement of a law (Law on the Press of July 8, 1946, Articles 15 to 20) that requires prior authorization for the importation and distribution of "newspapers, books and other publications issued abroad in the languages of our peoples, or intended for their use." Hungary banned the Hungarian-language New York newspaper in 1947, and Poland stopped the entry of seventeen Polish-language newspapers from the United States in 1946. By 1948 Poland had stopped the entry of all Polish-language newspapers from abroad, a total of eighty-two from the United States, Britain, and France. In 1947 thirty newspapers from abroad had been banned.[100]

"The education of public opinion being . . . a matter of such grave import to the common good," says Article 40.6(1)(i) of the Irish Constitution "the State shall endeavor to ensure that organs of public opinion, such as the radio, the press, the cinema, while preserving their rightful liberty of expression, including criticism of Government policy, shall not be used to undermine public order or morality or the authority of the State." It is for this reason that some states have chosen to censor the press and films and to prohibit listening to foreign broadcasts. The Syrian

Constitution of 1953 (Article 13(3)) has a similar statement, as has Article 22 of the Portuguese Constitution.

Quoting Braas and Dor, *La Constitution*, No. 202, Belgium reported to the Human Rights Division of the United Nations in 1946:

Propaganda by broadcasting could obviously not have been foreseen by the authors of the Constitution, from either the political or the moral point of view. "In Belgium, the legislature has attempted to find a satisfactory solution for the problem by conferring on the executive a kind of right of supreme police control over all broadcasts."

Under this system, "The State claims the power to restrict, in a general and permanent fashion, and even in cases not provided for by the penal law, the right of uttering opinions by broadcasting. . . .

"However ingenious and tempting such a system may appear at first sight, it nevertheless gives rise to grave apprehensions in certain circles, which are greatly alarmed by the threat which it offers to a principle which has remained inviolable since 1831."

It must also be remembered that broadcast propaganda in Belgium conducted from abroad raises a delicate problem — that of control of the right to listen to communications coming from abroad. That problem, which was solved by the occupying Power during the period 1940–1944 by an absolute ban, has not yet been studied since the war.[101]

The ban referred to in the preceding paragraph was similar to that existing in Germany during the war. The Law of September 1, 1939 (the day Germany marched on Poland), says: "Sec. 1. Listening intentionally to foreign radio transmitters is forbidden." Section 3 states that the regulations do not apply to actions undertaken in the line of duty. This did not satisfy Dr. Josef Goebbels, and in January 1942 he wrote in his diary: "At last all government departments are in accord about regulating the listening to foreign broadcasts. . . . That is imperative, for especially in so-called government circles the number of defeatists and gripers is legion. It is not true that these circles can take it when unpleasant news reaches them. They are the very ones who are most susceptible; therefore it is they who must be especially protected against defeatist tendencies." Japan, too, imposed severe penalties on anyone listening to foreign broadcasts.[102]

More recently, during the civil war in China, both the Nationalist government and the Communist government imposed severe penalties on those who were caught listening to each other's broadcasts. Later the Communist government branded the Voice of America as reactionary and forbade listening to it.[103]

But in peacetime, listening to foreign broadcasts is permissible in all countries as a rule, at least as far as any written law is concerned.[104] There have been many reports from Iron Curtain countries that listeners to Western radio broadcasts are severely punished. The reports have been firmly denied by the governments concerned. The Czech delegate to the Mexico City short-wave conference, for instance, said that there were at least two million radio receivers in Czechoslovakia and there was no government attempt to control propaganda from the West. Yet the previous year the Communist-controlled Central Action Committee had warned that persons who organized mass meetings to listen to unfriendly foreign broadcasts might be purged from public life.[105] On July 15, 1951, the Prague newspaper *Lidove Noviny* wrote: "We have already spoken of the spiteful atmosphere created in our country by the inciting foreign broadcasts. Listening to them is not prohibited by the law but there are certain moral rules which ought to be observed. The vicious voice incites to murder. Whoever listens to it places himself between the two camps and gets near to the camp of the warmongers. It is impossible to remain in the middle, the choice cannot be avoided. The mere passive listening to the Western lies affects the moral strength of the listener. Even if he swore a hundred times that he does not agree with everything that the imperialists and their servants do, be it in Korea or here in our country, the fact that he thinks their voice worthy to be listened to makes him one of them." On August 28, 1951, a Czech engineer by the name of Krousky was sentenced to six years' imprisonment for "plotting against the Republic by listening to and spreading slanderous and inciting reports of the Western broadcasts." And on October 28, 1952, a certain Kulhavy was quoted to have "justified his way of life," which included the murder of a security officer, by listening to the Voice of America and Radio Free Europe.[106]

In 1948 the Hungarian Foreign Ministry protested against a statement made by George V. Allen, then assistant secretary of state for public affairs, which alleged that it was a crime in Hungary to listen to and disclose the contents of Voice of America broadcasts. Later Allen said that the measures were not in the form of an actual legal or police restriction on listening, but were against "inciting against the Hungarian democracy." A new Hungarian protest stated that "everyone in this country is free to listen to what broadcasts he pleases," and it denied that anyone had been arrested in the matter.[107]

The government caught up with listeners in a different fashion. Three

Hungarians, for instance, were given from two to four years in prison for spreading "unfounded rumors" that Hungary would devalue 100 forint notes. They had heard this over the Voice of America and BBC. The Communist party newspaper *Szabad Nép* commented that these "were not the only ones who listen with devotion to the Voice of America." [108]

The situation was similar in Poland. United States Ambassador Lane received a letter from some relatives in the United States of a Polish woman whose son had been sentenced to four years' imprisonment for, among other things, listening to the American radio.[109] In April 1953 a Warsaw court sentenced a Pole to two years' imprisonment for allowing people to listen to broadcasts by the Voice of America and the BBC.[110] Two Poles, Joachim Schaak and Helmut Sadowski, were found guilty on October 26, 1953, of organizing "groups to listen to broadcasts of the Neo-Nazi RIAS radio in West Germany, which is spreading anti-Polish propaganda directed against our Recovered Territories." They were sentenced to death and fifteen years' imprisonment, respectively.[111]

The Iron Curtain countries are not alone in bringing social and other pressure to bear to deter people from listening to foreign broadcasts. At the hearings before a subcommittee of the Senate Committee on Foreign Relations on the overseas information programs of the United States, Gerald F. P. Dooher, acting chief of the Near Eastern division of the International Broadcasting Service, told Senator Hickenlooper that "in Greece today I don't think anyone will admit listening to a Communist radio. The Greek Government takes a very strong attitude toward people who admit such things." [112]

One way some states control listening to foreign radio programs is by prohibiting the repetition of news received on the radio from abroad. Sometimes the law is not intended to control propaganda but rather to protect copyright. This probably is the intention of the General Radio Regulations of the Union of South Africa which say that "Any person who, without the permission in writing of the Postmaster-General, publishes any news or information in print, or gives any news or information to any other person for such publication, shall, if the only source from which he has received such news or information is by radio, be guilty of an offence." This type of law can, however, be used to control propaganda by radio, as in the case of Hungary.[113] Germany probably had the original law forbidding the passing on of propaganda likely to harm the state that is heard on a foreign radio program. Section 2 of the Decree on Extraordi-

161

nary Measures Concerning Radio of September 1, 1939, read: "Whoever intentionally circulates news emanating from foreign transmitters which is apt to endanger the power of resistance of the German people shall be punished by confinement in a penitentiary, or in especially serious cases by death."

In Bulgaria, under Article 17 of the Law of March 25, 1948, "all are free to listen to broadcast programmes in Bulgaria, and everyone may own a receiving-set." However, "any listener wishing to use a receiving-set must obtain a permit therefor and pay the subscription fee pertaining thereto." Failure to observe this regulation is punishable by a fine of 500 to 500,000 levas and two to ten years' imprisonment. Similarly, all receiving sets must be declared in Yugoslavia under the decree of January 15, 1948, the penalty for nondeclaration being a fine. In Romania the laws are more elaborate. Chapter I of Decree No. 216, published in *Buletinul Oficial* No. 32 of May 23, 1949, reads: "Article 15. No one may install, keep, sell, operate or construct a receiver or loudspeaker for reception by coils and amplifying tubes [i.e., a wireless receiving set] without a written authorization from the Broadcasting Board. . . . Article 16. Such authorization shall be obtained by the filing of a printed application blank, either directly with the Broadcasting Board or with the post office . . . [accompanied by the subscription fee] Article 17. The authorization is personal and non-transferable. The subscriber is authorized to use the receiver or loudspeaker only at the place and for the purpose indicated and for the period covered by the fee paid. Any change in the domicile of the subscriber must be reported to the Broadcasting Board. . . ." In Hungary there is a big difference in the license fees paid by owners of the wired radio systems (6 forints), the owners of "people's radios" which can receive only certain preset stations (30 forints), and the owners of radios equipped with short-wave band (60 forints).[114] In the Soviet Union under section 191 of the Criminal Code owners of unlicensed private radio receivers, or those who put their receivers to some other use than that for which they were licensed, are subject to punishment.

In Turkey, under a law of June 23, 1947, receiving sets and the transfer of sets must be authorized, and Article 8 states that "the consent of the appropriate military authority must be obtained before a license is issued to any foreigner living in the military areas defined by the Cabinet."

All countries with state-owned radio broadcasting systems must reimburse themselves in some way for their expenditures. The best method so far discovered is through license fees. However, Terrou and Solal point out, while a tax or a fee for the ownership or use of a receiving set is justifiable in most countries, "the collection of this fee involves declarations and supervisory measures that may appreciably restrict the right to information. . . . We have seen the extremely detailed form the regulations sometimes take (even amounting, sometimes, to a sort of prior authorization), the extensive supervisory measures that they institute, and the severe penalties for which they provide. The least that can be said is that such methods of tax-collecting pave the way for more far-reaching interference, in this matter of the free reception of information." [115]

One wonders, for instance, what purpose the radio-receiving licenses in Tanganyika and Uganda serve. Permits are required by law; but they are granted free on application to the postmaster. In Italy and several Latin American states the manufacturer or distributor, or both, must keep a register of the names and addresses of all purchasers of receiving sets. Here again the possibilities of control can be imagined.[116]

Another control is the type to be found in the laws of Afghanistan and Turkey. Article 35 of the Afghanistan Act of December 31, 1950, Concerning the Press says that "The importation of radio receivers is subject to the provisions of special legislation." The Turkish Act on Radio of June 23, 1947, makes "all equipment and apparatus for transmitting or receiving by means of electro-magnetic waves any kinds of images, signals, or sounds . . . a government monopoly." During the Sino-Japanese War, the Japanese government prevented the people from listening to Chinese and Russian broadcasts by forbidding the sale of sets with short-wave bands and licensing the sale of sets with only limited receiving ability.[117]

In 1950 the Hungarian government ordered the mass production of "people's sets" designed to pick up only Hungarian and Soviet broadcasts. At the same time the Hungarian postal department offered to remove the short-wave bands from the older receivers owned by Hungarians. This was done by a house-to-house canvass and the owner had to make a special request for the short-wave band to be retained — an excellent deterrent. At about this time, too, the Hungarian post office started installing telephonic radios, which are loudspeakers on which only the Hungarian radio may be heard. By the end of 1952 telephonic radio was in operation in 230 cities and villages, with more than 100,000 subscribers.[118] The idea itself, of course, antedated wireless transmission.[119]

7

Extraterritorial Control of Propaganda

THE discussion in the previous chapter dealt with the municipal laws governing crimes committed in the state's own jurisdiction. The crimes included those committed against foreign states, their rulers, or their subjects; but the situs of the crime was always taken to be where the crime was committed. How does a state react to propaganda activities from abroad against itself or its inhabitants? What of propaganda crimes committed abroad by its own citizens? In other words, what besides the territorial principle determines the jurisdiction a state will assume? Will the state assume jurisdiction over its nationals wherever they may be in the case of offenses committed by them? Has it jurisdiction — under the protective principle and the passive personality principle respectively — over persons committing offenses against its national interests or its nationals? Or has it jurisdiction — under the universality principle — no matter who commits the crime or where, so long as it has custody of the person?

With respect to territorial jurisdiction, the Harvard Advisory Committee on Research in International Law prepared a draft convention on jurisdiction with respect to crime, Article 3 of which read: "A State has jurisdiction with respect to any crime committed in whole or in part within its territory. This jurisdiction extends to (a) Any participation outside its territory in a crime committed in whole or in part within its territory; and (b) Any attempt outside its territory to commit a crime in whole or in part within its territory." [1] The competence of a state to try persons whether citizens or aliens for crimes committed on its territory is universally accepted, the committee pointed out. [2]

In regard to crimes committed abroad the effect of which, however,

164

takes place within the state, the "objective territorial principle" establishes the right of the state to assume jurisdiction, according to the advisory committee. This is not what was referred to above as the passive personality principle. The question is not whether a national was hurt, but whether the crime was consummated within the state. A good example of the distinction appears in the Cutting case.[3]

A United States citizen while in Texas published what was alleged to be a libel in a Texas newspaper against a Mexican citizen resident in Mexico. The American citizen, Cutting, later crossed the border into Mexico, was arrested, tried, and convicted by a Mexican court under Article 186 of the Mexican Penal Code, which reads in part: "Penal offenses committed in a foreign country by . . . a foreigner against Mexicans, may be punished in the Republic (Mexico) and according to its laws, subject to the following conditions: I. That the accused be in the Republic, whether he has come voluntarily or has been brought by extradition proceedings. . . . IV. That the breach of law of which he is accused, shall have the character of a penal offense, both in the country in which it was committed and in the Republic." The United States government protested on the ground that "It nowhere appears that the Texas publication was ever circulated in Mexico so as to constitute the crime of defamation under the Mexican law." The United States conceded that "It is not now, and has not been contended, by this Government, as seems to have been assumed in some of the arguments put forth in behalf of the Mexican Government, that if Mr. Cutting had actually circulated in Mexico a libel printed in Texas, in such manner as to constitute a publication of the libel in Mexico within the terms of the Mexican law, he could not have been tried and punished for this offense in Mexico. Oftentimes, the question where a libel may actually have been printed is a matter of small moment, the real offense being the publication or circulation. I shall, therefore, pass this question by as having nothing to do with the present case."[4]

It is on this point that J. B. Moore rested his dissenting opinion in the *S.S. Lotus* case before the Permanent Court of International Justice.[5] He accepted the "objective territorial principle" as established in international law.[6] But he rejected the "passive personality principle" on which Article 6 of the Turkish Penal Code, similar to Article 186 of the Mexican Penal Code, is based. The "passive personality principle" is asserted by Italy as well as by Turkey and Mexico.[7]

165

Other states claim jurisdiction over certain crimes only. Thus Israel provides under its Crime of Genocide (Prevention and Punishment) Act, 1950 (Section 5), that "A person committing outside Israel an act which is an offence under this Act may be prosecuted and punished in Israel as if he had committed the act in Israel." Switzerland will punish a person "subject to special responsibility" who commits an offense in a foreign country through the press.[8]

The United States and Britain will not recognize jurisdiction based on the "passive personality principle," except in certain specific cases, such as injury to the state through counterfeiting.[9] Both these states are firm believers, however, in the "objective territorial principle." In *Strassheim v. Daily*, for instance, the United States court held: "Acts done outside a jurisdiction, but intended to produce and producing detrimental effects within it, justify a State in punishing the cause of the harm as if he had been present at the effect, if the State should succeed in getting him within its power." [10]

An example of a British case based on the "objective territorial principle" is *R. v. Coombes*. Here the court held that a person who fired a shot outside British territory and killed a person in England could be tried in England.[11]

Attempts made outside the territory of a state to commit a crime within its territory are considered to have been made within the jurisdiction of the state in a number of countries. An offense begun in one jurisdiction and completed in another may be "dealt with, inquired of, tried, determined and punished in either jurisdiction in the same manner as if the offense had been actually and wholly committed there," says a United States law dealing with communications.[12] The United Kingdom assumes similar jurisdiction.[13]

Almost all states claim some jurisdiction over their nationals wherever they may be. Few, however, claim jurisdiction over all offenses committed by them abroad. One of those states that does is the Democratic Republic of Germany which has the following provision in its Defense of Peace Act of December 15, 1950 (Article 10(3)): "The Supreme Court of the Democratic Republic of Germany shall have jurisdiction even when the offence is committed by German citizens outside the territory of the Democratic Republic of Germany, and when the offender has no domicile or residence in the territory of the Democratic Republic of Germany." A few other states also claim such total jurisdiction. Section 2 of the Penal

Code of the RSFSR puts socially dangerous acts of citizens within the jurisdiction of the Russian courts ño matter where they are committed. The Harvard Research Committee pointed out that in the Soviet Union "socially dangerous" acts are made coextensive with criminal offenses. This is true in the light of section 6 of the same code. But the note appended to the section explains that an act is not an offense under this section which "has lost, because of its manifestly minor importance and the absence of harmful consequences, its socially dangerous character." Finland takes the same attitude, and excludes minor offenses from the comprehensive jurisdiction of the courts.[14]

Many states will assume jurisdiction over their citizens if the offense is one that is punishable both in the state where it was committed and under the *lex fori*. Some of these same states plus a few others will punish nationals who are abroad if the crimes they have committed are of a certain degree of severity, while other states assume jurisdiction only over those crimes committed by their nationals that are extraditable.

Finally, crimes of a specific nature, when committed by nationals abroad, are punishable by some states. These will be considered here as they apply to the problem of propaganda. The British attitude is that "Ordinary offences committed by subjects of the King in countries outside his dominions, or on the high seas in foreign ships, cannot be said to be against the King's peace or against his crown and dignity, and therefore by the common law, and apart from statute, English courts have no jurisdiction in such cases. Treason forms an exception to this rule." [15] This does not mean that Parliament, the supreme lawmaking body in the land, could not, if it so desired, formulate laws placing the subjects of the king under the jurisdiction of the courts wherever they may be and whatever their crime. In the Sussex peerage case, 11 Cl. and Fin. 85 at 146 the court said: "An Act of the English Legislature can have no binding force beyond, or out of, the realm of England; and if by this is meant only, that it can have no obligatory force upon the subjects of another State, the position is no doubt correct in its full extent; but it is equally certain that an Act of the Legislature will bind the subjects of this realm, both within the kingdom and without, if such was its intention." [16] In the United States the courts will assume jurisdiction over citizens who have committed crimes abroad, if that crime is treason.[17]

As long as he is on British territory, or as long as he enjoys the protection of the British state, an alien owes allegiance to Britain under the laws

167

of England. This is also true if the alien goes abroad under the protection of a British passport. In the celebrated case of *Joyce v. Director of Public Prosecutions,* William Joyce was tried and convicted of treason for adhering to the king's enemies while he was under British protection. His crime was, among other things, that he had broadcast what was described as propaganda over the German radio to British troops and civilians. His defense was that he was born in the United States of Irish parents. But the court held that since he had described himself as a British subject in applying for a British passport, under which he had traveled to Germany, he enjoyed the protection of the Crown, and hence owed allegiance to it.[18]

Several states claim jurisdiction over aliens who are engaged in some public function for them, even though they commit a crime abroad. The Argentine Penal Code of 1921, Article 1, for instance, states that the code may be applied "2. In case of crime committed abroad by agents or employees of Argentine authorities in the performance of their duties." [19] This is important to the study of the control of international propaganda, because many states employ local or nonlocal aliens in their propaganda activities abroad.

Propaganda activities favoring a foreign state by a citizen from abroad are punishable under the laws of a number of states. In other words, the state assumes jurisdiction over its nationals for acts committed abroad. The case of *Joyce v. Director of Public Prosecutions* was quoted above as a recent British case. A similar case in the United States was Gillars v. United States (1950), 182 F.2d 962. Gillars was an American citizen who was convicted on the charge of treason for participating in a German propaganda program designed to weaken the morale of Americans during World War II. Chile punishes its nationals for propaganda activities abroad that are likely to be harmful to the state, as will Czechoslovakia, Romania, Spain, and Switzerland. The Swiss provision is contained in the Federal Act Amending the Swiss Penal Code of October 5, 1950, Article 6, which reads: "Any person who conducts propaganda aimed at disturbing or modifying illegally the order based on the constitution of the confederation or of a canton, or assists such propaganda, especially if it emanates from abroad, shall be liable to imprisonment or to a fine." Germany had such provisions in its Criminal Code, but these were repealed on January 30, 1946.[20]

Some states threaten with loss of citizenship those nationals who assist a foreign government against the state. Honduras, Mexico, and Nicaragua have put the threat into their constitutions. Until 1946, German law made such activity a treasonable offense under Section 91(b) of the Criminal Code. In Bolivia (Constitution, Article 44) "Rights of citizenship are suspended . . . thirdly, for accepting employment from a foreign Government without permission of the Senate. . . ." A Brazilian loses his nationality for the same offense. The Dominican Republic has a constitutional provision similar to that of Bolivia. The United States, like Brazil and a few other countries, deprives citizens of their citizenship for entering the service of a foreign government without prior authorization. Elsewhere, as for example in Nicaragua, Norway, and Turkey, voting rights are lost for such activities. In Turkey the owner of a newspaper or magazine must not have served a foreign state without permission of his government. An Egyptian loses his nationality if he serves a foreign government with which Egypt is at war, or with which it has no diplomatic relations. If he enters the employment of a foreign government or international organization and refuses to leave when ordered by his government, the Egyptian also loses his citizenship. In Venezuela a citizen is considered a traitor to his country if he serves a foreign government in time of war. A naturalized citizen can lose his citizenship for disloyalty to his adopted country in many states. And Romania will deprive even natural-born citizens of their citizenship for disloyalty. In Bulgaria, "a person may be deprived of Bulgarian nationality: 1. If he unlawfully crosses the frontiers of the country," according to the Bulgarian Nationality Act of March 6, 1948, Article 8. For this offense, other states in the Soviet sphere of influence also deprive nationals of their citizenship. The same penalty applies to those who refuse to return home from abroad within a prescribed time limit after they are officially summoned home. The right to go abroad is also restricted in Finland and the Democratic Republic of Germany, while the United States makes it unlawful for a member of a Communist organization to apply for or use a passport.[21]

The question of the status of an *émigré* who assists some foreign state in the preparation and dissemination of propaganda directed at both his own homeland and other countries is a very important one. Many of these expatriates lose their citizenship through accepting employment from the government of a foreign power, many for the very act of leaving their country — generally without permission — or for refusing to return when ordered to do so. The majority of them can, of course, be punished for engaging in propaganda activities harmful to their countries. But the question is, can they be tried for treason should they ever be caught? If they are deprived of their citizenship they presumably no longer owe allegience to their country. In that case, whatever else they could be tried for it would not be treason. Yet this need not necessarily be the case. A Bulgarian law, for instance, says that "Loss of Bulgarian nationality does not imply release from the fulfilment of the obligations towards the State incumbent on Bulgarian citizens." [22] This question has a number of ramifications that cannot be considered here. It would be difficult to contest the right of a state to assume jurisdiction over its former citizens and to apply any law it wished.

A large number of states will even prosecute aliens for crimes against the external or internal security of the state, or crimes that are otherwise harmful to the state, committed outside the national territory. The competence of the state here is based on the "protective principle," which is distinguishable from the "passive personality principle" discussed above by the fact that the state itself is harmed instead of just a national.

Great Britain and the United States, according to the Harvard Research Committee on Jurisdiction with Respect to Crime, are practically the only states which have declined to extend the jurisdiction of their courts over aliens who commit crimes against the integrity of the state from abroad.[23] Referring to the British case of Gurdyal Singh (Sirdar) v. Faridkote (Rajah) (1894) A.C. 670, Halsbury writes: "Generally speaking, except in the case of piracy *jure gentium*, no person who is not a subject of the King can be tried in England in respect of any act he commits outside the King's dominions." [24] In the American Banana Co. v. United Fruit Co. (1909), 213 U.S. 347 at 356, the court held that "For another jurisdiction, if it should happen to lay hold of the actor, to treat him according to its own notions rather than those of the place where he did the acts, not only would be unjust, but would be an interference with the authority of another sovereign, contrary to the comity of nations, which the other state concerned justly might resent." However, these were civil cases. In U.S. v. Bowman (1922), 260 U.S. 94 at 97, the court said that "the same rule of interpretation should not be applied to criminal statutes which are, as a class, not logically dependent on their locality for the Government's jurisdiction, but are enacted because of the right of the Government to defend itself against obstruction, or fraud wherever perpetrated. . . ." The judge goes on to say "especially if committed by its own citizens, officers or agents." But he does not exclude aliens. In U.S. *ex rel.* Majka v. Palmer

170

(1933), 67 F. 2d 146, a Pole was ordered deported for perjuring himself before a United States consul in Poland. Although this is given by the Harvard Research Committee as an example of the assumption of jurisdiction by United States courts over crimes committed abroad by aliens, the analogy might break down because the perjury was committed at the United States consulate, which has extraterritorial rights and may be considered U.S. territory. The court said that "A crime against the United States committed outside its territorial boundaries but within the limits of its consular jurisdiction may also be reason for deporting the alien, particularly where, as in this case, the act made it possible for him to enter and it might otherwise have been impossible for him to do so."

In the case of *Molvan v. Attorney-General for Palestine*, which came before the Privy Council in London, the British court of last resort upheld the ruling of the Palestine Supreme Court that the High Commissioner for Palestine was empowered to confiscate a foreign ship that was bringing illegal immigrants to Palestine. The ship was intercepted one hundred miles from Palestine by a British destroyer and escorted to Haifa. The court argued: "The question . . . is whether there is any principle of international law which is violated by an Ordinance which, in the circumstances in which this Ordinance was passed, penalizes persons of whatever nationality or wherever resident, who abet or are deemed to abet an offence against its laws. It is to be observed that, so far as their own persons are concerned, they cannot be punished so long as they remain outside the jurisdiction. The question therefore narrows down to this, whether they may be penalized by the forfeiture of their property which is within the jurisdiction. Their Lordships have not been referred to any decision nor to any textbook of authority which suggests that the enactment by a State of a penalty so expedient, if not essential, for the purpose of preventing an unlawful invasion of its territory, is contrary to any established principle of international law." [25]

While most states will try an alien guilty of harming the integrity of the state from abroad if that alien is within their physical custody, a few will go so far as to prosecute an alien in absentia. Among them are Albania, Belgium, Italy, Paraguay, Poland, and Uruguay.[26]

171

8

Control by Diplomacy

THERE are several popular definitions of diplomacy [1] and several technical definitions. [2] For purposes of this chapter, the *Oxford English Dictionary* definition is adequate: "Diplomacy is the management of international relations by negotiation; the method by which these relations are adjusted and managed by ambassadors and envoys. . . ."

If state A were to disseminate propaganda in or regarding state B, the latter could, if it objected to the propaganda, settle the resulting dispute through negotiation— diplomacy. If this failed, and state B still desired satisfaction, it could, if state A were willing, submit the dispute to an international claims commission or some international tribunal for adjudication. The consent of both parties to the dispute is a *sine qua non*. [3] If state A were unwilling, and state B considered the matter serious enough to be a *casus belli*, it could bring the dispute to the attention of the Security Council of the United Nations (under the United Nations Charter, Article 35(1), or Article 35(2) if it is not a member of the UN), and the Security Council could investigate the dispute (Article 34) and recommend or take appropriate measures (Article 36 and Chapter VII).

Of course, if the Security Council refused or failed to take action to the satisfaction of state B, and the latter were unwilling or unable to resort to the force of arms, it would have to revert to the preliminary steps recommended by the Charter, viz., "negotiation, enquiry, mediation, conciliation, arbitration, judicial settlement, resort to regional agencies or arrangements, or other peaceful means" (Article 33).

State B would not be able to sue state A in its own courts, since a state cannot be sued in foreign courts under a long-standing rule of customary international law. Nor can a state claim jurisdiction over a second sovereign state, in accordance with the rule *par in parem non habet imperium*. It is assumed, of course, that state A has not voluntarily submitted itself to the jurisdiction of the courts of state B.

State B could not bring suit against state A in the latter's courts, as the dissemination of propaganda by state A would be regarded as an "act of state" not subject to the jurisdiction of the court.[4] "The transactions of independent states with each other," writes Lord Halsbury,[5] "are governed by other laws than those which municipal courts administer; such courts have neither the means of deciding what is right, nor the power of enforcing any decision which they may make. Hence, the courts of this country, whether of law or equity (Doss v. Secretary of State for India in Council (1875) L.R. 19 Eq. 509; 38 Dig. 8, *18*) have no jurisdiction to adjudge upon acts committed by one sovereign state toward another in the exercise of its sovereign power (Coorg (Rajah) v. East India Co. (1860), 29 Beav. 300; 38 Dig. 9, *34*). . . ."

Oppenheim writes that "the simplest means of settling State differences, and that to which States as a rule resort before they make use of other means, is negotiation."[6] Naturally, negotiation does not preclude the invocation of law or dependence upon whatever law may be applicable. Law and diplomacy "are not mutually exclusive procedures."[7]

Protest

Diplomatic protests or representations may range all the way from the statement that the protesting government "cannot remain indifferent to" the behavior or actions of some other government, to a simple ultimatum. Protests are registered "(a) to make known that the protesting state does not approve of the behavior or actions of another state; (b) to make known that the protesting state does not recognize certain acts; (c) to preserve the rights of the protesting state."[8] International law definitely recognizes the principle of "extinctive prescription," that is to say, loss of rights by a state that fails to protest against the contravention of its rights. On the other hand, protest without further action will not necessarily preserve the rights of a state.

Since World II, diplomatic protests, especially against the propaganda activities of another state, have served yet another purpose. Many are lodged today merely for their propaganda value, and are therefore a form of counterpropaganda. Both the protesting state and the state with which the protest is lodged know this. Hence it is not uncommon for the reply to the protest to be couched in terms that will have the maximum propaganda effect — a sort of counterpropaganda in the second degree.[9]

The reactions evoked by diplomatic protests differ according to when, how, and why the protests are made, who makes them, and to whom. Before the world had aligned itself behind the two mighty protagonists of "westernism" and "communism", a protest from a large state to a small state usually brought forth a hurried apology, possibly a *démenti*, and a promise to desist from the nefarious practice, or to stop what the smaller state admitted to be the "illegal" activities of private individuals within its borders. In 1834, for instance, the Swiss government was forced to expel aliens in Switzerland who had been carrying on propaganda hostile to its powerful neighbors, when the latter protested.[10] When Austria-Hungary in 1909 demanded of diminutive Serbia that it "repudiate all idea of interfering or attempting to interfere with the destinies of the inhabitants of any part whatever of Austria-Hungary," and that it "eliminate without delay from public instruction in Serbia . . . everything that serves or might serve, to foment the propaganda against the Austro-Hungarian Monarchy," Serbia denied fomenting anything, but promised to remove officers guilty of such behavior.[11] A small state, on the other hand, would simply have to wink at the propaganda activities of larger states directed against it. United States Consul Clement Stanislaus Edwards, writing from Kovno, Lithuania, on August 17, 1923, said: "With reference to Soviet propaganda carried on in Lithuania and aimed at overthrowing the existing order, the officials are somewhat reticent. It is freely admitted that there has been considerable propaganda of this kind, but there is hesitancy in charging the Soviet Russian government with direct responsibility, or in expressing more than a vague suspicion that the Soviet representative or members of his staff have been engaged in it."[12]

Large states among themselves would treat protests according to their relationship with the protesting government. Great Britain refused in 1803 to prevent French royalist refugees in England from disseminating propaganda detrimental to the French republic.[13] Germany gruffly rejected an Austrian protest which alleged that it was giving aid to Austrian Nazis in a "terroristic campaign against the Austrian Government." It denied intervention in Austrian affairs and scolded Austria for taking the matter to the League of Nations before it had had a chance to investigate the allegation.[14]

Uruguay, on the other hand, closed a radio station that broadcast counterrevolutionary propaganda to Argentina in an attempt by an ousted government to regain control from a general who had seized power. But the diplomatic exchanges had reached the point of an open threat of war by Argentina. Similarly, after many diplomatic notes had passed back and forth, France tracked down and dismantled a secret radio station in Nice that broadcast anti-Fascist propaganda to northern Italy in 1929.[15] The United States extended its "sincere regrets" to the Italian people when in January 1931 United States General Smedley D. Butler made disparaging remarks about Mussolini at a banquet. The United States admitted that the remarks were unwarranted on the part of an officer on active duty, and General Butler was reprimanded.[16]

The attitude toward protests before World War II was also governed by whether the alleged propaganda emanated from public or private sources. Except when a very large state protested to a small state — in which case cognizance was taken of the protest regardless of the source of the exceptionable propaganda — an attempt was made by the protesting state to link the source to the government, or at least to show that the government condoned the activity. This was especially true after World War I. The theory is, apparently, that a state is not necessarily responsible for the propaganda activities of private individuals unless it is shown to be an accomplice.

The United States ambassador to Germany protested against statements in the German press on March 4 and 5, 1937, that were uncomplimentary to American women. "The connection between the newspaper and those in control of German governmental affairs was seemingly regarded as sufficient to justify such action on the ground that the latter were inspirers of the offensive statements," writes Hyde.[17] For years after the founding of the Comintern in 1919 and before its dissolution in 1943, many states tried unsuccessfully to make Russia admit responsibility for its propaganda activities all over the world. But the Soviet Union persisted in saying that it "Cannot take upon itself and has not taken upon itself obligations of any kind with regard to the Communist International."[18] This statement followed a formal protest by the United States, which cited the Roosevelt-Litvinov agreement of 1933. Similar protests were lodged by Britain, Italy, Latvia, and Japan at this time.[19]

As relations between the West and the countries in the Soviet sphere deteriorated, not only was propaganda stepped up, but the protests that

175

were occasionally lodged began to fall on deaf ears, or were themselves molded into weapons of propaganda as mentioned above. While the protests evoked some response in 1946, the year 1947 marked the turning point as the world entered the Cold War era. Especially indicative of the times was the behavior of the smaller states. These quickly aligned themselves behind one or the other of the two major powers, and from the shelter of the latter's strength flouted the protests that were at first showered upon them. At the same time they dared now to register their own displeasure at the propaganda activities of great powers in the opposite camp.

Thus in January 1947 Poland protested to Britain against the broadcasts emanating from the BBC in London. "Our government," said a Polish foreign office spokesman, "cannot but consider that the Polish-language broadcasts coming from London — their whole tone of hatred and provocation — have something to do with inciting people in this country to murder one another. We consider that the authors of these broadcasts share responsibility for part of the bloodshed in Poland." [20] A year later Poland again protested both to Britain and the United States for broadcasting the speeches of former Vice-Premier Stanislaw Mikolajczyk over the BBC and the Voice of America.[21] Both these protests were against activities carried on abroad by official agencies of a foreign government.

In June 1946 Poland had protested to Britain about the latter's propaganda activities within Poland itself. The note referred to a British news bulletin that carried news about Poland. The curt British reply pointed out that Poland was at liberty to circulate any material it desired through its embassy in London.[22]

Certain propaganda activities of private individuals are easily controlled through the municipal laws of a state. Others are not. The dissemination of propaganda by persons or groups not directly connected with any government has been the subject of diplomatic protests in recent years. The contrast between Greece's reaction to Soviet protests in August 1946 and, less than eight months later, in April 1947 is revealing. In the earlier instance the Soviet ambassador in Greece protested against attacks on Russia in the Greek press and a ban in some Greek districts against Soviet motion pictures. Acting Greek Foreign Minister Stephanos Stefanopoulos promised to prosecute the two royalist newspapers involved, although he insisted that the newspapers might have been provoked to make attacks on Russia by articles that had appeared in the Russian press. Nevertheless, the Greek government prosecuted two editors, who were sentenced to seven months in jail for publishing "libelous statements against Premier Stalin and Soviet Russia." The following April, on the other hand, when the Soviet government again sent a note of protest to Greece, this time in connection with an allegedly "faked" interview with Stalin published in a Greek newspaper, the Greek government was less accommodating. President Truman had proclaimed less than a month previously his doctrine of what became known as the "containment of communism." Greece replied that 1) the newspaper was an antigovernment publication; 2) the Greek press was free to publish whatever it liked; and 3) a Tass denial had been published by all Greek newspapers.[23]

By 1948 the Cold War had reached the stage where a small country like Denmark was brave enough to make representations to the Soviet Union about allegations in Russian newspapers that Denmark had formed a secret alliance with the West. In its reply Moscow informed the Danish government that it was "not too enthusiastic about the way in which Russia is being treated by the Danish press." A Soviet note to the Netherlands alleging violation of a United Nations resolution banning war propaganda was rejected by the Dutch government. The note referred to an article that had appeared in a Dutch newspaper, discussing possible Russian tactics should war break out. The Netherlands replied that the article did not violate any Dutch law.

It has become customary to reject or ignore protests against propaganda activities not only when the states involved are on different sides of what is today known as the Iron Curtain, but also when both states are outside the Iron Curtain. Thus Egyptian protests against articles that discussed King Farouk's love affairs in the Swiss press went unanswered, and the newspapers went unpunished. Even a protest by the powerful United States addressed to Syria — not an unfriendly state at the time — brought no satisfaction. The United States note objected to three articles appearing in the Syrian press which suggested that American diplomatic officials had been responsible for a bomb explosion on the grounds of the United States legation. The United States helpfully pointed out to the Syrian government that it could apply a press law which provided for "the prohibition of articles or items calculated to menace friendly relations with foreign states and punishment for publication of such material." The Syrian foreign minister informed the United States legation, however, that the Syrian press was free, and that the American press had published much exaggerated news of Syria. Behind the Iron Curtain less deviationism is tolerated. A Yugoslav protest to Czechoslovakia in 1947 regarding articles on Yugoslavia appearing in Prague periodicals brought the immediate response that the Czech cabinet was drafting a law that would "prevent irresponsible press attacks damaging the fundamental interests of the state." [24]

Many of the strongest representations are made against the permission by one state of propaganda activities on its territory by refugees from the protesting state. A series of notes were sent by Poland to Czechoslovakia just before World War II, protesting against the activities of Polish Communist fugitives directed at Poland from Czechoslovak soil. Czechoslovakia admitted most of the charges and promised to take the necessary steps to stop the activities. Poland did not consider the measures sufficient, however, and sent a new note, since "the Czechoslovak Government did not consider seriously enough the warning included in the Polish note of March 22."

Since World War II, the activities of Radio Free Europe have been an especially sore spot with the countries against which they are aimed. Both Czechoslovakia and Hungary have protested vehemently.[25] Two points emerge from these protests. The first is that what is most effective is the use of expatriates from the countries concerned in the preparation and transmission of the programs. The second point worth noting is that an attempt is made to link the propaganda agency with the United States government.[26]

To increase the propaganda value of a protest, a copy of the note is occasionally sent to the United Nations. Thus a Russian note to the United States charged that an article by General George C. Kenney in *Newsweek* discussing bases from which an attack on the Soviet Union might be contemplated, violated the General Assembly's resolution against warmongering. A copy of the note was sent to the secretary-general of the United Nations. The American reply pointed out that in the Soviet Union, where the press was admittedly controlled by the government, articles attacking the United States often appeared. It was true that the United States government had agreed to "promote, by all means of publicity and propaganda available to them, friendly relations among nations. . . . The Government of the United States is actively pursuing this policy. This Government, however, cannot accept the view expressed in the Embassy's note to the effect that governments which accepted the resolution should bear responsibility for acts committed on their territories which by their nature violate the resolution. . . . Any attempt on the part of the Government of the United States to control or suppress articles of this type appearing in the public press would be a violation of the right of freedom of the press which is guaranteed by the constitution of the United States." Russia attempted to squeeze every ounce of propaganda value out of the resolution on warmongering, and later introduced an unsuccessful motion in the United Nations to reprimand the United States and Britain for infractions by the American and British press of this General Assembly resolution.[27]

The question has been raised whether a protest is warranted before an actual violation of a nation's rights, integrity, or honor has taken place, but after some action on the part of a state — such as enabling legislation — makes such a violation possible or probable.[28] A case in point is the Russian note to the United States protesting against a $100-million item in the Mutual Security Act of 1951. The $100 million had been set aside for the support of "democratic elements in Eastern Europe." Russia claimed that the provision of the money for this purpose violated the Roosevelt-Litvinov agreement of 1933 which guaranteed against interference in the internal affairs of the Soviet Union by the United States and vice versa. The act, said the Russian note, "constitutes crass intervention of the United States in the internal affairs of other countries. . . . At the same time it represents unparalleled violation of the standards of international law and is incompatible with the normal relations between countries and respect of state sovereignty." The United States reply referred to the many breaches of the Roosevelt-Litvinov agreement by Russia. It accused the Kremlin of having tried to subvert and overthrow the United States government ever since the agreement was signed, primarily but not exclusively through local Communist parties. The MSA provision, on the other hand, was permissive rather than mandatory. Like NATO, the MSA was defensive, the reply said. "The organization would not have been necessary if, since the end of World War II, the USSR had not adopted an aggressive and threatening attitude toward the individual countries of the free world," all of which had now joined NATO for their common defense.[29] To get its full value out of the protest, the Soviet Union put the matter to the United Nations, but was rebuffed. The General Assembly voted 39 to 5 with 11 abstentions against the Soviet resolution to condemn the United States.[30]

The attitude toward protests against propaganda activities has changed since the turn of the century, and especially since World War II. "States have the right to require of any State which . . . permits enemies of public order to make of its territory a *foyer* of conspiracy or propaganda against them that it . . . suppress their operations," wrote Alphonse Rivier in 1896.[31] Others agreed that states had the right to require other states to curb hostile propaganda, especially that carried on by refugees.[32] This contrasts very markedly with the present-day attitude that representations against propaganda are ridiculous or plain counterpropaganda. "Foreign listening" behind the Iron Curtain, wrote the Free Europe Committee in its publication *News from Behind the Iron Curtain*, "is so prevalent that the Communists have had to resort to more direct methods. They have even gone to the rather comical extreme of 'protesting' to Western governments."[33]

Diplomatic Restriction

There is no doubt that a state has the right to make any laws regarding the entry, exclusion, and expulsion of aliens that it deems necessary, although certain great powers have claimed the right to question and request indemnity for the arbitrary expulsion of their subjects by smaller states. In Ben Tillett's case, Tillett, a British subject, was detained for expulsion by the Belgian police because he had entered Belgium "to organize the international federation of dockers there, and to foment a strike." Britain claimed compensation from Belgium. The arbitrator decided to disallow the claim and said that "the right of a State to exclude from its territory foreigners when their dealings or presence appears to compromise its security cannot be contested." In exercising this right the government may detain the foreigner in order "not to lose sight of" him.[34]

The expulsion of newspaper correspondents or their nonadmission by states which dislike what the correspondents or the publications they represent write about them are too numerous to be listed. Spain, for instance, voided the *New York Times* correspondent's credentials because it objected to the "general tone" of his coverage. Similarly, Yugoslavia ousted the Reuters' correspondent — a United States citizen — for "tendentious reporting of Yugoslav news." Sometimes a correspondent is expelled for disobeying police regulations or contravening a law. Yugoslavia expelled a Swiss correspondent for attempting to leave Belgrade for the provinces without permission of the ministry of information.[35] If the correspondent is a national of the state in which he is working, he is subject to arrest in most totalitarian states if the government is dissatisfied with the tenor of his coverage, even, or perhaps especially, if he represents a foreign newspaper or agency.[36]

While every state has the right to protect its subjects abroad, an individual or a corporation is in a foreign state on tolerance alone and not by right.[37] Radio Free Europe was granted the right to build its transmitters and to operate from Germany by the United States authorities in Germany. It had been informed by the West German government before the latter gained its sovereignty that it could continue its operations in Germany under a German license, after the United States withdrawal. But, RFE was told, it would have to be careful not to damage German interests. Already the government had found some of the broadcasts objectionable, and Germany would watch it more closely in the future.[38]

The question may be asked, can a government carry on propaganda activities in a foreign state? There appeared to be some doubt in certain states about the position of a governmental propaganda agency until recently. Yugoslavia, in asking the United States to close its information center in Belgrade in 1946, said that it had served as a "center of anti-regime propaganda, inciting the Yugoslavs to open treason." Furthermore, USIS was "acting as a private news service," and was therefore subject to censorship and other restrictions. The USIS center was immediately closed. Acting Secretary of State William L. Clayton admitted the sovereign right of Yugoslavia to order the closing, but he said that the State Department would take up the democratic "issue of whether the people of one country are to be denied access to the opinions of and information about other peoples." [39]

In October 1949 Iran published a decree enabling the government to close all foreign cultural and educational institutes in the provinces, and to restrict the activities of such centers in Teheran. Except for language lessons, all cultural activities including lectures and the showing of films required the prior sanction of the ministry of education.[40] The decree was not enforced until more than two years later. In February 1952 Iran decided to invoke the decree and ordered the closing of all foreign cultural institutes that were not directly attached to a foreign embassy. This meant the closing of the British Council centers in Isfahan and Meshed,[41] two Soviet institutes in Meshed and Tabriz, and an Indian institute in Zahidan. The USIS center, on the other hand, formed a part of the United States mission and was not affected.[42] It is not entirely clear whether Iran excluded those centers that were officially connected with a foreign diplomatic service because it was uncertain of its rights or for some other reason. But it is obvious that it could have found nothing better about which to be uncertain if its aim was to discriminate against Britain and Russia.[43]

The British attitude toward the right of governments to engage in propaganda activities in foreign countries is not absolutely clear. Apparently Britain distinguishes between the rights of a purely cultural agency — even one that is controlled by the government — such as the British Council, and a setup such as the British Information Services which also disseminates political information. The former has no more rights, it would appear from British behavior, than has a purely private institution. To the latter Britain seems prepared to grant diplomatic immunity. This is strange in the light of the undiplomatic treatment given to the BIS by countries in the Soviet bloc. On May 11, 1950, for instance, a written question was put to the secretary of state for the home department, J. Chuter Ede, asking "if he has considered evidence of Communist propaganda issued since 24th April by the Press department of the Soviet Embassy in London in 'Soviet News,' a copy of which has been sent to him; and, in view of the continuation of this propaganda, if he will take steps to stop the publication of 'Soviet News' in future." Mr. Ede's reply was short: "I have no power to take such action." [44] When Britain decided to order the closing of the Tass monitoring service in London, it did so on the excuse that the "conditions under which special facilities were accorded to TASS to operate the station during the war no longer apply." [45]

The Polish protest against the circulation of news concerning Poland by the British embassy was, at first, rejected by Britain. The Polish embassy in London, the British note countered, had the right to circulate anything it wished, and exploited that right. But the Polish government was adamant. It threatened to arrest the people who distributed the British bulletin unless the embassy complied. Britain had no alternative but to concede, and it assured Poland that the British Information Services would not comment on Polish internal affairs in the future.[46]

During the trial of Vogeler and Sanders in Hungary, the British embassy in Budapest received a note from the Hungarian government saying that it had become evident that the British Council had been actively engaged in espionage. The note requested that the British Institute be closed. Since the residence permits of the British members of the staff were simultaneously withdrawn, Britain had no option but to comply. In retaliation the Hungarian government was asked to close the Hungarian Cultural Institute in London.[47]

A few weeks later the Czechoslovak government requested Britain to close both the British Information Office and the British Institute in Prague. The Czechoslovak government and police had been acting in an openly unfriendly manner toward the council and the BIS, and the British ambassador had inquired on April 24, 1950, about the intentions of the government in regard to Czech-British cultural relations. Without referring to the British inquiry, the ministry of foreign affairs replied in a note dated May 12, 1950, that the offices were to be closed by noon of May 13 because "the British Government had been using Czechoslovak citizens and the BBC in a campaign of defamation of the Czechoslovak Government." In the same note Czechoslovakia denounced the Anglo-Czech cultural treaty of June 1947.[48] The British government answered by requesting Czechoslovakia to close its Czechoslovak Institute in London. On the pretext that the British Council had "failed to strengthen cultural relations between the two countries," Bulgaria asked the council to close its offices in June 1950.[49]

While Russia did not demand the closing down of the Russian-language weekly *British Ally*, published in Moscow by the British Information Services, Soviet restrictions made publication impossible, and it was discontinued in September 1950. After it had stopped appearing, the Russians charged that it had published articles of "propaganda for a new war." [50]

In China, the British Council's withdrawal was due partly to administrative interference by the Chinese Communist government — the difficulties in staffing institutes and the replacing of staff members because the government refused to grant them entry or re-entry visas, the restrictions placed on the movement of British personnel within the country, and the trouble the council experienced in importing necessary materials — and partly to the increasing cost of running the centers. By the end of 1952 the British Council had completely withdrawn from Communist China.[51]

The attitude of the United States about the right of governments to engage in propaganda activities abroad appears to be that, while the activities are legitimate diplomatic practice, all states have the sovereign right to control the propaganda activities of foreign diplomatic agents. The United States Information Agency forms a part of the diplomatic missions abroad; yet whenever the United States has been ordered to close a USIA center, it has done so promptly, even though under protest. In all cases the United States government has taken prompt retaliatory action, ordering the closing of that country's own information offices in the United States.

The first government to request the United States to close its USIS center was the Yugoslav government in September 1946 as mentioned above. The center was in fact closed under protest two days later. After a month of negotiations, the USIS was permitted to reopen its center on three conditions: 1) only information on life and culture in the United States was to be given; 2) nothing was to be done against the interests of Yugoslavia and its press laws; 3) a copy of all bulletins was to go to Yugoslav government offices and the information bureau.[52]

Czechoslovakia was the next state to give trouble to the USIS. In February 1948, the Czech police confiscated a notice in the window of the Prague office of the USIS, which told of a protest of British, American, and French correspondents against a Czech order to "rely mainly on official sources" for their news. A few days later the Czech authorities refused postal facilities to the USIS for the distribution of two issues of its news bulletin. In November 1949 the Czech post office informed the United States embassy that an edition of the information bulletin had been confiscated because it carried "an alarmist report menacing the security of state and public order." After that, all news bulletins put out by the USIS had to be submitted to the Czech government for prepublication censorship. Things came to a head early in 1950 when four Czech nationals employed by the USIS in Prague were arrested and, according to the United States embassy in Czechoslovakia, forced to make statements denouncing the USIS and its officials for abuse of their diplomatic privileges. The Czech nationals were accused of being traitors to their country, and two of them were sentenced to fifteen and eighteen years of imprisonment, respectively, for "espionage and plotting against the Czechoslovak Republic." On April 19, 1950, the Czechoslovak ministry of foreign affairs ordered the United States government to close its information center in Prague, which it did.[53]

When a rural leader was murdered in Poland in 1948, a Polish government spokesman attributed the murder and other violence to the "inflammatory broadcasts" of the Voice of America and the BBC. A campaign against the USIS reading room resulted in a drop of 50 per cent in the number of visitors at the center.[54] In March 1949 the Polish foreign office requested the recall of the attaché in charge of the USIS, because its news bulletin had referred to Poland as a "Soviet satellite." [55] In August 1951 the Polish government ordered the United States embassy to close the USIS and stop its activities, including its English and Polish-language wireless bulletins, its film showings, and its library functions. As a retaliatory measure, the United States ordered the closing of the Polish Research and Information Service in New York.[56] Poland did so, but not without protest. "The Polish Government considers this action of the United States Government as completely illegal and unjustified and categorically protests against it," the Polish ministry of foreign affairs wrote in a note to the United States embassy in Warsaw on August 14, 1951. "The Polish Information Office in New York has only served to enlighten the American people on Polish problems," the note continued. "While the PRIS has kept its activities strictly within the limits of the law of the country on whose territory it was active, while it observed fundamental rules and principles of international law, the USIS flagrantly violated them on Polish territory," the note said.[57]

Communist China ordered the closing of the five USIS offices on the Chinese mainland in July 1949. The United States reply was to increase the broadcasts of the Voice of America to China in Mandarin and Cantonese.[58]

After a "series of restrictions, insults, and harassments" experienced by the American legation in Bulgaria, the United States decided to break off diplomatic relations with the Bulgarian government on February 20, 1950. This followed a systematic campaign of persecution against Bulgarian nationals employed by the legation who were charged with "espionage for a foreign power." Although the American minister at Sofia interceded in behalf of the condemned employees and offered the Bulgarian government sworn affidavits testifying to the harmless nature of the duties of the Bulgarian employees, his efforts were to no avail, and it is thought that the accused were sentenced to death and executed. One of the charges against the Bulgarians was that they were working for an "enemy" legation.[59]

An exchange of notes took place in April 1950 between the United States legation at Bucharest and the Romanian foreign ministry regarding the activities of the USIS, which resulted in the closing of the center in Bucharest. The Romanian government charged that the activities of the USIS were not a "normal diplomatic function," but that rather "the former American Information Office [was] constituted as an organization with membership cards." The Romanians were referring to the library cards issued to all those who borrowed books from the USIS library. The USIS was accused of being "devoted to espionage, subversion of dissident elements of the Romanian population, propagation of retrograde social attitudes, misrepresentation of America, and incitement to war." According to the Romanian foreign ministry, "in the month of February 1950 alone, ninety percent of the contents of the Bulletin consisted of war propaganda and slander against the Romanian People's Republic and its allies." A Romanian national, who had been secretary at the information center, was put on trial and charged with espionage performed at the direction of the United States representatives.[60]

In the same way the offices of the USIS in Budapest were forced to close in July 1951. The recent trial of Archbishop Josef Groesz, the Hungarian note said, proved that legation officials had "carried out spying activities on the premises of the USIS." It requested the recall of three legation members because the trials had proved that the "nine employees of the Budapest Legation, ignoring the basic principles of international law and abusing their diplomatic rights, had intervened in Hungary's internal affairs." Not only the USIS library but also a motion picture theater used by the service — "cover organizations for spying activities" the note called them — was ordered closed. Hungary did not demand it, but the United States voluntarily stopped its daily news bulletin. The note also charged that the United States supported Hungarian Fascists abroad (especially in West Germany) and permitted them to use Voice of America facilities. When the United States refused to recall its three legation members, Hungary declared them *personae non gratae* thus forcing the United States to withdraw them. The United States protested against this action on the part of the Hungarian government. The U.S. note said in part: "The activities of the United States Legation in Hungary have been legitimate in every respect and in full conformity with international diplomatic practice. The United States Government concludes, therefore, that the conduct of the United States Legation officials has been called into question only to serve the propaganda aims of the Hungarian Government." [61]

The United States stopped publication of its Russian-language magazine *Amerika* voluntarily on July 15, 1952. But in doing so, the State Department pointed out in a note to the Soviet government that it had been forced to take this step because of the "progressive restriction" exercised on the circulation of the magazine by the USSR despite an agreement signed in 1944 guaranteeing free circulation to the publication. The Russians claimed that *Amerika* had lost circulation because of its anti-Russian propaganda. This, Wilson Compton, assistant secretary of state for public affairs, said, was ridiculous, as the Russians precensored everything that went into the magazine. "*Pravda* and other official Soviet organs," said Compton, "made more than forty vitriolic attacks on the magazine in order to frighten away Soviet readers." Since the United States felt it had been forced to cease publication of *Amerika* against its will, it requested the Soviet Union to stop circulating its news bulletins in the United States. The United States note said in part: "In view of the evident unwillingness of the Soviet Government to reciprocate the privileges granted by the Government of the United States to Soviet publications, the Soviet Government is requested to suspend immediately the publication and distribution in the United States of the U.S.S.R. Information Bulletin and supplements thereto." The Soviet government complied under protest, charging the United States with trying to prevent the dissemination in the United States of "truthful information about the Soviet Union." [62]

There are no American information centers or libraries behind the Iron Curtain today; outside the Soviet sphere of influence, however, no incidents involving the USIA have been reported. To help solve one of the problems, United States policy has been to replace aliens employed by the State Department abroad with United States citizens. This has served to protect both the local citizens against punishment by their governments, and the United States itself against internal sabotage and espionage. [63]

There appears to be general recognition of the principle that the recall of a diplomatic agent may be requested for interference with the internal affairs of a state. [64] Should the home government refuse to recall its minister, the receiving state may decide to dismiss him. [65] A state has various means short of physical force of making a diplomat leave, although the threat of force is not unknown in diplomatic history. [66]

If a diplomatic officer or a government information specialist working abroad is treated in an unfriendly manner by local authorities, his government is likely to employ retortion. Retortion is the term used when the retaliation for an inequitable act is an act of the same nature. Frequently, in the field of propaganda, retortion takes the form of a request for the recall of a diplomatic official or an order to close a cultural institute or information office as the result of a similar request or order by the state against which the retaliatory action is being taken. Retortion is the term also for the original action of asking a state to recall an official or to close a propaganda center, even if the reason for the request is of a different order altogether. The reason may be that the state is engaged in objectionable propaganda internally or externally, for instance through radio.

Nonrecognition

The recognition *vel non* of new governments is a problem that has involved a great deal of controversy. Some publicists have looked upon recognition as a right, others as a duty. Some have said that recognition is a legal matter, others that it is political. Oppenheim, who believes strongly that recognition is essentially a legal matter,[67] nevertheless admits that "it is unavoidable that political considerations may from time to time influence the act or refusal of recognition." As far as the municipal courts are concerned, the question of recognition has been left largely up to the executive branch of the government, and in this sense it is a political function.[68] However, this does not answer the question whether recognition must be granted as a duty in international law once certain conditions of statehood or of government have been fulfilled. The International Commission of American Jurists, meeting in Rio de Janeiro in 1927, believed that it was a duty. Article 8 of the draft convention which they drew up read: "A government is to be recognized whenever it fulfills the following conditions: (1) Effective authority with a probability of stability and consolidation, the orders of which, particularly as regards taxes and military service, are accepted by the inhabitants. (2) Capacity to discharge pre-existing international obligations, to contract others, and to respect the principles established by international law." [69]

If we accept this draft convention, then recognition is a legal matter subject only to the conditions of effective authority and the capacity (but not necessarily the will) to discharge international obligations and to observe international law. It follows that once these conditions are fulfilled, recognition becomes mandatory, almost automatic, and declarative of an existing fact. But what if the state is unwilling to respect the principles of international law even though it has the capacity to do so? Then surely the existence and the recognition of the state or its government becomes an anomaly.[70] For recognition means no more than that the recognizing state believes the new state or government has joined the community of nations, which it has not if it fails to observe the law of nations.

It is highly improbable that any state or government, whether new or old, would completely abrogate the rules of international intercourse, although it is true that some have been guilty of breaches of certain accepted principles of international behavior. Louis L. Jaffe has pointed out that "No individual can withdraw himself from the sway of social control. His personality and responsibility depend not on his willingness to perform, but on his capacity as an individual. And it is questionable whether any state today would be suffered to declare that it does not acknowledge the empire of international law, that it withdraws from the international community, or, if a new state, that it is not minded to accede." If, however, a state or government were to take this attitude, it would not make any difference whether it was new or old. But in that case, Jaffe continues, "non-recognition should be considered not as a denial of international personality, but as a sanction, as a mode of compelling an international personality to perform its duties. Non-recognition thus becomes one of the weapons along with war and retaliation for bringing delinquent nations to book." [71] J. L. Brierly agrees. "It has . . . been pointed out that non-recognition as practised to-day (that is to say, when it is used for some ulterior political purpose, and not because the stability of the government in question is really a matter of doubt) differs very little from the breaking off of diplomatic relations, and this seems to be true so far as the international consequences of either are concerned; and that it may be largely a matter of chance, depending on whether it is a new or an old government which displeases us, which will be used." [72]

There are many who agree with Jessup [73] that "the withholding of recognition has . . . become a political weapon wielded to force a new government to make concessions to the demands of the recognizing state." Warren Austin, former United States delegate to the United Nations Security Council, told the Syrian delegate on May 18, 1948, quite flatly: "I should regard it as highly improper for me to admit that any country on earth can question the sovereignty of the United States of America in the exercise of that high political act of recognition of the *de facto* status of a State. Moreover, I would not admit here, by implication or by direct answer, that there exists a tribunal of justice or of any other kind, anywhere, that can pass judgment upon the legality or the validity of that act of my country." [74]

If recognition is a political matter, there can be no duty to recognize. Each state can decide whether and when it will recognize a new state or

189

government, and each state can choose its own conditions for granting recognition. In that case nonrecognition can be used as a form of retortion [75] against nations that fail to live up to certain desirable standards. It must be remembered, however, that nonrecognition cannot then be excused on legal grounds. For if it is, recognition becomes a legal not a political matter, and the fulfillment of the legal prerequisites would make recognition a duty rather than a right on the part of the recognizing state.

It may, of course, be said that the United States' refusal to recognize the Communist government in China was due to the Communists' disregard of their international obligations in the treatment of United States consular officials and citizens. The United States refused until 1933 to recognize Soviet Russia for three reasons. The first was that the Soviet government had confiscated the property of American citizens without compensation. The second reason was that Russia had repudiated its obligations to the United States, and the third and "most serious is the continued propaganda to overthrow the institutions of this country." [76] One authority concedes that "the refusal of the Soviet Union to fulfil its international obligations has been shown to be a breach of [international] law, which justified the retorsion of refusal to recognize;" that "the confiscation of foreign private property without compensation [was] a breach of international law, which justified the refusal of recognition by the established states [Altstaaten];" that the Soviet states "are responsible for the international illegality of revolutionary propaganda, and, here, too, cannot evade the consequence that one is justified as a form of retorsion in refusing to recognize them." [77] But if these are the reasons why the United States failed to recognize China and the Soviet Union, then recognition is a legal matter and not a "high political matter," as Warren Austin put it. Furthermore, nonrecognition was, in these cases, a reprisal rather than a retortion, since had the legal requirements for recognition been fulfilled, nonrecognition would have been illegal.

In the opinion of this writer political considerations have generally been the decisive factor in recent times in the recognition of new states and governments. But most states have, illogically, attempted to justify nonrecognition by seeking legal grounds for it. For present purposes, however, it makes little difference whether recognition is a legal or a political matter. In the former case nonrecognition would be a reprisal, in the latter it would be a retortion. Whether in reprisal or as a retortion, nonrecognition has been and can be used by states to control international propaganda.

It should be mentioned that while recognition may be upon conditions, this does not make recognition conditional. In other words, recognition is not subject to withdrawal for breach of the condition or conditions. Once given, it is deemed absolute, and the most that could be done would be to sever diplomatic relations, which is not a withdrawal of recognition. This is important in the light of the argument used by President Roosevelt in 1933, when he recognized Soviet Russia, that recognition prepared the diplomatic ground for surmounting existing difficulties.

The classical example of nonrecognition of a new government because of its international propaganda activities was the attitude of most states toward the Soviet Union. Lenin himself opened the first propaganda campaign on November 28, 1917, in a broadcast addressed to all the belligerent states. He addressed himself directly to the peoples, exhorting them to resistance and revolt against their countries' diplomacies.[78] "The program of the Communist Party is the program not only of liberating the proletariat of one country; it is the program of liberating the proletariat of the world, for such is the program of the 'International Revolution'," wrote N. Bukharin, member of the Central Executive Committee and the Politburo, in 1918. Kamenev, vice-president of the People's Commissars of the USSR, wrote in the Petrograd *Krasnaya Gazeta* on July 18, 1920: "Yes, this is a conspiracy. But it is a conspiracy that cannot be crushed; one in which millions participate, which is supported by tens of millions — a conspiracy in which the reason of history finds embodiment and which, therefore, is destined to triumph in the end." [79]

When a number of nations protested,[80] the Soviets claimed that the Third International (the Comintern) was responsible for the propaganda, and that the Comintern was an independent organization over which the Soviets had no control, and for which the state could not be held responsible.[81] The world was not impressed. Said a report to the United States Department of State: "To deny the assertion that the so-called Soviet government is intimately connected with the Communist International is to repudiate the published statement of one of the principal spokesmen of Bolshevism, Steklov. To deny that the Russian Communist Party dominates and controls the so-called Soviet government is to repudiate statements of Zinoviev and the resolutions of the Twelfth Congress of the Party. To deny that there is a working connection between the Communist International and the Red International Trade Unions is to repudiate the official records published by those bodies. To deny that the Communist International and the Red International of Trade Unions are indulging in international revolutionary propaganda aimed at the overthrow of the existing order is to repudiate their published proclamations." [82]

Nevertheless, it was not long before a number of governments began to recognize the new state. The first were the contiguous states, and more especially those which had themselves only recently come into being. They recognized Soviet Russia in 1920 and 1921.[83] Their treaties of recognition included a clause in all but two cases forbidding the organization or encouragement of hostile groups on each other's territory.[84]

A series of provisional recognitions followed a trade agreement between Great Britain and the Soviet government on March 16, 1921. Britain considered its agreement as no more than *de facto* recognition. Lloyd George commented on it in the House of Commons on March 22, 1921: "This is purely a trading agreement, recognizing the Soviet government as the de facto government of Russia, which it undoubtedly is. I do not suppose anyone looking at the facts of the last two or three years could possibly challenge that. They have as complete control over that vast territory as any government could possibly have under present conditions, and therefore they have to be recognized as the de facto government of that empire." [85] The agreements were all conditional and each included a clause similar to the following: "The present agreement is subject to the fulfilment of the following conditions: (a) That each party refrains from hostile action or undertakings against the other, and from conducting outside of its own borders any official propaganda, direct or indirect, against the institutions" of the other.[86] Germany followed with a provisional agreement relating to the treatment of prisoners of war signed on May 6, 1921, Article XV(2) of which said: "They are duty bound, in particular, to avoid all forms of agitation or propaganda directed against the government or the public institutions of the host state." [87] Similarly, the Norwegian preliminary agreement with the "Soviet Republic of Russia" of September 2, 1921, included in Article 8 the pledge of the parties to "abstain from any political propaganda and not to interfere with the internal affairs of the respective country." [88] These were followed by agreements with Austria,[89] Italy,[90] Czechoslovakia,[91] and Denmark.[92]

On July 23, 1923, the Union of Soviet Socialist Republics was founded, and Foreign Commissar Chicherin invited foreign states to recognize the new central government.[93] In the meantime Britain had found that the 1921 formula was too narrow, and proposed in a note of May 29, 1923, that "the Soviet Government undertakes not to support with funds or in any other form persons or bodies or agencies or institutions whose aim is to spread discontent or to foment rebellion in any part of the British Empire."[94] The Russian government accepted the proposal in a note of June 9, 1923.

Early in 1924 Great Britain became the first in a long list of states that granted final *de jure* recognition to the newly created Union of Soviet Socialist Republics. British recognition came in an exchange of notes on February 1, 1924. Paragraph 5 of the British note read: "It is also obvious that truly amicable relations cannot be regarded as finally established so long as one Party has reasons to suspect the other Party of conducting propaganda against its interests and directly for the overthrow of its institutions." The Russian reply of February 8 included: "At the same time and in full agreement with the point of view of the British Government, the Union Government declares that the abstention from interference with the internal affairs of the other country constitutes the necessary condition for mutual confidence and friendly relations between the two countries."[95] A treaty was signed on August 8, 1924, following the exchange of notes, which contained provisions in Article 16 pledging both parties "to refrain and restrain all persons and organizations under their direct or indirect control, including organizations in receipt of financial assistance from them, from any act overt or covert liable in any way whatsoever to endanger the tranquillity or prosperity of any part of the territory of the British Empire or the Union of Soviet Socialist Republics, or intended to embitter the relations of the British Empire or the Union with their neighbours or any other countries."[96]

This treaty was never ratified. On October 15, 1924, Zinoviev, chairman of the Third International, was alleged to have written his revolutionary letter to the Central Committee of the British Communist party, calling on the party to create "cells in all the units of the troops, particularly among those quartered in the large centres of the country" who would become the "future directors of the British Red Army."[97] Prime Minister Stanley Baldwin's Cabinet refused to ratify the treaty, and diplomatic relations were broken completely in 1927. On December 21, 1929, diplomatic relations between the two states were re-established through an exchange of notes which reciprocally reaffirmed the pledge to abstain from propaganda contained in Article 16 of the unratified treaty of August 8, 1924.[98]

The British recognition was soon followed by that of other important states of the world.[99] The United States was the one notable exception. For the reasons discussed above, the United States refused to recognize the Soviet Union until November 1933. President Franklin D. Roosevelt's argument for recognition was the same as that used by the *New York Times* against recognition in 1924.[100] His view was: "One must first prepare the diplomatic ground through recognition. Upon it one could then build with the hope of successfully surmounting the existing difficulties." [101] In his note of November 16, 1933, Foreign Commissar Litvinov wrote: "Coincident with the establishment of diplomatic relations between our two governments it will be the fixed policy of the Government of the Union of Soviet Socialist Republics: 1. To respect scrupulously the indisputable right of the United States to order its own life within its own jurisdiction in its own way and to refrain from interfering in any manner in the internal affairs of the United States, its territories or possessions. 2. To refrain, and to restrain all persons in government service and all organizations of the government or under its direct or indirect control, including organizations in receipt of any financial assistance from it, from any act overt or covert liable in any way whatsoever to injure the tranquillity, prosperity, order or security of the whole or any part of the United States, its territories or possessions, and, in particular, from any act tending to incite or encourage armed intervention, or any agitation or propaganda having as an aim, the violation of the territorial integrity of the United States, its territories or possessions, or the bringing about by force of a change in the political or social order of the whole or any part of the United States, its territories or possessions." [102]

President Roosevelt stated in reply that "it will be the fixed policy of the Executive of the United States within the limits of the powers conferred by the Constitution and the laws of the United States to adhere reciprocally to the engagements above expressed." [103]

Lawrence Preuss suggested that "the obligations are not reciprocal, since no change in the American law, which is now inadequate to enforce such pledges as are made in the Russian note, is contemplated." [104] But a closer study of Litvinov's note will show that, as later history corroborated, the USSR had not promised much, and certainly not more than the United States itself was able to abide by. The United States, it is true, has no power to gag the press or individuals. But Russia did not promise to restrain individuals. Its promises applied to the Soviet government and "persons in government service and all organizations of the government or under its direct or indirect control." This the United States has every power to restrain, and in fact did restrain until after World War II. The sentiment expressed in the notes clearly refuted government-sponsored propaganda while remaining silent about propaganda of unofficial organizations and individuals.

As was shown above, the controversy with the Soviet government, at least until the outbreak of the Cold War, has generally centered on the question whether the Comintern and the Communist party are directly or indirectly controlled by the Russian government.[105] Since World War II, of course, both governments have given free rein to their propaganda activities aimed at the other party.

Romania and Czechoslovakia both recognized Soviet Russia on June 9, 1934.[106] Bulgaria followed on July 23, 1934. Here, too, a clause was inserted guaranteeing mutual respect for the sovereignty of the contracting states, and a pledge to refrain from propaganda against each other.[107]

The Soviet attitude toward nonrecognition was expressed by Litvinov in a note to Herbette, French ambassador in Moscow, on August 31, 1928, on the occasion of the signing of the Kellogg Peace Pact: "The Soviet government believes that there should also be put among the non-pacific means that are forbidden by the covenant such means as a refusal to resume normal pacific relations between nations or breaking such relations, for acts of that character, by setting aside the pacific means which might decide differences, aggravate relations and contribute in creating an atmosphere that is conducive to the unleashing of wars." E. M. Borchard appears to agree with him. Refusal to recognize a new government, says he, is not only contrary to international law, but it is a hostile and unfriendly act, a *casus belli*.[108]

Other Sanctions

Protests, diplomatic restrictions, and nonrecognition are all retaliatory responses of governments to the noxious actions or attitudes of other governments or of their subjects. As Charles Cheney Hyde puts it: "On occasions, when their differences with others have not been adjusted by amicable means, aggrieved States not infrequently have recourse to non-amicable measures for the purpose of obtaining desired redress or of removing the cause of controversy. Such measures may or may not lead to war." [109] These "non-amicable measures" are merely retortions or reprisals. The original grievance against which a state is retaliating is, however, often lost in the convolutions of history.

The Cold War which is being fought today by the two major camps of the world began almost imperceptibly. It is hard to designate the date or the act that finally brought it on. Suddenly the world woke up to the fact that there was a Communist camp that looked upon a Western chancellery as an "enemy legation," [110] and a camp of the Western democracies, where even the courts looked upon the Soviet Union as a "hostile nation." [111] In such an atmosphere nations are more prone to take offense, and adjustments are more likely to be of a nonamicable nature. But the adjustments are often not of the immediate wrong. This is generally minor and could easily be settled by less drastic measures. The retaliatory measures are taken rather because of the rankling disagreement that caused the original split between the East and the West.

The examples are numerous, as mentioned earlier, of foreign correspondents who were asked to leave a state which sensed animosity in their attitudes toward it. Occasionally a correspondent is told that he must go because of his prejudices; at other times more subtle excuses are offered. Thus an AP reporter was expelled from Hungary on charges of espionage and smuggling. A *New York Times* correspondent was ordered to leave Bulgaria because he had failed to register with the police as an alien. The London *Daily Mail* correspondent was ousted from Czechoslovakia for predicting a Communist *coup d'état* in Slovakia, while the AP reporter was forced to leave because of "misbehavior." In Bulgaria, the AP newsgathering facilities were simply cut off without further explanation. The *New York Times* wrote that a UP correspondent returning from Saudi Arabia had said that "King Ibn Saud, with the full cooperation, and perhaps at the instigation of the United States Army, State Department and oil company officials, had banned all American newspaper correspondents from his country." [112]

A state's right to decide to whom it will grant an entrance visa and to whom it will deny one has been fully exploited by most governments. The principle is well established that a state may forbid the entrance of aliens into its territory at will. Russia "punished" the BBC by barring its correspondent from the Soviet Union. Czechoslovakia denied four British correspondents entry visas to cover its elections, and, although a UP and a

Reuters correspondent had their visas renewed by Czechoslovakia, AP was completely excluded. When the United Nations committee hearings on Palestine were being held in Lebanon, Jewish journalists from Palestine were denied entry to cover the hearings; they were admitted, however, following United Nations intervention in their behalf. When Poland strongly protested to the United States for refusing to grant visas to four Polish newsmen, it was discovered that the American ambassador in Poland, Stanton Griffis, had himself handled the cases. "He believed," wrote the *New York Times*, "that there was no point in allowing a newspaper man to go to the U.S. when, he expected, the dispatches sent by the correspondent would be persistently critical. The Ambassador held this view," the *New York Times* continued, "despite the professed American policy of supporting freedom for all correspondents to report whatever and however they choose." Similarly the Czech embassy in Washington criticized the United States government for refusing visas to five Czech correspondents. The State Department replied that access to eastern European countries was often denied Americans.[113]

Diplomatic pressure is sometimes exercised to prevent certain types of unwelcome propaganda. When there was talk among certain American advertisers of the possibility of using radio facilities in Iceland, Ireland, or on the European continent to broadcast radio commercials to England, the British government said that while it would not jam these foreign commercial broadcasts, it would discourage them and use "its influence wherever necessary" to prevent them.[114]

The United States has generally been freer with its economic pressure and sanctions. In September 1945 former President Herbert Hoover outlined the limitations he would set on the aid that the United States "must" give toward world recovery. He said the aid should be "conditioned upon the willingness of other countries to cease trade conspiracies against us and to halt their propaganda against the American way of life." Russia successfully silenced American radio correspondents in Moscow by refusing to let them use its short-wave facilities on the pretext that its own "heavy winter schedule of short-wave programs" would not permit it. Poland disrupted British and American cultural activities in the country by organizing a campaign against the British Council and the USIA reading rooms. Fear of reprisals caused the number of readers to drop appreciably.[115]

An example of successful diplomatic bargaining was the Vogeler case.

Robert A. Vogeler, an American businessman, was arrested in Hungary for espionage. His release was secured by the United States after it had promised to stop Voice of America broadcasts to Hungary on the official Hungarian wave length. On April 7, 1951, the United States ended its relays into Hungary through Munich, and transmitted on a channel that did not interfere with the Hungarian radio.[116]

The diplomatic behavior of nations must be taken as evidence of the existence of an international custom. True, states veer from the accepted international behavior of the times occasionally; but if they do so long enough, and if enough of them do it, international custom itself is shown to have changed. International customs develop slowly or rapidly, according to the activity involved and the spirit of the times. International custom in regard to propaganda grew very slowly at first. It gained speed during and after World War I, and appears to have erupted into its present status after gaining tremendous momentum during and since World War II. Why this has happened can be understood by studying the history of international propaganda. That it has happened is incontrovertible. To ignore the change is to ignore the facts, and it would then be futile to seek a modus vivendi with international propaganda: without knowing the problem one cannot find a solution.

$\{\int$

9

International Propaganda in Retrospect and Prospect

PROPAGANDA, it has been shown, is a term that is subject to many definitions. The definitions appear to be in agreement about one thing only: that propaganda attempts to influence the thinking of people. There is general agreement that propaganda is aimed at the minds of people, and that the attempt is to direct or strengthen their thinking along predetermined lines. While courts of law will accept the common definitions of words, they cannot pass judgment when the common definition is vague and uncertain. Occasionally, courts in the United States, for instance, have let the jury decide whether the activities of defendants were the same as those described in a law. Expert testimony is received. But in this regard both the bench and the jury cannot help but be influenced by the national sentiment of the day. This means that what is accepted as manifestly hostile propaganda in one state may be considered in quite a different light in another, or at least it may be condoned as warranted. As has been pointed out, the impact of what is said depends not so much on what is said as on the degree of friendship between the states involved.

Further complicating matters are the many treaties and resolutions that have been signed positively calling upon the signatories to engage in certain types of propaganda activities. Some of these have used the term propaganda in this connection,[1] while others have merely provided for freedom of expression in general or of a particular nature, without using the term. Thus it is not only permissible but, occasionally, desirable that states engage in activities designed to influence the thinking of people —

199

their own nationals and others — about other states. The question then is whether the content of the propaganda is in agreement with the spirit of the treaty or resolution.

Much of the time it is very hard to tell what the tendency of a state's propaganda is. The content of a present-day propaganda program is far too subtle most of the time. Often it is of a nonpolitical nature, while many of the news releases and broadcasts of states contain slanted factual news and editorials on which they base their propaganda campaigns. Most, if not all of this is inspired, subsidized, and, generally, organized by the state. Of course, all communications media are potential propaganda media. Much of the propaganda contained in them is similarly too subtle to be dubbed generically as tendentious.

But let us assume a state decides that the propaganda of another state is manifestly tendentious of something undesirable. It would then, possibly, go to the numerous treaties that have been signed and look for one that bans the specific type of propaganda it feels has been perpetrated upon it. It will find that no resolution directly mentioning propaganda was ever adopted by the League of Nations. The United Nations condemns war propaganda, and propaganda likely to provoke a threat to the peace. It also recommends that measures be studied to combat false and distorted information likely to injure friendly international relations. But the United Nations does not define the two types of propaganda, and obviously each state will interpret its propaganda in the light of its own ideology.

A number of bilateral treaties were signed before World War II by certain states, especially with Russia, in which "propaganda against the other party" was banned. No such bilateral treaties have been signed since the war. But here again, propaganda against the other party will have to be defined. No state would normally admit that it is engaging in propaganda against another party. It is merely telling the truth about the other party (and itself). An international tribunal would find it difficult to adjudicate on the basis of the extant definitions. Furthermore, Russia might well plead innocent of a breach of the treaty under the *clausula rebus sic stantibus*, pointing to the fact that a cold war was being waged by the parties concerned, or that international propaganda had become so universal since the treaty was signed as to have become customary international behavior. Each contracting party might also claim violation of the treaty by the other without fear of contradiction.

Finally, the International Convention Concerning the Use of Broadcasting in the Cause of Peace could be adduced by the state. But only thirteen states have ratified it, and it has other weaknesses which have been discussed above.

The problem of hostile international propaganda has often come before the League of Nations and the United Nations, and many have argued both there and in writings that there ought to be some legislation outlawing hostile propaganda. This in itself is proof of the fact that no international law as yet exists making hostile propaganda a crime. The arguments of such protagonists of the theory as John B. Whitton and Vernon B. Van Dyke that hostile propaganda by states is a delict in international law are subject to various criticisms. Whitton advocates that warmongering propaganda on the part of states and individuals be banned.[2] On the other hand, he says that states should be allowed to conduct propaganda in support of a "licit" war; propaganda to promote aggressive wars is out, of course.[3] Elsewhere he asserts: "No state can be condemned for urging its own people to rise up and meet an unprovoked aggression. The same is true if the state is urging one foreign power to resist an unprovoked attack threatened by another foreign power."[4] The problems raised by these suggestions are obvious. Every war is licit from the point of view of the belligerent. Charles G. Fenwick has pointed out: "while jurists have been attempting to reconcile the conflict between the right of self-defense possessed by one state with the right of independence belonging to another, governments have gone ahead and done what they thought they had a right to do without finding any great difficulty in formulating a legal justification for their conduct. Thus a conflict of view has arisen not only in the field of theory, but between the jurists of one country and those of another, depending upon the foreign policies of their respective governments."[5]

Vernon B. Van Dyke adds the following footnote: "Note should be made of the fact that this statement refers to the spreading of propaganda within foreign countries. Governments are free in certain circumstances to issue and circulate within their own territory pronouncements which other governments regard as hostile to their interests (for instance, a declaration that another government is guilty of aggression), but aside from releasing the news via the radio and press, it is doubtful whether direct, official steps could legally be taken to make a foreign people cognizant of such pronouncements, unless it be done as a measure of reprisal."[6] Modern communications make this exception almost meaningless.

Whenever the problem of international propaganda has come up, its illegality in international law has been defended on two grounds: that hostile propaganda was an intervention in the affairs of another state, and that hostile international propaganda was injurious to international peace.

A number of treaties exist that do not specifically mention propaganda, but which forbid intervention by one state in the affairs of another. These have often been interpreted as banning hostile international propaganda. But is propaganda a form of intervention? "Intervention may or may not involve the use of force," writes Jessup.[7] But his examples of intervention without the use of force exclude propaganda, which is merely an attempt to influence people's thinking. A state may intervene in the affairs of another without the use of force, he says, "by lending open approval, as by the relaxation of an arms embargo, to a revolutionary group headed by individuals ready to accept the political or economic dominance of the intervening state. It may be accomplished by the withholding of recognition of a new government, combined with various forms of economic and financial pressure until the will of the stronger state prevails through the resignation or overthrow of the government disapproved."[8] Brierly is specific: "A mere tender of advice by one state to another about some matter within the competence of the latter to decide for itself would not be an intervention in this sense, though it might be popularly so described; the interference must take an imperative form; it must either be forcible or backed by the threat of force."[9] When it is the latter, the question is no longer one of mere propaganda. Oppenheim's definition is along the same lines, and Lauterpacht concurs: "Intervention can take place in the external as well as in the internal affairs of a State. It concerns, in the first case, the external independence, and in the second either the territorial or the personal supremacy. But it must be emphasised that intervention proper is always *dictatorial* interference, not interference pure and simple."[10]

The second argument that hostile international propaganda is injurious to international peace is one that puts the cart before the horse. Hostile international propaganda is merely an outward manifestation of an international illness. As well outlaw international misunderstandings as the fulminations that disclose them. Furthermore, the same argument that applies to the difficulty of defining propaganda in general also applies to a definition of propaganda designed to injure international harmony.

The state that considers itself injured by hostile international propaganda might then turn to international custom, as evidence of a general practice accepted as law. Here it would find that a protest was treated according to the relative sizes of the states before World War II. That is, small states were quick to admit their guilt to large states, large states generally ignored or rejected the protests of small states, and states of about the same size treated protests according to their current foreign policy. Since the war, however, with the world divided into two large camps, things have changed, and small states, even in the same camp, have been known to reject the protests of large states regarding their propaganda activities or those of their subjects. If states have continued to register their protests since World War II, they have apparently done so merely for the publicity or propaganda value of the protest.

Does this show a change in international custom? In the fifth edition of Oppenheim's *International Law*, Lauterpacht commented: "The series of statements and speeches made in the years 1936 and 1937 by representatives of Germany, Italy, and Russia, and containing violent attacks on the Governments and Institutions of the countries concerned, must be regarded as exceptional and as evidencing a suspension, in this matter, of the operation of an accepted rule of International Law in the relations of these States." [11] This comment is missing in the seventh edition. Perhaps it is no longer necessary, considering how widespread such propaganda has become. The argument is as false, however, as the popular interpretation of the proverb the "exception proves the rule," proves being taken to mean "establishes." The correct translation from the Latin — "the exception *tests* the rule" — is more pertinent. Here an exception rapidly developed into a custom.

An analogy may be drawn from the attitude of publicists toward propaganda in wartime. J. M. Spaight, for instance, considered it illegal to incite the civilian population in wartime in his *War Rights on Land*, a book published in 1911.[12] Thirteen years later, in the same author's *Air Power and War Rights*, he legitimizes war propaganda, because of the practice of the belligerents in World War I.[13] Lauterpacht writes: "The legitimacy, formerly controversial, of inciting enemy subjects to rise against the Government in power is now no longer disputed. During the First World War the belligerents displayed vigorous activity in that direction. Since then, the increased possibility of disseminating propaganda by aircraft and, above all, the advent of broadcasting, have revealed the wide potentialities of this weapon." [14] Hyde says much the same thing.[15] This argument should also hold true for international propaganda in peacetime.

Turning to the general principles of law recognized by civilized nations, the state that considered itself injured by hostile international propaganda would find much comfort. There is a great deal of municipal legislation on propaganda and allied subjects. But a closer examination of these laws will show that they tend to protect the state on whose books they are far more frequently than they protect foreign states. In other words, it is all right most of the time if the propaganda is directed against some other state, so long as it does not harm the state which enacted the law.

When a state protects other states against hostile propaganda, it does so for one or both of two reasons. The first is the hope of reciprocity, which is the reason why immunity is granted to foreign diplomats. The second is the fear of reprisals. Large states grant no greater immunities to foreign states or their officials than they do to their own citizens and organizations. In the totalitarian countries these immunities may be great because the rights of the people are few, since the state will not stand for much independent action on the part of its citizens. In the free nations the immunities are few because the freedoms are many. Small states, fearing reprisals, grant fewer immunities to their own citizens and organizations than they do to foreign citizens and organizations.

The majority of laws that protect other states or their officials, protect them against defamation. While the propagandist may use almost any words or terms in his propaganda, not all propaganda is defamatory. In fact, propaganda has never been defined as "that which is defamatory." Libel and slander are merely incidental to propaganda, if they exist in it, and as such, they may be crimes according to the municipal law of the country in which the propagandist conducts his propaganda. But it has never been suggested that libel and slander ought to be international crimes. And even if they were delicts in international law, there is no more reason to outlaw propaganda with them than there is to outlaw the press and broadcasting because they are occasionally guilty of defamation.

This is not to say that the means do not exist to control propaganda that might cause international disunity, accelerate the advent of war, or injure the feelings of foreign states, their governments, peoples, or officials. The domestic laws of most nations — probably all nations — contain provisions for the control of propaganda, and here propaganda is interpreted in the light of the ideology of the state. States can also control propaganda activities with certain results and certain undesirable beneficiaries. Their laws provide controls over the media of communication, the content, the disseminator, and the manner of reception. The courts of many states will assume jurisdiction in cases where they consider that a crime has been committed under the laws of the state, (a) if the perpetrator is within their physical jurisdiction, (b) if he is a national of the state, and (c) even if he is an alien outside the physical jurisdiction of the state.

Aliens outside the physical jurisdiction of a state are of special interest, since they, more often than not, are the propagandists engaged in hostile international propaganda. Following a war, such aliens often fall into the hands of a state that has considered itself injured by international propaganda. What would be the fate of these aliens?

Obviously, an international crime must be one that is internationally recognized as a crime — for instance, piracy, the white slave trade, traffic in opium.[16] Propaganda, which involves controversy, cannot be included because there is generally no agreement about the criminality of its content. However, propaganda can become a crime once agreement is reached on the criminality of the content. Such agreement is possible following a war, when the defendants all belong to one side of the controversy, and the plaintiffs, who are also the judges, belong to the other side. This was the case, following World War II, in the Nuremberg trials. "We can save ourselves from . . . pitfalls if our test of what legally is crime gives recognition to those things which fundamentally outraged the conscience of the American people," Justice Robert H. Jackson stated.[17]

It should be remembered that the Nuremberg trials will serve and were intended to serve as a precedent. "I think also that through these trials we should be able to establish that a process of retribution by law awaits those who in the future similarly attack civilization," said Justice Jackson.[18] The standards laid down at Nuremberg were intended to have universal application: "We may not, in justice, apply to these defendants because they are German, standards of duty and responsibility which are not equally applicable to the officials of the Allied Powers and to those of all nations. Nor should Germans be convicted for acts or conduct which, if committed by Americans, British, French or Russians, would not subject them to legal trial and conviction." [19]

Will the law of Nuremberg apply also to propaganda? Apparently it was intended to. Not only were certain actions criminal at Nuremberg, but incitement to action was also an indictable offense. Thus Fritzsche's broadcasts were found to be noncriminal, as they were "not intended to incite the German People to commit atrocities on conquered peoples," said the court.[20] Streicher's publications, on the other hand, constituted "incitement to murder and extermination at the time when Jews in the East were being killed under the most horrible conditions." [21] And it was just as wrong for the propagandists to influence their own people as it was to influence foreign nationals.[22]

The principles of international law recognized in the charter and judgment of the Nuremberg tribunal were formulated by the International Law Commission on the direction of the United Nations General Assembly. On December 12, 1950, the principles were presented to the General Assembly, which invited the comments of member states.[23] Nothing further has been done about them. Nothing is likely to be done, since to accept the Nuremberg charter and judgment is as much as to say *vae victis* — woe to the vanquished!

One cannot, it has been shown, speak of the control of propaganda as such. At best the controls that exist are designed to check the act, and only secondarily the advocacy of or incitement to the act. Propaganda cannot and should not be divorced from the act it attempts to promote.

The almost universal acceptance of democracy, at least in theory, has resulted in an equally universal attempt to influence the masses in whom the power resides. As communications improved, the methods used to influence whole nations were refined. The immediate reaction of governments was to look upon this propaganda with horror. Speeches were made; recommendations to outlaw propaganda were put forward; treaties were signed. For it was apparent in those states where the people had a meaningful vote that they might be persuaded to vote not in the best interests of their own state, but for the advancement of some other state. The dictatorship, on the other hand, feared that the people might be induced to rise up and throw off their shackles.

Before long, however, it was seen that propaganda was too intangible to control internationally. Besides, its powers became universally recognized, and no state was willing to give up its right to present its point of view and make known its cause among the nations. For anything a state might say officially or through unofficial sources was dubbed propaganda, which, in fact, it was, for why should a state want to say it if not to influence others in its own interest?

The tendency since World War I has been to tighten municipal laws designed to protect a state against undesirable propaganda from without or within, while at the same time there has been a steady increase in the scientific and organized dissemination of propaganda. While this means that a state has no control over propagandists not within its physical grasp, it can, if it desires, control incoming propaganda at the receiving end through the channels and media of communication. At the same time the state is left with a freer hand in conducting its own propaganda activities. Because of changing ideologies, even within a state, the subtleties of modern propaganda, and the difficulty of definition, it is inconceivable that international law will ever control propaganda, no matter what its content, so long as the sovereignty of states is recognized. The control of propaganda will remain in the municipal laws of states and the bargaining power of diplomacy.

Notes and Index

Notes

Chapter 1. Historical Background

[1] Cf. I. G. Flügel, *Vollständiges Englisch-Deutsches und Deutsch-Englisches Wörterbuch,* Vol. 1 (Leipzig, 1847), defining propaganda: " . . . originally [applied] to the spreading of religious principles, in most recent times also to the spreading of political or revolutionary principles."

[2] Decree of November 19, 1792, *Archives parlementaires de 1787 à 1860,* Vol. 53, p. 474.

[3] Albert Sorel, *L'Europe et la Révolution Française (1889–1904),* Vol. 3 (Paris, 1893), p. 227. Author's translation.

[4] Robert Redslob, *Histoire des grands principes du droit des gens* (Paris, 1923), p. 308.

[5] *Archives parlementaires de 1787 à 1860,* Vol. 58, pp. 141, 152, 133; Vol. 62, p. 3.

[6] Article 119. *Gazette Nationale ou Le Moniteur Universel,* No. 178, June 27, 1793, in *Réimpression de l'ancien Moniteur* (mai 1789–novembre 1799), Vol. 16 (Paris, 1840), p. 736.

[7] Harold Nicolson, *Diplomacy* (London, 1950), p. 168.

[8] U.S. Department of State, *Papers Relating to the Foreign Relations of the United States (1923)* (Washington, 1938), Vol. 2, p. 769.

[9] *Ibid.,* p. 766.

[10] From a letter of Charles Evans Hughes to Samuel Gompers, president of the American Federation of Labor, July 19, 1923. American Foundation, Committee on Russian-American Relations, *The United States and the Soviet Union: A report on the controlling factors in the relation between the U.S. and the Soviet Union* (New York, 1933), p. 39.

Chapter 2. Definition of Propaganda

[1] The definitions are to be found in the following works: William Albig, *Public Opinion* (New York, 1939), p. 286; F. C. Bartlett, *Political Propaganda* (Cambridge, Eng., 1940), pp. 5–6; Charles Bird, *Social Psychology* (New York, 1940), p. 308; A. Gordon Dewey, "Report of Conference on Pressure Groups and Propaganda," quoted in Violet Edwards, *Group Leader's Guide to Propaganda Analysis* (New York, 1938), p. 40; Leonard W. Doob, *Propaganda: Its Psychology and Technique* (New York, 1935), p. 75; Leonard W. Doob, *Public Opinion and Propaganda* (New York, 1948), p. 240; Knight Dunlap, *Social Psychology* (Baltimore, 1925), p. 247; Harold Gosnell quoted in Ralph D. Casey, "Some Attempts to Define Propaganda," unpublished mimeographed notes, No. 17, p. 2; John Hargrave, *Propaganda the*

Mightiest Weapon of All: Words Win Wars (London, 1940), p. 53; Captain Liddell Hart in preface to Sidney Rogerson, *Propaganda in the Next War* (London, 1938), p. viii; Edgar H. Henderson, "Toward a Definition of Propaganda," *Journal of Social Psychology,* Vol. 18 (August 1943), p. 83; E. Pendleton Herring quoted in Casey, *op. cit.,* No. 18, p. 2; Institute for Propaganda Analysis in Violet Edwards, *op. cit.,* p. 41; Harold D. Lasswell, "Propaganda," *Encyclopedia of the Social Sciences,* Vol. 12 (New York, 1944), p. 521; Harold D. Lasswell and Dorothy Blumenstock, *World Revolutionary Propaganda* (New York, 1939), p. 10; Harold D. Lasswell, Ralph D. Casey, and Bruce Lannes Smith, *Propaganda and Promotional Activities* (Minneapolis, 1935), p. 3; Richard S. Lambert, *Propaganda* (London, 1938 [1939]), p. 9; Alfred McClung Lee, *How to Understand Propaganda* (New York, 1952), p. 6; F. E. Lumley, *The Propaganda Menace* (New York, 1933), p. 44; Gorham Munson, *Twelve Decisive Battles of the Mind* (New York, 1942), p. 15; Norman J. Powell, *Anatomy of Public Opinion* (New York, 1951), p. 7; O. W. Riegel, *Mobilizing for Chaos: The Story of the New Propaganda* (New Haven, 1935), p. 199; David B. Truman, *The Governmental Process — Political Interests and Public Opinion* (New York, 1951), pp. 222–223; J. L. Woodward in Casey, *op. cit.* No. 19, p. 2; Quincy Wright in Casey, *op. cit.,* No. 20, p. 3; Kimball Young, *Social Psychology — An Analysis of Social Behavior* (New York, 1931), p. 653.

[2] (1942), 43 F.S. 507 at 510.

[3] Quoted in *New York Times,* May 17, 1950, p. 3, col. 5.

[4] "Symposium on Civil Liberties," *American Law School Review,* Vol. 9 (April 1941), p. 888.

[5] United Nations, *Yearbook on Human Rights for 1946* (Lake Success, N.Y., 1947), p. 261.

[6] 56 Stat. 248 at 250 (April 29, 1942).

[7] Neutral verbs used are publish, disseminate, teach, utter, assert, express, express oneself, circulate, make a statement, display, publicly exhibit, present, spread, send, transmit, acquaint, communicate, distribute, reproduce, instruct, issue, promulgate, sell, cause to be heard. Weighted words often used are advocate, plead in favor of, defend by argument, support, vindicate, recommend, incite, stir up, make, do, use, employ, conduct or engage in propaganda, spur, urge, counsel, promote, excite, provoke, be guilty of, attack, uphold, instigate, foment, encourage, facilitate, favor, justify, defend, prevail upon, indoctrinate, influence, abet, preach, advise.

[8] Prohibited among the objects of propaganda are libel, slander, defamation, abuse, hatred, ridicule, holding up to contempt, insulting, intimidation, harassing, coercion, bringing into public disrepute, or offending a person, group, race, color, religion, creed, sect, class, reigning prince, head of state, president, diplomatic or consular representative of a foreign power, or a member of a political assembly. Also prohibited by some laws are propaganda to bring about rioting; war; a breach of the peace; violence; disaffection toward the government; an offense against a government or person; a crime; opposition to the constitutional regime; acts prejudicial to relations with foreign countries; acts liable to punishment; acts prejudicial to public interest; crimes against the peace, stability, integrity, and independence of the government; treason; insurrection; resistance to law; mutiny; overthrow or destruction of the government; aid to rebels; aid and comfort to the enemy; prejudicing the authority or credit of the state. Other laws prohibit the spreading of false rumors, reports, or news; subversive ideas or doctrines; distorted facts; Communist or anarchist doctrine. International agreements have been signed enjoining the contracting parties to promote international understanding and cooperation, cultural and intellectual exchange through literature, science, art, music, theater, and history.

[9] Among these are printed matter, writing, written matter, word of mouth, pictorial form, spoken or written words, signs, visible representation, shout, gesture, drawing, painting, emblem, picture, any form, publication, information, symbol, any medium,

oral form, visual form, graphic form, pamphlet, photograph, cinematographic film, theatrical work, phonograph record, radio broadcast, lecture, book, periodical, speech, newspaper, press, magazine, pulpit, document, mail, interstate or international commerce, advertisement, article, news report, news.

[10] Leubuscher v. Commissioner of Internal Revenue (1932), 54 F. 2d 998 at 1000. The same dictionary definition of advocate is used in Butash v. State (Indiana), 9 N.E. 2d 88 at 90; the word "incite" is also defined as meaning "to move into action, to stir up; to spur on or urge on."

[11] State v. Quinlan (1914), 86 N.J.L. 120 at 123; also followed in State v. Gibbs (1946), 4 A. 2d 300 at 301.

[12] (1942), 43 F.S. 507 at 510.

[13] U.S. v. German-American Vocational League, Inc. (1945, 1946), 153 F. 2d 860 at 865; U.S. v. Pelley (1942), 132 F. 2d 170.

[14] (1945, 1946), 153 F. 2d 860 at 865.

[15] (1942), 132 F. 2d 170 at 181.

[16] Harold D. Lasswell, "Propaganda," *Encyclopedia of the Social Sciences*, Vol. 12, p. 526.

[17] Harold D. Lasswell, "The Strategy of Soviet Propaganda," in Daniel Lerner, ed., *Propaganda in War and Crisis* (New York, 1951), p. 27.

[18] *New York Times*, April 21, 1950. It may be pertinent to add that Hitler did not advocate the use of the "big lie" in propaganda, as he is often thought to have done. What he said was that people are taken in by the great lie, a fact which is known to "all great lying artists and societies of this world . . . and [they] therefore also villainously employ [these tactics]."

[19] W. Phillips Davison, "The Role of Research in Political Warfare," *Journalism Quarterly*, Vol. 29 (Winter 1952), p. 22.

[20] Edward W. Barrett, *Truth Is Our Weapon* (New York, 1953), p. 65; Ralph K. White, "The New Resistance to International Propaganda," *Public Opinion Quarterly*, Vol. 16 (Winter 1952–53), p. 540.

[21] See Powell, *Anatomy of Public Opinion*, pp. 415, 440.

[22] H. G. Nicholas, "Propaganda," *Chambers's Encyclopaedia*, Vol. 11 (London, 1950), p. 254.

[23] *New York Times*, May 23, 1947, p. 11, col. 4.

[24] *New York Times*, December 17, 1947, p. 11, col. 6.

[25] Quoted in Powell, *op. cit.*, p. 476.

[26] *Leslie's Weekly*, Vol. 126 (June 29, 1918), p. 902.

[27] Riegel, *Mobilizing for Chaos: The Story of the New Propaganda*, p. 200.

[28] *Time*, Vol. 38 (December 1, 1941), p. 25.

Chapter 3. Propaganda Agencies

[1] *New York Times*, April 21, 1950, p. 1, col. 4.

[2] U.S. Senate, Committee on Foreign Relations, *Overseas Information Programs of the United States*, 83rd Congress, 1st session, Report No. 406 (June 15, 1953), pp. 2, 50; and *New York Times*, January 7, 1951, p. 21, col. 1.

[3] U.S. Senate, *Overseas Information Programs* . . . p. 48.

[4] *U.S. Information Agency News*, Vol. 3 (December 1956), p. 5.

[5] *Ibid.*, p. 280.

[6] U.S. Senate, *Overseas Information Programs* . . . p. 59.

[7] For a fairly comprehensive list of private propaganda activities conducted by U.S. nationals and groups, see the semiannual reports of the International Information Administration, the last of which — the 11th — appeared in June 1953, and the semiannual reports of the United States Information Agency which succeeded them.

[8] U.S. Senate, Sub-Committee of the Committee on Foreign Relations, *Hearings on Overseas Information Programs of the United States,* 83rd Congress, 1st session, (Washington, 1953), p. 625. See also pp. 622–633, 1402–1411.

[9] Statement submitted to the Senate Sub-Committee of the Committee on Foreign Relations, *ibid.,* p. 705.

[10] Office memorandum from John Scott to *Time*'s publisher, James A. Linen, dated October 28, 1953, p. 72.

[11] *Ibid.,* p. 74.

[12] Hansard, *Parliamentary Debates,* Commons, Fifth Series, 331:1909 (February 16, 1938).

[13] *New York Times,* December 18, 1945, p. 16, col. 3.

[14] See R. H. Coase, *British Broadcasting: A Study in Monopoly* (Cambridge, Mass., 1950), p. 17.

[15] U.S. Senate, *Hearings on the Overseas Information Programs* . . . p. 107.

[16] *Ibid.,* pp. 834–835, 1250.

[17] Radio Free Europe, Audience Analysis Section, mimeographed Special Report No. 12 (March 1957), containing excerpts from a report published by International Research Associates, Inc., New York.

[18] March 20, 1935.

[19] Hansard, *Parliamentary Debates,* Commons, Fifth Series, 331:1948 (February 16, 1938).

[20] From the preamble to the charter. British Council, *Report on the Work of the British Council for the Year Ended 31st March 1952* (London, 1952), p. i.

[21] *The British Council Report for 1940–41,* quoted in Ruth E. McMurry and Muna Lee, *The Cultural Approach. Another Way in International Relations* (Chapel Hill, 1947), pp. 152–153.

[22] *The Spectator,* Vol. 186 (March 2, 1951), p. 271.

[23] Britain does not otherwise maintain an official news agency. Reuters has often been thought to be government connected, or at least subsidized. It has flatly denied this allegation on every occasion. See *New York Times,* January 6, 1946, p. 23, col. 1; also, United Nations, *Freedom of Information,* Vol. 1 (New York, 1950), p. 48.

[24] Phyllis Hamlin, ed., *The Anglo-American Year Book 1953,* 41st ed. (London, 1953), pp. 44–45.

[25] Glavlit is often mentioned by writers on Russia's propaganda activities. Glavlit is an abbreviation for the Main Administration for Literary and Publishing Affairs, and it is responsible for the censoring of all informational materials. A Glavlit representative is to be found in every administrative district of Russia, down to the smallest unit. Its activities assure uniformity in the dissemination of fact and opinion throughout the country and it also exercises strict control over information leaving the country. But, although this means that virtually all information specialists become merely the tools of the Russian government, the effect of Glavlit is indirect, and it cannot be called a government propaganda agency.

[26] For as reliable an account of Soviet propaganda as is available in the U.S., see F. Bowen Evans, *Worldwide Communist Propaganda Activities* (New York, 1955).

[27] U.S. Senate, *Hearings on Overseas Information Programs* . . . pp. 1111, 1425. Figures given by Evans, *op. cit.,* p. 67, are 63 hours of weekly broadcasts by the Soviet Union to North America both in 1953 and 1954.

[28] See Alan M. G. Little, "The Soviet Propaganda Machine," *Department of State Bulletin,* Vol. 25 (September 3, 1951), p. 369; U.S. Senate, *Hearings on Overseas Information Programs* . . . pp. 124, 830, 1111; Evans, *op. cit.,* pp. 60–68.

[29] The entire staff of the Soviet diplomatic mission in Israel, for example, is

said to be paid with money earned from the sale of Soviet literature in that country. U.S. Senate, *Overseas Information Programs* . . . 83rd Congress, 1st session, Report No. 406, p. 120.

[30] In Krajina v. Tass Agency (1949), 2 All E.R. 274, the British appellate court recognized the immunity of Tass as the agency of a foreign sovereign state. The defendant claimed to be immune from process, and presented in evidence the statute establishing Tass, clause 1 of which reads: "TASS is the central information organ of the U.S.S.R., and is attached to the Soviet People's Commissars of the U.S.S.R." The Soviet ambassador in London testified that "Tass Agency constitutes a department of the Soviet state."

[31] See *New York Times,* October 25, 1924, p. 1, col. 3; November 29, 1924, p. 3, col. 2.

[32] Quoted in U.S. House of Representatives, Committee on Foreign Affairs, *The Strategy and Tactics of World Communism,* Report of the Sub-Committee No. 5, House Document No. 619, 80th Congress, 2nd session (Washington, 1948), pp. 166, 167.

[33] *Ibid.,* pp. 208, 210.

[34] *Ibid.,* p. 128.

[35] *New York Times,* September 19, 1950, p. 17, col. 4.

[36] "The Red Network," *News from Behind the Iron Curtain,* Vol. 2, No. 8 (August 1953), p. 65.

[37] Evans, *op. cit.,* pp. 63, 68.

[38] *The Minneapolis Star,* January 25, 1954, p. 5, col. 7.

Chapter 4. The Teachings of the Publicists

[1] Emer de Vattel, *Le Droit des Gens,* Vol. 2, Chap. 4, Sec. 56, quoted in Vernon B. Van Dyke, "The Responsibility of States in Connection with International Propaganda," unpublished doctoral dissertation (University of Chicago, 1937), p. 272. Cf. also Vattel, *op. cit.,* Vol. 2, Sec. 53, p. 143, and Vol. 3, Sec. 180, pp. 344–345.

[2] William O. Manning, *Commentaries on the Law of Nations,* A New Revised Edition (London, 1875), p. 134.

[3] F. F. Martens, *Traité de Droit International,* Vol. 1, Alfred Léo, trans., (Paris, 1883–1887), Sec. 74; Paul L. E. Pradier-Fodéré, *Traité de Droit International Public Européen et Américain,* Vol. 1 (Paris, 1885–1906), Sec. 238; Carlos Calvo, *Le Droit International Théorique et Pratique,* Vol. 1, 5th ed. (Paris, 1896), Sec. 108, and Vol. 3, Sec. 1298, p. 156; Alphonse P. O. Rivier, *Principes du Droit des Gens,* Vol. 1 (Paris, 1896), Sec. 31, and Vol. 3, Sec. 397; Antoine Pillet, *Les Lois Actuelles de la Guerre* (Paris, 1898), pp. 97–98; Heinrich Triepel, *Völkerrecht und Landesrecht* (Leipzig, 1899), p. 340; Henry Wager Halleck, *Halleck's International Law,* Vol. 1, 3rd ed., revised by Sir G. Sherston Baker, Bt. (London, 1908), Sec. 14, p. 363; James M. Spaight, *War Rights on Land* (London, 1911), pp. 146–150; John Westlake, *International Law,* Vol. 1, 2nd ed. (Cambridge, Eng., 1913), p. 318, and Vol. 2, p. 83; P. Quincy Wright, *The Enforcement of International Law Through Municipal Law in the United States* (Urbana, 1916), p. 69; Ellery C. Stowell, "Respect Due to Foreign Sovereigns," *American Journal of International Law,* Vol. 31 (April 1937), p. 302; E. C. Stowell, *Intervention in International Law* (Washington, D.C., 1921), pp. 378, 384; Paul Fauchille, *Traité de Droit International Public,* Vol. 1, 8th ed. (Paris, 1922), Secs. 255, 441(24), 472, and Vol. 2, Sec. 1088; Robert Redslob, *Histoire des Grands Principes du Droit des Gens* (Paris, 1923), p. 379; William E. Hall, *A Treatise on International Law,* 8th ed., A. Pearce Higgins, ed. (Oxford, 1924), Sec. 91, p. 339; Scipione Gemma, "Les Gouvernements de Fait," *Recueil des Cours de l'Académie de Droit International,* Vol. 4 (1924-III), p. 365; H. Lauterpacht, "Revolutionary Propaganda by Governments," *Grotius So-*

ciety Transactions, Vol. 13 (1928), p. 146; A. Verdross, "Die Völkerrechtliche Verantwortlichkeit für die Handlungen der Russischen Kommunistischen Partei und der 3. Internationale," *Zeitschrift für Oeffentliches Recht,* Vol. 9 (1930), p. 580; Lawrence Preuss, "International Responsibility for Hostile Propaganda against Foreign States," *American Journal of International Law,* Vol. 28 (October 1934), pp. 652, 668; L. Oppenheim, *International Law,* Vol. 1, 5th ed., H. Lauterpacht, ed. (London, 1937), Sec. 121, p. 231; Vernon Van Dyke, "Responsibility of States for International Propaganda," *American Journal of International Law,* Vol. 34 (January 1940), p. 73; Charles Cheney Hyde, *International Law: Chiefly as Interpreted and Applied by the United States,* Vol. 1, 2nd revised ed. (Boston, 1945), Sec. 217D, p. 724; John B. Whitton, "Propaganda and International Law," *Recueil des Cours de l'Académie de Droit International,* Vol. 72 (1948-I), p. 570.

⁴ Fauchille, *op. cit.,* Vol. 1, Sec. 255; cf. Sir Robert Phillimore, *Commentaries upon International Law,* Vol. 1 (London, 1854), Sec. 392, p. 437. See also Théophile Funck-Brentano and Albert Sorel, *Précis du Droit des Gens* (Paris, 1877), p. 216; Stowell, *Intervention in International Law,* p. 390.

⁵ See Preuss, "International Responsibility for Hostile Propaganda against Foreign States," *op. cit.,* pp. 663, 668. Cf. also Whitton, "Propaganda and International Law," *op. cit.,* p. 569; C. L. Bouvé, "The National Boycott as an International Delinquency," *American Journal of International Law,* Vol. 28 (January 1934), p. 37; J. Spiropolous, *Die de facto-Regierung im Völkerrecht* (Kiel, 1926), p. 172; Clyde Eagleton, *The Responsibility of States in International Law* (New York, 1928), p. 40.

⁶ Vattel, *op. cit.,* Vol. 2, Chap. 6, Sec. 72; Field, *Outlines of an International Code,* 2nd ed. (New York, 1876), Sec. 207; Bluntschli, *Das moderne Völkerrecht der civilisierten Staaten als Rechtsbuch dargestellt* (Nordlingen, 1878), Sec. 396, p. 229; Pradier-Fodéré, *Traité de Droit International Public Européen et Américain,* Vol. 1 (Paris, 1885–1906), Sec. 260; Rivier, *Principe du Droit des Gens,* Vol. 1 (Paris, 1896), Sec. 20, p. 266; Calvo, *op. cit.,* Vol. 3, Sec. 1298, p. 156; Kleen, *Lois et Usages de la Neutralité d'après le Droit International Conventionnel et Coûtumier des Etats Civilisés,* Vol. 1 (Paris, 1898–1900), p. 161; Liszt, *Das Völkerrecht systematisch dargestellt,* Vol. 3, 5th ed. (Berlin, 1907), Sec. 125; *ibid.,* 12th ed., Max Fleischmann, ed. (Berlin, 1925), p. 118; Fauchille, *op. cit.,* Vol. 1, Sec. 295, p. 498; Redslob, *op. cit.,* Sec. 102e, p. 511; Cavaglieri, in *Annuaire de l'Institut de Droit International,* Vol. 1 (1927), p. 152; Mannzen, *Sowjetunion und Völkerrecht: die Fragen der Anerkennung der Schulden, der Auslandspropaganda, und des Aussenhandelsmonopols* (Berlin, 1932), pp. 49–50; Hyde, *op. cit.,* Vol. 1, 2nd revised ed., Sec. 192, p. 606. Karl Strupp, *Wörterbuch des Völkerrechts und der Diplomatie,* Vol. 1 (Berlin, 1924), pp. 495–496, should perhaps be added to this list. Strupp says that since a state alone has sovereign power over its territory it must protect the integrity of foreign states against injury by private individuals within its jurisdiction. Eduard Zellweger, in *Die völkerrechtliche Verantwortlichkeit des Staates für die Presse — Unter besonderer Berücksichtigkeit der schweizerischen Praxis* (Zurich, 1949), p. 32, adds that Strupp is among those who say that "the action of the individual in itself is not a breach of international law; but the failure of the state to prevent or punish the delict is. . . ."

⁷ Hyde, *op. cit.,* Vol. 1, p. 724.

⁸ Eagleton, *op. cit.,* p. 80. This passage was also quoted by the arbitral tribunal in the Trail Smelter arbitration (final decision), *American Journal of International Law,* Vol. 35 (October 1941), p. 716.

⁹ Eagleton, *op. cit.,* p. 93.

¹⁰ Stowell, "Respect due to Foreign Sovereigns," p. 301, and *Intervention in International Law,* p. 378.

¹¹ Triepel, "Die auswärtige Politik von Privatpersonen," *Zeitschrift für Ausländisches Oeffentliches Recht und Völkerrecht,* Vol. 9 (1939), p. 26, quoted by

Zellweger, *op. cit.*, p. 74, and *Völkerrecht und Landesrecht* (Leipzig, 1899), p. 340.

[12] De Louter, *Le Droit International Public Positif*, Vol. 1 (London, 1920), pp. 244, 248.

[13] Hall, *op. cit.*, 8th ed., Sec. 7, p. 50, Sec. 65, p. 269.

[14] Zellweger, *op. cit.*, pp. 35, 41, 42, 75.

[15] Anzilotti, *Cours de Droit International*, 3rd ed. (Paris, 1929), pp. 490, 491. See also pp. 485–486.

[16] Oppenheim, *op. cit.*, Vol. 1, 5th ed., Sec. 164, p. 294, Sec. 127a, pp. 238–239 (also 7th ed., pp. 259–260).

[17] *Ibid.*, Sec. 316, p. 539, Sec. 121, pp. 231–232.

[18] Phillimore, *op. cit.*, Vol. 1, Sec. 392, p. 437, Vol. 2, Sec. 29, p. 35.

[19] Gemma, "Les Gouvernements de Fait et Leur Légitimation dans l'Ordre International," *Recueil des Cours de l'Académie de Droit International*, Vol. 4 (1924-III), p. 365; Bourquin, "Crimes et Délits contre la Sûreté des Etats Etrangers," *Recueil des Cours de l'Académie de Droit International*, Vol. 16 (1927-I), p. 233; Lauterpacht, "Revolutionary Activities by Private Persons against Foreign Governments," *American Journal of International Law*, Vol. 22 (January 1928), pp. 107, 126, 129; Dickinson, "The Defamation of Foreign Governments," *American Journal of International Law*, Vol. 22 (October 1928), pp. 840–844; Verdross, "Die Völkerrechtliche Verantwortlichkeit für die Handlungen der russischen Kommunistischen Partei und der 3. Internationale," *Zeitschrift für Oeffentliches Recht*, Vol. 9 (1930), p. 580; Preuss, "International Responsibility for Hostile Propaganda against Foreign States," *op. cit.*, pp. 649, 668; Van Dyke, "Responsibility of States for International Propaganda," *loc. cit.*: ". . . aside from special treaty provision [a state] is under no responsibility with respect to private propaganda activities proceeding from its territory."

[20] Radulesco, "Les délits pour lesquels il convient d'admettre la compétence universelle," *Revue Internationale de Droit Pénal*, Vol. 9 (1er–2e trimestres, 1932), pp. 24–42; de Vabres, "Pour quels délits convient-il d'admettre la compétence universelle?" *Revue Internationale de Droit Pénal*, Vol. 9 (3e–4e trimestres, 1932), pp. 315–335.

[21] Radulesco, *op. cit.*, pp. 38, 39–40.

[22] De Vabres, *op. cit.*, pp. 321–322.

Chapter 5. Control by International Agreement

[1] Charles G. Fenwick, *International Law*, 3rd ed. (New York, 1948), p. 77.

[2] Georg Schwarzenberger, *International Law (International Law as Applied by International Courts and Tribunals)*, Vol. 1, 2nd ed. (London, 1949), p. 194, quoting series A of the Judgments and Orders of the Permanent Court of International Justice. There are, it is true, occasions when third states are affected by treaties. But this is either through their accession or adhesion to the treaty, in which case they are no longer third states; or indirectly through being hurt by the fulfillment of the treaty by the parties to it (e.g. in the Island of Palmas case (1928), see Manley O. Hudson, ed., *Cases and Other Materials on International Law*, 2nd ed. (St. Paul, 1936), pp. 361–369. For a complete discussion see Ronald F. Roxburgh, *International Conventions and Third States* (London, 1917). Of course, as Roxburgh points out, "It frequently happens that a treaty becomes the basis of a rule of customary law, because all the states which are concerned in its stipulations have come to conform habitually with them, under the conviction that they are legally bound to do so. In this case third states acquire rights and incur obligations which were originally conferred and imposed by treaty, but have come to be conferred and imposed by a rule of law," p. 112. But here we have entered the realm of Article 38(b) of the statute of the Inter-

national Court of Justice, viz., "international custom, as evidence of a general practice accepted as law."

[3] Phillip C. Jessup, *A Modern Law of Nations* (New York, 1950), p. 134; this would appear both from the "Opening Statement for the United States of America" referred to by Jessup, and from the judgment, which includes the following language: "The question is, what was the legal effect of this pact [the Kellogg-Briand Pact]? The nations who signed the pact or adhered to it unconditionally condemned recourse to war for the future as an instrument of policy, and expressly renounced it. After the signing of the pact, *any nation* resorting to war as an instrument of national policy necessarily involves the proposition that *such a war is illegal in international law*; and that *those who plan and wage such a war*, with its inevitable and terrible consequences, are committing a crime in so doing." — International Military Tribunal, *Trial of the Major War Criminals before the International Military Tribunal*, Vol. 22, November 14, 1945 — October 1, 1946 (Nuremberg, 1948), p. 463. Italics added.

[4] Joseph Berry Keenan and Brendan Francis Brown, *Crimes against International Law* (Washington, 1950), pp. 76–77, and all of Chapter V. "The reduction of the natural law obligation to treaty form, of course, has the effect of adding a quasi-statutory obligation and of creating a legal custom, if the process is repeated," p. 77.

[5] See Schwarzenberger, *A Manual of International Law* (New York, 1950), p. 91.

[6] See Jessup, *A Modern Law of Nations,* p. 135; cf. Oppenheim, *International Law*, Vol. 1, 7th ed., p. 834.

[7] International Military Tribunal, *op. cit.,* Vol. 22, pp. 465–466.

[8] *In re Baba Masao (1947),* in H. Lauterpacht, ed., *Annual Digest and Reports of Public International Law Cases, 1947* (London, 1951), p. 206.

[9] Florence E. Allen, *The Treaty as an Instrument of Legislation* (New York, 1952), pp. 23–25.

[10] The Cherokee Tobacco (1870), 78 U.S. 616.

[11] P.C.I.J., *Collection of Judgments,* Series B, No. 15, p. 27.

[12] Quoted in the Harvard Law School, Research in International Law, *American Journal of International Law,* Vol. 29 (1935), Supplement, Part III, p. 1038.

[13] *Ibid.,* pp. 977–978.

[14] Union Interparlementaire pour l'Arbitrage International, *Documents Préliminaires,* XIXe Conférence, Stockholm, August 19–21, 1914 (Brussels, 1914), p. 55.

[15] Section 2 (b) (2) of the resolution; 27 countries were represented.

[16] Quoted in O. W. Riegel, *Mobilizing for Chaos: The Story of the New Propaganda* (New Haven, 1935), p. 170.

[17] *Ibid.,* pp. 171–172, 176.

[18] League of Nations, *Quarterly Bulletin,* Vol. 4, No. 1 (1932), p. 44.

[19] Belgium, Bulgaria, Czechoslovakia, Egypt, France, Greece, Italy, Lithuania, Poland, Portugal, Romania, Spain, Switzerland, and Yugoslavia.

[20] League of Nations, *Quarterly Bulletin,* Vol. 2, No. 8 (1930), p. 375.

[21] Quoted by Vernon Van Dyke, "Responsibility of States for International Propaganda," *American Journal of International Law,* Vol. 34 (January 1940), p. 72n.

[22] League of Nations, *VII Political* (1931), Doc. A.14.1931.VII.8, pp. 32, 43.

[23] League of Nations, *IX Disarmament* (1931), 1931.IX.19, pp. 2–3, (1932) 1932.IX.18, pp. 1–2.

[24] League of Nations, *Official Journal, Minutes of Council,* 15th year, No. 12 (December 1934), p. 1759.

[25] League of Nations, *IX Disarmament* (1935), 1935.IX.4, p. 702. Article 2(2) quoted is the first of three alternatives. The third alternative is much shorter and reads: "Inciting public opinion by direct public propaganda with a view to forcing the State to embark upon a war of aggression."

[26] Cf. the resolution of the League which reads: "The Assembly: 1. Expresses its

gratitude to the international and national Press organisations for their views upon the problem of preventing 'the spread of false information which may threaten the peace of the world and the good understanding between nations'." — League of Nations, *IX Disarmament* (1932), 1932.IX.56.

[27] See Whitton, "Propaganda and International Law," *Recueil des Cours de l'Académie de Droit International,* Vol. 72 (1948-I), pp. 600–601. Article 2(4) of the Charter reads: "All Members shall refrain in their international relations from the threat or use of force against the territorial integrity or political independence of any state, or in any other manner inconsistent with the Purposes of the United Nations."

[28] United Nations, *Yearbook of the United Nations, 1947–1948* (Lake Success, N.Y., 1949), pp. 91–93.

[29] *United Nations Weekly Bulletin,* Vol. 3, No. 19 (November 4, 1947), p. 580; United Nations documents A/C.3/162, L/AC.7/SR.17.

[30] *New York Times,* October 28, 1947, p. 1, col. 6; November 4, 1947, p. 1, col. 1.

[31] United Nations, *Official Records of the General Assembly, Second Session, Resolutions* (Doc. A/519) (Lake Success, N.Y., 1948), p. 14; *Yearbook of the United Nations, 1947–1948,* pp. 91–93. Resolution 110(II). Measures to be taken against propaganda and the inciters of a new war.

[32] *Yearbook of the United Nations, 1947–1948,* pp. 133–135.

[33] United Nations, *Yearbook on Human Rights for 1947,* p. 441.

[34] *New York Times,* November 30, 1947, p. 56, col. 6. To show the Eastern bloc that they did not approve of warmongering, distortion, falsification, and slanderous information, despite their opposition to legal control of these practices, the United States, Canada, the United Kingdom, the Netherlands, Sweden, Mexico, and China (Nationalist government), condemned the practices in a joint resolution and appealed to news personnel to avoid them. — *New York Times,* April 7, 1948, p. 16, col. 6.

[35] The new resolution read: "*The General Assembly* 1. *Reaffirms* its resolutions 110(II) and 290(IV), paragraph 8, which condemn all propaganda against peace and recommend the free exchange of information and ideas as one of the foundations of good neighbourly relations between the peoples; 2. *Declares* that such propaganda includes: (1) Incitement to conflicts or acts of aggression; (2) Measures tending to isolate the peoples from any contact with the outside world, by preventing the press, radio and other media of communication from reporting international events, and thus hindering mutual comprehension and understanding between peoples; (3) Measures tending to silence or distort the activities of the United Nations in favour of peace or to prevent their peoples from knowing the views of other States Members." — United Nations General Assembly, Fifth Session, Doc. A/1532, November 21, 1950. This resolution was adopted by 49 votes to 0, with 7 abstentions. — United Nations, *Official Records of the General Assembly, Sixth Session,* Supp. No. 1 (Doc. A/1844) (New York, 1951), p. 65. Paragraph 8 of Resolution 290(IV) referred to above reads: "*The General Assembly* calls upon every nation . . . 8. *To remove* the barriers which deny to peoples the free exchange of information and ideas essential to international understanding and peace." — United Nations, *Official Records of the General Assembly, Fourth Session, Resolutions* (Doc. A/1251) (Lake Success, N.Y., 1949), p. 13.

[36] Quoted by John B. Whitton, "U.N. Conference on Freedom of Information and the Movement against International Propaganda," *American Journal of International Law,* Vol. 43 (January 1949), pp. 81, 83.

[37] United Nations Documents A/925, A/CN.4/SR.25.

[38] Quoted in Louis B. Sohn, ed., *Cases and Other Materials on World Law* (Brooklyn, 1950), p. 274.

[39] *Yearbook of the United Nations, 1951,* pp. 846–849.

[40] Schwarzenberger, *International Law,* Vol. 1, p. 528.

[41] See Sei Fujii v. State (1952), 242 Pac. (2d) 617 at 620.

[42] Hans Kelsen, *The Law of the United Nations* (London, 1950), p. 29.

[43] (1952), 242 Pac. (2d) 617 at 621.

[44] Cf. Kelsen, *op. cit.,* pp. 95–98, 293.

[45] Case of Agricultural Labor (1922), in which the Permanent Court of International Justice said that "no measure can be applied in any country that does not see fit to adopt it." — Quoted by Schwarzenberger, *op. cit.,* pp. 506–507.

[46] See Free Zones of Upper Savoy and the District of Gex (1929 and 1932), quoted by Schwarzenberger, *op. cit.,* p. 194, and other cases *loc. cit.*

[47] Author's translation. G. Fr. de Martens, *Nouveau Recueil Général de Traités,* IIIe série edited by Heinrich Triepel, Vol. 13 (Leipzig, 1925), p. 249, Vol. 20 (1930), p. 72.

[48] Martens, *op. cit.,* Vol. 30 (1935), p. 644. Author's translation.

[49] Quoted by Charles G. Fenwick, "Intervention by Way of Propaganda," *American Journal of International Law,* Vol. 35 (October 1941), p. 626.

[50] Resolution 8 quoted *ibid.,* p. 628.

[51] Quoted *ibid.,* pp. 628–630.

[52] *United Nations Treaty Series,* Vol. 21 (1948), p. 97.

[53] *American Journal of International Law,* Vol. 46, No. 2 (April 1952), pp. 43, 45.

[54] The signatories constitute what is known as the Council of Europe and comprise Belgium, Denmark, France, the Federal Republic of Germany, Iceland, Ireland, Italy, Luxembourg, the Netherlands, Norway, the Saar, Turkey, and the United Kingdom, signing in Rome on November 4, 1950, and Greece and Sweden, signing in Paris on November 28, 1950. — United Nations, *Yearbook on Human Rights for 1950,* pp. 418–422.

[55] Riegel, *op. cit.,* pp. 27–28.

[56] UN Doc. E/CN.4/Sub.1/110 of March 28, 1950, p. 9.

[57] Quoted in Manley O. Hudson, *Cases and Other Materials on International Law* (St. Paul, 1951), p. 227, from Scott, *Resolutions of the Institute,* p. 164.

[58] Hudson, *op. cit.,* p. 227.

[59] C. C. Hyde, *International Law, Chiefly as Interpreted and Applied by the United States,* Vol. 1 (New York, 1922), p. 331.

[60] Oppenheim, *International Law,* Vol. 1, 5th ed., H. Lauterpacht, ed. (London, 1937), p. 413.

[61] Quoted by G. H. Hackworth, *Digest of International Law,* Vol. 4 (Washington, 1942), p. 275.

[62] *American Journal of International Law,* Vol. 35 (April 1941), Supplement, p. 59.

[63] Quoted in Hackworth, *op. cit.,* Vol. 4, p. 282.

[64] *Yearbook of the United Nations, 1947–1948* (Lake Success, N.Y., 1949), pp. 932, 940.

[65] 55 Stat. 1005 at 1006, Article I.4.

[66] An organization of radio stations that encouraged the use of radio as a medium of interstate understanding, mediated conflicts and fostered treaties for the control of propaganda. In 1939 the International Broadcasting Union had 60 members, comprising 900 stations with an estimated 300 million listeners. — Arno Huth, *Radio Today, The Present State of Broadcasting in the World,* Geneva Studies, Vol. 12 (Geneva, 1942), pp. 138ff.

[67] United Nations Document E/CN.4/Sub.1/104, p. 5.

[68] League of Nations, *Quarterly Bulletin,* Vol. 1, No. 16 (1926), p. 603; League of Nations, *Official Journal,* 7th year, No. 9 (September 1926), p. 1191.

[69] League of Nations, *Official Journal, Special Supplement,* No. 66 (1928), pp.

32–33, 48, No. 64 (1928), p. 473; United Nations Document E/CN.4/Sub.1/104, p. 5.

[70] League of Nations, *Official Journal, Special Supplement,* No. 93 (1931), p. 115; League of Nations, *Official Journal,* 15th Year, No. 1 (January 1934), pp. 167–171.

[71] For the text of the convention see the *American Journal of International Law,* Vol. 32 (July 1938), Supplement, pp. 113–120.

[72] Brazil, Chile, Denmark, Egypt, Estonia, France (including French colonies, protectorates, mandates by accession on January 14, 1939), India, Luxembourg, the Netherlands (including Surinam, Curaçao), New Zealand, Norway, Switzerland, the United Kingdom of Great Britain and Northern Ireland (including dependent territories by accession on July 14, 1939).

[73] Australia (including territories of Papua, Norfolk Island, and mandates), Burma, El Salvador, Finland, Ireland, New Hebrides, Southern Rhodesia, Sweden, the Union of South Africa (including the mandate of South-West Africa). See United Nations Document E/CN.4/Sub.1/104, p. 3.

[74] They are Albania, Argentina, Austria, Belgium, Dominican Republic, Colombia, Spain, Greece, Romania, Lithuania, Czechoslovakia, Mexico, Turkey, the USSR, and Uruguay. Argentina informed the United Nations secretary-general, when the latter inquired for purposes of a report, that although it had not ratified the convention, "the decisions adopted in" the convention "are applied in the Republic." — United Nations Document E/CN.4/Sub.1/104, p. 3.

[75] United Nations Document E/CN.4/Sub.1/104, p. 21.

[76] Belgium's reservation was: "The Delegation of Belgium declares its opinion that the right of a country to jam by its own means improper transmissions emanating from another country, in so far as such a right exists in conformity with the general provisions of international law and with the conventions in force, is in no way affected by the convention." Spain wrote: "The Spanish Delegation declares that its Government reserves the right to put a stop by all possible means to propaganda liable adversely to affect internal order in Spain and involving a breach of the convention, in the event of the procedure proposed by the convention not permitting of immediate steps to put a stop to such breach." The Russian reservation stated: "The Delegation of the Union of Soviet Socialist Republics declares that, pending the conclusion of the procedure contemplated in Article 7 of the convention, it considers that the right to apply reciprocal measures to a country carrying out improper transmissions against it, in so far as such a right exists under the general rules of international law and with the conventions in force, is in no way affected by the convention. The Delegation of the Union of Soviet Socialist Republics declares that its Government, while prepared to apply the principles of the convention on a basis of reciprocity to all the contracting states, is nevertheless of opinion that certain of the provisions of the convention presuppose the existence of diplomatic relations between the contracting parties, particularly in connection with the verification of information and the forms of procedure proposed for the settlement of disputes. Accordingly, the Government of the Union of Soviet Socialist Republics is of opinion that, in order to avoid the occurrence of differences or misunderstandings between the states parties to the convention which do not maintain diplomatic relations with one another, the convention should be regarded as not creating formal obligations between such states." — *American Journal of International Law,* Vol. 32 (July 1938), Supplement, pp. 119–120.

[77] See United Nations Document E/CN.4/Sub.1/104, p. 19.

[78] Quoted by Whitton, "Propaganda and International Law," *op. cit.,* p. 620.

[79] Article 8: "No state has the right to intervene in the internal or external affairs of another." — Thomas A. Bailey, *A Diplomatic History of the American People* (New York, 1946), p. 737.

[80] Manley O. Hudson, *International Legislation,* Vol. 7 (Washington, D.C., 1941),

p. 407; Howard S. LeRoy, "Treaty Regulation of International Radio and Shortwave Broadcasting," *American Journal of International Law*, Vol. 32 (October 1938), p. 729.

[81] By Bolivia, Brazil, Chile, Colombia, Paraguay, Peru, Uruguay, Venezuela. — United Nations Document E/CN.4/Sub.1/105, p. 28.

[82] *Ibid.*; LeRoy, *op. cit.*, p. 730. By January 1, 1946, Argentina, Bolivia, Chile, Paraguay, and Venezuela had ratified the Santiago agreement. The Santiago agreement was itself replaced by the Inter-American Radio Agreement, which was adopted in July 1949 in Washington, D.C. Here states were more widely represented: Argentina, Bolivia, Brazil, Canada, Chile, Colombia, Costa Rica, Cuba, Dominican Republic, El Salvador, Ecuador, the U.S.A., Guatemala, Honduras, Mexico, Nicaragua, Panama, Uruguay, and Venezuela. — United Nations, *Yearbook on Human Rights for 1950* (New York, 1952), p. 429.

[83] *American Journal of International Law*, Vol. 35 (January 1941), Supplement, pp. 44, 46–47.

[84] *New York Times*, October 3, 1947, p. 50, col. 1; April 8, 1949, p. 7, col. 5; April 10, 1949, p. 33, col. 3; April 11, 1949, p. 8, col. 7; Marie Louise Smith, "High Frequency Broadcasting — Another Attempt at World Agreement," *The Department of State Bulletin*, Vol. 22 (April 3, 1950), pp. 533–535. Miss Smith writes: "The relative channel hour assignments provided for the major countries are as follows: The U.S.S.R. 660 (plus 120 for the Ukraine and Byelorussia); the United Kingdom 437; India 350; France 235; and the United States 202. . . . The assignment of 202 frequency hours to the United States represents a reduction of 30 percent from the present level of frequency usage and almost a 50 percent reduction from our requirements as originally submitted." By way of explanation it should perhaps be added that, unlike the United States, the USSR and India, for technical and geographic reasons, use the high frequencies for domestic broadcasting as well as for international services.

[85] *New York Times*, April 5, 1950, p. 3, col. 1; May 14, 1950, p. 4, col. 4.

[86] *Yearbook of the United Nations, 1947–1948*, p. 928. Russia was a signatory of this agreement.

[87] *New York Times*, March 14, 1950, p. 8, col. 6; March 24, 1950, p. 12, col. 4. Of course, there were protests. Bulgaria complained to the Geneva Bureau of Broadcasting that both the United States and France were violating the Copenhagen allocation of wave lengths. — *New York Times*, March 30, 1950, p. 14, col. 6. The Ukraine accused the United States at a meeting of the Third Committee of the United Nations of sabotaging the Copenhagen Convention by using twenty-two priority wave lengths in its broadcasts which had been assigned to Russia. — "Assembly Condemns Radio Jamming," *United Nations Bulletin*, Vol. 10 (January 1, 1951), p. 44. And again, later in 1951, the Russians charged the United States with "radio piracy" by "illegally seizing radio wavelengths and thus jamming the broadcasts of Russia." — *New York Times*, August 14, 1951, p. 11, col. 4. In October 1951 a Soviet motion branding the United States broadcasts as a "flagrant violation of national sovereignty of countries concerned" was rejected by the International Telecommunication Union by 37 to 9 votes. By "foreign broadcasts" the Soviets probably meant broadcasts emanating from radio stations based on non-U.S. territory. Russia charged that the United States had more than a thousand frequencies in thirty-seven countries. Britain, charged the USSR, had 250 frequencies in ten countries. — *New York Times*, October 6, 1951, p. 5, col. 4.

[88] "Assembly Condemns Radio Jamming," *op. cit.*, p. 43; *New York Times*, May 3, 1949, p. 4, col. 5; May 4, 1949, p. 13, col. 3.

[89] "Assembly Condemns Radio Jamming," *op. cit.*, pp. 43–45.

[90] See Hackworth, *Digest of International Law*, Vol. 4, pp. 275, 276, 277, 278, 279, 283, 288–91, 293. An exception to this was made in regard to wartime broad-

casts. A commission of jurists met in Washington in February 1922 to consider the revision of the rules of warfare, and recommended — although their countries (the United States, Britain, France, Italy, Japan, and the Netherlands) never adopted — a resolution, Article 1 of which read: "In time of war the working of radio stations shall continue to be organized, as far as possible, in such manner as not to disturb the services of other radio stations. This provision does not apply between the radio stations of opposing belligerents." — *Ibid.*, p. 315. The Inter-American Neutrality Committee at Rio de Janeiro recommended in more positive terms on June 22, 1940, the adoption of the following resolution: "Article VII. Broadcasting stations of the neutral State, which are technically equipped to do so, may interfere with messages sent or broadcasts made in violation of these rules [i.e., that radio diffusion should not contain information of a military character or propaganda relative to the hostilities contrary to neutrality]. . . ." — *American Journal of International Law,* Vol. 35 (January 1941), Supplement, p. 47. As a matter of fact, during World War II all the major powers used jamming as a tactical weapon against enemy military communications, although the Allies never jammed the regular broadcasts of the enemy as Germany, Italy, and Japan did. — Edward W. Barrett, *Truth Is Our Weapon* (New York, 1953), p. 116.

[91] *Yearbook of the United Nations 1947–1948,* p. 940. In the Cairo revision of the general radio regulations annexed to the International Telecommunication Convention signed on April 8, 1938, Article 7, section 4(2) had read: "The administrations concerned shall conclude the necessary agreements to avoid interference and, when needed, shall, for this purpose, in conformity with the procedure which will be agreed among them in bilateral or regional agreements, call upon organs of expert investigation or of expert investigation and conciliation. . . ." — 54 Stat. 1417.

[92] Egypt, France, and Yugoslavia. — *New York Times,* May 17, 1950, p. 3, col. 5; August 10, 1950, p. 8, col. 3; December 15, 1950, p. 22, col. 3.

[93] *New York Times,* December 15, 1950, p. 22, col. 3. The previous year Russian delegate Vyshinsky had said at a United Nations General Assembly meeting that Russia's reason for jamming American broadcasts was that the untruths in the broadcasts might make the Russian people react so violently that cooperation between the two countries would suffer. — *New York Times,* November 17, 1949, p. 9, col. 3; "Assembly Condemns Radio Jamming," *op. cit.,* pp. 44, 43. The reservations with which Belgium and Spain signed the International Convention Concerning the Use of Broadcasting in the Cause of Peace fourteen years earlier might be noted here. See discussion above.

[94] *New York Times,* May 3, 1949, p. 4, col. 5. As were also protests lodged by the U.S. ambassador in Moscow requesting the Soviet government to take "effective remedial measures" to stop the jamming. — *New York Times,* March 21, 1948, p. 5, col. 2; June 14, 1949, p. 15, col. 1. By August 1949 the Voice of America was broadcasting on 110 channels, while the Russians were blotting out the broadcasts on 250 stations with 90 per cent effectiveness. — *New York Times,* August 9, 1949, p. 11, col. 1. Besides the 250 ground-wave (that is, local) jammers, Russia used 100 sky-wave (long distance) jammers. By early 1950 it had increased its ground-wave jammers to 500, and these were more than doubled by late 1950. There were 200 long-range jammers in use late in 1950. Barrett estimated that 10,000 Russian technicians were employed in jamming operations. — Barrett, *op. cit.,* pp. 117, 120–121. The best the United States could do under the circumstances was to try to invent new techniques to help surmount the jamming. — *New York Times,* January 1, 1951, p. 15, col. 5. The Hungarian government won a round with the Voice of America on this count when it agreed to release Robert A. Vogeler, the U.S. businessman arrested for espionage, if, among other things, the Voice of America stopped broadcasting on the official Hungarian wave length. This the United States agreed to do. It ended its relays into Hungary through Munich, and transmitted on a channel

that did not interfere with the Hungarian radio. — *New York Times,* April 29, 1951, p. 1, col. 4.

[95] Charles G. Fenwick, *International Law,* 3rd ed. (New York, 1948), p. 455.

[96] See comment on Article 27 of the Harvard draft convention on the law of treaties, *American Journal of International Law,* Vol. 29, Supplement, pp. 1077–1096, 1083.

[97] See Ware v. Hylton (1796), 3 Dallas, 199 at 261; *In re* Thomas (1874), 23 Fed. Cases, 927.

[98] One U.S. senator demanded that a peace offensive be launched against Russia through guided missiles and remotely controlled planes carrying propaganda leaflets. — *New York Times,* April 14, 1949, p. 2, col. 2. Another senator suggested that messages of friendship be sent to Russia in balloons. — *New York Times,* May 16, 1949, p. 3, col. 7.

[99] *American Journal of International Law,* Vol. 32 (January 1938), Supplement, pp. 21–22.

[100] U.S. Department of State, *Proceedings of the International Civil Aviation Conference, Chicago, Illinois, November 1 — December 7, 1944,* Vol. 1 (Washington, 1948), pp. 147–148.

[101] Article 35(a), *ibid.,* p. 156.

[102] "Paragraph 2.11. *Dropping Objects.* A pilot in command of an aircraft shall not permit anything to be dropped from the aircraft in flight that might create a hazard to persons or property on the ground or water." — International Civil Aviation Organization, *Standards and Recommended Practices. Rules of the Air,* Annex 2 to the Convention on International Civil Aviation (Montreal, September 1948), p. 11.

[103] See Whitton, "Propaganda and International Law," *op. cit.,* p. 594.

[104] Quoted by Van Dyke, "Responsibility of States for International Propaganda," *op. cit.,* p. 59.

[105] Leonard Shapiro, *Soviet Treaty Series,* Vol. 1, 1917–1928 (Washington, D.C., 1950), p. 4.

[106] See Article 4 of the alleged secret treaty signed by Germany and the RSFSR at Brest-Litovsk on December 22, 1917. — *Ibid.,* p. 381. A similar secret treaty, alleged to have been signed in Berlin by Germany and the RSFSR on May 28 — July 8, 1920, provided in articles 5 and 10 that each party refrain from propaganda activities in the territory of the other. — *Ibid.,* p. 382.

[107] Preamble paragraph (a), *ibid.,* p. 102, in which the parties promise to refrain from "official propaganda direct or indirect" outside their own borders against the other party, especially in the British dependencies and in the independent states that had formerly been a part of the Russian empire.

[108] This treaty was also signed by the Byelorussian Soviet Socialist Republic and the Ukrainian Soviet Socialist Republic. Under Article 5 of the treaty the parties undertake to respect one another's sovereignty and to "refrain from all agitation, propaganda or interference of any kind." — *Ibid.,* p. 107.

[109] Article 8, in which the parties promise to "abstain from any political propaganda and not to interfere with the internal affairs of the respective country." — *League of Nations Treaty Series,* Vol. 7 (1921), pp. 294, 298.

[110] Preamble paragraph (a), which is similar to the treaty signed with Britain on March 16, 1921. — Shapiro, *op. cit.,* p. 158.

[111] Article 8, *ibid.,* p. 174. A similar treaty was signed by Czechoslovakia with the Ukraine the following day (June 6), in which Article 8 was identically worded. — Martens, *Nouveau Recueil Général de Traité,* Vol. 18 (1928), p. 649.

[112] Shapiro, *op. cit.,* p. 227. Similar pledges were signed by the USSR with China on May 31, 1924, Article 6, *ibid.,* p. 242; the Three Autonomous Eastern Republics of China (the Mukden government) on September 20, 1924, Chapter 2, *ibid.,* p.

279; Germany on October 12, 1925, Exchange of notes No. 2, Martens, *op. cit.*, Vol. 15 (1926), p. 405; and Afghanistan on August 31, 1926, Article 2, *ibid.*, Vol. 18 (1928), p. 327.

[113] *Ibid.*, Vol. 19 (1929), p. 4.

[114] Shapiro, *op. cit.*, p. 351.

[115] Article 3, Martens, *op. cit.*, Vol. 28 (1934), p. 327.

[116] Article 5, *ibid.*, Vol. 29 (1934), p. 29.

[117] *The Times* (London), June 11, 1934, p. 12, col. 5; Martens, *op. cit.*, Vol. 36 (1938), p. 680.

[118] Paragraph 1, Martens, *op. cit.*, Vol. 30 (1935), p. 50.

[119] Shapiro, *op. cit.*, p. 148. Similar treaties were signed by Russia with Germany on May 6, 1921, Article 15, *League of Nations Treaty Series*, Vol. 6 (1921), p. 277; Norway on September 1, 1921, Article 8(1), Shapiro, *op. cit.*, p. 132; Germany on November 5, 1922, Article 7, *ibid.*, p. 199 (this treaty was co-signed by the other independent Soviet Socialist states), and Denmark on April 23, 1923, Article 5(1), *ibid.*, p. 206.

[120] Preamble paragraph (b), Shapiro, *op. cit.*, p. 102.

[121] Article 5, *ibid.*, p. 107.

[122] Preamble paragraph (a), *ibid.*, p. 158.

[123] Quoted by Preuss, "International Responsibility for Hostile Propaganda against Foreign States," *American Journal of International Law*, Vol. 28 (October 1934), p. 662.

[124] Article 5, providing that "all organizations in receipt of any financial assistance" shall refrain from "any act overt or covert liable in any way whatsoever to endanger the order or security in any part of the territories of Japan or the U.S.S.R." — *League of Nations Treaty Series*, Vol. 34 (1925), p. 32.

[125] Preuss, *op. cit.*, p. 663; Martens, *op. cit.*, Vol. 20 (1930), p. 9.

[126] Quoted by Preuss, *op. cit.*, p. 662.

[127] Shapiro, *op. cit.*, p. 94.

[128] *United Nations Treaty Series*, Vol. 12 (1948), p. 400. Other such treaties were signed by the USSR with China on August 14, 1945, Article 5, *ibid.*, Vol. 10 (1947), p. 336; Romania on February 4, 1948, Article 5, *ibid.*, Vol. 48 (1950), p. 198; Hungary on February 18, 1948, Article 5, *ibid.*, Vol. 48 (1950), p. 172; Bulgaria on March 18, 1948, Article 5, *ibid.*, Vol. 48 (1950), p. 145; and Finland on April 6, 1948, Article 6, *ibid.*, Vol. 48 (1950), p. 158.

[129] *League of Nations Treaty Series*, Vol. 11 (1922), p. 50. Similar provisions were contained in the treaties signed by Soviet Russia and Germany on May 28, 1920, Article 9, Shapiro, *op. cit.*, p. 382 (this was an alleged secret treaty); Lithuania on July 12, 1920, Article 4(1), *League of Nations Treaty Series*, Vol. 3 (1921), p. 122; Latvia on August 11, 1920, Article 4(2), Heinrich Freund, *Russlands Friedens- und Handelsverträge 1918–1923* (Leipzig, 1924), p. 96; Persia on February 26, 1921, Article 5, *League of Nations Treaty Series*, Vol. 9 (1922), p. 400; Turkey on March 16, 1921, Article 8, Martens, *op. cit.*, Vol. 16 (1927), p. 37; Mongolia on November 5, 1921, Article 3(1), Freund, *op. cit.*, p. 129; Finland on June 1, 1922, Article 5(2) (this referred specifically to the activities of groups or individuals in the frontier zone "whose actions appear likely to disturb the neighborly and peaceful relations existing on the frontier"), Shapiro, *op. cit.*, p. 173; China on May 31, 1924, Article 6, paragraph 1, *ibid.*, p. 242; Persia on October 1, 1927, Article 4, paragraph 3 (paragraph 2 of the same article reads: "Should the citizens of either of the Contracting Parties in the territory of the other Party engage in any propaganda or campaign prohibited by the authorities of this latter Party, the Government of that territory shall have the right to put a stop to the activities of such citizens and to impose the statutory penalties") *ibid.*, p. 341; Afghanistan on June 24, 1931, Article 3, Martens, *op. cit.*, Vol. 28 (1934), p. 327; and paragraphs 3 and 4 of the Roosevelt-Litvinov exchange of

notes of November 16, 1933, in which the United States and Russia mutually pledge not to permit the establishment on their territories of organizations claiming to be the government of the other party, quoted by Preuss, *op. cit.*, p. 662n.

[130] *League of Nations Treaty Series,* Vol. 174 (1937), p. 131.

[131] *New York Times,* July 12, 1936, p. 20, col. 2.

[132] Article 4, Martens, *op. cit.,* Vol. 34 (1938), p. 331.

[133] *League of Nations Treaty Series,* Vol. 190 (1938), p. 25; Martens, *op. cit.,* Vol. 35 (1938), p. 657.

[134] Signed in Bangkok on June 12, 1940; *League of Nations Treaty Series,* Vol. 203 (1940–1941), p. 423.

[135] Section 2(iii) (a) and (b), United Nations Document E/CN.4/Sub. 1/105, p. 29.

[136] Article 1, *United Nations Treaty Series,* Vol. 37 (1949), p. 282.

[137] *Ibid.,* pp. 295, 327.

[138] *League of Nations Treaty Series,* Vol. 9 (1922), p. 249. Similar treaties were signed by Great Britain, Iraq, and Turkey on June 5, 1926, Article 12 (dealing especially with propaganda activities in the frontier zone between Turkey and Iraq), Martens, *op. cit.,* Vol. 18 (1928), p. 335; Greece and Turkey on October 30, 1930, Article 3, *ibid.,* Vol. 36 (1938), p. 683; Danzig and Poland on August 13, 1932 (in which the government of Poland promises to prohibit economic propaganda against Danzig), Protocol II, *ibid.,* Vol. 28 (1934), p. 650; Persia and Turkey on November 5, 1932, Article 5, *ibid.,* Vol. 30 (1935), p. 689; Saudi Arabia and Iraq on April 2, 1936 (stressing the prohibition of political agitation by refugees), *League of Nations Treaty Series,* Vol. 174 (1937), p. 131; and Italy and Yugoslavia on March 25, 1937, Article 4, Martens, *op. cit.,* Vol. 34 (1938), p. 331.

[139] *League of Nations Treaty Series,* Vol. 190 (1938), p. 27; Martens, *op. cit.,* Vol. 36 (1938), p. 682.

[140] Article 2 of the treaty of April 20, 1942; *United Nations Treaty Series,* Vol. 10 (1947), p. 118.

[141] Article 1, *ibid.,* Vol. 9 (1947), p. 376.

[142] Article 6, *ibid.,* Vol. 23 (1948–1949), p. 158.

[143] United Nations Document E/CN.4/Sub.1/105, p. 29.

[144] Article 1(b), *United Nations Treaty Series,* Vol. 87 (1951), p. 355.

[145] United Nations, *Yearbook on Human Rights for 1950,* p. 444.

[146] League of Nations, *IX Disarmament* (1931), 1931.IX.19, p. 4; John B. Whitton, "Radio after the War," *Foreign Affairs,* Vol. 22 (January 1944), p. 313.

[147] See Eduard Zellweger, *Die völkerrechtliche Verantwortlichkeit des Staates für die Presse* . . . p. 122.

[148] See Ignaz Rothenberg, *The Newspaper* (London, 1946), p. 5.

[149] *United Nations Treaty Series,* Vol. 83 (1951), p. 356.

[150] See the treaty with Italy, Part II, Sec. I, Article 15; with Hungary, Part II, Sec. I, Article 2.1; with Bulgaria, Part II, Sec. I, Article 2; with Romania, Part II, Sec. I, Article 3.1; with Finland, Part II, Sec. I, Article 6; Permanent Statute of the Free Territory of Trieste, Annex VI to Italian Peace Treaty, Article 4.— United Nations Documents E/CN.4/Sub.1/105, p. 9.

[151] *United Nations Treaty Series,* Vol. 19 (1948), p. 57.

[152] Article 1; signatories are Belgium, Denmark, France, Ireland, Italy, Luxembourg, the Netherlands, Norway, Sweden, and the United Kingdom. — United Nations Document E/CN.4/Sub.1/105, p. 10.

[153] *Yearbook on Human Rights for 1949,* p. 312; United Nations, *Yearbook on Human Rights for 1950,* p. 421.

[154] Cf. Article 17: "Nothing in this Convention may be interpreted as implying for any State, group or person any right to engage in any activity or perform any

act aimed at the destruction of any of the rights and freedoms set forth herein or at their limitation to a greater extent than is provided for in the Convention." — *Ibid.,* p. 422. The signatories of the convention are the states that signed the statute of the Council of Europe plus the Federal Republic of Germany (West Germany), Iceland, the Saar, and Turkey. The convention was subsequently signed by Greece on November 28, 1950, at which time Sweden also signed. — *Ibid.,* p. 418.

[155] Article 30 states that these rights may not be used to destroy the rights and freedoms referred to in the declaration.

[156] Kelsen, *The Law of the United Nations,* p. 39.

[157] United Nations Document E/CN.4/Sub.1/105, pp. 7–8; Louis B. Sohn, ed., *Cases and Other Material on World Law,* p. 1213; United Nations, *Yearbook on Human Rights for 1950,* p. 482.

[158] Preamble to the Recommendations, quoted by Robert R. Wilson, "International Law and Proposed Freedom of Information," *American Journal of International Law,* Vol. 39 (October 1945), p. 792.

[159] Section 8. — United Nations Document A/1251, p. 13; United Nations Document A/1844, p. 65; United Nations Document A/1532, p. 1.

[160] *New York Times,* April 19, 1949, p. 10, col. 6. Need it be pointed out that there is hardly a situation that does not relate directly, if it must be, "to the protection or national defense of a country"?

[161] *New York Times,* May 15, 1949, p. 14, col. 1.

[162] *New York Times,* April 3, 1948, p. 9, col. 1. Perhaps it should be pointed out that the entire work of the 12-man Sub-Commission on Freedom of Information and of the Press, set up under the Economic and Social Council's Commission on Human Rights on March 23, 1947, has so far gone unrecognized — if approval represents recognition.

[163] Article 11 of the Cultural Treaty of the Arab League. — United Nations Document E/CN.4/Sub.1/105, p. 20.

[164] United Nations Document A/519, p. 14; United Nations, *Everyman's United Nations,* 4th ed. (New York, 1953), p. 157.

[165] Article 31. — United Nations Document E/CN.4/Sub.1/105, p. 11.

[166] *United Nations Treaty Series,* Vol. 70 (1950), p. 252. The original signatories of the league were Egypt, Iraq, Transjordan, Lebanon, Saudi Arabia, Syria, and Yemen.

[167] United Nations Document E/CN.4/Sub.1/105, p. 10.

[168] United Nations, *Yearbook on Human Rights for 1950,* pp. 406, 410.

[169] United Nations Document E/CN.4/Sub.1/104, p. 5.

[170] *American Journal of International Law,* Vol. 32 (1938), Supplement, p. 116.

[171] U.S. Department of State, *Conference Series,* No. 19 (1934), p. 279.

[172] LeRoy, "Treaty Regulation of International Radio and Shortwave Broadcasting," *op. cit.,* p. 729.

[173] *Ibid.,* p. 730.

[174] *American Journal of International Law,* Vol. 35 (April 1941), Supplement, p. 61.

[175] *New York Times,* September 20, 1945, p. 4, col. 8; September 26, 1945, p. 14, col. 4; United Nations, *Yearbook on Human Rights for 1950,* p. 429.

[176] Shapiro, *Soviet Treaty Series,* p. 381.

[177] League of Nations, *IX Disarmament* (1931), 1931.IX.19, p. 4.

[178] *United Nations Treaty Series,* Vol. 54 (1950), pp. 235, 242–244, Vol. 67 (1950), pp. 279, 288–292, Vol. 65 (1950), pp. 203, 210–214, 217, 224–226, Vol. 73 (1950), pp. 223, 231–234, Vol. 67 (1950), p. 293, Vol. 65 (1950), pp. 265, 266–268.

[179] Such clauses were included in the treaties signed by China with the Dominican

Republic on May 11, 1940, Article 4, *United Nations Treaty Series,* Vol. 10 (1947), p. 293; Cuba on November 12, 1942, Article 6, *ibid.,* p. 251; Costa Rica on May 5, 1944, Article 6, *ibid.,* Vol. 14 (1948), p. 436; Mexico on August 1, 1944, Article 6, *ibid.,* p. 448; Ecuador on January 6, 1946, Article 5, *ibid.,* Vol. 12 (1947), p. 241; the Philippines on April 18, 1947, Article 6, *ibid.,* Vol. 11 (1947), p. 366.

[180] *United Nations Treaty Series,* Vol. 68 (1950), pp. 157, 161–163.

[181] *Ibid.,* Vol. 17 (1948), p. 27.

[182] *Ibid.,* Vol. 34 (1949), pp. 88–91. Article 1 reads: "The aim of this agreement is to establish firmly and to develop by permanent contact between the two parties, the good relations existing between the two countries in the spheres of education, science, art and general culture." Article 13 says that "The Contracting Parties will consult with each other for the purpose of preserving and developing their common cultural interests abroad." It should be remembered that Czech Foreign Minister Jan Masaryk plunged to his death on March 10, 1948, almost exactly a year later; and that President Eduard Beneš resigned on June 7, 1948, rather than sign the new Communist constitution.

[183] *Ibid.,* Vol. 32 (1949), pp. 41–43. Article 11 of this treaty reads: "The Contracting Governments will assist each other in making the culture of each territory better known in the other territory by means of: (a) books, periodicals and other publications; (b) lectures and concerts; (c) art exhibits and other exhibitions of a cultural nature; (d) dramatic performances; (e) radio, films, gramaphone records and other mechanical means." Article 12 is unusual: "The Contracting Governments will be careful to draw the attention of authors and publishers to all inaccuracies appearing in the textbooks used in either country which have a bearing on the other."

[184] *Ibid.,* Vol. 41 (1949), p. 5.

[185] *Ibid.,* Vol. 46 (1950), pp. 61–67; *The Times* (London), May 13, 1950, p. 4, col. 5; *United Nations Treaty Series,* Vol. 34 (1949), pp. 35–39; Articles 12 and 13 of this treaty are identical to Articles 11 and 12 of the treaty with Belgium quoted above; *ibid.,* Vol. 33 (1949), pp. 110–113, Vol. 12 (1948), pp. 105, 128. Article 17 of this treaty reads: "The two Governments shall ensure that all education textbooks reflect the friendly relations which exist between the two countries."

[186] Article 7 of the Yugoslav treaty with Czechoslovakia of April 27, 1947.— *United Nations Treaty Series,* Vol. 33 (1949), p. 62.

[187] *Ibid.,* Vol. 10 (1947), pp. 24–26; Vol. 33 (1949), pp. 49, 60–62; Vol. 46 (1950), pp. 26–30; Zellweger, *op. cit.,* p. 126; *United Nations Treaty Series,* Vol. 15 (1948), p. 136; Vol. 25 (1949), pp. 258–260; Vol. 33 (1949), pp. 91–99; Vol. 46 (1950), pp. 48–52; Vol. 33 (1949), pp. 73, 82–86; Vol. 25 (1949), pp. 292–296; Vol. 46 (1950), pp. 143, 152.

[188] Zellweger, *op. cit.,* pp. 127, 125.

[189] See Article 5 of USSR treaty with Romania of February 4, 1948, *United Nations Treaty Series,* Vol. 48 (1950), p. 198; with Hungary of February 18, 1948, *ibid.,* p. 172; and with Bulgaria of March 18, 1948, *ibid.,* p. 145.

[190] U.S. Congress, *Congressional Record,* June 2, 1948 (80th Congress, 2nd session), Vol. 94, Part 5, pp. 6931, 6935.

[191] United Nations, *Yearbook on Human Rights for 1950,* p. 443.

[192] Article 3; *United Nations Treaty Series,* Vol. 87 (1951), p. 355.

[193] United Nations, *Yearbook on Human Rights for 1949,* p. 323.

[194] *New York Times,* June 12, 1952, p. 10, col. 3.

Chapter 6. Control by Municipal Law

[1] See Hilton v. Guyot (1895), 159 U.S. 113.

[2] *American Journal of International Law,* Vol. 18 (1924), p. 835.

NOTES

[3] See Oppenheim, *International Law*, Vol. 1, 5th ed., pp. 28–29; Schwarzenberger, *International Law*, Vol. 1, p. 19.

[4] Schwarzenberger, *loc. cit.*

[5] West Rand Central Gold Mining Co., Ltd. v. The King (1905), 2 K.B. 391.

[6] E.g., Article 26 of the Greek Code of Civil Procedure which states that the Greek courts are not competent in actions brought against foreign sovereigns. — E. W. Allen, *The Position of Foreign States before National Courts* (New York, 1933), p. 291. This is in keeping with the generally recognized principle that *par in parem imperium non habet*. Cf. also *Bergman v. de Sieyes* in *Annual Digest* (1947), p. 151, in which the court quoted from *Ex parte* Baiz, 135 U.S. 403. Referring to Section 252, Title 22, of the U.S.C.A., the court held in the latter case that the act was "drawn from the statute 7 Anne, ch. 12, which was declaratory simply of the law of nations, which, Lord Mansfield observed in Heathfield v. Chilton, 4 Burr. 2016, the Act did not intend to alter and could not alter."

[7] Cf. Article 25 of the Basic Law of the Federal Republic of Germany of 1949: "The general rules of international law form part of federal law. They take precedence over the laws and directly create rights and duties for the inhabitants of the federal territory." — United Nations, *Yearbook on Human Rights for 1948*, p. 82. Similarly the Constitution for the State of Württemberg-Hohenzollern of 1947 states: "Article 7(1). The universally accepted rules of international law are binding components of the law of the state. They are binding on the state and on individual citizens." — *ibid*. (1947), p. 113. Article I, section 8, clause 10 of the U.S. Constitution has been interpreted to recognize international law as part of the general body of the law of the United States. "The Congress shall have power . . . to define and punish . . . offenses against the law of nations."

[8] Quoted by George A. Finch, *The Sources of Modern International Law* (Washington, D.C., 1937), p. 90.

[9] *American Journal of International Law*, Vol. 29 (1935), Supplement, Part II, "Jurisdiction with Respect to Crime," pp. 444–445.

[10] (1779), 1 C. Rob. 196.

[11] *American Journal of International Law*, Vol. 35 (1941), p. 684.

[12] Italy-Venezuela, Mixed Claims Commission, 1903, quoted in Hudson, *Cases and Other Materials on International Law*, 2nd ed. (St. Paul, Minn., 1936), p. 1142. The umpire wrote: "On examining the general subject we find that by all nations and from the earliest period has it been considered that as between individuals an end to disputes should be brought about by the efflux of time. Early in the history of the Roman law this feeling received fixity by legislative sanction. In every country have periods been limited beyond which actions could not be brought. In the opinion of the writer these laws of universal application were not the arbitrary acts of power, but instituted because of the necessities of mankind, and were the outgrowth of a general feeling that equity demanded their enactment." — *ibid., pp. 1142–1143.

[13] The Russian Indemnity case (1912), James Brown Scott, *Hague Court Reports* (New York, 1916), p. 298.

[14] Permanent Court of International Justice, *Collection of Judgments,* Series A, No. 10 (Judgment No. 9) (Leyden, 1927), pp. 20, 21.

[15] The fundamental laws referred to here and below are Afghanistan, Constitution of October 31, 1931, Art. 23; Albania, Constitution of July 4, 1950, Art. 20; Andorra, no constitution; Argentina, Constitution of May 1, 1853, restored May 1, 1956, upon revocation of the Constitution of March 11, 1949, Arts. 14, 32; Australia, Constitution Act of July 9, 1900, applying the British Bill of Rights of 1689; Austria, Federal Constitution, Act of October 1, 1920, with amendments of 1925 and 1929, Art. 149 of which makes the Fundamental Law of December 21, 1867, concerning the general rights of the citizen, a part of the Constitution, Art. 13;

Belgium, Constitution of February 7, 1831, Art. 18; Bhutan, no constitution; Bolivia, Political Constitution of November 23, 1945, as amended on September 20, 1947 and November 26, 1947, Art. 6; Brazil, Constitution of September 18, 1946, Art. 141(5); Bulgaria, Constitution of December 4, 1947, Art. 88; Burma, Constitution of September 24, 1947, Art. 17; Cambodia, Constitution of May 6, 1947, Art. 9; Canada, applies provisions of the British Bill of Rights of 1689; Ceylon, applies provisions of the British Bill of Rights of 1689; Chile, Political Constitution of September 18, 1925, Art. 10; People's Republic of China, Constitution of September 20, 1954, Art. 87; Republic of China, Constitution of January 1, 1947, Art. 11; Colombia, Political Constitution of February 16, 1945, Art. 42; Costa Rica, Political Constitution of November 7, 1949, Art. 29; Cuba, Constitutional Law of April 4, 1952, Arts. 33, 40; Czechoslovakia, Constitution of June 9, 1948, Secs. 18, 20, 21; Denmark, Constitution of June 5, 1953, Art. 77; Dominican Republic, Constitution of January 10, 1942, Art. 6(5); Ecuador, Constitution of December 31, 1946, Art. 187(11); Egypt, Constitution of June 23, 1956, Arts. 44, 45; Ireland, Constitution of December 29, 1937, Art. 40.6(1)(i); Ethiopia, Constitution of November 4, 1955, Art. 41; Finland, Form of Government of July 17, 1919, Art. 10; France, Constitution of September 28, 1946, reaffirming the Declaration of the Rights of Man and of the Citizen, August 26, 1789, Arts. 10, 11; Democratic Republic of Germany, Constitution of March 19, 1949, Art. 9; Federal Republic of Germany, Basic Law of May 23, 1949, Arts. 5, 18; Greece, Constitution of December 22, 1951, Sec. 14; Guatemala, Constitution of March 1, 1956, Arts. 44, 57; Haiti, Constitution of the Republic of Haiti of November 25, 1950, Art. 19; Honduras, Political Constitution of March 28, 1936, Art. 59; Hungary, Constitution of August 20, 1949, Art. 55; Iceland, Constitution of June 17, 1944, Art. 72; India, Constitution of February 21, 1948, adopted with amendments November 26, 1949, Art. 13; Indonesia, Provisional Constitution of August 15, 1950, Art. 19; Iran, Constitutional Law of October 8, 1907, Art. 20; Iraq, Constitution of March 21, 1925, Art. 12; Israel, no constitution; Italy, Constitution of January 1, 1948, Art. 21; Japan, Constitution of November 3, 1946, Arts. 19, 21; Jordan, Constitution of January 8, 1952, Art. 15; People's Republic of Korea, Constitution of September 8, 1948, Art. 13; Republic of Korea, Constitution of July 12, 1948, Art. 13; Kuwait, no constitution; Laos, Constitution of May 11, 1947, Preamble; Lebanon, Constitution of May 23, 1926, Art. 13; Liberia, Constitution of July 26, 1847, Art. 1, sec. 15; Libya, Constitution of October 7, 1951, Arts. 22, 23, 24; Liechtenstein, Constitution of October 5, 1921, Art. 40; Luxembourg, Constitution of October 17, 1868, Art. 24; Mexico, Political Constitution of February 5, 1917, Arts. 6, 7; Monaco, Constitution of January 5, 1911, Art. 10; Mongolian People's Republic, Fundamental Law of June 20, 1940, as amended September 28, 1944 and February 1949, Art. 98; Morocco, no constitution; Nepal, Interim Government of Nepal Act of March 30, 1951, as amended 1954, Sec. 16; Netherlands, Constitution of August 24, 1815, reissued by decree of January 22, 1947, Chap. I, Art. 7; New Zealand, Constitution Act of 1852 applying the British Bill of Rights of 1689; Nicaragua, Political Constitution of November 1, 1950, Art. 113; Norway, Constitution of May 17, 1814, Art. 100; Oman and Masqat, no constitution; Pakistan, Constitution of February 29, 1956, Sec. 8; Panama, Constitution of March 1, 1946, Art. 38; Paraguay, Constitution of July 10, 1940, Art. 19; Peru, Political Constitution of April 9, 1933, Arts. 59, 63; Philippines, Constitution of February 8, 1935, Art. III, sec. 1(8); Poland, Constitution of July 22, 1952, Art. 71; Portugal, Political Constitution of March 19, 1933, as amended up to June 11, 1951, Art. 8; Qatar, no constitution; Romania, Constitution of September 24, 1952, Art. 85; El Salvador, Political Constitution of September 7, 1950, Art. 158; San Marino, Electoral Law of November 18, 1926, no provision; Saudi Arabia, Constitutional Documents of August 29, 1926, December 29, 1931, September 18, 1932, no provisions; Spain, Charter of July 16, 1945, Art. 12; Sudan, Self-Government Statute of March 21, 1953, Art. 7; Sweden, Constitution of June 6, 1809, as amended up to 1953, Arts. 85, 86; Switzerland, Federal Constitution of September 12, 1848, Art. 55; Syria, Constitution of September 5, 1950 (restored in 1954 when Constitution of July 10, 1953 was repealed), Arts. 14, 15; Thailand, Constitution of December 19, 1932 (restored November 26, 1951, when Constitution of March 23, 1949, was repealed), as amended up to and including March 12, 1952, Chap. II, Sec. 26; Tunisia, no constitution; Turkey, Constitution of January 10, 1945, Arts. 70, 77; Union of South Africa, Act to Constitute the Union of South Africa, September 20, 1909, applying the British Bill of Rights of 1689; USSR, Fundamental Law of December 5, 1936, Art. 125; United Kingdom, Bill of Rights of 1689; U.S.A., Constitution of September 17, 1787, Amendment Art. I; Uruguay, Constitution of October 26, 1951, Art. 29; Vatican City, Constitutional Laws of June 7, 1929, Art. 8; Venezuela, Constitution of April 11, 1953, Art. 35(7), Democratic Republic of Viet Nam, Constitution of November 8, 1946, Art. 10; Republic of Viet Nam, Constitution of October 26, 1956, Arts. 15, 16; Yemen, no constitution; Yugoslavia, Constitutional Act of January 13, 1953, amending Constitution of January 31, 1946, Art. 27 (retained unchanged).

[16] Article 40 of the same constitution increases the freedom granted by saying, "The legal, governmental or any other enactment regulating the exercise of the rights guaranteed by this Constitutional Law shall, if it diminishes, restricts or impairs any of those rights, be null and void."

[17] Article 10 of the French Constitution says: "No man is to be interfered with because of his opinions, not even because of his religious opinions, provided his avowal of them does not disturb public order established by law."

[18] Article 23 of the Libyan Constitution reads: "Freedom of the press and of printing shall be guaranteed within the limits of the law."

[19] Article 15 guarantees freedom of the press again "within the limits of the law."

[20] Although the United States Constitution has been interpreted as not making "basic civil liberties the peculiar privilege or rights of American citizens" — see United Nations, *Yearbook on Human Rights, 1946*, p. 324 — the courts have ruled at other times that aliens are not protected by the first ten amendments until they have become bona fide residents of the U.S. — see F. Turner v. Williams (1904), 194 U.S. 279; Fong Yue Ting v. U.S. (1892), 149 U.S. 698 at 724; Wong Wing v. U.S. (1898), 163 U.S. 228 at 231.

[21] Constitution of December 1, 1946.

[22] Article 5(1). Also Berlin, Constitution of September 1, 1950, Article 8(2); Bavaria, Constitution of December 1, 1946, Article 112 (2); Hesse, Constitution of December 1, 1946, Article 13; Hanseatic Town of Bremen, Constitution of October 12, 1947, Article 15.

[23] United Nations, *Yearbook on Human Rights, 1949*, p. 162.

[24] In this chapter, only one or two typical examples of each type of law will be given. Similar laws of other states will be listed under the last footnote at the end of each section.

[25] The United States Deficiency Appropriation Act of October 22, 1913, reads: "No money appropriated by any Act shall be used for the compensation of any publicity expert unless specifically appropriated for that purpose." — 5 U.S.C. 54. Also "No book or document not having to do with the ordinary business transactions of the Executive Department shall be printed on the requisition of any executive department or unless the same shall have been expressly authorized by Congress." — 44 U.S.C. 219a. Section 11 of the Appropriation Act of March 1, 1919 reads: "That hereafter no journal, magazine, periodical, or other similar publication shall be printed and issued by any branch or officer of the government service unless the same shall have been specifically authorized by Congress. . . ."

— 40 Stat. 1212, 1270. Act of May 6, 1939, Section 6, as amended 53 Stat. 683 at 989; 39 U.S.C. 321b forbids the mailing of printed matter under government frank by any agency to any person except on special request, with certain exceptions.

Acts of violence against state and/or government: Australia, Commonwealth Crimes Act; Austria, Penal Code of May 27, 1852, amended to 1948, Art. 58(c); Chile, Act Regarding the Permanent Defense of Democracy, Act No. 8987 of September 3, 1948, Art. 2; China, Publications Law of July 8, 1937, Art. 21(2); Czechoslovakia, see *New York Times*, June 2, 1951, p. 12, col. 6; Denmark, Penal Code of April 15, 1930, sec. 100; Ecuador, Constitution, Art. 94(8); France, Act Concerning the Freedom of the Press of July 29, 1881, Art. 24; Democratic Republic of Germany, Constitution of Thuringia, Art. 6; Republic of Germany, Law No. 5 of September 21, 1949, of the Council of the Allied High Commissioner, Art. 2(1); Greece, Resolution XV of November 25, 1946, para. 3 (in force to November 25, 1948); Guatemala, Decree No. 666 of September 24, 1949, Art. 126(1); India, Penal Code of 1868, as amended, sec. 124A; Israel, Criminal Code Ordinance, United Nations, *Yearbook on Human Rights, 1948*, pp. 128–129; Italy, Law No. 1546 of December 3, 1947, Art. 8; Korea, Revised National Security Law of December 23, 1949, Arts. 1 and 3; Liechtenstein, Defense of the State Act of March 14, 1949, Art. 19(2), 3; Mexico, Constitution, Art. 20(6); New Zealand, Crimes Act of 1908, sec. 118; Nicaragua, Constitution of 1948, Art. 97; Pakistan, Penal Code of 1868, as amended, sec. 124a; Peru, Law of Internal Security, Decree-Law No. 11049 of July 1, 1949, Art. 1(c), 1(n), 3; Poland, see trial of Joachim Schaak and Helmut Sadowski in "Current Developments," *News from Behind the Iron Curtain*, Vol. 3, No. 1 (January 1954), p. 49; Saar, Nationality Act of July 15, 1948, Art. 18.1(a), Act to Supplement and Amend the *Strafgesetzbuch*, July 19, 1950, Art. 90(1); Spain, Decree of December 23, 1944, amended July 17, 1946, Arts. 120, 215, 217, 218, 251(1); Switzerland, Decree of the Federal Council Reinforcing the Penal Provisions for the Protection of the State, October 29, 1948, Art. 13; Federal Act amending the Swiss Penal Code, October 5, 1950, Art. 272(2); Syria, Constitution of 1953, Art. 13(3); USSR, Criminal Code of RSFSR, Art. 58(1); United Kingdom, in R. v. M'Hugh (1901), 2 I.R. 569 at 578; Singapore, Sedition Ordinance No. 18 of 1939; U.S.A., Sedition Act of 1798, 1 Stat. 596; Alien Registration Act of June 28, 1940, sec. 2(a), 54 Stat. 670 at 671; Appropriation Act of May 31, 1941, 55 Stat. 212; Act to Revise, Codify and Enact into Positive Law "Title 18 U.S.C." secs. 2383, 2384, 2385, 62 Stat. 683 at 808; U.S. v. Dennis *et al.* (1950), 183 F. 2d 201; Customs Laws, 19 U.S.C. 1305; Postal Laws, 18 U.S.C. 344; Yugoslavia, Law on the Press of July 8, 1946, Art. 11(2), 11(3).

Subversion; attacks on national interests and/or dignity: Afghanistan, Act Concerning the Press of December 31, 1950, Art. 18; Argentina, see *New York Times*, September 29, 1948, p. 11, col. 1; see *New York Times*, September 15, 1949, p. 4, col. 5; Belgium, Constitution, Art. 14; Ceylon, Citizenship Act No. 18 of 1948, sec. 22; Chile, Act Regarding the Permanent Defense of Democracy, No. 8987 of September 3, 1948, arts. 3(1), 25; Czechoslovakia, Constitution, secs. 20(2), 37(1); Act No. 194 of July 13, 1949, Concerning Acquisition and Loss of Czechoslovak Nationality, Art. 7.1 (a); Dominican Republic, Act No. 5906 of July 5, 1949, Art. 30; Penal Code, Art. 368; Act No. 1951 of March 2, 1949, for the Regulation of Public Entertainment and Radio Broadcasts, Art. 2; Ecuador, Constitution, Art. 187(11); Egypt, Penal Code of July 31, 1937, Art. 188; Federal Republic of Germany, Constitution, Art. 5(3); Greece, Constitution of 1911, Art. 14; Hungary, Act 1946, No. VII, of March 22, 1946, Concerning the Defense of the Order of the State and the Republic by Criminal Law, Art. 2(c); Act II of May 18, 1950, Containing General Provisions of the Penal Code, Art. 4(b); India, West Bengal Security Act of 1948, sec. 7.1(a), 7.2; Constitution, Sec. 19(2); Iran, see *New York Times*, March 10,

1949, p. 11, col. 2; Act Concerning the Press, February 1908, sec. 40; Iraq, Press Law of 1933; Italy, Constitution, Art. 278; 1931 Law on Public Security, Art. 112; Japan, Criminal Code of October 6, 1947, Art. 232; 1952 Law on the Prevention of Subversive Activities; Lebanon, see *New York Times,* July 24, 1950, p. 15, col. 5; Liechtenstein, Defense of the State Act of March 14, 1949, Art. 19(3), 19(4); Mexico, Criminal Code of the Federal District of Mexico, 1931, Art. 360(II); New Zealand, Crimes Act of 1908, sec. 118; Nicaragua, Constitution of 1948, Art. 19; Law on Freedom to Express and Disseminate Opinions of 1953; Pakistan, Fundamental Rights of the Citizens of Pakistan and Matters Relating to Minorities, October 6, 1950, Art. 9(2); Peru, Internal Security Law, Decree-Law No. 11049 of July 1, 1949, Art. 26; Portugal, Decree-Law No. 34:938 of September 22, 1945, Art. 4(3); Decree-Law No. 24:426 of December 31, 1945, Art. 2(7); Saar, Ordinance on Provisional Press Regulations, March 9, 1948, Art. 10(1); Spain, Decree of December 23, 1944, amended July 17, 1946, Arts. 131, 132, 163, 164, 251(2); Sweden, Constitutional Act Relating to the Freedom of the Press, April 5, 1949, Chap. VII, Art. 4(5); Switzerland, Decree of the Federal Council Reinforcing the Penal Provisions for the Protection of the State, Art. 10; Turkey, Law Concerning the Press, amended September 20, 1946, Art. 30; Penal Code, Art. 158; United Kingdom, R. v. Lambert and Perry (1810), 2 Camp. 398; 15 Dig. 637, 6780; R. v. Tutchin (1704), 14 State Tr. 1095, C.C.R.; R. v. Cobbett (1804), 29 State Tr. 1; Yugoslavia, Law on the Press of July 8, 1946, Art. 11(8).

[25] Argentina, Penal Code, as amended in 1949, Art. 244; Chile, Law of March 20, 1925; Colombia, Decree 3000 of 1954; Democratic Republic of Germany, Constitution, Art. 6; Federal Republic of Germany, Penal Code, Art. 187a; Greece, Decree of July 1953; India, Press Law of 1954; Italy, Press Law of February 8, 1948; Nicaragua, Law on Freedom to Express and Disseminate Opinions of 1953; Spain, Penal Code, Decree of December 23, 1944, amended July 17, 1946, Arts. 218(2) 244, 245; Sweden, Constitutional Act Relating to the Freedom of the Press, April 5, 1949, Chap. VII, Art. 4(6), 4(9); Switzerland, Criminal Code, December 21, 1937, in force since January 1, 1942, Art. 259; Turkey, Penal Code, Art. 159; Law Concerning the Press, September 20, 1946, Art. 34(b); United Kingdom, R. v. Tutchin (1704), 14 State Tr. 1095; Aliens Restriction (Amendment) Act, 1919 (9 & 10 Geo. 5, c. 92) sec. 3(1), 3(2); U.S.A., Alien Registration Act of 1940, sec. 2(a)(1), 54 Stat. 670 at 671; 62 Stat. 683 at 808, sec. 2385; Espionage Act of 1917, 40 Stat. 219, amended by Act of March 3, 1921, 41 Stat. 1359.

[26] Earl of Halsbury, *Halsbury's Laws of England*, Vol. 9, p. 388.

[28] Afghanistan, Constitution, Art. 23; Albania, Constitution, Arts. 15, 18; Austria, Penal Code of May 27, 1852, amended to 1948, Art. 302; Belgium, Constitution, Art. 14; Belgian Congo, Legislative Order No. 254/Telec. on Telecommunications, August 23, 1940, Art. 27(5); Brazil, Constitution, Art. 141(33); Bulgaria, Constitution, Arts. 71, 78; Burma, Constitution, Art. 21(4); Canada, Saskatchewan Bill of Rights Act, 1947, Art. 14(1); Costa Rica, Constitution of 1871, Art. 36; Czechoslovakia, Constitution, Sec. 37(2); Penal Code of July 12, 1950, Arts. 83, 118; Egypt, Penal Code of July 31, 1937, Art. 176; Ireland, Constitution, Art. 40.6(1) (i); Democratic Republic of Germany, Constitution, Arts. 6, 41; Saxony-Anhalt, Constitution, Art. 8(3); Mark Brandenburg, Constitution, Arts. 8(1), 24, 62(2); Mecklenburg, Constitution, Arts. 7, 86; Saxony, Constitution, Art. 8; Thuringia, Constitution, Arts. 6, 73(2); Defense of Peace Act of December 15, 1950, Art. 1; Federal Republic of Germany, Bavaria, Constitution, Art. 119; Greece, Constitution of 1911, Art. 14; Hungary, Act 1946, No. VII of March 22, 1946, Art. 2(d); India, Penal Code of 1868, as amended, Arts. 153(a), 505(c); Constitution, Sec. 25(2); Iran, Constitution, Art. 20; Israel, The Crime of Genocide (Prevention and Punishment) Act, 1950, Arts. 3(a), 8; Korea (South), Constitution, Art. 12; Luxembourg, Constitution, Art. 19; Mexico, Constitution, Art. 130; Regulation Regarding Radio Broad-

casting Stations, February 6, 1942; Netherlands, Penal Code of 1886, as amended to 1947, Art. 137(c), 137(d); Norway, Constitution, Art. 100; Pakistan, Penal Code of 1868, as amended, Art. 153a; Paraguay, Constitution, Art. 35; Poland, Polish Military Penal Code, Decree of the Polish Committee of National Liberation of September 23, 1944, Art. 102(1); Romania, Constitution, Art. 17; Determination and Punishment of Certain Infringements of the Law of the Status of Nationalities, Law No. 630 of August 6, 1945, Art. 8; El Salvador, Constitution, Art. 157; Spain, Penal Code, Decree of December 23, 1944, amended July 17, 1946, Art. 218(3), 218(4), 218(5); Sudan, Penal Code, Chap. 21, Offenses Relating to Religion; Sweden, Constitutional Act Relating to the Freedom of the Press, March 23, 1949, Chap. VII, Art. 4(10); Switzerland, the *Bundesratsbeschluss* of January 20, 1939; Constitution, Arts. 51, 52; Syria, Constitution of 1930, Art. 19; Union of South Africa, Act of 1927; Riotous Assemblies Act No. 27 of 1914; USSR Criminal Code, Art. 59(7); Byelorussian SSR, Constitution, Art. 98; United Kingdom, R. v. Gathercole (1838), 2 Lewin, C.C. 237; R. v. M'Hugh (1901), 2 I.R. 569 at 578; British Act of Uniformity of 1548 and 1558, 2 & 3 Edw. 6, c. 1, sec. 3; 1 Eliz. c. 2, sec. 3; U.S.A., New Jersey, N.J.S.A. 2:157 B-5; State v. Klapprott (1941), 127 N.J.L. 395; 22 A. 2d 877; Massachusetts, Mass. Laws, Chap. 272 (1943), sec. 98(c); Connecticut, Revised Statutes, Chap. 417, para. 8376 (1949); Indiana, Indiana Statutes, para. 10-904-914 (Burns 1933), sec. 10-9058; People v. Eastman (1907), 81 N.E. 459 at 460; Illinois Stat., Chap. 38, para. 471; Yugoslavia, Constitution, Arts. 21, 25(4); Law on the Press, July 8, 1946, Art. 11(1); Law of May 24, 1945, Prohibiting the Incitement of National and Religious Hatreds and Discord, Arts. 2, 5.

[29] Terrou and Solal, *Legislation for Press, Film and Radio* (Paris, 1951), p. 297.

[30] Van Dyke, "Responsibility of States for International Propaganda," *American Journal of International Law*, Vol. 34 (January 1940), pp. 69–70.

[31] C. C. Hyde, *International Law*, Vol. 2, 2nd revised ed., pp. 1249–1250.

[32] (1938), 100 F. (2d) 961; 69 App. D.C. 281; upheld in 59 S.Ct. 488; 306 U.S. 640; L.Ed. 1040.

[33] In regard to the protection of consular representatives, it is uncertain whether an international tribunal would grant them the same protection granted to diplomats; but the General Claims Commission in the Francisco Mallen claim (1927) between Mexico and the United States held that "the government of the consul's residence should exercise greater vigilance in respect to their security and safety," as "foreign governments are sensitive regarding the treatment accorded their representatives." — Quoted by Schwarzenberger, *International Law*, Vol. 1, p. 97.

[34] Act Concerning the Press, February 1908, section 40. This law is interpreted by Iranian courts to apply to presidents of states as well, as witness the suspension of the Teheran weekly *Hemleh* for publishing a cartoon attacking President Celal Bayar of Turkey. — See *Minneapolis Tribune*, April 14, 1952, p. 13, col. 8.

[35] Two cases in 1935 came up with conflicting findings regarding the problem of distinguishing between the office and the person of the head of a foreign state. The first, Public Prosecutor v. G. (Holland, District Court of Maastricht, June 17, 1935), was a criminal action for insulting Adolf Hitler at a public meeting. The accused said in his defense that he had criticized Hitler not in his capacity as head of the German Reich, but for his actions as leader of the National Socialist party. The court held that Hitler was a political person in the latter capacity, "whose actions are, and must be susceptible of criticism without being treated as an insult to the Head of the State." In the second case, Public Prosecutor v. B. (Court of Appeal of Arnhem, October 31, 1935) the defense claimed that insulting statements made by him against Hitler alluded to the latter's actions before his accession to Führer of the Reich, and that Hitler combined in himself the qualities of Führer and party leader. The court held, however, that "the law did not distinguish whether the insult related to the period before or after the assumption of the dignity of Head of the State. The

NOTES

second defence could not be admitted on the ground that the personality of a Head of State could not be split up into different functions." Both these cases are quoted by Lauterpacht, *Annual Digests and Reports of International Law Cases, 1935,* pp. 24–25.

[36] Decree of March 26, 1924. See *New York Times,* October 8, 1938, p. 5, col. 1.

[37] Queen v. Most (1881), 7 Q.B.D. 244; King v. Antonelli and Barberi (1905), 70 J.P. 4.

[38] Theodore Schroeder, *Where Speech Is Not Free — in the U.S.A.; An Appeal to the Record* (Mays Landing, N.J., 1944), p. 36.

[39] Harold J. Berman, *Justice in Russia. An Interpretation of Soviet Law* (Cambridge, Mass., 1950), p. 276.

[40] King v. Antonelli and Barberi (1905), 70 J.P. 4.

[41] Quoted by Lawrence Preuss, "International Responsibility for Hostile Propaganda against Foreign States," *American Journal of International Law,* Vol. 28 (October 1934), p. 650n.

[42] An 1897 case discussed by Zellweger, *Die völkerrechtliche Verantwortlichkeit des Staates für die Presse . . .* pp. 67–68, in which Paul Brousse, publisher of an anarchist paper, the *Avantgarde,* was found not guilty of seditious libel against a foreign state.

[43] Laws of New Jersey, 1902 act, a supplement to an act entitled "An Act for the Punishment of Crimes" (Revision of 1908), approved June 14, 1898, Chapter 133, p. 405, quoted by Schroeder, *op. cit.,* p. 37.

[44] Hansard, *Parliamentary Debates,* Commons, Fifth Series, 217:175, 390 (May 8 and 10, 1928).

[45] Afghanistan, Act Concerning the Press of December 31, 1950, Art. 19; Australia, Customs (Cinematographic Films) Regulations; Austria, Penal Code of May 27, 1852, amended to 1948, Arts. 66, 494(a); Belgium, Law of March 12, 1858, Art. 3; Canada, Criminal Code of 1892, as amended, sec. 135; China, Criminal Code, Art. 116; Colombia, Act No. 29, Concerning Press Regulations of December 15, 1944, Art. 46; Costa Rica, Police Code of August 21, 1941, Chap. III, Art. 87; Cuba, Code of Social Defense of 1938, Art. 162; Czechoslovakia, Penal Code of July 12, 1950, Art. 126; Denmark, Penal Code of April 15, 1930, sec. 108; Dominican Republic, Act No. 2279 Relating to Exiles or Political Refugees, February 22, 1950, Art. 1; Penal Code, Art. 369; Act No. 5906 of July 5, 1949, Art. 31; Egypt, Penal Code of July 31, 1937, Art. 181; France, Act Concerning the Freedom of the Press of July 29, 1881, Arts. 36, 60(1); Germany, Criminal Code, secs. 102 (repealed), 103(a), 104; Greece, Law No. 5060 of 1931 Regarding Press Matters, Art. 18; Constitutional Act No. 87, Art. 1(a); Guatemala, Law on the Spread of Thought by Methods of Publicity, April 24, 1947, Art. 47; Iran, Act Concerning the Press, February 1908, secs. 40, 41; Israel, Criminal Code Ordinance; Italy, Penal Code, Art. 297; Japan, Criminal Code, Arts. 90, 232; Liechtenstein, Defense of the State Act of March 14, 1949, Arts. 12, 13; Mexico, 1931 Criminal Code of the Federal District, Art. 360.II; Netherlands, Penal Code of 1886, as amended to 1947, Arts. 117, 119; New Zealand, The Crimes Act, 1908, Art. 120; Norway, Penal Code, Art. 96; Peru, Penal Code, Art. 299; Saar, Ordinance on Provisional Press Regulations, March 9, 1948, Art. 10(1); Sweden, Constitutional Act Relating to the Freedom of the Press, April 5, 1949, Chap. VII, Art. 4(7); Switzerland, Federal Act Amending the Swiss Penal Code, October 5, 1950, Arts. 296, 297; Penal Code of 1853, Arts. 41, 42; Executive Regulation of the Cinemas and Theaters Act, May 2, 1949, Art. 39(c); Decree of March 26, 1924; *Bundesblatt* (1921), Vol. 2, p. 389; Penal Code of December 21, 1937, as amended, Art. 299; USSR, Criminal Code of 1927, Art. 58(1); United Kingdom, King v. Gordon (1787), 22 Howell's State Tr. 213 at 233; King v. Vint (1799), 27 Howell's State Tr. 627 at 641–642; King v. Peltier (1803), 28 Howell's State Tr. 529 at 617; Offenses Against the Person Act of 1861,

sec. 4; Queen v. Most (1881), 7 Q.B.D. 244; King v. Antonelli and Barberi (1905), 70 J.P. 4; U.S.A., New Jersey, a supplement to an act entitled "An Act for the Punishment of Crimes" (Revision of 1908), approved June 14, 1898, Chap. 133, p. 405; U.S. Neutrality Law of June 15, 1917, U.S.C. Title 18, Chap. II, sec. 25; Uruguay, Penal Code of December 4, 1933, Art. 138; Vatican, Constitutional Law of June 7, 1929, Art. 4; Yugoslavia, Law on the Press of July 8, 1946, Art. 11(5).

[46] Kennerly v. Hennessy (1914), 68 Fla. 138 at 139; 66 So. 729.

[47] (1930), 112 Conn. 121; 151 A. 349; cf. People v. Eastman (1907), 81 N.E. 459 at 460.

[48] Afghanistan, Act Concerning the Press of December 31, 1950, Arts. 14, 15; Argentina, Security Law of October 1950, Art. 8; Austria, Penal Code of May 27, 1852, as amended to 1948, Art. 65(b), 308; Belgium, Act of March 25, 1891, amended by Act of July 28, 1934; Belgian Congo, Legislative Order No. 254/Telec. on Telecommunications, August 23, 1940, Art. 27; Brazil, Penal Code, Arts. 508, 509, 510; Burma, 1947 Public Order Preservation Act, sec. 5; Cambodia, Constitution, Art. 9; Canada, Criminal Code of 1892, as amended, Art. 136; Chile, Act Regarding the Permanent Defense of Democracy, Act No. 8987 of September 3, 1948, Art. 4; China, Publications Law of July 8, 1937, Art. 21(3); Colombia, Decree No. 1966 of 1946, Regulating Radiocommunications Services, Art. 10; Cuba, Code of Social Defense of 1938, Art. 163(b); Czechoslovakia, Penal Code of July 12, 1950, Act No. 86 of 1950, Art. 127; Act No. 124 of 1933, sec. 2(2); Denmark, Penal Code of April 15, 1930, sec. 136; Dominican Republic, Act No. 5906 of July 5, 1949, in Pursuance of Act No. 1951 of March 2, 1949, Art. 31; Constitution, Art. 5; Egypt, Penal Code of July 31, 1937, Arts. 171, 176, 188; Finland, see *New York Times* January 25, 1947, p. 4, col. 3; France, Act Concerning the Freedom of the Press of July 29, 1881, Arts. 23, 27; Germany, Criminal Code, sec. 90(f) (repealed January 30, 1946); Federal Republic of Germany, Constitution, Art. 9(2); Greece, Law No. 5060 of 1931 Regarding Press Matters, Art. 18; Resolution XV of November 25, 1946; Decree of July 1953; Guatemala, Government Decree No. 673 of July 1907, Vol. 26 (Criminal Penalties); Decree No. 666 of September 24, 1949, Art. 126; Law on the Spread of Thought by Methods of Publicity of April 24, 1947, Art. 43; Hungary, Act 1946, No. VII, March 22, 1946, Arts. 3, 4(1); Iceland, see United Nations, *Freedom of Information*, Vol. 1 (New York, 1950), p. 10; India, Penal Code of 1868 as amended, Art. 505(b); Preventive Detention Act, 1950, Act No. IV of 1950, amended by the Preventive Detention Ordinance No. XIX of 1950, Arts. 3(1), 12(1); Indonesia, Penal Code of 1848, Art. 171; Iran, Act Concerning the Press of February 1908, secs. 27, 32; Israel, Civil Wrongs Ordinance, 1944; Criminal Code Ordinance, 1936; Italy, Law No. 1546 of December 3, 1947, Art. 6; 1931 Law on Public Security, Arts. 112, 113; Japan, Law Implementing the Japanese Constitution and Containing Partial Amendments of the Criminal Code of October 6, 1947, Art. 230(2); Liechtenstein, Defense of the State Act of March 14, 1949, Arts. 3, 19; Luxembourg, Cour. Lux., January 27, 1906, Pas. VII, p. 359; Mexico, Constitution, Arts. 6, 20(6); Norway, Penal Code, Chap. XXIII; Constitution, Art. 100; Pakistan, Telegraph Act of 1885, amended in 1950, Art. 29; 1952 Public Security Act; Panama, Decree No. 469 of February 20, 1950, published in *Gaceta Oficial* No. 11130, February 28, 1950, Art. 22; Peru, Law of Internal Security, Decree-Law No. 11049 of July 1, 1949, Art. 1(b); Saar, Ordinance on Provisional Press Regulations of March 9, 1948, Art. 10(1); Spain, Decree of December 23, 1944, amended July 17, 1946, Arts. 253, 281(1); Sweden, Constitutional Act Relating to the Freedom of the Press of April 5, 1949, Chap. VII, Art. 4(8), 4(9); Constitution, Art. 86; Switzerland, Decree of the Federal Council Reinforcing the Penal Provisions for the Protection of the State, October 29, 1948, Art. 8; Federal Act Amending the Swiss Penal Code, October 5, 1950, Art. 272(2); Criminal Code, December 21, 1937, in force since January 1, 1942, Art. 259; Syria,

see *New York Times*, August 15, 1947, p. 6, col. 3; Thailand, Press Law of 1941; Turkey, Law Concerning the Press, amended September 20, 1946, Art. 34; Law Concerning the Press Amending Art. 161 of the Penal Code, 1954 amendment; Union of South Africa, Riotous Assemblies Act of 1914; United Kingdom, Public Order Act of 1936, sec. 5; R. v. M'Hugh (1901), 2 I.R. 569 at 578; R. v. Krause (1902), 66 J.P. 121; 14 Dig. 109, *798*; R. v. Banks (1873), 12 Cox, C.C. 393; 14 Dig. 97, *676*; R. v. Ransford (1874), 13 Cox, C.C. 9, C.C.R.; 14 Dig. 108, *786*; U.S.A., Kennerly v. Hennessy (1914), 68 Fla. 138 at 139; 66 So. 729; State v. Gardner (1930), 112 Conn. 121; 151 A. 349; People v. Eastman (1907), 81 N.E. 459 at 460; Postal Laws, 18 U.S.C. 344; Espionage Act of June 15, 1917, sec. 2, 40 Stat. 217 at 230; Venezuela, Constitution, Art. 37; Yugoslavia, Law on the Press of July 8, 1946, Art. 11(8).

[49] *International unrest*: Austria, Penal Code of May 27, 1852, as amended to 1948, Art. 58(c); Belgium, Act of March 12, 1858; Royal Decree of July 19, 1926, completed by Royal Decree of December 3, 1934; Belgian Congo, Legislative Order No. 254/Telec. on Telecommunications, August 23, 1940, Art. 27; Brazil, Penal Code, Arts. 508, 509, 510; Chile, Act No. 8987 of September 1948, Art. 2(8); Colombia, Decree No. 1966 of 1946 Regulating Radiocommunications Services, Art. 10; Act No. 29 Concerning Press Regulations of December 15, 1944, Art. 30; Cuba, Code of Social Defense of 1938, Art 163(c); Czechoslovakia, Penal Code of July 12, 1950, Act No. 86 of 1950, Art. 128.1; Denmark, Public Press Act of April 13, 1938; Dominican Republic, Act No. 1951 of March 2, 1949, Art. 2; Finland, Decree on the Press and other Publications, No. 898 of December 30, 1946, Art. 1; Decree Regarding Restrictions of Personal Freedom, No. 899 of December 30, 1946, Art. 1; France, Act Concerning the Freedom of the Press of July 29, 1881, Art. 24; Germany, Criminal Code, sec. 90 (f), (h), Repealed by Law No. 11, January 30, 1946; Democratic Republic of Germany, Thuringia, Constitution, Art. 6; Democratic Republic of Germany, Constitution, Art. 5; Defense of Peace Act of December 15, 1950, Art. 1; Federal Republic of Germany, Constitution, Arts. 9(2), 26(1); Berlin, Constitution, Art. 21(1); Württemberg-Hohenzollern, Constitution, Art. 8; Guatemala, Law on the Spread of Thought by Methods of Publicity, April 24, 1947, Art. 43(c); Hungary, Act 1946 No. VII, March 22, 1946, Concerning the Defense of the Order of the State and the Republic by Criminal Law, Art. 4(1); Act II of May 18, 1950, Containing General Provisions of the Penal Code, Art. 4(b); India, Preventive Detention Act, 1950, Act No. IV of 1950, as amended by the Preventive Detention Ordinance No. XIX of 1950, secs. 3(1) (a), 12(1); Constitutional Amendment of June 1951, Art. 19(a)(2); Iran, Act Concerning the Press of February 1908, sec. 27; Japan, Broadcasting Act No. 132, May 2, 1950, Art. 5; Liechtenstein, Defense of the State Act of March 14, 1949, Art. 3; Luxembourg, Act Mitigating Certain Penalties Attached to Convictions for Offenses against the External Security of the State, March 31, 1950, Art. 21; Mexico, Regulations Regarding Radio Broadcasting Stations, February 6, 1942; Constitution, Art. 20(6); Nicaragua, Constitution of January 21, 1948, Art. 7; Norway, Penal Code, Chapter 23; Pakistan, Survey of Human Rights, sec. 14; 1952 Public Security Act; 1950 Public Safety Act; Panama, Decree No. 469 of February 20, 1950, *Gaceta Oficial* No. 11130 of February 28, 1950, Art. 22(f); Paraguay, Constitution, Art. 41(3); Peru, see Francis Deak and Philip C. Jessup (eds.), *A Collection of Neutrality Laws, Regulations and Treaties of Various Countries* (Washington, D.C., 1939), p. 872; Law of Internal Security, Decree-Law No. 11049 of July 1, 1949, Arts. 1(b), 132; Romania, Constitution, Art. 96; Saar, Nationality Act of July 15, 1948, Art. 18(1)(a); Spain, Decree of December 23, 1944, amended July 17, 1946, Arts. 132, 251(4); Sudan, Penal Code, Chap. X; Sweden, Constitutional Act Relating to the Freedom of the Press of April 5, 1949, Chap. VII, Art. 4(9); Press Act of 1812, Art. 3(9); Switzerland, Federal Act Amending the Swiss Penal

Code, October 5, 1950, Arts. 4, 272(2); Decree of the Federal Council Reinforcing the Penal Provisions for the Protection of the State, October 29, 1948, Art. 13; Penal Code of December 21, 1937, Title 16, Arts. 296–301; Concession for the Use of the Radio Broadcasting Stations of the Federal Post and Telegraph Administration, November 30, 1936, sec. 9(1); Federal Decree of March 26, 1924; Syria, see *New York Times*, May 5, 1950, p. 7. col. 6; Turkey, Law Concerning the Press, as amended on September 20, 1946, Art. 34.I(a); Penal Code, Art. 140; Union of South Africa, see United Nations, *Yearbook on Human Rights for 1947*, p. 305; USSR, Criminal Code, Art. 58(1); United Kingdom, King v. Gordon (1787), 22 Howell's State Tr. 213 at 233; King v. Vint, 27 Howell's State Tr. 529 at 618; U.S.A., Trial of William Cobbett for Libel (1797), Francis Wharton, *State Trials of the United States During the Administrations of Washington and Adams* (Philadelphia, 1849), p. 322 at 324; Uruguay, see League of Nations Document Conf/E.R.P./1st session/P.V.1(1)–9(1), p. 18; Yugoslavia, Law on the Press of July 8, 1946, Art. 11(5).

War propaganda: Argentina, Penal Code of 1921, Art. 219; Belgium, Penal Code of 1867, Art. 123; Bolivia, Penal Code of 1834, Art. 160; Brazil, Constitution, Art. 141(5); Burma, Constitution, Arts. 211, 212; Costa Rica, Penal Code of 1924, Art. 448; Cuba, Code of Social Defense of 1938, Art. 163(a); Czechoslovakia, Act No. 165 of December 20, 1950, Concerning the Defense of Peace, Art. 1(1) and (2); Act No. 86, Penal Code of July 12, 1950, Art. 98; Law for the Defense of the Republic, March 19, 1923, sec. 3; Ecuador, Constitution, Art. 94(9); France, Penal Code of 1810, Arts. 84, 85; Democratic Republic of Germany, Constitution, Art. 6; Defense of Peace Act of December 15, 1950, Arts. 1, 2, 3, 5, 6, 7; Saxony-Anhalt, Constitution, Art. 8(3); Mark Brandenburg, Constitution, Arts. 8(2), 24; Mecklenburg, Constitution, Art. 7; Saxony, Constitution, Art. 8; Thuringia, Constitution, Art. 6; Federal Republic of Germany, Constitution, Art. 26(1); Hesse, Constitution, Art. 69; Württemberg-Hohenzollern, Constitution, Art. 8; Italy, Penal Code of 1930, Art. 244; Constitution, Art. 11; Japan, Criminal Code as amended in 1947, Arts. 81, 93; Constitution, Art. IX; Luxembourg, Penal Code of 1879, Art. 123; Mexico, Penal Code of 1931, Art. 125; Nicaragua, Constitution of 1948, Arts. 7, 97; Law of July 31, 1948, Art. 23; Panama, Penal Code of 1922, Art. 106; Paraguay, Penal Code of 1914, Art. 139; Poland, Defense of Peace Act of December 29, 1950, Arts. 1, 2; Penal Code, Art. 113; Portugal, Penal Code of 1886, Art. 148; Romania, Penal Code of 1864, Arts. 74, 75; Spain, Penal Code of 1928, Art. 253; Penal Code of 1932, Art. 134; Decree of December 23, 1944, amended July 17, 1946, Art. 127; USSR, Peace Defense Law, USSR Supreme Soviet, March 12, 1951; Uruguay, Penal Code of 1889, Art. 139; Venezuela, Constitution, Art. 37.

[50] (1950) 183 F. 2d 201. In June 1957 the United States Supreme Court re-examined the language of the Smith Act when it reversed the conviction by a federal district court in southern California of fourteen alleged Communists. In *Yates, Steinberg, Stack, et al. v. U.S.* (see *New York Times*, June 18, 1957, pp. 24 and 25) the Supreme Court construed "organize" narrowly, in the sense of "establish" or "found." The district court had permitted the broad interpretation of a "continuing process." It held that mere proof of membership, or even leadership, in the Communist party is not enough for a Smith Act conviction. It also stated that in advocating the violent overthrow of a government, a person must advocate action, present or future, not merely a theoretical desirability, to violate the Smith Act.

[51] *New York Times*, May 16, 1950, p. 20, col. 5.

[52] Re Meunier (1894), 2 Q.B. 415, 24 Dig. 874, *37*.

Propaganda benefiting parties and doctrines: Afghanistan, Act Concerning the Press of December 31, 1950, Art. 14; Albania, Constitution, Article 38; Argentina, Constitution of 1949, Arts. 15, 21; Austria, Penal Code of May 27, 1852, amended to 1948, Art. 65; Belgium, Constitution, sec. 13; Brazil, Constitution, Art. 141, secs.

NOTES

5, 13; Ruling of the Supreme Electoral Court, No. 211 of January 7, 1948; Bulgaria, Act of July 23, 1949; Constitution, Art. 87; Burma, Constitution, Article 17; Canada, see United Nations, *Yearbook on Human Rights for 1946*, p. 57; Chile, Act No. 8987 of September 3, 1948, Arts. 1, 2(2), 9; Law No. 9341 on Electoral Registers Codified by Presidential Decree No. 3030 of July 4, 1949, Arts. 1, 2, 25; China, Publications Law of July 8, 1937, Art. 21(1); Costa Rica, Constitution, Art. 98; Czechoslovakia, Constitution, Art. 37(1), 37(2); Penal Code of July 12, 1950, Arts. 81(1), 82, 83(1), 83(2); Dominican Republic, Act No. 5906 of July 5, 1949, Art. 30; Constitution, Art. 103; Act No. 1951 of March 2, 1949, for the Regulation of Public Entertainment and Radio Broadcasts, Art. 4; Law No. 1443 Prohibiting Communist, Anarchist and Other Anti-Constitutional Associations, June 14, 1947, Arts. 1, 2; Egypt, Decree-Law No. 117 of 1946, Art. 98(b), 98(c); France, Act of July 28, 1894, Art. 1; Democratic Republic of Germany, Saxony-Anhalt, Constitution, Art. 8(3); Mark Brandenburg, Constitution, Arts. 8(2), 24; Saxony, Constitution, Art. 8; Mecklenburg, Constitution, Art. 7; Thuringia, Constitution, Art. 6; Federal Republic of Germany, Constitution, Arts. 9(2), 16(2), 18, 143; Hesse, Constitution, Art. 17; Greece, Resolution 15 of November 24, 1946, sec. 1; Hungary, Act 1946, No. VII of March 22, 1946, Arts. 1, 2; Israel, Criminal Code Ordinance, see United Nations, *Yearbook on Human Rights for 1948*, pp. 128, 129; Italy, Constitution, Arts. 283, 290; Law No. 1546 of December 3, 1947, Art. 3; Liechtenstein, Defense of the State Act of March 14, 1949, Art. 19(1); Mexico, Regulation Regarding Radio Broadcasting Stations of February 6, 1942; New Zealand, Crimes Act of 1908, sec. 118; Nicaragua, Constitution of 1950, Arts. 21(3), 116; Constitution of 1948, Art. 100; Panama, Resolution No. 1 of April 29, 1950, *Gaceta Oficial* No. 11241, July 14, 1950; Decree No. 469 of February 20, 1950, art. 22(f); Decree-Law No. 13 of May 26, 1950, *Gaceta Oficial* No. 11202, May 29, 1950; Act No. 12 of February 9, 1950, *Gaceta Oficial* No. 11139, March 11, 1950; Peru, Law of Internal Security, Decree-Law No. 11049 of July 1, 1949, Art. 1(d), 1(n), 1(o), Art. 25; Electoral Statute, Legislative Decree No. 11172 of September 30, 1949, Arts. 7, 95, 96, 98; Constitution, Art. 53; Poland, Constitution, Declaration of Rights and Liberties, sec. 5; Romania, Constitution, Art. 96; Saar, Constitution, Art. 10; El Salvador, Constitution, Arts. 158, 160; Spain, Constitution, Art. 12; Penal Code, Decree of December 23, 1944, amended July 17, 1946, Arts. 163, 164, 251(3); Switzerland, Decree of the Federal Council Reinforcing the Penal Provisions for the Protection of the State, October 29, 1948, Arts. 6, 8 (rescinded by Act of October 5, 1950); Syria, Constitution of 1953, Art. 13(3); Turkey, Turkish Law Regarding the Formation of Associations of June 5, 1946, Art. 9(a); Union of South Africa, Suppression of Communism Act of June 26, 1950; USSR, Criminal Code, Article 58(10); Criminal Code of RSFSR, Art. 58(1), Ukrainian Criminal Code, Art. 58(1); United Kingdom, R. v. Wilkes (1769), 4 Burr. 2527, H.L.; R. v. Harvey (1823), 2 B. & C. 257; U.S.A., Hatch Act, 18 U.S.C., sec. 61(i), 54 Stat. 611 at 620; Internal Security Act of 1950, secs. 2, 3, 64 Stat. 987 at 989; U.S. v. Dennis *et al.* (1950), 183 F. 2d 201; Emergency Relief Appropriation Act of June 26, 1940, 54 Stat. 611 at 620, sec. 15(f); Yugoslavia, Constitution, Art. 43; Law on the Press of July 8, 1946, Art. 11(4).

[58] Chile, Act No. 8987 of September 3, 1948, Art. 2(5), 2(6); Republic of China, Regulations Governing the Suppression of Rebellion, Revised and Promulgated on April 26, 1950, Art. 7; Egypt, Decree-Law No. 117 of 1946, Art. 98(c); Germany, Penal Code, sec. 91(b) (repealed January 30, 1946); Democratic Republic of Germany, Defense of Peace Act, December 15, 1950, Art. 2(2); Greece, Resolution XXXI of October 17, 1947; Haiti, Constitution, Art. 18; Liechtenstein, Defense of the State Act of March 14, 1949, Art. 3; New Zealand, British Nationality and New Zealand Citizenship Act, September 6, 1948, sec. 23(3)(b); Paraguay, Constitution, Art. 37; Peru, Decree-Law No. 11049 of July 1, 1949, Art. 1(e); Spain, Decree of December 23, 1944, amended July 17, 1946, Arts. 126, 129, 251; Sweden, Constitu-

tional Act Relating to the Freedom of the Press, March 23, 1949, Chap. VII, Art. 4(1); Switzerland, Decree of the Federal Council Reinforcing the Penal Provisions for the Protection of the State, October 29, 1948, Arts. 6, 10 (rescinded October 5, 1950); Federal Act amending the Swiss Penal Code of October 5, 1950, Arts. 266a, 271(1), 272(1), 275(b); USSR, Criminal Code, Art. 58(1a); United Kingdom, R. v. Casement (1917), 1 K.B. 98, C.C.A.; 14 Dig. 128, *1002*; U.S.A., Act to Revise, Codify and Enact into Positive Law "Title 18 U.S.C.," secs. 953, 954, 62 Stat. 683 at 744; sec. 958 at 745; Espionage Act of 1917, sec. 3, 40 Stat. 219, amended by Act of March 3, 1921, 41 Stat. 1359; 50 U.S.C. sec. 33; U.S. v. Burgman (1949), 87 F.S. 568 at 571; Gillars v. U.S. (1950), 182 F. (2d) 962; the "Little Brooklyn Cases" of June 18, 1941, U.S. Federal Communications Commission, *Federal Communications Commission Reports* (Washington, D.C., 1943), Vol. 8, p. 577; Yugoslavia, Law on the Press of July 8, 1946, Art. 11(6).

[54] Tomoya Kawakita v. U.S. (1951), 190 F. (2d) 506 at 515.

[55] See the British case of R. v. Casement (1917), 1 K.B. 98 at 130; also R. v. Lynch (1903), 1 K.B. 444.

[56] Halsbury, *Halsbury's Laws of England*, Vol. 9, p. 293; R. v. Charnock, King and Keyes (1696), 12 State Tr. 1377 at 1452.

[57] See Joyce v. Director of Public Prosecution (1946), A.C. 347.

[58] Gillars v. U.S. (1950) 182 F. (2d) 962.

[59] Cf. *Department of State Bulletin*, Vol. 22 (March 6, 1950), pp. 351–356.

[60] Albania, Constitution, Art. 36; Argentina, Constitution, Art. 103; Austria, Penal Code of May 27, 1852, amended to 1948, Art. 58(c); Bolivia, Constitution, Art. 25; Bulgaria, Constitution, Arts. 90, 93; Czechoslovakia, Constitution, sec. 30(1); Ecuador, Constitution, Art. 187(11); Germany, Criminal Code, Arts. 80–93 (repealed by Law No. 11 of January 30, 1946); Haiti, Constitution, Art. 18; Hungary, Constitution, Art. 61(1), 61(2); Mongolian People's Republic, Constitution, Art. 91; Paraguay, Constitution, Art. 37; Romania, Constitution, Art. 36; Spain, Constitution, Art. 20; Sweden, Constitutional Act Relating to the Freedom of the Press of March 23, 1949, Chap. VII, Art. 4(1); Syria, Constitution of 1953, Art. 27; USSR, Constitution, Art. 133; Criminal Code, Art. 58(1a); Byelorussian SSR, Constitution, Art. 108; RSFSR, Constitution, Art. 137; Ukrainian SSR, Constitution, Art. 113; Uzbek SSR, Constitution, Art. 132; Kazakh SSR, Constitution, Art. 110; Lithuanian SSR, Constitution, Art. 105; Moldavian SSR, Constitution, Art. 106; Latvian SSR, Constitution, Art. 105; Kirghiz SSR, Constitution, Art. 104; Tadjik SSR, Constitution, Art. 120; Turkmen SSR, Constitution, Art. 110; Karelo-Finnish SSR, Constitution, Art. 106; Georgian SSR, Constitution, Art. 146; Azerbaijan SSR, Constitution, Art. 140; Armenian SSR, Constitution, Art. 108; Estonian SSR, Constitution, Art. 105; United Kingdom, R. v. Casement (1917), 1 K.B. 98 at 130; R. v. Lynch (1903), 1 K.B. 444; R. v. Charnock, King and Keyes (1696), 12 State Tr. 1377 at 1452; Joyce v. Director of Public Prosecution (1946), A.C. 347; U.S.A., U.S. v. Burgman (1949), 87 F.S. 568 at 571; Tomoya Kawakita v. U.S. (1951), 190 F. (2d) 506 at 515; Gillars v. U.S. (1950), 182 F. (2d) 962; Constitution, Art. III, sec. 3(1); Act to Revise, Codify and Enact into Positive Law "Title 18 U.S.C." sec. 2381, 62 Stat. 683 at 807; Act of March 4, 1909, sec. 1, 35 Stat. 1088; Espionage Act of June 15, 1917, sec. 2, 40 Stat. 217 at 230; Customs Law, 19 U.S.C. 1305; Postal Law, 18 U.S.C. 344; Guam, Organic Act, sec. 5(e); Venezuela, Constitution of Cojedes, Art. 7.

[61] Communications Act of 1934, revised to September 1, 1948, sec. 301.

[62] Decree No. 1966 of 1946 regulating Radiocommunications Services, Art. 1.

[63] See Leslie John Martin, "The Rise and Development of Agence France-Presse," *Journalism Quarterly*, Vol. 27 (Spring 1950), pp. 197–206.

[64] See Bronislaw Kusnierz, *Stalin and the Poles* (London, 1949), p. 298.

[65] *Controlling the medium through state ownership*: Albania, Constitution, Art.

28; Argentina, Constitution of 1949, Art. 37(IV); Bolivia, Constitution, Art. 6(g); Bulgaria, Constitution, Art. 79; Chile, Constitution, Art. 10(7); Colombia, Decree No. 1966 of 1946 regulating radiocommunications services, Art. 1; Constitution, Art. 41; Czechoslovakia, Constitution, secs. 14(2), 22(1); Federal Republic of Germany, Constitution, Art. 7(1); Greece, Constitution, Art. 16; Guatemala, Constitution, Arts. 79, 81; Haiti, Constitution, Art. 23; Iran, Constitution, Art. 18; Jordan, Constitution, Art. 21; Korea (South), Constitution, Art. 16; Lebanon, Constitution, Art. 16; Mexico, Constitution, Art. 3; Panama, Decree No. 469 of February 20, 1950, Art. 1; Constitution, Art. 79; Syria, Constitution of 1953, Art. 23; Thailand, Constitution, sec. 63; Turkey, Constitution, Art. 80; USSR, See Krajina v. Tass Agency (1949), 2 All Eng. L.R. 274; U.S.A., Communications Act of 1934, revised to September 1, 1948, sec. 301; Venezuela, Constitution, Arts. 53, 55; Yugoslavia, Constitution, Art. 38.

[66] Alex Inkeles, *Public Opinion in Soviet Russia. A Study in Mass Persuasion* (Cambridge, Mass., 1951), p. 251.

[67] *New York Times*, June 4, 1947, p. 9, col. 1.

[68] *Controlling the medium through registration*: Australia, Queensland, Printers and Newspapers Act, amended 1953; Belgium (forbids), Constitution, Art. 18; Brazil, Constitution, Art. 141(5); Czechoslovakia, Constitution, sec. 21; Press Law of June 1947; Dominican Republic, Act No. 5906 of July 5, 1949, Art. 4; Egypt, Press Law of 1941, amended 1949; France (forbids), Law of July 23, 1881, Art. 5; Lebanon, Decree No. 2464 of May 6, 1924; Law of Association of 1909; Liechtenstein, Constitution, Art. 40; Paraguay, Constitution, Art. 31; Saar, Ordinance on Provisional Press Regulations, March 9, 1948, Art. 2; Spain, Decree of December 23, 1944, amended July 17, 1946, Art. 165(2); Sudan, Press Ordinance 1930, as amended; Syria, Press Law of May 11, 1954; Turkey, Law Regarding the Formation of Associations, June 5, 1946, Art. 4; United Kingdom, Newspaper Libel and Registration Act of 1881; U.S.A., Communications Act of 1934, sec. 301(c) and (d); Uruguay (forbids), Law of June 20, 1935, Art. 2; Vatican, Constitution, Art. 8.

[69] *The Times* (London), October 25, 1949, p. 3, col. 4.

[70] *Controlling the medium through other restrictions*: Australia, War Precautions Act, Repeal Act of 1934; Belgium, Royal Decree of June 28, 1930; Brazil, Constitution, Art. 18; Colombia, Constitution, Art. 42; Decree No. 109, Regulating the Execution of Act No. 29 of 1944, January 24, 1945, Arts. 1, 4; Denmark, Constitution, Art. 86; Dominican Republic, Act No. 5906 of July 5, 1949, Arts. 7, 40, 46; Egypt, Royal Rescript No. 42 of April 19, 1923, Art. 98(c); France, Decree for the Repression of Foreign Propaganda, April 21, 1939, Arts. 1, 2, 13; Act Concerning the Freedom of the Press, July 29, 1881, Art. 14; Federal Republic of Germany, Law No. 5 of the Allied High Commission for Germany, September 21, 1949, Art. 3(2); Guatemala, Law on the Spread of Thought by Methods of Publicity of April 24, 1947, Art. 37; Iran, Decree of October 24, 1949; Italy, Decree-Law No. 428 of April 3, 1947; Lebanon, Decree No. 3080; Luxembourg, Constitution, Art. 25; Peru, Law of Internal Security, Decree-Law No. 11049 of July 1, 1949, Art. 1(e); Spain, Decree of December 23, 1944, amended July 17, 1946, Art. 177; Switzerland, Order of the Federal Council Respecting the Relaxation of Measures Restricting the Establishment of New Newspapers, Periodicals, and Press and News Agencies of March 8, 1946, Art. 4; United Kingdom, see Halsbury, *Halsbury's Laws of England*, Vol. 25, p. 474; Sarawak, Defence Regulations; U.S.A., Communications Act of 1934, revised to September 1, 1948, sec. 310(a)(5); *In re* The Yankee Network, FCC Docket No. 5640, FCC Public Notice No. 46566, January 17, 1941; the "Little Brooklyn Cases" (June 18, 1941), U.S. FCC, *Federal Communications Commission Reports* (March 1, 1940–August 1, 1941), Vol. 8, p. 577; Espionage Act of 1917, sec. 2, 40 Stat. 217 at 230; Yugoslavia, Law on the Press of July 8, 1946, Art. 12.

[71] Arthur Mayer, "A Movie Exhibitor Looks at Censorship," *Reporter*, Vol. 10 (March 2, 1954), pp. 36–37.

[72] *New York Times*, November 30, 1949, p. 14, col. 3; January 25, 1947, p. 4, col. 3; September 25, 1947, p. 23, col. 2; July 24, 1950, p. 15, col. 5; August 5, 1947, p. 19, col. 2.

[73] See *Washington Post and Times Herald,* December 30, 1956, p. B3, col. 1.

[74] Criminal Code, sec. 89; see also secs. 88 to 90e, all now repealed.

[75] See Decree of the Presidium of the Supreme Soviet of the USSR on Responsibility for Disclosure of State Secrets, June 4, 1947, secs. 1, 3, 6, and 7, United Nations, *Yearbook on Human Rights for 1947*, p. 311; also "Decision of the Council of Ministers of the USSR on Information Constituting State Secrets," secs. 6, 7, 8, 9, 12, and 14, *ibid.*, p. 312; Criminal Code, Art. 193(24), 193(25).

[76] 10 & 11 Geo. 5, c. 75, Halsbury, *op. cit.*, Vol. 9, pp. 328–332.

[77] 62 Stat. 683 at 736, 737, secs. 793, 794; Internal Security Act of 1950, 64 Stat. 987 at 991, sec. 4(b).

[78] *New York Times*, April 19, 1950, p. 14, col. 6.

[79] Quoted by Ignaz Rothenberg, *The Newspaper. A Study in the Workings of the Daily Press and Its Laws* (London, 1946), p. 4.

[80] Directions for the Use of the Swiss News Broadcasting Service, July 5, 1939, sec. A(b), United Nations, *Freedom of Information*, Vol. 2 (New York, 1950), p. 121.

[81] United Nations, *Freedom of Information*, Vol. 1 (New York, 1950), p. 39.

[82] *Controlling the content through censorship*: Afghanistan, Act Concerning the Press, December 31, 1950, Art. 36; Argentina, Decree of May 14, 1946, Arts. 3, 4, 123; Australia, Objectionable Literature Act of 1954; Belgium, Constitution, Art. 35(5); China, Publications Law of July 8, 1937, Art. 24; Colombia, Constitution, Art. 42; Cuba, Decree No. 141 of January 24, 1942; Dominican Republic, Act No. 1951 of March 2, 1949, for the Regulation of Public Entertainment and Radio Broadcasts, Art. 1; Act No. 5906 of July 5, 1949, Art. 43; Ecuador, Constitution, Art. 94(10); Federal Republic of Germany, Law No. 5 of the Council of the Allied High Commission of September 21, 1949, Arts. 1, 2(2); Constitution, Art. 10; Greece, Constitution, Art. 1(14); Haiti, Constitution, Art. 19; India, West Bengal Security Act, 1948, modified up to November 1, 1948, Arts. 8.1(c) and (d), 9.1(a); Iraq, Press Law of 1933; Mexico, Law of February 6, 1942; Peru, Constitution, Art. 65; El Salvador, Constitution, Art. 158; Spain, Decree of December 23, 1944, amended July 17, 1946, Art. 165(2) para. 2; Switzerland, Order of December 16, 1949, of the Canton of Vaud, on cinemas, Art. 11; Syria, Constitution of 1953, Art. 14(3); Thailand, Constitution, sec. 35; Union of South Africa, Public Safety Act of 1953; United Kingdom, Children and Young Persons (Harmful Publications) Act of March 1955; Defence Regulations, 2D and 94B (rescinded); Sarawak, Defence Regulations.

Mandatory publication and right of reply: Afghanistan, Act Concerning the Press, December 31, 1950, Art. 17; Australia, Broadcasting Act; Belgium, Decree of June 28, 1930, Art. 16; Brazil, Constitution, Art. 141(5); Chile, Act Regarding the Permanent Defense of Democracy, Act No. 8987 of September 3, 1948, Art. 22; Colombia, Decree 3000 of 1954; Cuba, Presidential Decree No. 2273 of August 3, 1950, on the Right of Correction in Radio Broadcasting; Czechoslovakia, Law of July 10, 1933; France, Law on Freedom of the Press, July 29, 1881, as modified by the Law of September 29, 1919, Art. 13; Germany, Press Law of May 7, 1874, sec. 11; Guatemala, Law on the Spread of Thought by Methods of Publicity, April 24, 1947, Art. 34; Italy, Act No. 47 of February 8, 1948, to Issue Provisions Regarding the Press, Art. 8; Japan, Broadcasting Act No. 132 of May 2, 1950, Art. 4; Lebanon, Order No. 2464 of May 6, 1924, Art. 19; Norway, Criminal Code, sec. 430; Peru, Law on the Press, November 30, 1945, amended December 14, 1945, Art. 7; Portugal, Constitution, Arts. 8(20), para. 2, 23; Saar, Ordinance on Provisional Press Regulations, March 9, 1948, Art. 8(1); Syria, Constitution of 1953, Art. 14(5); Yugoslavia, Law on the Press, July 8, 1946, Art. 10.

State secrets: Argentina, Security Law of October 1950, Arts. 2, 6; China, Criminal Code, Arts. 109–111; France, Penal Code, as amended by Daladier Decree of 1939, Arts. 81, 86; Germany, Criminal Code, secs. 88, 89, 90 (repealed); Art. 353c; Poland, Decree No. 437 of October 26, 1949, on the Protection of State and Official Secrets, Art. 4; Turkey, Penal Code, Art. 140; Union of South Africa, Riotous Assemblies Act; USSR, Decree of the Presidium of the Supreme Soviet of the USSR on Responsibility for Disclosure of State Secrets, June 4, 1947, secs. 1, 3, 6, 7; Decision of the Council of Ministers of the USSR on Information Constituting State Secrets, secs. 6, 7, 8, 9, 12, 14; Criminal Code, Art. 193(24) and (25); United Kingdom, Official Secrets Act of 1920, 10 & 11 Geo. 5, c. 75; U.S.A., 62 Stat. 683 at 736, 737, secs. 793, 794; Internal Security Act of 1950, 64 Stat. 987 at 991, sec. 4(b) and (c).

Conformity: Cuba, Constitution, Art. 51; Czechoslovakia, Constitution, Sec. 14; Democratic Republic of Germany, Constitution, Art. 37; Guatemala, Constitution, Art. 80; Liechtenstein, Constitution, Art. 15; Mexico, Constitution, Art. 3; Panama, Constitution, Art. 79; Switzerland, Directions for the Use of the Swiss News Broadcasting Service, July 5, 1939, sec. A(b); Syria, Constitution of 1930, Art. 20; Thailand, Constitution, Sec. 36.

[83] See *Minneapolis Star*, March 15, 1954.

[84] *New York Times*, February 21, 1948, p. 4, col. 7.

[85] World Publishing Co. v. Minahan (1918), 70 Okla. 107; 173 P. 815; L.R.A. 1918 F. 283.

[86] Folwell v. Miller (1906), 145 F. 495 at 497; 10 L.R.A., N.S., 332; 7 Ann. Cas. 455; Rex v. Clerk (1728), 1 Barn. 304; Vizetelly v. Mudie's Select Library (1900), 2 K.B. 170; 69 L.J.Q.B. 654.

[87] 61 A. (2d) 143 at 147. On the other hand, Wachenfeld, J. (dissenting), said: "Free and unimpeded broadcasting is desirable but adequate responsibility should be fully provided for. A broadcasting company cannot allow the passing parade of known and unknown voices to utilize its facilities and then seek immunity simply because it acted in good faith and exercised reasonable care."

[88] A similar case is Summit Hotel Co. v. National Broadcasting Co. (1939), 337 Pa. 182; 8 A. (2d) 302; 124 A.L.R. 968.

[89] Coffey v. Midland Broadcasting Co. (1934), D.C. 8 Fed. Supp. 889; Sorenson v. Wood (1932), 123 Neb. 348; 243 N.W. 82 at 83; 82 A.L.R. 1098; Miles v. Louis Wasmer, Inc. (1933), 172 Wash. 466; 2 P. (2d) 847.

[90] *New York Times*, March 9, 1949, p. 9, col. 5; June 22, 1951, p. 5, col. 5.

[91] *New York Times*, April 19, 1950, p. 14, col. 6.

[92] Union of South Africa, *New York Times*, February 5, 1950, p. 21, col. 1.

Citizenship: Afghanistan, Constitution, Art. 23; Australia, Wireless Telegraphy Act of 1942; Brazil, Constitution, Art. 160; China, Publications Law amended and promulgated by the National Government on July 8, 1937, Art. 13; Colombia, Decree No. 1966 of 1946, Regulating Radiocommunications Services, Art. 15; Act No. 29 Concerning Press Regulations of December 15, 1944, Art. 13; Czechoslovakia, Act No. 94 of March 24, 1949, Art. 6; Dominican Republic, Act No. 5906 of July 5, 1949, Art. 43(d); France, Ordinance Concerning the Organization of the French Press, August 26, 1944, Art. 3; Greece, Constitution, Art. 14; Guatemala, Law on the Spread of Thought by Methods of Publicity, April 24, 1947, Art. 36; Italy, Act No. 47 of February 8, 1948, To Issue Provisions Regarding the Press, Art. 3; Mexico, Constitution, Art. 130; Poland, Press Law of November 21, 1938, Art. 10; Saar, Ordinance on Provisional Press Regulations, March 9, 1948, Art. 5; Sweden, Constitutional Act Relating to the Freedom of the Press, April 5, 1949,

Chap. V, Arts. 1, 2; Chap. VI, Art. 1; Switzerland, Order of the Federal Council Respecting the Relaxation of Measures Restricting the Establishment of New Newspapers, Periodicals, and Press and News Agencies, March 8, 1946, Arts. 1, 4; Turkey, Law Concerning the Press, as amended September 20, 1946, Art. 12(a); U.S.A., Communications Act of 1934, revised to September 1, 1948, sec. 310(a); Yugoslavia, Law on the Press of July 8, 1946, Art. 7.

Assigning responsibility: Belgium, Constitution, Art. 18; Press Decree of July 20, 1931, Art. 2; Dominican Republic, Act No. 5906 of July 5, 1949, Arts. 41, 43, 44; Egypt, Press Law of 1936, Art. 11; France, Act Concerning the Freedom of the Press of July 29, 1881, Art. 42; Greece, Constitution, Art. 1(14); Guatemala, Law on the Spread of Thought by Methods of Publicity, April 24, 1947, Art. 33; Haiti, Penal Code, Arts. 314, 315; India, West Bengal, Security Act of 1948, modified up to November 1, 1948, Act III of 1948, Arts. 7(2), 8(1) (a); Iran, Constitution, Art. 20; Act Concerning the Press of February 1908, sec. 48; Italy, Act No. 47 of February 8, 1948, to Issue Provisions Regarding the Press, Art. 3; Lebanon, Law of May 8, 1948; Luxembourg, Constitution, Art. 24; Act of July 20, 1869, Art. 17; Cour. Lux. January 5, 1917, Pas. X, p. 4; Mexico, Constitution, Art. 7; Law of April 12, 1917, Art. 23; Nicaragua, Constitution of 1948, Art. 97; Peru, Constitution, Art. 63; Saar, Ordinance on Provisional Press Regulations of March 9, 1948, Art. 14; Spain, Decree of December 23, 1944, amended July 17, 1946, Art. 165; Sweden, Constitutional Act Relating to the Freedom of the Press, April 5, 1949, Chap. V, Art. 2, Chap. VIII, Art. 10; Switzerland, Federal Act Amending the Swiss Penal Code, October 5, 1950, Art. 27(1), (3), (6); United Kingdom, Rex v. Clerk (1728), 1 Barn. 304; Vizetelly v. Mudie's Select Library (1900), 2 K.B. 170; 69 L.J.Q.B. 654; U.S.A., Kelly v. Hoffman (1948), 61 Atl. (2d) 143 at 147; Summit Hotel Co. v. National Broadcasting Co. 337 Pa. 182; 8 A. (2d) 302; 124 A.L.R. 968; Coffey v. Midland Broadcasting Co., D.C. 8 Fed. Supp. 889; Sorenson v. Wood, 123 Neb. 348; 243 N.W. 82 at 83; 82 A.L.R. 1098; Miles v. Louis Wasmer, Inc., 172 Wash. 466; 2 P. (2d) 847; Crane v. Bennett (1904), 177 N.Y. 106; 69 N.E. 274; Smith v. Utley (1896), 92 Wis. 133; 65 N.W. 744; Youmans v. Smith (1897), 153 N.Y. 214 at 219; 47 N.E. 265; Staub v. Van Benthuysen (1884), 36 La. Ann. 467; Arnold v. Ingram (1912), 151 Wis. 438; 138 N.W. 111; World Publishing Co. v. Minahan (1918), 70 Okla. 107; 173 P. 815; L.R.A. 1918F, 283; Folwell v. Miller (1906), 145 F. 495 at 497; 10 L.R.A., N.S., 332; 7 Ann. Cas. 455.

Other restrictions: Afghanistan, Constitution, Art. 21; Argentina, Act No. 12908 of 1946, establishing a Statute for Professional Journalists, Art. 3(a); Austria, Penal Code of May 27, 1852, as amended to 1948, Art. 308; Belgium, Law of February 12, 1897; Brazil, Constitution, Art. 141(5); Burma, Constitution, Art. 26; Chile, Act Regarding the Permanent Defense of Democracy, Act No. 8987 of September 3, 1948, Art. 24; Colombia, Constitution, Art. 11; Decree No. 1966 of 1946 Regulating Radiocommunications Services, Art. 38; Costa Rica, Constitution, Art. 19, para. 2; Cuba, Constitution, Art. 56; Denmark, Act No. 147 Concerning the Use of the Press, April 13, 1938, sec. 1, sub-sec. 2; Notification of July 6, 1946, of the Ancillary to the Civil Penal Code Concerning Treason and other Activities Detrimental to the Nation, sec. 6.1(8); Ecuador, Law on the Status of Aliens, February 20, 1947, Arts. 4, 20, 29(6); India, 1951 Press (Objectionable Matter) Act; Lebanon, Press Law of 1948; Liechtenstein, Defense of the State Act of March 14, 1949, Art. 27; Constitution, Art. 31; Mexico, Constitution, Art. 33; Nicaragua, Constitution of 1950, Arts. 25, 26; Panama, Constitution, Art. 81; Paraguay, Constitution, Art. 31, 36; Peru, Law on the Press of November 30, 1945, amended December 14, 1945, Art. 5; Poland, Constitution of March 17, 1921, Art. 95; El Salvador, Constitution, Art. 20; Spain, Decree of December 23, 1944, amended July 17, 1946, Art. 132, para. 2; Sweden, Constitutional Act Relating to the Freedom of the Press, April 5, 1949, Chap. VI, Art. 3; Switzerland, Constitution, Art. 70; Turkey, Law

Concerning the Press, amended September 20, 1946, Art. 12(h); Press Act of April 25, 1951, Art. 2; Penal Code of 1886, amended to 1947, Art. 119; amended to 1954, Art. 104; Union of South Africa, see *New York Times*, February 5, 1950, p. 21, col. 1; United Kingdom, Aliens Restrictions (Amendment) Act, 1919, 9 & 10 Geo. 5, c. 92, sec. 3(2); U.S.A., 52 Stat. 631, amended in 1939, 53 Stat. 1244; (1942) 56 Stat. 248; (1950) 64 Stat. 399 at 400, sec. 2(a); 54 Stat. 1201, sec. 2(a); 18 U.S.C.A. sec. 15(a) (Supp. 1942), amended 1948, 62 Stat. 683 at 808, sec. 2386; (1948) 62 Stat. 683 at 743; 37 Stat. 553 (1912), amended by 47 Stat. 1486 (1933); 39 U.S.C. secs. 233, 234 (1940); Foreign Agents Registration Act of 1938, as amended, sec. 4(b); Internal Security Act of 1950, 64 Stat. 987 at 991, secs. 7(a), (b), 10(1), (2), 12; Wisconsin Statutes (1939), secs. 12(12), (14); Act of October 16, 1918, 40 Stat. 1012, as amended to 1950; Internal Security Act of 1950, 64 Stat. 1006, sec. 22; Venezuela, Constitution, Art. 21; Yugoslavia, Law on Associations, Meetings and Other Assemblies of June 21, 1946, amended April 2, 1947, Art. 25; Constitution, Art. 28, para. 9.

[93] *New York Times*, February 29, 1948, p. 1, col. 8; January 11, 1950, p. 5, col. 3; November 28, 1948, p. 32, col. 6; December 24, 1946, p. 8, col. 7; January 12, 1951, p. 6, col. 3; January 11, 1949, p. 7, col. 5; September 25, 1947, p. 5, col. 4; January 10, 1950, p. 34, col. 6.

[94] 19 U.S.C. 1305.

[95] See *New York Times*, July 19, 1950, p. 23, col. 6.

[96] Note on Basic Human Rights, United Nations, *Yearbook on Human Rights, 1949*, p. 288.

[97] Bronislaw Kusnierz, *Stalin and the Poles* (London, 1949), p. 294.

[98] *New York Times*, August 16, 1947, p. 6, col. 8; September 19, 1946, p. 5, col. 1.

[99] Austria, Act Concerning the Press of April 7, 1922, as amended.

[100] *New York Times*, April 3, 1947, p. 3, col. 6; December 10, 1946, p. 28, col. 1; February 13, 1948, p. 12, col. 3.

[101] United Nations, *Yearbook on Human Rights, 1946*, pp. 38–39.

[102] Louis P. Lochner, ed., *The Goebbels Diaries* (New York, 1948), p. 40; Barrett, *Truth Is Our Weapon*, p. 13.

[103] *New York Times*, December 26, 1948, p. 34, col. 5; November 14, 1950, p. 6, col. 6; April 16, 1950, p. 34, col. 5.

[104] The only peacetime law that has come to the writer's attention imposing a fairly stiff fine on anyone caught listening to a foreign broadcast is one in Transjordan effected in 1947. This was at a time when there was great tension between Transjordan and Syria over King Abdullah's Greater Syria plan. Transjordanians were forbidden to listen to the Damascus radio.—*New York Times*, September 25, 1947, p. 5, col. 4.

[105] *New York Times*, April 9, 1949, p. 28, col. 4; April 2, 1948, p. 7, col. 3.

[106] Quoted in "The Red Network," *News from Behind the Iron Curtain*, Vol. 2, No. 8 (August 1953), pp. 58, 59.

[107] *New York Times*, July 6, 1948, p. 1, col. 2; July 10, 1948, p. 1, col. 6; July 13, 1948, p. 18, col. 5.

[108] *New York Times*, November 12, 1949, p. 4, col. 5. See also November 24, 1952, p. 1, col. 4, which points out that while there is no law in Hungary against listening to foreign broadcasts, people are often arrested on trumped-up charges.

[109] Arthur Bliss Lane, *I Saw Poland Betrayed* (Indianapolis, 1948), pp. 211–212.

[110] *Minneapolis Sunday Tribune*, April 26, 1953, p. 5, col. 5.

[111] "Current Developments," *News from Behind the Iron Curtain*, Vol. 3, No. 1 (January 1954), p. 49. It should be noted that the Soviet Union, too, has no formal law forbidding listening to foreign broadcasts.—Inkeles, *Public Opinion in Soviet Russia* . . . p. 251n.

[112] U.S. Senate, Sub-Committee of the Committee on Foreign Relations, *Hearings*

on Overseas Information Programs . . . 82nd Congress, 2nd session (March 6–May 13, 1953), p. 1465.

[113] See *New York Times,* November 24, 1952, p. 1, col. 4.

[114] "The Red Network," *op. cit.,* pp. 58, 62.

[115] Terrou and Solal, *Legislation for Press, Film and Radio,* p. 207.

[116] Cf. the confiscation of all radio tubes during the Brazilian revolution of 1930, after the names of all purchasers of receiving sets had been procured from the distributors.—Heber Blankenhorn, "The Battle of Radio Armaments. Broadcasting and International Friction," *Harper's Magazine,* Vol. 164 (December 1931), pp. 87–88.

[117] Harwood L. Childs and J. B. Whitton, eds., *Propaganda by Short Wave* (Princeton, 1942), p. 11. In 1940, 70 per cent of the radios in Japan had four tubes, 26 per cent had three tubes and 2 per cent had fewer than three and more than five tubes.— *New York Times,* August 10, 1945, p. 3, col. 5.

[118] *New York Times,* June 19, 1950, p. 5, col. 3; October 9, 1950, p. 3, col. 5; *News from Behind the Iron Curtain,* Vol. 2 (February 1953), p. 47.

[119] *Printed matter*: Afghanistan, Act Concerning the Press of December 31, 1950, Art. 33; Constitution, Art. 23; Austria, Act Concerning the Press of April 7, 1922, as amended; Belgium, Act of April 11, 1936; Belgian Congo, Ordinance of the Governor-General of March 5, 1922, approved by Decree of August 6, 1922, as amended, Art. 1; China, Publications Law of July 8, 1937, Art. 31; Czechoslovakia, Act No. 94 of March 24, 1949, Art. 4; Government Ordinance No. 72 of 1933; Denmark, Press Law, Art. 14; Denmark, Act No. 147 Concerning the Use of the Press of April 13, 1938, secs. 1(2), 5; Egypt, Decree-Law of 1936, Arts. 2, 21, 22; Finland, see *New York Times,* December 24, 1946, p. 8, col. 7; France, Act Concerning the Freedom of the Press, July 29, 1881, as amended by Decree-Law of May 6, 1939, Art. 14; Germany, Law No. 5 of the Council of the Allied High Commission, September 21, 1949, Art. 6; Criminal Code, sec. 83(4) (repealed); Iran, Act Concerning the Press of February 1908, sec. 16; Jordan, see *New York Times,* September 25, 1947, p. 5, col. 4; Lebanon, Order No. 2464 of May 6, 1924; Law of May 8, 1948, Art. 23; Saar, Ordinance on Provisional Press Regulations of March 9, 1948, Art. 10(2); Sweden, Constitutional Act Relating to the Freedom of the Press of March 23, 1949, Chap. IX, Art. 5, Chap. XIII, Arts. 1, 3; Switzerland, Canton of Vaud, Law of December 14, 1937, amended by Law of November 19, 1940; United Kingdom, Singapore, Undesirable Publication Ordinance, No. 19 of 1938; U.S.A., 19 U.S.C. 1305; Yugoslavia, Law on the Press of July 8, 1946, Arts. 15–20.

Radio Signals: Afghanistan, Act of December 31, 1950, Concerning the Press, Art. 35; Bulgaria, Law of March 25, 1948, Art. 17; Ireland, Constitution, Art. 40.6(1)(i); Germany, Decree on Extraordinary Measures Concerning Radio of September 1, 1939, secs. 1, 2; Portugal, Constitution, Arts. 8(20), para. 2, 22; Romania, Decree No. 216 published in *Buletinul Oficial* No. 32 of May 23, 1949, Chap. I, Arts. 15, 16, 17; Syria, Constitution of 1953, Art. 13(3); Turkey, Law of June 23, 1947, Arts. 1, 8; USSR, Criminal Code (RSFSR), sec. 191; United Kingdom, Tanganyika Territory, Wireless Telegraph Ordinance, Chap. 124.

Chapter 7. Extraterritorial Control of Propaganda

[1] *American Journal of International Law,* Vol. 29 (1935), Supplement, Part II, p. 480.

[2] See national codes listed *ibid.,* pp. 481–482.

[3] See case of Cutting in J. B. Moore, *Digest of International Law,* Vol. 2 (Washington, D.C., 1906), pp. 228–242.

[4] *Ibid.,* pp. 230–231, 235–236.

[5] See the case of the *S.S. Lotus* (No. 10), Permanent Court of International Jus-

tice, *Collection of Judgments* (Leyden, 1927), Series A, No. 10, Judgment No. 9, pp. 65–94.

[6] Cf. his statement: "But it appears to be now universally admitted that, where a crime is committed in the territorial jurisdiction of one State as the direct result of the act of a person at the time corporeally present in another State, international law, by reason of the principle of constructive presence of the offender at the place where his act took effect, does not forbid the prosecution of the offender by the former State, should he come within its territorial jurisdiction."—*Ibid.*, p. 73.

[7] *Ibid.*, pp. 65, 94. Turkey took Article 6 of its penal code verbatim from Article 10 of Italy's code.—*Ibid.*, p. 9.

[8] Penal Code of December 21, 1937, as amended, articles 347, 348. The provisions of these articles are rather vague.

[9] It would seem, however, that the British court was pretty close to accepting the "passive personality principle," if it did not indeed accept it, in Phillips v. Eyre (1870), L.R. 6 Q.B. Cases 1, 28: "As a general rule, in order to found a suit in England for a wrong alleged to have been committed abroad, two conditions must be fulfilled. First, the wrong must be of such a character that it would have been actionable if committed in England. . . . Secondly, the act must not have been justifiable by the law of the place where it was done."

[10] Strassheim v. Daily (1911), 221 U.S. 280 at 285; similar cases are State v. Hall (1894), 114 N.C. 909; 8 Harv. L.R. 494; Simpson v. State (1893), 92 Georgia 41 at 45: ". . . a criminal act begun in one State and completed in another renders the person who does the act liable to indictment in the latter;" Commonwealth v. Macloon (1869), 101 Mass. L, 7; Commonwealth v. Smith (1865), 11 Allen 243 at 259; Adams v. The People (1848), 1 Comstock (N.Y.) 173; U.S. v. Davis (1837), 2 Sumn. 482; Commonwealth v. James Blanding (1825), 3 Pick. 304. In the last case, a libel published in a newspaper printed in another state and circulating in Massachusetts was competent and conclusive evidence of a publication in Massachusetts.

[11] R. v. Coombes (1786), 1 Leach 388; 14 Dig. 134, *1068*; similar cases are R. v. Ellis (1889), 1 Q.B. 230, C.C.R.; 14 Dig. 135, *1079*; Regina v. Nillins (1884), 53 L.J. (M.C.) 157; Rex v. Godfrey (L.R. 1923) 1 K.B. 24; R. v. Holmes (1883), 12 Q.B.D. 23, C.C.R.; 14 Dig. 136, *1085*.

[12] The Communications Act of 1934, revised to September 1, 1948, sec. 505.

[13] R. v. De Marny (1907), 1 K.B. 388, C.C.R.; 14 Dig. 91, *606*.

[14] *American Journal of International Law*, Vol. 29 (1935), Supplement, Part II, p. 524. Jules Patouillet (trans.), *Les Codes de la Russie Soviétique. IV Code Pénal de la R.S.F.S.R.* (Paris, 1935), p. 9.

[15] Halsbury, *Halsbury's Laws of England* (London, 1931), Vol. 8, p. 536.

[16] See also R. v. Sawyer (1815), 2 C. & K. 101; the Zollverein (1856) Swabey, 96 at 98, in which the court assumed jurisdiction over British subjects for crimes committed abroad. For a case of treason committed abroad by a British subject who was punished as soon as he came within the British jurisdiction, see R. v. Casement (1917), 1 K.B. 98 at 130.

[17] See Tomoya Kawakita v. U.S. 72 S.Ct. 950 at 962, in which the court held: "An American citizen [even though he be a dual citizen] owes allegiance to the United States wherever he may reside." See also U.S. Nationality Act of 1940, sec. 401(h), 54 Stat. 1137 at 1169.

[18] Joyce v. Director of Public Prosecutions (1946), A.C. 347; (1946), 1 All E.R. 186, 351.

[19] *American Journal of International Law*, Vol. 29 (1935), Supplement, Part II, p. 540.

[20] In this connection the German *Reichsgericht* on December 23, 1889, held that sedition had been committed by a person who shouted across the border from French

territory into Germany: "Vive la France!"—*Entscheidungen in Strafsachen,* Vol. 20 (December 23, 1889), p. 146.

[21] Constitution, Article 10, paragraph 3. These two states merely say that "Every citizen has the right to emigrate. This right may be restricted only by virtue of a law of the Republic." But from such a provision to the enactment of a law is a short step. Cf. Czechoslovakia, which also says in its constitution that "The right to emigrate abroad may not be restricted, except by virtue of an Act."—Sec. 7(2). Cf. on the other hand, the provisions of the constitutions of Costa Rica (Article 22), Bavaria (Article 190(2)), Honduras (Article 67), Indonesia (Article 9(2)), and Japan (Article 22) which say that "Everyone has the right to leave the country and—being a citizen or resident—to return thereto."—Quoted from the Indonesian Constitution. U.S.A., Internal Security Act of 1950, Sec. 6(a), 64 Stat. 987 at 991.

[22] Bulgarian Nationality Act of March 6, 1948, Article 7.

[23] *American Journal of International Law,* Vol. 29 (1935), Supplement, Part II, p. 546.

[24] Halsbury, *op. cit.,* Vol. 9, p. 65.

[25] (1946) 13 P.L.R. 523; (1948) A.C. 351, in Lauterpacht, *Annual Digest (1946),* p. 58.

[26] *American Journal of International Law,* Vol. 29 (1935), Supplement, Part II, pp. 546–551.

Chapter 8. Control by Diplomacy

[1] Harold Nicolson, *Diplomacy* (London, 1950), pp. 13–16, discusses five interpretations of the term.

[2] Sir Ernest Satow, *A Guide to Diplomatic Practice,* 3rd ed., revised by H. Ritchie (London, 1932), pp. 1–4.

[3] See Georg Schwarzenberger, *International Law,* Vol. 1 (London, 1949), pp. 388–403.

[4] See G. H. Hackworth, *Digest of International Law,* Vol. 2 (Washington, 1941), pp. 16–19.

[5] Halsbury, *Halsbury's Laws of England,* Vol. 26, 2nd ed. (London, 1931), p. 248.

[6] Oppenheim, *International Law,* Vol. 2, pp. 6–7. An attempt to settle the dispute by negotiation need not precede its submission to an international tribunal for adjudication. "If one of the parties to a dispute considers it impossible to achieve a settlement by way of negotiation, the Court cannot lightly override such an opinion." — Schwarzenberger, *op. cit.,* Vol. 1, p. 415. Occasionally arbitration precedes diplomatic negotiation. Cf. Article 15 of the Convention on Cultural and Educational Relations, signed at Sofia between Czechoslovakia and Bulgaria on June 20, 1947, which reads: "Any dispute as to the application or interpretation of the present Convention will be settled through the diplomatic channel, if the Permanent Mixed Commission fails to reach an agreement."—*United Nations Treaty Series,* Vol. 46 (1950), p. 34.

[7] Philip C. Jessup, *A Modern Law of Nations* (New York, 1950), p. 3.

[8] Oppenheim, *op. cit.,* Vol. 1, pp. 690–691.

[9] An example is the U.S. note to Russia of September 25, 1947, protesting against an article by a Russian writer, Boris Gorbatov, in the *Literary Gazette* of Moscow attacking President Truman. The note said, among other things: "I cannot recall that Dr. Goebbels, of unsavory memory, at the height of our common struggle against Nazi Germany ever stooped to greater ridicule and vituperation against the head of an enemy country than has Mr. Gorbatov against the chief executive of a friendly and allied state. In this connection, I would never have believed that a Soviet writer would permit himself, or be permitted, to draw an analogy between the President of the United States and our recent common enemy, Hitler." Earlier in

the note the U.S. ambassador said: "I have been obliged with the deepest regret to witness in the Soviet press an increasing flood of half truths, distortions of truth and utter falsehoods about my country and my government. I have tried to overlook this incendiary press campaign, feeling that to take issue with a myriad false or incorrect statements would simply be adding fuel to the flame of hatred toward my country which the Soviet press has apparently undertaken to kindle in the hearts of the Soviet people."

In his reply, Molotov refused to take responsibility for articles appearing in Russian newspapers, and accused U.S. Ambassador W. Bedell Smith of undertaking a "general evaluation of the Soviet press" and obtaining a "completely perverted picture" of it. "Despite your allegation," Molotov continued, "the Soviet press more than the press of any other country whatsoever, especially aims to elucidate broadly as possible the actual situation and true facts of the life of other countries, attaching special significance to the strengthening of friendly relations between peoples." This, said Mr. Molotov in his note, was by no means true of the American press, "which is so widely encouraged by the most reactionary circles in the U.S.A. and which not only from day to day inserts lying and slanderous articles regarding the U.S.S.R. and its statesmen, but also inflames hostility between peoples, and which does not meet with any serious support whatsoever in the U.S.A., which is of course, Mr. Ambassador, well known to you regarding which there are not two different opinions in international democratic circles. . . ."—U.S. House of Representatives, *The Strategy and Tactics of World Communism*, Supp. II, pp. 88–89. Occasionally a recipient of a note does not have the patience to formulate a telling reply, as when the Russian representative on the Allied Council in Austria rebuked the United States for not conforming to the Copenhagen Frequency Agreement. The American High Commissioner Walter J. Donnelly merely said, "This protest seems better adapted for a radio comedian's broadcast than for the Allied Council agenda."— *New York Times*, December 9, 1950, p. 5, col. 4.

[10] Foreign Office, *British and Foreign State Papers*, compiled by Lewis Hertslet, Vol. 24 (London, 1835–1836), p. 999.

[11] Foreign Office, *Collected Diplomatic Documents Relating to the Outbreak of the European War* (London, 1915), pp. 5–8, 506–514; Vernon Van Dyke, "Responsibility of States for International Propaganda," *American Journal of International Law*, Vol. 34 (January 1940), p. 62; Melosh Bogičević, *Die auswärtige Politik Serbiens, 1903 bis 1914* (Berlin, 1928–1931), Vol. 2, p. 87.

[12] U.S. Department of State, *Papers Relating to the Foreign Relations of the United States (1923)*, Vol. 2 (Washington, D.C., 1938), p. 772.

[13] John B. Whitton, "Propaganda and International Law," *Recueil des Cours de l'Académie de Droit International*, Vol. 72 (1948-I), p. 595.

[14] *New York Times*, February 3, 1934, p. 6, col. 3.

[15] Heber Blankenhorn, "The Battle of Radio Armaments. Broadcasting and International Friction," *Harper's Magazine*, Vol. 164 (December 1931), p. 88.

[16] Ellery C. Stowell, "The General Smedly B. Butler Incident," *American Journal of International Law*, Vol. 25 (April 1931), p. 321.

[17] C. C. Hyde, *International Law . . .*, Vol. 1, 2nd revised ed., Sec. 217, p. 709n.

[18] U.S. Department of State, *Press Releases*, Vol. 13, No. 309 (August 31, 1935), p. 150.

[19] *New York Times*, September 4, 1935, p. 15, col. 6.

[20] *New York Times*, February 1, 1947, p. 4, col. 6. This protest, which was rejected by the British government, might be contrasted with another formal protest made by Poland to Britain in 1933. At that time a speaker in a New Year's Eve broadcast on the BBC had made a derogatory remark about Poland. The postmaster general said in Parliament that while he was responsible for matters of general policy, he did not interfere in matters of detail. However, Sir John Reith, then chief

executive of the BBC, called on the Polish minister in London on his own initiative, and soon thereafter the BBC announced that a friendly settlement had been arranged. The matter was thus taken out of the hands of the British Foreign Office.— See William A. Robson, "The Progress of Socialization in England," *Foreign Affairs*, Vol. 11 (April 1933), p. 506.

[21] *New York Times*, February 11, 1948, p. 18, col. 7.

[22] *New York Times*, June 21, 1946, p. 3, col. 7.

[23] *New York Times*, August 28, 1946, p. 3, col. 7; April 6, 1947, p. 31, col. 3.

[24] *New York Times*, March 16, 1948, p. 15, col. 2; June 11, 1948, p. 11, col. 3; February 15, 1950, p. 21, col. 7; May 5, 1950, p. 7, col. 6; May 4, 1950, p. 8, col. 3; December 21, 1947, p. 10, col. 1. Needless to say, this was before Tito developed "Titoist" tendencies.

[25] *New York Times*, April 4, 1938, p. 1, col. 2; May 7, 1938, p. 5, col. 6; July 29, 1938, p. 6, col. 5; Barrett, *Truth Is Our Weapon*, p. 96.

[26] See "The Red Network," *News from Behind the Iron Curtain*, Vol. 2, No. 8 (August 1953), p. 59. According to the *New York Times*, the Czech note handed to the U.S. ambassador charged: "The United States had violated international agreements by having allowed Czechoslovak 'traitors' to use its radio facilities for 'anti-Czechoslovak hostile activity.' This charge was aimed specifically at the new Radio Free Europe. . . . 'The Czechoslovak Government protests most strongly . . . and expects to be informed of the [remedial] measures the United States Government has taken.' The six-page note devoted considerable space to the charge that the United States radio stations were broadcasting 'false news and reports and propaganda of incitation against Czechoslovakia. One that is particularly notorious . . . is the American short-wave broadcasting station, hypocritically called "Free Europe",' it said. . . . 'In violation of international agreements, it uses a wave length that has been allotted to stations in other countries. The seriousness of this form of hostile activity is increased by the fact that the United States uses traitors . . . from the ranks of the mercenary Czechoslovak emigration for the broadcasts,' the note said." The note cited U.S. press reports to prove that Radio Free Europe was operated by the U.S. government rather than by private individuals. Radio Free Europe denied that it was using unauthorized wave lengths. It claimed that it had an arrangement with the U.S. State Department for the use of its wave lengths. —*New York Times*, May 23, 1951, p. 19, col. 3. It must be remembered, however, that the U.S. had refused to abide by the European wave-length awards of the Copenhagen Convention.

[27] *New York Times*, June 11, 1948, p. 11, col. 3; June 30, 1948, p. 5, col. 1; July 13, 1949, p. 14, col. 4.

[28] Britain, for instance, insisted that the Canal Tolls Act of 1912, giving the President the authority to proclaim and collect discriminatory tolls in the Panama Canal not only violated the Hay-Pauncefote Treaty, but that Britain had a right to protest the act, even before actual injury had been suffered by Britain.—Quincy Wright, "The Denunciation of Treaty Violators," *American Journal of International Law*, Vol. 32 (Summer 1938), p. 530.

[29] *New York Times*, November 22, 1951, p. 1, col. 5, p. 13, col. 2; November 23, 1951, p. 1, col. 6; December 20, 1951, p. 18, col. 4; December 21, 1951, p. 11, col. 3.

[30] *New York Times*, November 23, 1951, p. 16, col. 5; November 24, 1951, p. 4, col. 6; December 22, 1951, p. 4, col. 2.

[31] Alphonse Rivier, *Principes du droit des gens*, Vol. 1 (Paris, 1896) p. 266.

[32] E.g., Heinrich Triepel, Carlos Calvo, Paul Fauchille, L. Oppenheim, and H. Lauterpacht.

[33] "The Red Network," *loc. cit.*, p. 59.

[34] Foreign Office, *British and Foreign State Papers*, Vol. 92 (London, 1899), p. 105.

NOTES

[35] *New York Times*, April 18, 1951, p. 24, col. 5; July 18, 1948, p. 32, col. 6; January 14, 1946, p. 4, col. 4.

[36] Cf. the arrest of three Reuters correspondents in Belgrade who were Yugoslav nationals.—*New York Times*, September 24, 1946, p. 11, col. 1. While the diplomatic representative of the state where the newspaper is published will often intercede in behalf of a local correspondent, his intercession is generally futile.

[37] See Oppenheim, *op. cit.*, Vol. 1, 5th ed., Chapter VII, pp. 540–549. For an extreme view on the freedom of states to treat aliens as they wish, see T. Baty, *The Canons of International Law* (London, 1930), pp. 119–134.

[38] *New York Times*, November 28, 1952, p. 34, col. 8.

[39] *New York Times*, September 25, 1946, p. 1, col. 6; September 27, 1946, p. 12, col. 4; September 28, 1946, p. 1, col. 3.

[40] *The Times* (London), October 25, 1949, p. 3, col. 4. The British Council had five provincial institutes in Iran, while the Russian equivalent, VOKS, had two or three. The United States had three provincial centers.

[41] The one Briton teaching under British Council auspices in an Iranian institute in Shiraz, and another teaching at the University of Tabriz were temporarily not affected.

[42] *The Times* (London), February 5, 1952, p. 3, col. 5; February 6, 1952, p. 3, col. 3.

[43] Upon Iran's severing of diplomatic relations with Britain, which had been strained for more than a year, the last remaining British Institute was closed in Teheran.—*The Times* (London), October 23, 1952, p. 6, col. 4.

[44] Hansard, *Parliamentary Debates*, Commons, Fifth Series, 475:87 (May 11, 1950).

[45] *New York Times*, October 8, 1951, p. 1, col. 8.

[46] *New York Times*, June 21, 1946, p. 3, col. 7; July 20, 1946, p. 4, col. 7; September 5, 1946, p. 4, col. 7. Britain's submission saved the British Council from complete extinction behind the Iron Curtain. The British Institute in Warsaw remained the only center of the council in the countries of the Soviet bloc. In 1951 the council reported that the Polish attitude was "severe but civilized."—*The Times* (London), September 14, 1951, p. 2, col. 7.

[47] *The Times* (London), March 10, 1950, p. 5, col. 4; April 20, 1950, p. 4, col. 3; March 11, 1950, p. 5, col. 5. It should be pointed out that members of the British Council staff do not have diplomatic status, and Great Britain considers it to be an advantage to keep it that way.

[48] *The Times* (London), May 13, 1950, p. 4, col. 5; *The British Council Report for the Year 1950–1951*, pp. 12–13.

[49] *The British Council Report for the Year 1950–1951*, p. 13.

[50] *New York Times*, September 1, 1950, p. 4, col. 4; September 11, 1950, p. 16, col. 5.

[51] *The British Council Report for the Year 1951–1952*, pp. 8, 24; *The Times* (London), September 14, 1951, p. 2, col. 7; August 15, 1952, p. 4, col. 3; October 25, 1952, p. 3, col. 4.

[52] *New York Times*, October 31, 1946, p. 8, col. 6.

[53] *New York Times*, February 29, 1948, p. 1, col. 8; March 3, 1948, p. 10, col. 7; November 22, 1949, p. 3, col. 6; *Department of State Bulletin*, Vol. 22 (April 24, May 1, 1950), pp. 632, 684.

[54] *New York Times*, January 6, 1949, p. 18, col. 7.

[55] *Department of State Bulletin*, Vol. 20 (April 3, 1949), p. 432.

[56] *New York Times*, August 10, 1951, p. 1, col. 6.

[57] Ministry for Foreign Affairs of the Polish People's Republic, *Documents on the Hostile Policy of the United States Government Towards People's Poland* (Warsaw, 1953), pp. 174–175.

[58] *New York Times*, August 1, 1949, p. 9, col. 2.

[59] *Department of State Bulletin*, Vol. 22 (March 6, 1950), pp. 351–356.

[60] *Department of State Bulletin*, Vol. 22 (May 8, 1950), pp. 732–735; (May 15, 1950), p. 755.

[61] *New York Times*, July 3, 1951, p. 1, col. 6; July 4, 1951, p. 13, col. 4; July 3, 1951, p. 6, col. 6; July 6, 1951, p. 1, col. 7; July 8, 1951, p. 10, col. 1.

[62] *New York Times*, July 16, 1952, p. 1, col. 2; August 6, 1952, p. 4, col. 5; July 16, 1952, p. 1, col. 2; August 6, 1952, p. 4, col. 5. Both *Amerika* and the *USSR Information Bulletin* resumed publication by mutual agreement on October 22, 1956.—*New York Times*, October 23, 1956, p. 16, col. 5.

[63] *Department of State Bulletin*, Vol. 23 (July 10, 1950), p. 77.

[64] Fenwick, *International Law*, p. 478.

[65] *Ibid.*, p. 479; see examples in Satow, *A Guide to Diplomatic Practice*, pp. 260–283.

[66] In 1924 H. A. C. Cummins, in charge of the British legation in Mexico, was told that he must leave within ten days or compulsion would be used. When he refused to go, his food and telephonic communications were cut off. Similarly in 1931 the papal nuncio in Lithuania was declared *persona non grata* for "undue interference with the internal affairs of the country." When the Vatican failed to recall him, Lithuania threatened to expel him.—Satow, *op. cit.*, pp. 274–275.

[67] Oppenheim, *op. cit.*, Vol. 1, 5th ed., pp. 121–122.

[68] See *ibid.*, p. 122; this is especially true in Britain and the United States. Cf. The Gagara, Great Britain, Court of Appeal, 1919. L.R. (1919) P.D. 95; The Arantzazu Mendi, Great Britain, House of Lords (1939) A.C. 256: "Our State cannot speak with two voices on such a matter, the judiciary saying one thing, the executive another. Our Sovereign has to decide whom he will recognise as a fellow-sovereign in the family of States; and the relations of the foreign state with ours in the matter of State immunities must flow from that decision alone. . . ." In the United States, RSFSR v. Cibrario (1923), 235 N.Y. 255, 139 N.E. 259: "Who is the sovereign of a territory is a political question." Republic of China v. Merchants' Fire Assurance Corp. of New York (1929), 30 F. (2d) 278; Jones v. U.S. (1890), 137 U.S. 202, 11 S.Ct. 80: "Who is the sovereign, *de jure* or *de facto*, of a territory is not a judicial, but a political question, the determination of which by the legislative and executive departments of any government conclusively binds the judges, as well as all other officers, citizens and subjects of that government." U.S. v. Pink (1942), 315 U.S. 203, 62 S.Ct. 552; Z. & F. Assets Realization Corp. v. Hull (1941), 311 U.S. 470, 61 S.Ct. 351.

[69] Quoted by Fenwick, *op. cit.*, p. 170.

[70] See Oppenheim, *op. cit.*, Vol. 1, p. 122.

[71] Louis L. Jaffe, *Judicial Aspects of Foreign Relations: In Particular of the Recognition of Foreign Powers* (Cambridge, Mass., 1933), pp. 110–111.

[72] J. L. Brierly, *The Law of Nations: An Introduction to the International Law of Peace*, 4th ed. (Oxford, 1949), pp. 132–133.

[73] Jessup, *A Modern Law of Nations*, p. 57.

[74] Quoted by Edwin Dickinson, *Cases and Materials on International Law* (Brooklyn, 1950), p. 114.

[75] Not reprisal, as this is an act "otherwise illegal, performed by a State for the purpose of obtaining justice for an international delinquency by taking the law into its own hands."—Oppenheim, *op. cit.*, Vol. 2, 7th ed., p. 136. As nonrecognition would here be a political matter, there is no question of illegality.

[76] Exchange of notes between Secretary of State Hughes and Foreign Minister Chicherin, December 18, 1923, quoted by Peter Kleist, *Die völkerrechtliche Anerkennung Sowjetrusslands* (Königsberg, Prus., 1934), p. 99. For other exchanges of a similar nature see Fenwick, *op. cit.*, p. 166.

NOTES

[77] Kleist, *op. cit.*, pp. 85, 86, 92. Author's translation.

[78] *Ibid.*, p. 87.

[79] U.S. Department of State, *Papers Relating to the Foreign Relations of the United States (1923)*, Vol. 2 (Washington, D.C., 1938), pp. 769, 770.

[80] See the numerous diplomatic exchanges between the Soviets and the United States, the Baltic states, Great Britain, France, and Japan in U.S. Department of State, *Papers Relating to the Foreign Relations of the United States (1919 Russia)* (Washington, D.C., 1937), pp. 7, 16, 41, 88, 124, 156, 159, 161, 164, 165, 166, 194, 196, 600, 601, 602, 740.

[81] Kleist, *op. cit.*, pp. 90–91.

[82] U.S. Department of State, *Papers . . . (1923)*, Vol. 2, p. 785.

[83] They were Estonia, February 2, 1920; Lithuania, July 12, 1920; Latvia, August 11, 1920; Finland, October 14, 1920; followed by Persia, February 26, 1921; Afghanistan, February 28, 1921; Turkey, March 16, 1921; Poland, March 18, 1921; Mongolia, November 5, 1921.

[84] Kleist, *op. cit.*, pp. 92–93; Estonia: *League of Nations Treaty Series*, Vol. 11 (1922), Article 7(5), p. 50; Lithuania: *ibid.*, Vol. 3, (1921), Article 4(1), p. 122; Latvia: Heinrich Freund, *Russlands Friedens- und Handelsverträge 1918–1923* (Leipzig, 1924), Article 4(2), p. 96; Finland: *League of Nations Treaty Series*, Vol. 3 (1921), p. 6, no provision; Persia: Leonard Shapiro, *Soviet Treaty Series* (Washington, D.C., 1950), Vol. 1, Article 5, p. 93; Afghanistan: *ibid.*, p. 96, no provision; Turkey: G. F. de Martens, *Nouveau Recueil Général . . .*, 3e série, Vol. 16, Article 8, p. 37; Poland: *League of Nations Treaty Series*, Vol. 6 (1921), Article 5(2), p. 123; Mongolia: Freund, *op. cit.*, Article 3(1), p. 129.

[85] Quoted from Hansard, *Parliamentary Debates* in Kleist, *op. cit.*, p. 94.

[86] *League of Nations Treaty Series*, Vol. 4 (1921), p. 128.

[87] Kleist, *op. cit.*, p. 95.

[88] *League of Nations Treaty Series*, Vol. 7 (1921), pp. 294, 298.

[89] December 7, 1921. Article 14 of the "Provisional Agreement regarding Future Relations" says that "the delegations . . . shall be required to refrain from any kind of agitation or propaganda against the Government or the state organizations of the country in which they are temporarily resident."—Shapiro, *op. cit.*, p. 148.

[90] December 26, 1921, the Preamble of the "Preliminary Economic and Political Agreement" includes: "(a) That each of the two Parties abstains from every act or undertaking hostile to the other and refrains from engaging, outside of its own borders, in direct or indirect propaganda against the institutions of the Kingdom of Italy and of the Russian Republic of the Soviets. Under the term 'to engage in propaganda' are included assistance and encouragement given by one Party to any propaganda whatsoever carried on outside of its own borders."—*Ibid.*, p. 158.

[91] June 5, 1922; Article 8 of the "Provisional Treaty of Friendship and Commerce" reads: "The two Contracting Parties agree that their Governments will abstain from all propaganda directed against the Government, state institutions and other public institutions, and the socio-political system of the other Contracting Party, and that they will not take part in the socio-political differences which may arise in these states."—*Ibid.*, p. 174.

[92] April 23, 1923; Article 5 of the preliminary agreement with Denmark pledged the parties to "refrain from conducting, supporting or encouraging any political propaganda against the institutions of Denmark and Russia respectively."—*League of Nations Treaty Series*, Vol. 18 (1923), pp. 16, 20.

[93] Kleist, *op. cit.*, p. 97.

[94] Quoted by Lawrence Preuss, "International Responsibility for Hostile Propaganda against Foreign States," *American Journal of International Law*, Vol. 28 (October 1934), p. 662.

[95] Shapiro, *op. cit.*, p. 227.

[96] Martens, *op. cit.*, Vol. 20 (1930), p. 9.

[97] Quoted by Kleist, *op. cit.*, pp. 88–89.

[98] Preuss, *op. cit.*, p. 663; Martens, *op. cit.*, Vol. 20 (1930), p. 9.

[99] Italy, February 7, 1924; Norway, February 15, 1924; Austria, February 25, 1924; Greece, March 8, 1924; Danzig, March 13, 1924; Sweden, March 15, 1924; China (Peking), May 31, 1924; Denmark, June 18, 1924; Mexico, August 4, 1924; Hejaz, August 6, 1924; Hungary, September 5, 1924; China (Three Autonomous Eastern Republics, Mukden), September 30, 1924; France, October 28, 1924; Japan, January 20, 1925; Uruguay, August 21, 1926; Spain, July 28, 1933.—Kleist, *op. cit.*, p. 98; T. A. Taracouzio, *The Soviet Union and International Law* (New York, 1935), p. 264.

[100] Said the *New York Times* on October 29, 1924: "French recognition of the Soviet Government is on the new model created by MacDonald last winter. Recognition used to mean that the recognizing Government had satisfied itself that normal relations with the party of the second part were feasible and desirable. MacDonald's *de jure* recognition of Moscow established a form of international trial marriage. You recognized first and then you proceed to find out if you could live together."—Quoted by Kleist, *op. cit.*, p. 100.

[101] Kleist, *op. cit.*, p. 100.

[102] Quoted by Preuss, *op. cit.*, pp. 661–662.

[103] *Ibid.*

[104] *Ibid.*

[105] As a matter of fact, at the Genoa Economic Conference of 1922, the Soviet delegation refused to subscribe to any convention to prohibit propaganda by private organizations, as it claimed that it was impossible to forbid the activities of political parties and workers' organizations unless the activities were contrary to the municipal laws of the state in which they functioned.—France, *Documents Diplomatiques: Conférence Economique Internationale de Gênes* (Paris, 1922), pp. 99, 105, 118, 129.

[106] *The Times* (London), June 11, 1934, p. 12, col. 5; the treaty with Romania included: "The governments of our two states mutually guarantee full and total respect for the sovereignty of our respective states and abstention from any interference, whether direct or indirect, in each other's internal affairs and development, and especially from any agitation, propaganda and any form of intervention or support of same."—Martens, *op. cit.*, Vol. 36 (1938), p. 680. Author's translation.

[107] Martens, *op. cit.*, Vol. 30 (1935), pp. 49–50. Switzerland did not recognize the Soviet Union until 1946.—Ernest Rabel, *The Conflict of Laws: A Comparative Study*, Vol. 2 (Chicago, 1947), p. 88.

[108] Quoted by Jaffe, *Judicial Aspects of Foreign Relations* . . . pp. 102n, 147.

[109] C. C. Hyde, *International Law* . . . Vol. 2, 2nd revised ed. (Boston, 1945), p. 1654.

[110] See *Department of State Bulletin*, Vol. 22 (March 6, 1950), pp. 351–356.

[111] U.S. v. Rosenberg *et al.*, 195 F. (2d) 583 at 609.

[112] *New York Times*, November 4, 1947, p. 1, col. 2; February 12, 1948, p. 20, col. 4; July 9, 1947, p. 11, col. 4; September 23, 1950, p. 5, col. 6; April 23, 1950, p. 17, col. 2; March 6, 1948, p. 6, col. 3.

[113] *New York Times*, December 10, 1946, p. 5, col. 5; May 15, 1948, p. 2, col. 6; September 28, 1950, p. 21, col. 1; July 17, 1947, p. 10, col. 7; July 19, 1947, p. 5, col. 4; May 11, 1948, p. 18, col. 4; May 13, 1948, p. 11, col. 2; May 15, 1948, p. 5, col. 6; March 19, 1949, p. 7, col. 1.

[114] *New York Times*, May 5, 1946, II, p. 7, col. 5; July 17, 1946, p. 25, col. 1.

[115] *New York Times*, September 18, 1945, p. 1, col. 4; October 8, 1946, p. 1, col. 5; January 6, 1949, p. 18, col. 7.

[116] *New York Times*, April 29, 1951, p. 1, col. 4.

NOTES

Chapter 9. International Propaganda in Retrospect and Prospect

[1] Cf. Resolution 110(II) of the United Nations General Assembly.

[2] John B. Whitton, "Propaganda and International Law," *Recueil des Cours de l'Académie de Droit International*, Vol. 72 (1948-I), p. 645.

[3] *Ibid.*, p. 609.

[4] *Ibid.*, p. 598.

[5] Charles G. Fenwick, "Intervention: Individual and Collective," *American Journal of International Law*, Vol. 39 (October 1945), p. 646.

[6] Vernon B. Van Dyke, "Responsibility of States for International Propaganda," *American Journal of International Law*, Vol. 24 (January 1940), p. 65n.

[7] Jessup, *A Modern Law of Nations*, p. 172.

[8] *Ibid.*, pp. 172–173.

[9] Brierly, *The Law of Nations*, p. 284.

[10] Oppenheim, *International Law*, Vol. 1, 5th ed., pp. 249–250, 250n.

[11] *Ibid.*, p. 231n.

[12] J. M. Spaight, *War Rights on Land*, pp. 146–150.

[13] J. M. Spaight, *Air Power and War Rights,* pp. 308–310. Cf. p. 333 in 3rd ed. (1947).

[14] Oppenheim, *International Law,* Vol. 2, 7th ed., pp. 426–427.

[15] Hyde, *International Law . . .,* Vol. 3, 2nd revised ed., pp. 1838–1839.

[16] Even here it is perhaps more correct to say that a universal jurisdiction, rather than an international crime, is recognized.

[17] Quoted in Telford Taylor, "Nuremberg Trials, War Crimes and International Law," *International Conciliation,* No. 450 (April 1949), p. 251.

[18] Quoted *ibid.* The question here is not whether the Nuremberg trials constitute a legal precedent, thus changing existing international law. It is rather that the victors in a future war would probably bring to trial the leaders of the vanquished nations, vindicating themselves by pointing to the Nuremberg trials. Hans Kelsen says in this connection: "The Agreement of London applied only to subjects and organs of the vanquished European Axis Powers, not to subjects or organs of the states Members of the United Nations. Hence individual criminal responsibility for violation of the rules prohibiting war, as established by the Agreement, without the consent of the vanquished states will hardly be recognised as a principle of a new international law." — *The Law of the United Nations* (London, 1950), p. 738. Yet it is inconceivable that a major war of the future ending in the unconditional surrender of one of the belligerents would fail to be followed by war crimes trials.

[19] Quoted in Taylor, *op. cit.,* p. 353.

[20] Quoted *ibid.,* p. 271. The Soviet member of the International Military Tribunal, I. T. Nikitchenko, on the other hand, dissented. "I consider Fritzsche's responsibility fully proven," he said. "His activity had a most basic relation to the preparation and the conduct of aggressive warfare as well as to the other crimes of the Hitler regime." Nikitchenko pointed out that "the dissemination of provocative lies and the systematic deception of public opinion were as necessary to the Hitlerites for the realization of their plans as were the production of armaments and the drafting of military plans. Without propaganda, founded on the total eclipse of the freedom of press and of speech, it would not have been possible for German fascism to realize its aggressive intentions, to lay the groundwork and then to put to practice the War Crimes and the Crimes against Humanity." — International Military Tribunal, *Trial of the Major War Criminals . . .* pp. 353, 351.

[21] Quoted in Taylor, *op. cit.,* p. 271.

[22] See *ibid.,* p. 333. See also Quincy Wright, "The Crime of 'War-Mongering'," *American Journal of International Law*, Vol. 42 (January 1948), p. 129.

[23] *Yearbook of the United Nations, 1950,* p. 852. Relevant portions were: "Prin-

ciple I: Any person who commits an act which constitutes a crime under international law is responsible therefor and liable to punishment. Principle II: The fact that internal law does not impose a penalty for an act which constitutes a crime under international law does not relieve the person who committed the act from responsibility under international law. . . . Principle VI: The crimes hereinafter set out are punishable as crimes under international law: *a.* Crimes against peace: (i) Planning, preparation, initiation or waging of a war of aggression or a war in violation of international treaties, agreements or assurances; (ii) Participation in a common plan or conspiracy for the accomplishment of any of the acts mentioned under (i)."

Index

Access to information, 98, 106–7, 119, 145–46
Ackerman, Carl W., 26
Adams v. The People, 247n10
Administration of Central Broadcasting (USSR), 47
Aerial Navigation, Paris Convention on, 78
Aerial Warfare, Rules of, and propaganda leaflets, 88
Afghanistan: and freedom of speech, 116; restricts aliens, 118, 155, 243n92; controls disseminator, 118, 149, 244n92; protects sovereigns, 123, 127; protects national unity, 135; controls media, 140, 246n119; censorship in, 145, 242n82; right of reply in, 148, 242n82; restricts alien teachers, 155; restricts foreign publications, 157; controls importation of radios, 163; Constitution, 229n15; and subversion, 232n25; and propaganda against people, 233n28; protects foreign states, 235n45; bans propaganda causing unrest, 236n48; restricts doctrines, 238n52; controls radio, 246n119; recognizes RSFSR, 253n83
—and Iraq, Iran, and Turkey: treaty of *1937* on nonintervention, 92–93, 94
—and USSR: treaty of *1931* banning intervention, 91; treaty of *1926* banning intervention, 225n112; treaty of *1931* banning subversive propaganda, 225n129
Agence Anatolie, 141
Agence France-Presse, 141
Agerpress, 141

Aggression, encouragement forbidden, 118
Agitprop: controls Soviet propaganda, 46; organization of, 47
Agriculture, 50
Air: freedom of, 78; sovereignty of, 88–89
Air Power and War Rights, 203
Air waves, controlled by state, 140
Aircraft: propaganda by, 88, 89, 203; dropping objects from, 89
Albania: and freedom of speech, 115; controls education, 142; and jurisdiction over aliens abroad, 171; Constitution, 229n15; bans propaganda against people, 233n28; restricts doctrines, 238n52; bans treason, 240n60; controls media, 240–41n65
—and Yugoslavia: treaty of *1947* on cultural exchanges, 105
Albig, William, defines propaganda, 10, 11
Alexander I, King of Yugoslavia, 70
Algeria: and censorship, 145; access to information in, 146
Alien Registration Act (U.S.), 233n26
Aliens: propaganda by, banned, 75, 130–31; and civil rights, 119, 231n20; restricted, 119, 149, 154–55; relations with, forbidden, 136–37; banned from clergy, 150; jurisdiction over, 167–71, 205; expulsion of, 174, 180–88; admission of, 196–97
Aliens Restriction (Amendment) Act (Great Britain), 233n26

All-India Radio, 39

All-Slav Committee, 50–51

Allen, George V., 25, 28, 160

Allies, propaganda of, in World War II, 18

America Illustrated, 29

American Banana Co. v. United Fruit Co., 170

American Committee for Liberation from Bolshevism, Inc., 31, 33

American Forces Network, Hungarian listeners to, 40

American Peace Crusade, 51

Amerika: ceases publication in USSR, 186–87; mentioned, 24

Anarchy: incitement to, 57, 130; outlawed, 136

Anatolian Agency, 37

Andorra: and freedom of speech, 115; Constitution, 229n15

Anglo-Italian Accord of *1938*, 9

Anglo-Soviet Protocol of *1929*, 91

Anti-Bolshevist Struggle, Co-ordinating Center of, 33

Anzilotti, Dionisio, on responsibility for private propaganda, 59

Arab League, advocates cultural cooperation, 99, 100

Arabian states, and censorship, 145

Arantzazu Mendi, The, 252n68

Argentina: and freedom of speech, 116; and disrespect in press, 123; and treason, 138, 240n60; education in, 142; and responsibility of cable companies, 153; restricts aliens, 154, 155; and crimes abroad by aliens, 168; protests to Uruguay, 175; Constitution, 229n15; bans subversion, 232n25; protects officials, 233n26; bans propaganda causing unrest, 236n48; bans war propaganda, 238n49; restricts doctrines, 238n52; controls media, 241n65; censorship in, 242n82; and state secrets, 243n82; restricts disseminator, 244n92

Armaments, Conference for the Reduction and Limitation of, 70

Armed Forces Network, 30

Arnold v. Ingram, 244n92

Asia Foundation, 33

Assassination, incitement to, forbidden, 124

Assembly, freedom of, 143

Associated Press: refuses to sell services to government, 26; reporter expelled, 196; correspondent barred, 197; mentioned, 32

Associations: propaganda against international, banned, 131; subversive, banned, 135; registration of, 143

Austin, Warren, on recognition of states, 189, 190

Australia: protects friendly nations, 129; and Communist party, 135; requires broadcasting government communiqués, 147–48; Constitution Act, 229n15; protects state, 232n25; protects foreign states, 235n45; controls media, 241n68, 241n70; censorship in, 242n82; right of reply in, 242n82; restricts aliens, 243n92

Austria: and protests, 7, 174; calls news broadcasts propaganda, 19, 153; and freedom of speech, 116; protects security of state, 122, 232n25; protects heads of state, 127; protects foreign states, 129, 235n45; newsboys held responsible by USSR, 152; and importation of publications, 158; recognizes RSFSR, 192; Constitution, 229n15; bans propaganda against people, 233n28; bans propaganda causing unrest, 236n48, 237n49; restricts doctrines, 238n52; bans treason, 240n60; restricts disseminator, 244n92; controls printed matter, 246n119; recognizes USSR, 254n99

—and Czechoslovakia, treaty of *1921* banning subversion, 94

—and France, treaty on cultural exchanges, 105

—and Germany, treaty of *1936* on nonintervention, 92

—and RSFSR, treaty of *1921* banning propaganda by diplomats, 91

Austria-Hungary, and Serbia, 90, 174

Baba Masao, In re, 218n8

Baiz, Ex parte, 229n6

Baldwin, Stanley, 193

Balloons, propaganda by, 88, 89

Barrett, Edward W.: on propaganda of action, 18; heads International Information Administration, 27

Barthou, Louis, 70

Bartlett, F. C., 11

Bayard, Thomas F., 130

Beaverbrook, Lord, 34

Belgian Congo: protects convictions, 125; bans propaganda against people,

233n28; bans propaganda causing unrest, 236n48, 237n49; controls printed matter, 246n119

Belgium: and freedom of speech, 116, 155; bans subversion, 122, 232n25; bans propaganda through religion, 125; protects foreign states, 129, 235n45; and bond for publishers, 143; access to information in, 146; restricts disseminator, 150, 244n92; and broadcast restrictions, 159; and jurisdiction over aliens abroad, 171; expels British citizen, 180; Constitution, 230n15; bans propaganda against people, 233n28; bans propaganda causing unrest, 236n-48, 237n49; bans war propaganda, 238n49; restricts doctrines, 238n52; controls media, 241n68, 241n70, 246n-119; censorship in, 242n82; right of reply in, 242n82
—and Czechoslovakia, treaty of 1947 on cultural exchanges, 104
—and France, treaty of 1946 on cultural exchanges, 103–4
—and Italy, treaty of 1948 on cultural exchanges, 104
—and Netherlands, treaty of 1946 on cultural exchanges, 104
—and Norway, treaty of 1948 on cultural exchanges, 104
Ben Tillett's case, 180
Benton, William: cuts U.S. information program, 24; mentioned, 25
Berlin Airlift, used for propaganda, 18
Bessarabia, Soviet and Romanian propaganda in, 8
Bevin, Ernest, on propaganda, 34
Bhutan: and freedom of speech, 115; no constitution in, 230n15
Bible, propaganda in, 5
"Big Lie," 17
Binder, Carroll, 13
Bird, Charles, defines propaganda, 10, 11
Blumenstock, Dorothy, defines propaganda, 10
Bluntschli, Johann Kaspar, on responsibility for private propaganda, 58
Bolivia: propaganda against Paraguay, 18; and freedom of speech, 116, 119; outlaws Communist party, 135; and foreign government employ, 169; Constitution, 230n15; bans war propaganda, 238n49; bans treason, 240n60; controls media, 241n65

Bolsheviks, and radio propaganda, 7
Books, distribution of, 21, 25, 29, 43, 47–48
Borchard, E. M., on recognition of states, 195
Bourquin, Maurice, on responsibility for private propaganda, 60
Boycotts, incitement to, banned, 118, 125
Brande, W. T., Dictionary, 5
Brazil: and freedom of speech, 116, 117, 118–19; and race hatred, 117; and war propaganda, 118, 238n49; and right of reply, 119, 242n82; controls disseminator, 149, 149–50, 244n92; forbids press anonymity, 153; and foreign government employ, 169; Constitution, 230n15; bans propaganda against people, 233n28; bans propaganda causing unrest, 236n48, 237n49; restricts doctrines, 238–39n52; controls media, 241n68, 241n70; restricts aliens, 243n92; confiscates radio tubes, 246n116
—and Canada, notes of 1944 on cultural exchanges, 103
—and Chile, treaty of 1941 on cultural exchanges, 103
—and Dominican Republic, treaties of 1942 and 1945 on cultural exchanges, 103
—and Ecuador, treaty of 1944 on cultural exchanges, 103
—and Paraguay, treaty of 1941 on cultural exchanges, 103
—and Venezuela, treaty of 1942 on cultural exchanges, 103
Brest-Litovsk (alleged convention of 1917), endorses revolutionary propaganda, 102
Brest-Litovsk, Treaty of: peace negotiations broadcast, 7; mentioned, 90
Brierly, J. L.: on recognition of states, 189; on intervention, 202
British Act of Uniformity, 234n28
British Ally, 38, 183
British Broadcasting Corporation: Empire Service established, 8, 37; launches foreign-language programs, 9, 37; described, 34–40; charter of, 38–39; external services of, 39; in international law, 39; performance compared with Voice of America, 39–40; Hungarian listeners to, 40; broadcasts protested, 86, 176, 183, 184, 249–50n20; listen-

ing by Soviet satellites, 161; correspondent barred from USSR, 196
British Council: described, 35–44; established, 35, 40–41; aims of, 41; charter of, 41; history of, 41–42; activities of, 41–44; revenues of, 44; and Radio Free Europe compared, 44; compared with VOKS, 49; closed in Iran, 181, 251n40; rights in British view, 182; accused of espionage by Hungary, 182–83; closed in Bulgaria and China, 183; Polish reprisals against, 197; in Warsaw, 251n46; no diplomatic status, 251n47
British Information Services: established, 36; integrated with diplomatic missions, 36; activities of, 36–37; concedes to Poland, 182; treatment by Soviet bloc, 182; closed in Czechoslovakia, 183
British Institute. See British Council
British Library of Information, 36
British Life and Thought, 43
British News (Newsreel), 43
British Press Service, 36
Broadcasting. See Radio
Brussels Pact of 1948, encourages cultural exchanges, 97
Buenos Aires Convention of 1936, provides for exchange of students, 22
Bukharin, Nikolai, 8, 191
Bulgaria: and race hatred, 117; and freedom of speech, 117, 119; forbids chauvinism, 118; and imperialist aggression, 118; inhibits fascism, 136; and radio listening, 162; and illegal emigration, 169; responsibility of ex-citizens to, 170; bans British Council, 183; breaks diplomatic relations with U.S., 185; recognizes USSR, 195; expels correspondents, 196; Constitution, 230n15; bans propaganda against people, 233n28; restricts doctrines, 239n52; bans treason, 240n60; controls media, 241n65, 246n119
—and Czechoslovakia: treaty of 1947 on cultural exchanges, 105; on settlement of disputes, 248n6
—and Poland, treaty of 1947 on cultural exchanges, 105
—and USSR: treaty of 1934 banning intervention, 91; treaty of 1948 banning intervention, 225n128; on cultural cooperation, 228n189
Burgman v. de Sieyes, 229n6

Burma: and freedom of speech, 115–16; bans antireligious propaganda, 124–25; outlaws Communist party, 135; and censorship, 145; protects citizens abroad, 155; Constitution, 230n15; bans propaganda against people, 233n28; bans propaganda causing unrest, 236n48; bans war propaganda, 238n49; restricts doctrines, 239n52; restricts disseminator, 244n92
Butash v. State (Indiana), 213n10
Butler, General Smedley D., 175

Calvo, Carlos: on hostile propaganda, 57; on state responsibility for private propaganda, 58
Cambodia: and freedom of speech, 116; and war propaganda, 118; Constitution, 230n15; bans propaganda causing unrest, 236n48
Canada: no censorship in, 145; and radio offenses, 152; and British Bill of Rights, 230n15; bans propaganda against people, 233n28; protects foreign states, 235n45; bans propaganda causing unrest, 236n48; restricts doctrines, 239n52
—and Brazil, notes of 1944 on cultural exchanges, 103
Carnegie Foundation, 30
Carol, Prince of Romania, 130
Carroll, Wallace, 20
Casey, Ralph D., 212n1
Cavaglieri, A., and responsibility for private propaganda, 58
Censorship: in USSR, 46; United Nations attacks, 98–99; in wartime, 144; of telegrams, 144; discussed, 144–45; laws on, 242n82
Censorship, U.S. Office of, 23
Central Intelligence Agency (U.S.), 27
Central Office of Information (Great Britain), 35, 45
Central Powers, and RSFSR, treaty of 1918 banning propaganda, 90
Ceylon: protects state, 123; and British Bill of Rights, 230n15; bans subversion, 232n25
Chambers's Encyclopaedia, 18
Chauvinism, forbidden, 118, 123
Cherokee Tobacco Co., The, 218n10
Chicherin, Georghi Vasilievich, 192
Chile: and freedom of speech, 116; protects state, 123, 123–24, 232n25; bans propaganda causing unrest, 132, 236n-

48, 237n49; restricts aliens, 137, 155; controls education, 142; and propaganda by citizens abroad, 168; Constitution, 230n15; bans subversion, 232n-25; protects officials, 233n26; restricts doctrines, 239n52; bans propaganda favoring foreign states, 239n53; controls media, 241n65; right of reply in, 242n82; restricts disseminator, 244n92
—and Brazil, treaty of 1941 on cultural exchanges, 103
China: and Kuomintang propaganda, 8; treaties on cultural rights, 103; requires resident publisher, 149; forbids listening to foreign broadcasts, 159; protects state, 232n25; protects foreign states, 235n45; bans propaganda causing unrest, 236n48; restricts doctrines, 239n52; censorship in, 242n82; and state secrets, 243n82; restricts aliens, 243n92; controls printed matter, 246n119
—and Costa Rica, treaty of 1944 on cultural rights, 228n179
—and Cuba, treaty of 1942 on cultural rights, 228n179
—and Dominican Republic, treaty of 1940 on cultural rights, 227n179
—and Ecuador, treaty of 1946 on cultural rights, 228n179
—and Mexico, treaty of 1944 on cultural rights, 228n179
—and Philippines, treaty of 1947 on cultural rights, 228n179
—and USSR: treaty of 1924 banning intervention, 224n112; banning subversive propaganda, 225n129; banning intervention, 225n128
China (Mukden government), recognizes USSR, 254n99
—and USSR, treaty of 1924 banning intervention, 224n112
China (Peking government), recognizes USSR, 254n99
China, People's Republic of: broadcasts of, 54; and freedom of speech, 115; censorship in, 145; bans British Council, 183; bans USIS, 185; and recognition by U.S., 190; Constitution, 230n15
China, Republic of: and freedom of speech, 115; protects heads of friendly states, 127; condemns war propaganda and false news, 219n34; Constitution, 230n15; bans propaganda favoring foreign states, 239n53

Chronicle of Soviet Chess, 50
Chronicle of Soviet Fine Arts, 50
Chronicle of the Soviet Theater, 50
Citizens: and pro-enemy propaganda, 138, 168; jurisdiction over, abroad, 166–70; employed by foreign government, 186
Citizenship: and communication media, 118, 149–50; and free speech, 119; and offenses against state, 123
Classics of Democracy, 29
Clay, Lucius D., 32
Clayton, William L., 181
Clear and present danger test, 120
Cobbett, William, Trial of, 238n49
Coffee v. Midland Broadcasting Co., 243n-89, 244n92
Cold War, 17, 108, 176, 177, 195, 196
Colombia: and freedom of speech, 116, 117, 119; restricts aliens, 119, 149, 155, 243n92; bans official propaganda at home, 124; protects heads of state, 127; allocates radio frequencies, 140; and foreign newspaper subsidies, 143; controls media, 143, 241n65, 241n70; censorship in, 145, 242n82; restricts disseminator, 149, 244n92; Constitution, 230n15; protects officials, 233n26; protects foreign states, 235n45; bans propaganda causing unrest, 236n48, 237n-49; right of reply in, 242n82
Cominform: established, 52; abolished, 53; mentioned, 156
Comintern: program of, 8; established, 51; activities in Great Britain, 51–52, 193; abolished, 52; and USSR, 53; Russia rejects responsibility for, 175, 191; mentioned, 195
Common Council for American Unity, 31
Commonwealth v. James Blanding, 247n-10
Commonwealth v. Macloon, 247n10
Commonwealth v. Smith, 247n10
Communism: propaganda of, after World War I, 7, 8; propaganda of, 46; and loyalty to USSR, 53
Communist International. See Comintern
Communist party: program of, 8, 191; outlawed, 135; appoints Soviet newspaper staffs, 140; members restricted, 154, 244–45n92; and Soviet government, 195
Communist press: exploited by USSR, 48–49; anonymity forbidden in U.S., 153

Compton, Wilson, 27, 187

Conformity: insisted on, 146, 147; in education, 147; laws enforcing, 243n-82

Consensus of states, 111

Constitutions: and international law, 110; and freedom of speech, 115–20. See also individual states

Content, control of, 144–48

Cooperation with the American Republics, Inter-Departmental Committee on (U.S.), 22

Coorg (Rajah) v. East India Co., 173

Correspondence, by government with individuals, 93

Costa Rica: and freedom of speech, 116; protects foreign states, 127, 129, 235n-45; and political parties, 135, 239n52; and aliens, 155; Constitution, 230n15; bans propaganda against people, 233n-28; bans war propaganda, 238n49; restricts disseminator, 244n92; permits emigration, 248n21

—and China, treaty of 1944 on cultural rights, 228n179

Council of Europe, and freedom of expression, 97, 220n54

Crane v. Bennett, 244n92

Credit, endangering, forbidden, 133

Crime: international propaganda not a, 60–61, 108, 201; justification of, 132; incitement to, 132; abroad, jurisdiction of, 164–71; international, 205

Criticism, of foreign officials forbidden, 128–29

Cromwell, Oliver, 6

Crusade for Freedom, 32

Cuba: and freedom of speech, 116, 117; protects foreign states, 127, 129, 235n-45; and right of reply, 148, 242n82; restricts alien teachers, 155; Constitution, 230n15; bans propaganda causing unrest, 236n48, 237n49; bans war propaganda, 238n49; censorship in, 242n-82; and conformity, 243n82; restricts disseminator, 244n92

—and China, treaty of 1942 on cultural rights, 228n179

Cultural activities: educational exchanges, 22, 25, 30, 42–43, 46, 49–50, 103–5; of U.S., 22–23, 25–26, 30; of Great Britain, 36, 40–44; of USSR, 47–50; advocated, 99, 100, 103–5; treaties on, 103–5, 227–28n179, 228n189; treaty denounced, 183; mentioned, 22

Cultural Cooperation, Division of (U.S.), 23

Cultural Relations, Division of (U.S.), 23

Cummins, H. A. C., 252n66

Custom, and diplomatic behavior, 198

Cutting case, 165

Cyprus: and censorship, 145; access to information in, 146

Czechoslovak Institute, closed in London, 183

Czechoslovak Press Bureau, 141

Czechoslovakia: renounces treaty of 1947 with Britain, 105; and freedom of speech, 116; and race hatred, 117; forbids chauvinism, 118; forbids hostile activities abroad, 123, 168; protects state, 123, 232n25; protects national unity, 135; and treason, 138, 240n60; defines duties of citizen, 138; controls films, 141; controls media, 141, 142, 150, 241n65, 241n68, 246n119; supports wire service, 141; and information to foreign power, 146; controls book distribution, 150; restricts aliens, 150, 243n92; and foreign correspondents, 154, 196, 197; bans foreign publications, 155–56; and foreign broadcasts, 160; protests Radio Free Europe activity, 178, 250n26; reaction to protest, 178; bans British Information Services, 183; arrests nationals working for USIS, 184; bans USIS, 184; recognizes RSFSR, 192; recognizes USSR, 195; Constitution, 230n15; bans subversion, 232n25; bans propaganda against people, 233n-28; protects foreign states, 235n45; bans propaganda causing unrest, 236n-48, 237n49; bans war propaganda, 238n-49; restricts doctrines, 239n52; right of reply in, 242n82; and conformity, 243n-82; permits emigration, 248n21

—and Austria, treaty of 1921 banning subversion, 94

—and Belgium, treaty of 1947 on cultural exchanges, 104

—and Bulgaria: treaty of 1947 on cultural exchanges, 105; on settlement of disputes, 248n6

—and Great Britain, treaty of 1947 on cultural exchanges, 104

—and Poland, treaty of 1947 on cultural exchanges, 105

—and Romania, treaty of 1947 on cultural exchanges, 105

—and RSFSR, treaty of *1922* banning propaganda, 90
—and USSR, treaty of *1934* banning intervention, 91
—and Yugoslavia, treaty of *1947* on cultural exchanges, 105, 228n*186*

Daily Express (London), banned in Egypt, 156
Daily Graphic (London), banned in Egypt, 156
Daily Mail (London), correspondent expelled from Czechoslovakia, 196
Danzig, recognizes USSR, 254n*99*
—and Poland, treaty of *1922* banning subversive propaganda, 226n*138*
Danzig Railway case, 65
Davis, Elmer, heads Office of War Information, 23
Davison, W. Phillips, 18
Dedijer, Stevan (Yugoslav U.N. delegate), equates information and propaganda, 13
Defamation of officials, 204
Defense Department (U.S.), propaganda activities of, 30
Definition of words, in U.S. courts, 15–16
Democracy: and systematic propaganda, 7; propaganda against, banned, 123
Denmark: calls conference on accurate news, 68; and freedom of speech, 116; bans incitement to breach of law, 132; and Communist party, 135; helps film industry, 141; freedom of assembly in, 143; and press offenses, 151; and Danish-language publications abroad, 153, 158; restricts disseminator, 153–54, 244n*92*; responsibility of importer, 158; protests to USSR, 177; recognizes RSFSR, 192; Constitution, 230n*15*; protects state, 232n*25*; protects foreign states, 235n*45*; bans propaganda causing unrest, 236n*48*, 237n*49*; controls media, 241n*70*, 246n*119*; recognizes USSR, 254n*99*
—and Great Britain, treaty on subversives, 89
—and USSR, treaty of *1923* banning propaganda by diplomats, 225n*119*
De Vabres, H. Donnedieu, denies propaganda is international crime, 60–61
Dewey, A. Gordon, 211n*1*
Dickinson, Edwin D., and responsibility for private propaganda, 60
Dictatorship, and propaganda, 7

Dictionary of Science, Literature and Art, 5
Diplomacy: defined, 172; and propaganda, 207
Diplomatic protest. *See* Protest
Diplomats: activities of Soviet, 47; propaganda by, banned, 91, 225n*119*; protected against libel, 126, 127; recall of, 187
Disseminator: control of, 149–55, 158; laws on, 244–45n*92*
Doctrines, propaganda benefiting, 238–39n*52*
Documentaries. *See* Films
Domestic law. *See* Municipal law
Dominican Republic: and freedom of speech, 116, 117; protects friendly states, 127, 129, 235n*45*; bans propaganda by refugees, 130–31; censorship in, 145, 242n*82*; and radio responsibility, 152; and foreign government employ, 169; Constitution, 230n*15*; bans subversion, 232n*25*; bans propaganda causing unrest, 236n*48*, 237n*49*; restricts doctrines, 239n*52*; controls media, 241n*68*, 241n*70*; restricts aliens, 243n*92*; controls disseminator, 244n*92*
—and Brazil: treaty of *1942* on cultural exchanges, 103; treaty of *1945* on cultural exchanges, 103
—and China, treaty of *1940* on cultural rights, 227–28n*179*
Donnelly, Walter J., 249n*9*
Doob, Leonard W., defines propaganda, 10, 11–12
Doss v. Secretary of State for India in Council, 173
Dunlap, Knight, 10

Eagleton, Clyde, on responsiblity for private propaganda, 58
Eastern Extension, Australasia & China Telegraph case, 109
Echo, 45
Eco del Mondo, 45
Economic and Social Council (United Nations), condemns jamming, 86
Economic pressures, 197
Ecuador: and freedom of speech, 116; protects national interest, 123; and aliens, 155; Constitution, 230n*15*; protects state, 232n*25*; bans subversion, 232n*25*; bans war propaganda, 238n*49*; bans treason, 240n*60*; censorship in, 242n*82*; restricts disseminator, 244n*92*

—and Brazil, treaty of *1944* on cultural exchanges, 103

—and China, treaty of *1946* on cultural rights, 228n*179*

Ede, J. Chuter, 182

Education: and propaganda, 15; exchange of students, 22, 25, 30, 42–43, 46, 49–50, 103–5; treaties concerning, 107; control of, 141–43; and conformity, 147; alien teachers restricted, 155

Educational Exchange, Office of (U.S.), 25

Educational Exchange, U.S. Advisory Commission on, 25

Edwards, Clement Stanislaus, 174

Edwards, Violet, defines propaganda, 10, 11

Egypt: and freedom of speech, 116; protects foreign states, 127, 235n*45*; and Communist party, 135; controls media, 143, 241n*68*, 241n*70*, 246n*119*; and censorship, 145; bans British and American publications, 156; and employment by foreign states, 169; protests to Switzerland, 177; Constitution, 230n*15*; bans subversion, 232n*25*; bans propaganda against people, 233n*28*; bans propaganda causing unrest, 236n*48*; restricts doctrines, 239n*52*; bans propaganda favoring foreign states, 239n*53*; controls disseminator, 244n*92*

—and Yemen, treaty of *1945* banning subversion, 94

Eire. *See* Ireland

Eisenhower, Dwight D.: reorganizes U.S. information program, 27–28; on U.S. propaganda aims, 28; People-to-People program of, 29, 30; mentioned, 24

Eklogi, 45

Emigration: United Nations on, 98; illegal, 169; and responsibility of ex-citizen, 170; laws on, 248n*21*

En Guardia, 24

Encyclopedia of the Social Sciences, 10

Enemy, propaganda favoring, 137–38

Enemy Propaganda, Department of (Great Britain), abolished, 35

English-Speaking Union, activities of, 45–46

English-Speaking World, 46

Enlistment, urging foreign, forbidden, 137

Entertainment, control of, 143

Espionage Act (U.S.), 233n*26*

Estonia: protests to USSR, 7; and conformity, 146; recognizes RSFSR, 253n-*83*. *See also* USSR

—and RSFSR, treaty of *1920* banning private propaganda, 92

Ethics, journalistic code of, 68

Ethiopia: and freedom of speech, 115; Constitution, 230n*15*

Ethnic minorities, broadcasts to, 7

European Broadcasting Convention: (Copenhagen, *1948*) allocates medium and long waves, 85; infringement of protested, 222n*87*; (Lucerne, 1933) mentioned, 78

European Convention for the Protection of Human Rights and Fundamental Freedoms, 76–77

Expert testimony, and current sentiment, 16

Extinctive prescription, 173

Facts about the United States, 29

Fascism: propaganda of, banned, 105; outlawed, 136; anti-Fascist station closed, 175

Fauchille, Paul: and hostile propaganda, 57; and responsibility for private propaganda, 58; on freedom of air, 78

Fenwick, Charles G.: on treaties, 62, 87; on illicit wars, 201

Field, David Dudley, on responsibility for private propaganda, 58

Films: produced by U.S., 29; by Great Britain, 43; distributed by USSR, 49; documentaries, 141; industry state controlled, 141; and censorship, 144; barriers to importation of, 157–58

Finland: protests to USSR, 7; and freedom of speech, 116; protects international relations, 133; and censorship, 145; bans anti-Soviet newspapers, 156; and crimes abroad, 167; restricts foreign travel, 169; Constitution, 230n*15*; bans propaganda causing unrest, 236n-*48*, 237n*49*; controls printed matter, 246n*119*; recognizes RSFSR, 253n*83*

—and RSFSR, treaty of *1922* banning subversive propaganda, 225n*129*

—and USSR, treaty of *1948* banning intervention, 225n*128*

Folwell v. Miller, 243n*86*, 244n*92*

Fong Yue Ting v. U.S., 231n*20*

For a Lasting Peace, For a People's Democracy: established, 52; banned in France, 156

Ford Foundation, 30

Foreign Agents Registration Act (U.S.), 14, 154
Foreign Broadcasting Sector (USSR), 47
Foreign broadcasts, listening to, 158–63
Foreign ministers meetings: (1939) in Panama, 75; (1940) in Havana, 75–76
Foreign Operations Administration (U.S.), 28
Foreign policy, propaganda as instrument of, 7
France: propaganda during Revolution, 5–6; broadcasts abroad, 8; Polish propaganda in, 8; cooperates with England, 20; and freedom of speech, 116; protects foreign states, 126–27, 235n45; and anarchist propaganda, 136; controls wire services, 140–41; helps film industry, 141; controls media, 143, 241n68, 241n70, 246n119; controls disseminator, 149, 244n92; and press offenses, 150; bans Cominform organ, 156; and protests, 174, 175; closes anti-Fascist station, 175; Constitution, 230n-15; protects state, 232n25; bans propaganda causing unrest, 236n48, 237n49; bans war propaganda, 238n49; restricts doctrines, 239n52; right of reply in, 242n82; and state secrets, 243n82; restricts aliens, 243n92; recognizes USSR, 254n99
—and Austria, treaty on cultural exchanges, 105
—and Belgium, treaty of 1946 on cultural exchanges, 103–4
—and Italy, treaty of 1935, 75
—and Netherlands, treaty of 1947 on cultural exchanges, 105
—and Poland, treaty of 1947 on cultural exchanges, 105
—and Russia, treaty of 1801 on subversives, 89–90
—and USSR, treaty of 1932 banning intervention, 91
Francis, Robert J., compares BBC and Voice of America, 39–40
Free Asia, Committee for a, 31, 33
Free Europe Committee: activities of, 31–33; Crusade for Freedom, 32; Free Europe Exile Relations Division, 33; Free Europe Press, 33; Free Europe University in Exile, 33; mentioned, 45, 180. See also Radio Free Europe
Free Zones of Upper Savoy and the District of Gex case, 220n46
Freedom of Information and the Press,

United Nations Sub-Commission on, condemns jamming, 86
Freedoms, treaty on, 107
Friendly propaganda: United Nations advocates, 99; by radio, 101; treaty on, 105
Fritzsche, Hans, 205
Fulbright Act, 24, 25
Funk and Wagnall, defines propaganda, 12

Gagara, The, 252n68
Gemma, Scipione: on hostile propaganda, 57; on responsibility for private propaganda, 60
General Convention to Improve the Means of Preventing War, 69
Geneva Convention, 64
Genocide: propaganda forbidden, 125; Israel assumes jurisdiction for, 166
Gentlemen's Agreement (1938), bans harmful propaganda, 93
George, Lloyd, on recognition of RSFSR, 192
George III, King of England, 6
German Soviet Republic and RSFSR, treaty of 1919 endorsing Spartacist propaganda, 102
Germany: radio propaganda of, 6, 8; and protests, 7, 174, 175; denies responsibility for Nazi propaganda, 8; and World War II propaganda triumphs, 18; protects foreign diplomats, 127; protects foreign states, 129, 235n45; and treason, 139, 240n60; and state secrets, 146, 243n82; and responsibility of importer, 158; and foreign broadcasts, 159, 161–62; and aiding foreign states, 168, 239n-53; and propaganda by citizens abroad, 168; recognizes RSFSR, 192; propaganda by, 203; bans propaganda causing unrest, 236n48, 237n49; right of reply in, 242n82; controls printed matter, 246n119; controls radio, 246n119. See also Germany, Democratic Republic of; Germany, Federal Republic of
—and Austria, treaty of 1936 on nonintervention, 92
—and Italy, treaty of 1938 banning biased publications, 95
—and RSFSR: treaty of 1917 endorsing revolutionary propaganda, 102; treaty of 1920 banning subversive propaganda, 225n129; treaty of 1921 banning propaganda by diplomats, 225n119

—and USSR, notes of *1925* banning intervention, 225n*112*

Germany, Allied Control Council for, 139

Germany (British Zone), bans Soviet-sponsored newspapers, 156

Germany, Democratic Republic of: and freedom of speech, 116; and race hatred, 117, 125; and war propaganda, 118, 238n*49*; forbids boycotts, 118, 125; and loyalty to Constitution, 122; bans incitement to assassinate, 124; and enlistment in foreign army, 137; and censorship, 145; and crimes abroad, 166; restricts foreign travel, 169; Constitution, 230n*15*; protects state, 232n-*25*; protects officials, 233n*26*; bans propaganda against people, 233n*28*; bans propaganda causing unrest, 237n-*49*; restricts doctrines, 239n*52*; bans propaganda favoring foreign states, 239n*53*; and conformity, 243n*82*

—Mark Brandenburg: bans propaganda against people, 233n*28*; bans war propaganda, 238n*49*; restricts doctrines, 239n*52*

—Mecklenburg: bans propaganda against people, 233n*28*; bans war propaganda, 238n*49*; restricts doctrines, 239n*52*

—Saxony: bans propaganda against people, 233n*28*; bans war propaganda, 238n*49*; restricts doctrines, 239n*52*

—Saxony-Anhalt: b a n s propaganda against people, 233n*28*; bans war propaganda, 238n*49*; restricts doctrines, 239n*52*

—Thuringia: protects state, 232n*25*; bans propaganda against people, 233n*28*; bans propaganda causing unrest, 237n-*49*; bans war propaganda, 238n*49*; restricts doctrines, 239n*52*

Germany, Federal Republic of: and Radio Free Europe, 32–33, 181; and freedom of speech, 116; access to information in, 119, 146; requires loyalty to Constitution, 122; and international law, 229n*7*; Constitution, 230n*15*; bans subversion, 232n*25*; protects state, 232n-*25*; protects officials, 233n*26*; bans propaganda against people, 233n*28*; bans propaganda causing unrest, 236n-*48*, 237n*49*; bans war propaganda, 238n*49*; restricts doctrines, 239n*52*; controls media, 241n*65*, 241n*70*; censorship in, 242n*82*

—Bavaria: and freedom of speech, 119; bans propaganda against people, 233n-*28*; permits emigration, 248n*21*

—Berlin, bans propaganda causing unrest, 237n*49*

—Hesse: bans war propaganda, 238n*49*; restricts doctrines, 239n*52*

—Württemberg-Hohenzollern: on international law, 229n*7*; bans propaganda causing unrest, 237n*49*; bans war propaganda, 238n*49*

—and United States, treaty of *1952* permitting U.S. radio propaganda, 107

Gillars v. U.S., 168, 240n*53*, 240n*58*, 240n*60*

Glavlit, 214n*25*

Goebbels, Josef, 159

Gosnell, Harold, 211n*1*

Government communiqués, broadcast of, 119, 147–48

Great Britain: reaction to French propaganda, 6; and protests, 7, 9, 174, 175, 176, 182, 249–50n*20*; foreign-language broadcasts, 9, 35; reaction to Russian broadcasts, 9; cooperation with France, 20; attitude on propaganda, 34, 35, 182; Ministry of Information, 34; propaganda activities of, 34–46; propaganda in World War I, 34; propaganda between wars, 35; propaganda agencies of, 35–36, 44–45; activities of Comintern in, 51–52; and treaties, 65,66; condemns false news, 73, 219n*34*; bans incitement to mutiny, 124; bans hatred propaganda, 125; protects religion, 125; protects sovereigns, 128, 129; and propaganda against foreign states, 129–30, 235n*45*; bans breach of the peace, 131; protects its international relations, 133; and anarchists, 136; and treason, 138, 167–68, 240n*60*; controls media, 143, 241n*68*, 241n*70*, 246n*119*; and state secrets, 146; and press offenses, 152; restricts aliens, 155, 167–168; restricts foreign films, 157–58; and crimes abroad, 166; and objective territorial principle, 166; rejects passive personality principle, 166; and jurisdiction over citizens, 167; protects aliens, 168; and jurisdiction over aliens abroad, 170, 171; accused of war propaganda, 179; bans Tass monitoring service, 182; bans foreign institutes, 183; recognizes RSFSR, 192; recognizes USSR, 193–94; protests commercial broadcasts, 197; condemns war propaganda, 219n*34*;

INDEX

Bill of Rights, 231n*15*; protects state, 232n*25*; bans subversion, 233n*25*; protects officials, 233n*26*; bans propaganda against people, 234n*28*; bans propaganda causing unrest, 237n*48*, 238n*49*; restricts doctrines, 239n*52*; bans propaganda favoring foreign states, 240n*53*; censorship in, 242n*82*; and state secrets, 243n*82*; controls disseminator, 244n*92*, 245n*92*; controls radio, 246n*119*

—and Czechoslovakia: treaty of *1947* on cultural exchanges, 104; denounced, 183

—and Denmark, treaty on subversives, 89

—and Iraq and Turkey, treaty of *1926* banning subversive propaganda, 226n-*138*

—and Italy, treaty of *1938* banning harmful propaganda, 93

—and Norway, treaty of *1948* on cultural exchanges, 105

—and RSFSR: treaty of *1921* banning propaganda and subversion, 90, 91; notes of *1923* banning subversion, 91

—and Thailand, treaty of *1940* banning intervention, 93

—and USSR: notes of *1924* banning propaganda, 90; notes of *1929* banning subversion, 91; notes banning intervention, 193

Greece: and freedom of speech, 116; protects Crown, 117; protects foreign states, 127, 235n*45*; outlaws Communist party, 135; access to information in, 146; controls disseminator, 149, 244n*92*; restricts aliens, 149, 243n*92*; and listening to Communist broadcasts, 161; reaction to Soviet protest, 176–77; on jurisdiction over sovereigns, 229n*6*; Constitution, 230n*15*; bans subversion, 232n*25*; protects officials, 233n*26*; bans propaganda against people, 233n*28*; bans propaganda causing unrest, 236n-*48*; restricts doctrines, 239n*52*; bans propaganda favoring foreign states, 239n*53*; controls media, 241n*65*; censorship in, 242n*82*; recognizes USSR, 254n*99*

—and Lebanon: treaty of *1948* banning subversion, 95; permitting educational activities, 107

—and Serbia, treaties of *1867* and *1868* advocating subversive propaganda, 102

—and Turkey: treaty of *1938* banning subversion, 94; treaty of *1930* banning subversive propaganda, 226n*138*

Greek and Turkish Populations, Exchange of, case, 65

Gregory XV, Pope, 5

Griffis, Stanton, 197

Groesz, Archbishop Josef (of Hungary), 186

Guam, bans treason, 240n*60*

Guatemala: and freedom of speech, 116, 119; protects foreign states, 127, 235n-*45*; bans breach of peace, 131; forbids justifying crime, 132; censorship in, 145; controls media, 149, 241n*65*, 241n*70*; controls radio, 149; restricts aliens, 149, 243n*92*; Constitution, 230n-*15*; protects state, 232n*25*; bans propaganda causing unrest, 236n*48*, 237n*49*; right of reply in, 242n*82*; and conformity, 243n*82*; controls disseminator, 244n-*92*

Gurdyal Singh (Sirdar) v. Faridkote (Rajah), 170

Haiti: and freedom of speech, 116; censorship in, 145, 242n*82*; and press offenses, 151; Constitution, 230n*15*; bans propaganda favoring foreign states, 239n*53*; bans treason, 240n*60*; controls media, 241n*65*; controls disseminator, 244n*92*

Hall, William E.: on hostile propaganda, 57; on responsibility for private propaganda, 59

Halleck, Henry Wager, on hostile propaganda, 57

Halsbury, Lord, on jurisdiction of courts, 173

Hargrave, John G., defines propaganda, 11

Hart, B. H. Liddell, 11

Hatch Act (U.S.), 135

Heads of states, protected against propaganda, 126, 127

Heathfield v. Chilton, 229n*6*

Hejaz, recognizes USSR, 254n*99*

Henderson, Edgar H., defines propaganda, 10, 11

Herbette (French ambassador), 195

Herring, E. Pendleton, 10, 11

High Frequency Broadcasting Conference (Mexico City, *1948–1949*), allocates high frequency bands, 84

Hilton v. Guyot, 228n*1*

Hitler, Adolf: and international propaganda, 7; litigation in Netherlands, 234n*35*; mentioned, 20

Holmes, Oliver Wendell, 120

Honduras: and freedom of speech, 116; on citizens aiding foreign governments, 168; Constitution, 230n*15*; permits emigration, 248n*21*

Hong Kong, access to information in, 146

Hoop, The, on consensus of law, 111

Hoover, Herbert, on U.S. aid abroad, 197

Howe, Quincy, 157

Hungarian Cultural Institute, banned in London, 183

Hungary: Communist propaganda after World War I, 7; and listening to foreign broadcasts, 40, 160; and freedom of speech, 115; forbids propaganda against democracy, 123; protects national honor, 123; and war crimes, 132; operates film industry, 141; bans Hungarian-language newspaper, 158; bans rumors, 161; and radio sets, 162, 163; protests Radio Free Europe activity, 178; accuses British Council of espionage, 182; bans British Institute, 182–83; bans USIS, 186; protests to United States, 186, 198; expels correspondent, 196; and radio dispute with U.S., 198; arrests Robert Vogeler, 198; Constitution, 230n*15*; bans subversion, 232n*25*; bans propaganda against people, 233n-*28*; bans propaganda causing unrest, 236n*48*, 237n*49*; restricts doctrines, 239n*52*; and treason, 240n*60*; recognizes USSR, 254n*99*

—and Poland, treaty of *1948* on cultural exchanges, 105

—and USSR: treaty of *1948* banning intervention, 225n*128*; on cultural cooperation, 228n*189*

—and Yugoslavia: treaty of *1947* on cultural exchanges, 105; treaty of *1947* on friendly propaganda, 105

Hyde, Charles Cheney: and hostile propaganda, 57; on responsibility for private propaganda, 58; on control of radio waves, 78; on protection of foreign diplomats, 126; on state responsibility for press, 175; on wartime propaganda, 203; mentioned, 195

Iceland: and freedom of speech, 116; commercial radio in, 197; Constitution, 230n*15*; bans propaganda causing unrest, 236n*48*

India: and freedom of speech, 116, 117; protects state authority, 122; protects its foreign relations, 133; institutes closed in Iran, 181; Constitution, 230n-*15*; bans subversion, 232n*25*; protects state, 232n*25*; protects officials, 233n*26*; bans propaganda against people, 233n-*28*; bans propaganda causing unrest, 236n*48*, 237n*49*; censorship in, 242n*82*; controls disseminator, 244n*92*

—West Bengal: bans subversive opinion, 122; forbids prejudicial reports, 123

—and Pakistan, treaty of *1948* banning inflammatory propaganda, 93, 94–95

Indochina, outlaws Communist party, 135

Indonesia: and freedom of speech, 115; outlaws Communist party, 135; censorship in, 145; Constitution, 230n*15*; bans propaganda causing unrest, 236n-*48*; permits emigration, 248n*21*

—and Netherlands, treaty of *1949* on freedoms, 107

Inflammatory propaganda, banned by treaty, 93, 94–95

Information, access to, 98, 106–7, 119, 145–46. *See also* News

Information, Ministry of (Great Britain), 35

Information and Education, Office of (U.S.), 30

Information services, detrimental, forbidden, 137. *See also* individual states

Institute for Propaganda Analysis, 11

Institute of International Education, 30

Institute of International Law, on freedom of air, 78

Insults: to state, forbidden, 123; to officials, 124, 126–27, 128, 129; to convictions, banned, 125; to foreign states, 126

Inter-American Affairs, Coordinator of (U.S.), 23

Inter-American Affairs, Office of (U.S.), abolished, 23

Inter-American Association for Radio Broadcasting, 101

Inter-American Conference for the Maintenance of Continental Peace and Security, 76

Inter-American Conference for the Maintenance of Peace (Buenos Aires, *1936*), 83, 101

Inter-American Conference on Problems of War and Peace (Mexico City, *1945*), recommends freedom of expression, 98

Inter-American Neutrality Committee (Rio de Janeiro, *1940*), 84

Inter-American Radiocommunication Convention: (Havana, *1937*), on freedom of radio waves, 78–79; on cultural broadcasting, 101; (Rio de Janeiro, *1945*), on free circulation of news, 101

Inter-American Treaty of Reciprocal Assistance, 76

Internal Security Act (U.S.), 154

International Book Publishing Corp., 47, 48

International Broadcasting Union: on radio propaganda, 79–80; intervenes between Germany and Poland, 95; advocates friendly propaganda, 100; mentioned, 220n66

International Civil Aviation Convention (Chicago, *1944*), on air sovereignty, 88–89

International Commission of American Jurists, on recognition, 188

International Conference of American States (Montevideo, *1933*): bans intervention, 83; on positive radio propaganda, 101

International Convention Concerning the Use of Broadcasting in the Cause of Peace, 80–82, 83–84, 100, 200–1

International Court of Justice: on elements of international law, 55; on treaties, 63; and general principles of law, 110; mentioned, 56, 109

International crime, 205

International High Frequency Radio Conference (Florence, *1950*), allocates high frequencies, 85

International Information, Office of (U.S.), 25

International Information, U.S. Advisory Commission on, 25

International Information Administration, 27, 28

International Information and Cultural Affairs, Office of (U.S.), 24

International Information and Cultural Exchange, Office of (U.S.), 24

International Labor Organization, 67, 98

International law: elements of, 55; and propaganda, 55, 60–61, 108, 201, 205–6; need for monographs on, 56–57; treaties as source of, 62, 63, 87; and individuals, 64; and general principles of law, 109–12, 204; sources of, 109, 110; and constitutions, 110; and municipal law, 110, 112; and Nuremberg Trials, 205–6

International Law, 203

International Law Commission, 73, 206

International relations, protected, 118, 133

International Telecommunication Convention: (Atlantic City *1947*), on intercepting telegrams, 77; limits radio waves, 79; allocates broadcasting channels, 84; bans jamming, 86, 88; contravention of, 87; (Buenos Aires, *1952*), 77; (Cairo, *1938*), bans radio interference, 79, 223n91; (Madrid, *1932*), bans radio interference, 79; mentioned, 78

International Telecommunication Union, 85. *See also* International Telecommunication Convention

Internationale Echo, 45

Inter-Parliamentary Union, on propaganda and peace, 67

Intervention: through propaganda attacked, 73, 76, 83, 91–94, 193, 225n112; 225n128; defined, 202

Intourist (USSR), 49

Iran: and freedom of speech, 116; protects friendly sovereigns, 127; protects foreign officials, 128; protects its foreign prestige, 133; operates wire service, 141; and foreign institutes, 143, 181; and censorship, 145; and responsibility for press offenses, 151; and foreign publication ban, 156; Constitution, 230n15; bans subversion, 232–33n25; bans propaganda against people, 233n28; protects foreign states, 235n45; bans propaganda causing unrest, 236n48, 237n49; controls media, 241n65, 241n70, 246n119; controls disseminator, 244n92. *See also* Persia

—and Afghanistan, Iraq, and Turkey, treaty of *1937* on nonintervention, 92–93, 94

Iraq: and freedom of speech, 116, 119; restricts aliens, 119; and censorship, 145, 242n82; Constitution, 230n15; bans subversion, 233n25

—and Afghanistan, Iran, and Turkey, treaty of *1937* on nonintervention, 92–93, 94

—and Great Britain and Turkey, treaty of *1926* banning subversive propaganda, 226n138

—and Saudi Arabia, treaty of *1936* banning subversive propaganda, 92, 226n138

—and Transjordan, treaty of *1947* banning subversion, 94

—and Turkey, treaty of *1946* banning intervention and subversion, 93

Ireland: and freedom of speech, 116, 117, 119; controls public opinion, 117, 158; commercial radio in, 197; Constitution, 230n*15*; bans propaganda against people, 233n*28*; controls radio signals, 246-n*119*

—and United States: treaty of *1950* banning political activities, 95; on access to information, 106–7

Israel: and freedom of speech, 115; and genocide, 125, 166; protects foreign states, 129, 235n*45*; forbids subversion, 135; and censorship, 145; access to information in, 146; excludes foreign publications, 156; and offenses committed abroad, 166; no constitution in, 230n*15*; protects state, 232n*25*; bans propaganda against people, 233n*28*; bans propaganda causing unrest, 236n*48*; restricts doctrines, 239n*52*

Italy: and foreign broadcasts, 8, 9; and freedom of speech, 116; protects heads of state, 126–27; protects foreign sovereigns, 127; bans war propaganda, 134, 238n*49*; and film industry, 141; controls media, 143, 163, 241n*70*; access to information in, 146; controls disseminator, 149, 244n*92*; restricts aliens, 149, 171, 243n*92*; and members of Parliament, 151; and responsibility for press offenses, 151; registers radio owners, 163; and jurisdiction, 165, 171; protests to France, 175; recognizes RSFSR, 192; propaganda of, 203; Constitution, 230n*15*; protects state, 232n*25*; bans subversion, 233n*25*; protects officials, 233n*26*; protects foreign states, 235n*45*; bans propaganda causing unrest, 236n*48*; restricts doctrines, 239n*52*; right of reply in, 242n*82*; recognizes USSR, 254n*99*

—and Belgium, treaty of *1948* on cultural exchanges, 104

—and Germany, treaty of *1938* banning biased publications, 95

—and Great Britain, treaty of *1938* banning harmful propaganda, 93

—and RSFSR, treaty of *1921* banning propaganda and subversion, 90, 91

—and United States, treaty of *1948* on freedom of the press, 106

—and Yugoslavia, treaty of *1937* banning subversion, 92, 226n*138*

Italy (Gentini) v. Venezuela, 112

Jackson, Justice Robert H., 205

Jaffe, Louis L., on recognition of states, 189

Jamming: by USSR, 47, 85, 87, 88, 223n-*94*; banned, 79, 86; discussed, 85–88; countermeasures to, 87; mentioned, 197

Japan: U.S. view of, 19; and freedom of speech, 115; protects foreign sovereigns, 127–28; protects its international relations, 133; bans war propaganda, 134, 238n*49*; access to information in, 146; controls radio listening, 163; protests to USSR, 175; Constitution, 230n*15*; bans subversion, 233n*25*; protects foreign states, 235n*45*; bans propaganda causing unrest, 236n*48*, 237n*49*; right of reply in, 242n*82*; permits emigration, 248n*21*; recognizes USSR, 254n*99*

—and USSR, treaty of *1925* banning subversion, 91

Jessup, Phillip: on recognition of states, 189; on intervention, 202

Jones v. U.S., 252n*68*

Jordan: and freedom of speech, 116, 119; restricts aliens, 119; education in, 142; and censorship, 145; Constitution, 230n-*15*; controls media, 241n*65*, 246n*119*; restricts listening to foreign broadcasts, 245n*104*. *See also* Transjordan

Journalists, International Federation of, creates Tribunal of Honor, 67, 68

Journalists, International Organization of, recommends court of honor, 68

Joyce, William, 138, 168

Joyce v. Director of Public Prosecution, 168, 240n*57*, 240n*60*, 247n*18*

Jurisdiction: of Nuremberg Tribunal, 64; types of, 164, 165, 166, 170; over aliens abroad, 165, 170, 171, 205; over citizens abroad, 167; over illegal immigrants, 171; over foreign states, 172–73, 229n*6*

Kellogg-Briand Pact, 63, 195

Kelly v. Hoffman, 152, 244n*92*

Kelsen, Hans, on human rights, 97

Kennerly v. Hennessy, 236n*46*, 237n*48*

Kenney, General George C., 178

King v. Antonelli and Barberi, 235n*37*, 235n*40*, 236n*45*

King v. Gordon, 235n*45*, 238n*49*

King v. Peltier, 128, 235n*45*
King v. Vint, 235n*45*, 238n*49*
Kleen, Richard, 58
Korea, People's Republic of: and freedom of speech, 115, 119; restricts aliens, 119; Constitution, 230n*15*
Korea, Republic of: and freedom of speech, 116; bans revolutionary propaganda, 122; outlaws Communist party, 135; Constitution, 230n*15*; protects state, 232n*25*; bans propaganda against people, 233n*28*; controls media, 241n*65*
Korean War, 26
Krajina v. Tass Agency, 215n*30*, 241n*65*
Kun, Béla, 7
Kuwait: and freedom of speech, 115; no constitution in, 230n*15*
—and Saudi Arabia, treaty of *1942* banning subversion, 94

Lambert, Richard S., 212
Lang, Robert, 32
Laos: and freedom of speech, 116, 119; restricts aliens, 119; Constitution, 230n*15*
Larsen, Arthur, 28
Lasswell, Harold D.: defines propaganda, 10, 11; on propaganda and social order, 17
Latin America, propaganda in boundary disputes, 8
Latvia: protests to Russia, 175; recognizes RSFSR, 253n*83*. *See also* USSR
—and RSFSR, treaty of *1920* banning subversive propaganda, 225n*129*
Lauterpacht, H.: on hostile propaganda, 57, 203; on responsibility for private propaganda, 60; on air sovereignty, 78; on intervention, 202
Law. *See* Municipal law
Leaflets, propaganda by, 88
League of Nations: Covenant, 17; and propaganda, 56, 69, 71, 200, 201; press conference on propaganda, 67; and false news, 69; and war propaganda, 70; bans political terrorism, 70
Lebanon: and freedom of speech, 116; outlaws Communist party, 135; controls associations, 143; controls disseminator, 143, 244n*92*; controls media, 143, 241n*65*, 241n*68*, 241n*70*, 246n*119*; and censorship, 145; bars correspondents, 197; Constitution, 230n*15*; bans subversion, 233n*25*; right of reply in, 242n*82*

—and Greece: treaty of *1948* banning subversion, 95; permitting educational activities, 107
Lee, Alfred McClung, 11
Lemmon, Walter S., 31
Lenin, Nikolai, 7, 69, 102, 191
Letters from America Campaign, 31
Leubuscher v. Commissioner of Internal Revenue, 213n*10*
Libel: diplomats protected from, 126; heads of state protected against, 128; and breach of peace, 132; jurisdiction when committed abroad, 165; and propaganda, 204
Liberia: and freedom of speech, 116; Constitution, 230n*15*
Libya: and freedom of speech, 116; Constitution, 230n*15*
—Fezzan, admits foreign publications, 157
Liebknecht, Karl, 102
Liechtenstein: and freedom of speech, 116; protects state authority, 124; protects heads of states, 128; protects foreign states, 129, 235n*45*; restricts foreign information services, 137; and aliens, 155; Constitution, 230n*15*; protects state, 232n*25*; bans subversion, 233n*25*; bans propaganda causing unrest, 236n*48*, 237n*49*; restricts doctrines, 239n*52*; bans propaganda favoring foreign states, 239n*53*; controls media, 241n*68*; and conformity, 243n*82*; controls disseminator, 244n*92*
Liszt, Franz von, 58
Literary Gazette, 49
Lithuania: and Soviet propaganda, 174; recognizes RSFSR, 253n*83*. *See also* USSR
—and Poland, treaty of *1938* banning unfavorable propaganda, 95
—and RSFSR, treaty of *1920* banning subversive propaganda, 225n*129*
Litvinov, Maxim, 194, 195
Lord Haw-Haw. *See* William Joyce
Louter, Jan de, on responsibility for private propaganda, 59
Loyalty, enforced, 122, 169
Lumley, F. E., defines propaganda, 11
Luxembourg: and freedom of speech, 116; and freedom of assembly, 143; and press offenses, 151; Constitution, 230n*15*; bans propaganda against people, 233n*28*; bans propaganda causing unrest, 236n*48*, 237n*49*; bans war propa-

ganda, 238n49; controls media, 241n70; controls disseminator, 244n92

MacDonald, Lord, 34
Maine, Sir Henry Sumner, 111
Majka v. Palmer, 170–71
Malaya: outlaws Communist party, 135; and censorship, 145
Manning, William O., on anarchy, 57
Mannzen, Karl, 58
Marshall, George C., 24
Martens, F. F., 57
Marxist-Leninist doctrine, 53
Medical Chronicle, 50
Meunier, Re, 238n52
Mexico: and treaties, 65; and freedom of speech, 116; and war propaganda, 118, 219n34, 238n49; bans religious propaganda, 125, 150; protects foreign states, 128, 235n45; controls media, 143, 241n65; access to information in, 146; and conformity, 147, 243n82; restricts aliens, 150, 243n92; and immunity of Parliament, 151; and press offenses, 151; and jurisdiction, 165; and aiding foreign governments, 168; Constitution, 230n15; protects state, 232n25; bans subversion, 233n25; bans propaganda against people, 233n28; bans propaganda causing unrest, 236n48, 237n49; restricts doctrines, 239n52; censorship in, 242n82; controls disseminator, 244n92; recognizes USSR, 254n99
—and China, treaty of *1944* on cultural rights, 228n179
Mikolajczyk, Stanislaw, 176
Miles v. Louis Wasmer, Inc., 243n89, 244n92
Military courts, law of, 64
Molvan v. Attorney General for Palestine, 171
Monaco: and freedom of speech, 116; Constitution, 230n15
Mongolia, recognizes RSFSR, 253n83
—and RSFSR, treaty of *1921* banning subversive propaganda, 225n129
Mongolian People's Republic: and freedom of speech, 117; forbids imperialistic chauvinism, 118, 123; and treason, 138, 240n60; Constitution, 230n15
Morocco: and freedom of speech, 115; no constitution in, 230n15
Morrison, Herbert, 35
Moscow Foreign Language Publishing House, 48

Motion pictures. *See* Films
Mundt, Karl, 24, 25
Municipal law: and propaganda, 14–15, 204, 206–7; and treaties, 65; and international law, 109, 110, 111, 112; permitting propaganda, 114–20; protects states enacting it, 204. *See also* individual states
Munson, Gorham, 212
Murder, incitement to, banned, 132
Music Chronicle, 50
Musqat: and freedom of speech, 115; no constitution in Oman and, 230n15
Mussolini, Benito, 175
Mutiny, incitement to, 124
Mutual Security Agency (U.S.), 179

National Committee for a Free Europe. *See* Free Europe Committee
National honor, protected, 123
National interest, protected, 123
National law. *See* Municipal law
National unity, propaganda against, banned, 135
Nationalism: in Soviet propaganda, 53; forbidden, 118; propaganda against, forbidden, 123
Nazis: propaganda of, 8; propaganda restricted, 136, 138
Near East, broadcasts by Italy to, 9
Near East Arab Broadcasting Corporation, 37
Negotiation, in international diplomacy, 172–73
Nepal: and freedom of speech, 116; Constitution, 230n15
Netherlands: first to use short wave, 8; reaction to Soviet protest, 65, 177; and freedom of speech, 116; protects heads of friendly states, 128; access to information in, 146; and war propaganda, 219n34; Constitution, 230n15; bans propaganda against people, 234n28; and cases involving Adolf Hitler, 234–35n35; protects foreign states, 235n45
—and Belgium, treaty of *1946* on cultural exchanges, 104
—and France, treaty of *1947* on cultural exchanges, 105
—and Indonesia, treaty of *1949* on freedoms, 107
Neue Auslese, 45
New Times, 48
New York Times: correspondent expelled, 196; mentioned, 32

New Zealand: protects heads of states, 128; controls media, 143; Constitution Act, 230n*15*; protects state, 232n*25*; bans subversion, 233n*25*; protects foreign states, 235n*45*; restricts doctrines, 239n*52*; bans propaganda favoring foreign states, 239n*53*

News: as propaganda tool, 17; broadcasts called propaganda, 19, 153; accurate, 68, 83; false, condemned, 68–73, 200, 219n*34*; free circulation of, 99, 101; disturbing peace banned, 131, 132; by radio not publishable, 161

News, 48

News agencies, controlled, 140–41

News from Behind the Iron Curtain, 180

Newspapers. *See* Press

Newsreels. *See* Films

Newsweek: banned in Sudan, 156; USSR protests article in, 178

Nicaragua: and freedom of speech, 116; and racial propaganda, 122; outlaws communism and fascism, 136, 239n*52*; and censorship, 145; and aiding foreign governments, 168, 169; Constitution, 230n*15*; protects state, 232n*25*; bans subversion, 233n*25*; protects officials, 233n*26*; bans propaganda causing unrest, 237n*49*; bans war propaganda, 238n*49*; controls disseminator, 244n*92*

Nicholas, H. G., 18

Nicolson, Harold, 7

Nikitchenko, I. T., 255n*20*

Non-recognition. *See* Recognition

North American Regional Broadcasting Agreement (Havana, *1937*), regulates radio waves, 79

North Atlantic Fisheries case, 64

North Atlantic Treaty Organization, 179

Northcliffe, Lord, 35

Norway: and freedom of speech, 116; protects heads of states, 128; bans incitement to breach of law, 132; access to information in, 146; and aiding foreign governments, 169; recognizes RSFSR, 192; Constitution, 230n*15*; bans propaganda against people, 234n*28*; protects foreign states, 235n*45*; bans propaganda causing unrest, 236n*48*, 237n*49*; right of reply in, 242n*82*; recognizes USSR, 254n*99*

—and Belgium, treaty of *1948* on cultural exchanges, 104

—and Great Britain, treaty of *1948* on cultural exchanges, 105

—and RSFSR, treaty of *1921* banning propaganda, 90, 225n*119*

—and USSR, treaty of *1949* banning speech across border, 95

November Decree, 6

Nuremberg Trials: jurisdiction of, 64; and propaganda, 205; as precedent, 205, 255n*18*; and international law, 206

"Objective territorial principle," 165, 166

Offenses Against the Person Act (Great Britain), 235n*45*

Office of War Information, 23

Official Secrets Act (Great Britain), 146

Officials: propaganda against, 124, 126–31; propaganda by, 124; criticism of foreign, banned, 128–29

OGIZ, 48

Oman and Musqat: and freedom of speech, 115; no constitution in, 230n*15*

Oppenheim, L.: on hostile propaganda, 57, 203; on responsibility for private propaganda, 59–60; on words and deeds, 60; on negotiation, 173; on intervention, 202

Organization of American States: on intervention, 76; on cultural exchanges, 100

Organizations. *See* Associations

Overseas Information Services (Official) Committee (Great Britain), 36

Pakistan: and freedom of speech, 116, 117, 119, 120; protects courts, 117; protects its international relations, 118; restricts aliens, 119; protects public interest, 123; Constitution, 230n*15*; protects state, 232n*25*; bans subversion, 233n*25*; bans propaganda against people, 234n*28*; bans propaganda causing unrest, 236n*48*, 237n*49*

—and India, treaty of *1948* banning inflammatory propaganda, 93, 94–95

Palestine: jurisdiction over illegal immigrants, 171; mentioned, 197

Pan-American Convention (Montevideo, *1933*), 75

Pan-Slavic Movement, 50–51

Panama: and freedom of speech, 116; bans propaganda causing unrest, 131, 236n*48*, 237n*49*; restricts aliens, 155; Constitution, 230n*15*; bans war propaganda, 238n*49*; restricts doctrines, 239n*52*; controls media, 241n*65*; and conformity, 243n*82*; controls disseminator, 244n*92*

PAP (Polish press agency), 141

Paraguay: in propaganda struggle with Bolivia, 18; and treaties, 65; and freedom of speech, 116, 117; and race hatred, 117; forbids press anonymity, 119, 153; protects state security, 133; forbids propaganda favoring enemy, 137; and treason, 139, 240n*60*; and censorship, 145; and jurisdiction over aliens, 171; Constitution, 230n*15*; bans propaganda against people, 234n*28*; bans propaganda causing unrest, 237n-*49*; bans war propaganda, 238n*49*; bans propaganda favoring foreign states, 239n*53*; controls media, 241n*68*; controls disseminator, 244n*92*
—and Brazil, treaty of *1941* on cultural exchanges, 103

Parhaat, 45

Parliamentary immunity, 151

PARS (Iranian press agency), 141

Partisans of Peace, 51

Passive personality principle of jurisdiction, 164, 165, 166, 170

Peace: propaganda for, by USSR, 51; propaganda against, banned, 73; incitement to breach of, 131–32; news disturbing, banned, 132; and international propaganda, 202

Pedagogical Chronicle, 50

People, propaganda against, banned, 124–26

People-to-People program, 29, 30

People v. Eastman, 234n*28*, 236n*47*, 237n-*48*

Periodicals: published by U.S., 24, 29; published by Great Britain, 43, 45, 46; published by USSR, 48, 49, 50, 52, 156, 187

Permanent Court of Arbitration, 64, 112

Permanent Court of International Justice, 65, 110, 165

Permissive treaties on propaganda, 96–107

Persia, recognizes RSFSR, 253n*83*. *See also* Iran
—and RSFSR: treaty of *1921* banning religious propaganda, 91–92; banning subversive propaganda, 225n*129*
—and Turkey, treaty of *1932* banning subversive propaganda, 226n*138*
—and USSR, treaty of *1927* banning subversive propaganda, 90–91, 225n*129*

Peru: and freedom of speech, 116; and subversive propaganda, 122, 233n*25*; protects national unity, 135; and press offenses, 151; and press anonymity, 153; restricts correspondents, 154; Constitution, 230n*15*; protects state, 232n*25*; protects foreign states, 235n*45*; bans propaganda causing unrest, 236n*48*, 237n*49*; restricts doctrines, 239n*52*; bans propaganda favoring foreign states, 239n*53*; censorship in, 242n*82*; right of reply in, 242n*82*; controls disseminator, 244n*92*

Philippines: and freedom of speech, 115, 119; and censorship, 145; Constitution, 230n*15*
—and China, treaty of *1947* on cultural relations, 228n*179*

Phillimore, Sir Robert: on hostile governments, 57; on responsibility for private propaganda, 60

Phillips, Joseph B., on BBC, 39

Phillips v. Eyre, 247n*9*

Photo Review, 24

Pillet, Antoine, 57

Poland: and protests, 7, 19, 176, 178, 182, 249–50n*20*; and propaganda in France, 8; and war propaganda, 70, 238n*49*; and right of reply, 73; defends jamming, 86; and freedom of speech, 117; and race hatred, 117; controls media, 141; controls disseminator, 149, 244n-*92*; restricts aliens, 149, 155, 243n*92*; restricts foreign publications, 157, 158; and listening to foreign broadcasts, 161; and jurisdiction over aliens, 171; bans USIS, 184–85; and British and American cultural activities, 197; Constitution, 230n*15*; protects state, 232n*25*; bans propaganda against people, 234n-*28*; restricts doctrines, 239n*52*; and state secrets, 243n*82*; recognizes RSFSR, 253n*83*
—and Bulgaria, treaty of *1947* on cultural exchanges, 105
—and Czechoslovakia, treaty of *1947* on cultural exchanges, 105
—and Danzig, treaty of *1922* on subversive propaganda, 226n*138*
—and France, treaty of *1947* on cultural exchanges, 105
—and Hungary, treaty of *1948* on cultural exchanges, 105
—and Lithuania, treaty of *1938* banning unfavorable propaganda, 95

—and Romania: treaty of *1948* on cultural exchanges, 105; treaty of *1949* on cooperation, 105

—and RSFSR, treaty of *1921* banning propaganda, 90, 91

—and USSR, treaty of *1945* of cooperation and nonintervention, 92

—and Yugoslavia, treaty of *1946* on cultural exchanges, 105

Polish Research and Information Service, 185

Politburo, 46

Political activities, treaties ban, 95

Political parties: responsibility for propaganda of, 58; propaganda favoring, 134–36; internationally organized, banned, 136

Polskie Radio, agreement with Reichsrundfunkgesellschaft, 95, 102

Portugal: and freedom of speech, 116, 117–18, 119; protects its independence, 117; controls public opinion, 117–18, 158–59; and government communiqués, 119, 148; and right of reply in, 119, 242–43n82; restricts aliens, 119; bans subversion, 122, 233n25; protects national honor, 123; outlaws Communist party, 135; and censorship, 145; Constitution, 230n15; bans war propaganda, 238n49; controls radio, 246n119

Powell, Norman John: defines propaganda, 10; on efficacy of propaganda, 18

Pradier-Fodéré, Paul L. E., 57, 58

Prejudicial reports, banned, 123

Press: charged with lies, 19; Western, exploited by USSR, 51; and international misunderstanding, 66–67; importation restricted, 95, 155–58; treaty on freedom of, 106; and citizenship, 118, 149–50; anonymity in publishing, 119, 153; disrespect in, forbidden, 123; control of, 140; foreign subsidy of, 143; bond forbidden, 143; censorship of, 144–45; conformity in, 146; responsibility for, assigned, 150–53; correspondents restricted, 154, 155; responsibility of importer, 158; government responsibility for, 175; correspondents expelled, 180–81, 196–97

Press agencies, controlled, 140–41

Press Associations, International Union of, on false news, 68

Press-Non-Attack-Pact, 95

Preuss, Lawrence: on hostile propaganda, 57; on responsibility for private propaganda, 60, 130; on recognition of USSR, 194

Printed matter, 246n119

Private Cooperation, Office of (U.S.), 29

Private propaganda: agencies in U.S., 30–34; responsibility for, 58, 59, 60; controlled by treaty, 92

Propaganda: meanings of, 3; change in attitude toward, 4; uses of, 4; defined, 5, 10, 11, 12, 112, 113, 199; origin of, 5; as instrument of foreign policy, 7; and news, 13, 17, 19, 153; legal definition of, 13–16, 113, 199; methods of, 13, 17, 21–22; of word and deed distinguished, 18, 60; effectiveness compared, 54; expenditures compared, 54; encouraged, 96–107

Propaganda and Agitation, Department of. *See* Agitprop

Protective principle of jurisdiction, 164, 170

Protest: discussed, 173–80; propaganda value of, 173–74; types of, 173; reaction to, 174; change in attitude toward, 175–76, 179–80; and propaganda, 203

Psychological Operations Coordinating Committee (U.S.), 27

Psychological Strategy Board (U.S.), 27

Psychological warfare, 57

Public interest, protected, 123

Public opinion, controlled, 117–18, 158–59

Public Prosecutor v. B., 234n35

Public Prosecutor v. G., 234n35

Publication. *See* Books; Periodicals; Press; Printed matter

Qatar: and freedom of speech, 115; no constitution in, 230n15

Queen v. Most, 235n37, 236n45

Quirin, Ex parte, on international law and individuals, 64

R. v. Banks, 237n48

R. v. Casement, 240n53, 240n55, 240n60, 247n16

R. v. Charnock, King and Keyes, 240n56, 240n60

R. v. Clerk, 243n86, 244n92

R. v. Cobbett, 233n25

R. v. Coombes, 166, 247n11

R. v. Demarny, 247n13

R. v. Ellis, 247n11

R. v. Gathercole, 234n28
R. v. Godfrey, 247n11
R. v. Harvey, 239n52
R. v. Holmes, 247n11
R. v. Krause, 237n48
R. v. Lambert and Perry, 233n25
R. v. Lynch, 240n55
R. v. M'Hugh, 232n25, 234n28, 237n48
R. v. Nillins, 247n11
R. v. Ransford, 237n48
R. v. Sawyer, 247n16
R. v. Tutchin, 233n25, 233n26
R. v. Wilkes, 239n52
Race hatred: punishable, 117; propaganda to incite, 124–25
Racial propaganda, forbidden, 122
Radio: in international propaganda, 6, 7; short wave first used, 8; reception, control of, 40, 155–63; broadcasting hours compared, 47; Soviet programs relayed, 53; programs of People's Republic of China, 54; treaties on control of propaganda by, 77–88; used in cause of peace, 80–84, 200–1; broadcasting channels distributed, 84–85, 222n84, 222n87; and friendly propaganda, 100–1; propaganda permitted by treaty, 107; broadcasts endangering international relations forbidden, 133; under government control, 139–40; government communiqués on, 147–48; station ownership restricted, 149; responsibility for offenses on, 152–53; news not publishable, 161; and license fees, 162–63; importation controlled, 163; telephonic, 163; anti-Fascist station closed, 175; commercial, 197; Hungary-U.S. dispute over channels, 198
Radio España Independiente, 54
Radio Free Asia, 31, 33
Radio Free Europe: activities of, 32; rights in Germany, 32, 181; Hungarian listening to, 40; and British Council compared, 44; attacked by Poland, 86; freedom balloons, 88; Czech listening to, 160; activities protested, 178; attacked by Czechoslovakia, 250n26; mentioned, 31, 53. *See also* Free Europe Committee
Radio Free Greece, 54
Radio Free Japan, 54
Radio in American Sector. *See* RIAS
Radio jamming. *See* Jamming
Radio Liberation, 31, 33, 34
Radio Luxembourg, 31

Radio Moscow, Hungarian listening to, 40
Radio Nacional, attacked by Poland, 86
Radio Peking, 54
Radio Vilnius (Lithuania), 53
Radio waves, right to, 78
Radiodifusion Française, attacked by Poland, 87
Radulesco, Jean, on propaganda in international law, 60
Rakovski, Christian, 51
Rebellion, incitement to, forbidden, 129
Recognition: discussion of, 188–95; not conditional, 191; Soviet attitude toward, 195
Redslob, Robert, 57, 58
Refugees: propaganda by, banned, 130–31; and responsibility of ex-citizen, 170; hostile propaganda by, 174, 178, 180
Reichsrundfunkgesellschaft, agreement with Polskie Radio, 95, 102
Reith, Sir John, 249n20
Religion: propaganda of, banned, 91–92; incitement to hatred of, banned, 124–25; orders of, restricted, 125–26; propaganda through, banned, 125; protected, 125; aliens banned from ministry of, 150
Reports, prejudicial, banned, 123
Reprisal, 190, 196, 204
Republic of China v. Merchants' Fire Assurance Corp., 252n68
Responsibility: for press offenses, 143, 150–53, 158, 175; for radio offenses, 152–53; of cable companies, 153
Restriction, diplomatic, 180–88
Retortion, 187–88, 190, 196
Reuters, and government connections, 214n23
Revolutionary propaganda: by Communists, 8, 90; agreements endorsing, 102; banned, 122, 129, 130, 135
RIAS (Radio in American Sector): discussed, 29–30; Hungarian listening to, 40; transmitters permitted in Germany, 107; listening by Poles, 161
Riegel, O. W.: defines propaganda, 11; on successful propaganda, 19
Right of reply, 73, 119, 147–48, 242n82
Rivier, Alphonse, 57, 58, 180
Robespierre, 6
Rockefeller Foundation, 30
Romania: on hostile propaganda, 80; and freedom of speech, 117; forbids chauvinism, 118; protects its credit, 133; controls media, 141, 246n119; and radio

listening, 162; jurisdiction over citizens abroad, 168; and disloyalty, 169; bans USIS, 185–86; arrests national employed by U.S., 186; recognizes USSR, 195; Constitution, 230n15; bans propaganda against people, 234n28; bans propaganda causing unrest, 237n49; bans war propaganda, 238n49; restricts doctrines, 239n52; and treason, 240n60; controls radio, 246n119
—and Czechoslovakia, treaty of 1947 on cultural exchanges, 105
—and Poland: treaty of 1948 on cultural exchanges, 105; treaty of 1949 on cooperation, 105
—and USSR: treaty of 1934 banning intervention, 91; treaty of 1948 banning intervention, 225n128; on cultural cooperation, 228n189
—and Yugoslavia: treaty of 1947 on cultural exchanges, 105; treaty of 1947 on friendly propaganda, 105

Roosevelt, Franklin D., initiates U.S. propaganda activities, 22; on recognition of USSR, 191, 194
Roosevelt-Litvinov Agreement, 56, 175, 179
RSFSR v. Cibrario, 252n68
Ruhr, French and German propaganda in, 8
Rumors, banned, 161
Russia, treaty of 1801 with France on subversives, 89–90
Russian Indemnity case, 229n13
Russian Orthodox Church, 50, 51
Russian Soviet Federation of Socialist Republics: and crimes abroad, 167; states recognize, 192; and treason, 240n60. *See also* USSR
—and Austria, treaty of 1921 banning propaganda by diplomats, 91
—and Central Powers, treaty of 1918 banning propaganda, 90
—and Czechoslovakia, treaty of 1922 banning propaganda, 90
—and Denmark, treaty of 1923 banning propaganda by diplomats, 225n119
—and Estonia, treaty of 1920 on private propaganda, 92
—and Finland, treaty of 1922 banning subversive propaganda, 225n129
—and German Soviet Republic, treaty of 1919 endorsing Spartacist propaganda, 102
—and Germany: treaty of 1917 endorsing

revolutionary propaganda, 102; treaty of 1920 banning subversive propaganda, 225n129; treaty of 1921 banning propaganda by diplomats, 225n119
—and Great Britain: treaty of 1921 banning propaganda, 90, 91; notes of 1923 banning subversion, 91
—and Italy, treaty of 1921 banning propaganda, 90, 91
—and Latvia, treaty of 1920 banning subversive propaganda, 225n129
—and Lithuania, treaty of 1920 banning subversive propaganda, 225n129
—and Mongolia, treaty of 1921 banning subversive propaganda, 225n129
—and Norway, treaty of 1921 banning propaganda, 90, 225n119
—and Persia: treaty of 1921 banning religious propaganda, 91–92; banning subversive propaganda, 225n129
—and Poland, treaty of 1921 banning propaganda, 90, 91
—and Turkey, treaty of 1921 banning subversive propaganda, 225n129

Saar: protects state authority, 124; protects heads of states, 128; controls disseminator, 149, 244n92; restricts aliens, 149, 242n92; and press offenses, 152; protects state, 232n25; bans subversion, 233n25; protects foreign states, 235n45; bans propaganda causing unrest, 236n48; restricts doctrines, 239n52; controls media, 241n68, 246n119; right of reply in, 243n82
Sacre Congregatio de Propaganda Fide, 5
El Salvador: and freedom of speech, 116; Constitution, 230n15; bans propaganda against people, 234n28; restricts doctrines, 239n52; censorship in, 242n82; controls disseminator, 244n92
San Marino: and freedom of speech, 115; Electoral law, 230n15
Sanctions, 195–98
Sanders, Edgar, 182
Sarawak: controls media, 241n70; censorship in, 242n82
Sargeant, Howland: heads IIA, 27; heads American Committee for Liberation from Bolshevism, 34
Saudi Arabia: and freedom of speech, 115; bans U.S. correspondents, 196; Constitution, 230n15
—and Iraq, treaty of 1936 banning subversive propaganda, 92, 226n138

—and Kuwait, treaty of *1942* banning subversion, 94

Science, Education, and Art, Division of (U.S.), 23

Science in Britain, 43

Sciences in the USSR, 50

Scientific and Cultural Cooperation, Inter-Departmental Committee on (U.S.), 22, 23

Scott, John, 32

Security Council. *See* United Nations

Sei Fujii v. State: on United Nations Charter, 74; mentioned, 220n*41*

Serbia, reaction to Austro-Hungarian protest, 174

—and Austria-Hungary, treaty of *1881* banning government propaganda, 90

—and Greece, treaties of *1867* and *1868* advocating subversive propaganda, 102

Siam. *See* Thailand

Simpson v. State, 247n*10*

Singapore: and censorship, 145; protects state, 232n*25*; controls media, 246n*119*

Sino-Japanese War, 163

Slavic Committee of the USSR, 50–51

Slavyane, 51

Slovak News Agency, 141

Slovakia: wire service in, 141; mentioned, 196

Smith, H. Alexander, 25

Smith, Walter Bedell, 24, 249n*9*

Smith Act: re-examined by U.S. Supreme Court, 238n*50*; mentioned, 135

Smith-Mundt Act (U.S.), 25, 26

Smith v. Utley, 244n*92*

Solal, Lucien: on insulting foreign states, 126; on radio licensing, 163

Sorenson v. Wood, 243n*89*, 244n*92*

South African Broadcasting System, 31

South American Radio Communications Agreement (Santiago, *1940*), on accuracy, 83

South American Regional Convention on Radio Communications, renounced, 84

—(Buenos Aires, *1935*), on accuracy, 83

—(Rio de Janeiro, *1937*): on accuracy, 83; on positive radio propaganda, 101

Sovereign: protected, 117, 123, 127–29; jurisdiction over, 229n*6*

Sovfilm Movie Distributing Agency, 49

Sovfoto, 49

Soviet Anti-Fascist Youth Committee, 50

Soviet Architecture, 50

Soviet Friendship Societies, 50

Soviet Literature, 48

Soviet News, 182

Soviet Peace Committee, 50

Soviet Union, 48

Soviet Woman, 48

Soviet Women's Anti-Fascist Committee, 50

Sovinformburo, 49

Spaight, James M.: on hostile propaganda, 57; on wartime propaganda, 203

Spain: defines propaganda, 13–14; U.S. attitude toward, 20; and freedom of speech, 117; bans propaganda against state, 121, 123, 232n*25*; protects nationalism, 123; protects dignity of state, 124; protects government authority, 124; protects social class, 125; protests hostile agitation in U.S., 130; and war propaganda, 134, 238n*49*; protects national unity, 135; outlaws Communist party, 135; controls media, 141, 144, 241n*68*, 241n*70*; controls education, 143; and censorship, 144, 145, 242n*82*; jurisdiction over citizens abroad, 168; expels U.S. correspondent, 180; Constitution, 231n*15*; bans subversion, 233n*25*; protects officials, 233n*26*; bans propaganda against people, 234n*28*; bans propaganda causing unrest, 236n*48*, 237n*49*; restricts doctrines, 239n*52*; bans propaganda favoring foreign states, 239n*53*; and treason, 240n*60*; controls disseminator, 244n*92*; recognizes USSR, 254n*99*

Speech: across border forbidden, 95; freedom of, guaranteed in peace treaties, 96; international freedom of, 96; freedom of, recommended, 97, 98; freedom of, and anarchy, 114; freedom of, and responsibility, 114–15; freedom of, in world's constitutions, 115–20; freedom of, qualified in constitutions, 115–17, 155; freedom of, and abuses, 116–19; freedom of, and aliens, 118–19, 155; freedom of, and controls in weak states, 120–21; freedom of, in Belgium, 155

S.S. Lotus case, 112, 165, 246–47n*5*

Stalin, Josef, 20, 177

Stalin transmitter, 47

Stamps, and propaganda, 18

State: offenses against, forbidden, 121–24; security protected, 122, 133, 232n*25*

State, foreign: protected, 126, 127, 129–

30, 235n45; propaganda favoring, banned, 136–37, 168, 239–40n53; relaying information to, banned, 146; employment by, 169, 186; jurisdiction over, 172–73

State Literary Publishers (USSR), 48

State secrets, 146, 243n82

State v. Gardner, 132, 237n48

State v. Gibbs, 213n11

State v. Hall, 247n10

State v. Klapprott, 234n28

State v. Quinlan, 213n11

Staub v. Van Benthuysen, 244n92

Stefanopoulos, Stephanos, 176

Stevens, Leslie C., 33, 34

Stockholm Peace Petition, 51

Stowell, Ellery C.: on hostile propaganda, 57; on responsibility for private propaganda, 58

Strassheim v. Daily, 166, 247n10

Streibert, Theodore C., 28

Streicher, Julius, 206

Strupp, Karl, on responsibility for private propaganda, 216n6

Subversion: in British army, 51–52; treaties banning, 89–95, 225n129, 226n138; treaty advocating, 102; forbidden, 232n25

Subversive opinion, banned, 122

Subversive organizations, forbidden, 135

Suchov, Boris, 48

Sudan: and freedom of speech, 116; protects convictions, 125; bans U.S. magazines, 156; Constitution, 231n15; bans propaganda against people, 234n28; bans propaganda causing unrest, 237n49; controls media, 241n68

Summit Hotel Co. v. National Broadcasting Co., 243n88, 244n92

Supplements to British Book News, 43

Sussex Peerage case, 167

Sweden: and false news, 69, 219n34; and freedom of speech, 116, 119; restricts aliens, 119, 149, 150, 243n92; protects officials, 124, 233n26; protects heads of states, 128; controls media, 143, 246n119; controls disseminator, 149, 150, 158, 244n92; and press offenses, 151; forbids press anonymity, 153; importer responsible, 158; and war propaganda, 219n34; Constitution, 231n15; bans subversion, 233n25; bans propaganda against people, 234n28; protects foreign states, 235n45; bans propaganda causing unrest, 236n48, 237n49; bans prop-

aganda favoring foreign states, 239–40n53; and treason, 240n60; recognizes USSR, 254n99

Switzerland: protests Hungarian Communist propaganda, 7; and freedom of speech, 117, 119; protects state, 122, 123, 232n25; protects officials, 124, 233n26; bans incitement to boycott, 125; restricts religious orders, 125–26; protects foreign officials, 128–29; protects heads of state, 128; protects foreign states, 129, 235n45; ignores propaganda against foreign states, 130; protects international organizations, 131; and aliens, 137, 149, 174, 244n92; controls media, 143, 146–47, 241n70, 246n119; and conformity, 146–47, 243n82; controls disseminator, 149, 244n92; and press offenses, 151; and crimes abroad, 166, 168; and jurisdiction over citizens abroad, 168; expels propagandists, 174; reaction to protest, 174, 177; Constitution, 231n15; bans subversion, 233n25; bans propaganda against people, 234n28; bans propaganda causing unrest, 236n48, 237–38n49; restricts doctrines, 239n52; bans propaganda favoring foreign states, 240n53; censorship in, 242n82

Syria: and freedom of speech, 116, 119; restricts aliens, 119; and Communist party, 135; and censorship, 145, 242n82; excludes Jordanian newspapers, 156; controls public opinion, 158–59; reaction to U.S. protest, 177; Constitution, 231n15; protects state, 232n25; bans propaganda against people, 234n28; bans propaganda causing unrest, 236–37n48, 238n49; restricts doctrines, 239n52; and treason, 240n60; controls media, 241n65, 241n68, 246n119; and conformity, 243n82; right of reply in, 243n82; controls radio, 246n119

Tanganyika, controls radio, 163, 246n119

Tangier, propaganda in, 74–75

Tanjug, 141

Tass: described, 49; monitoring service closed, 182; immune as government agency, 215n30; mentioned, 141, 177

Telegraph, control of, 77, 143, 144

Telephonic radio, 163

Territorial jurisdiction, 164

Terrorist activity, banned, 70

Terrou, Fernand: on insulting foreign states, 126; on radio licensing, 163

Thailand: and freedom of speech, 116; protects Crown, 117; forbids propaganda by government, 124; Constitution, 231n15; bans propaganda causing unrest, 237n48; controls media, 241n65; censorship in, 242n82; and conformity, 243n82
—and Great Britain, treaty of 1940 banning intervention, 93

Third International. See Comintern

Time: on U.S. view of USSR, 20; banned, 156; mentioned, 32

Today, 45

Tomoya Kawakita v. U.S., 240n54, 240n60, 247n17

Trade Unions of the USSR, Central Council of, 50

Trail Smelter Arbitration case, 111

Transjordan, treaty of 1947 with Iraq banning subversion, 94. See also Jordan

Travel. See Emigration

Treason: in municipal laws, 137–39; committed abroad, 167–68

Treaties: as source of international law, 62; types of, 62; and third parties, 63, 217n2; and war crimes, 63; and individuals, 64; and municipal law, 65; and state responsibility, 65; limiting international propaganda, 66–96; abrogation of, 87; encouraging propaganda, 96–107; and propaganda, 199–200. See also individual states

Tribunal of Honor, press establishes, 67

Triepel, Heinrich: on hostile propaganda, 57; on responsibility for private propaganda, 58–59

Trotsky, Leon, 7

Truman, David B., defines propaganda, 10, 11

Truman, Harry S.: on truth and propaganda, 17; organizes postwar information activities, 23–24; launches Campaign of Truth, 26

Truman Doctrine, 177

Truth, Campaign of, launched, 26–27, 31

Tunisia: and freedom of speech, 115; no constitution in, 231n15

Turkey: and freedom of speech, 116, 119; restricts aliens, 119, 244n92; protects nationalism, 123; protects government authority, 124; and breach of peace, 132; and subversive organizations, 125;

outlaws Communist party, 135; controls wire service, 141; controls associations, 143; controls media, 143, 241n65, 241n68, 246n119; and censorship, 145; and information to foreign power, 146; controls disseminator, 154, 244–45n92; and radio set ownership, 162; controls radio manufacture, 163; and jurisdiction, 165; and foreign government employ, 169; Constitution, 231n15; bans subversion, 233n25; protects officials, 233n26; bans propaganda causing unrest, 237n48, 238n49; restricts doctrines, 239n52; and state secrets, 243n82; controls radio, 246n119; recognizes USSR, 253n83
—and Afghanistan, Iran, and Iraq, treaty of 1937 on nonintervention, 92–93, 94
—and Greece: treaty of 1930 banning subversive propaganda, 226n138; treaty of 1938 banning subversion, 94
—and Iraq, treaty of 1946 banning intervention, 93
—and Iraq and Great Britain, treaty of 1926 banning subversive propaganda, 226n138
—and Persia, treaty of 1932 banning subversive propaganda, 226n138
—and RSFSR, treaty of 1921 banning subversive propaganda, 225n129

Turner, F. v. Williams, 231n20

Uganda, and radio licenses, 163

Unification of Criminal Law, International Bureau for, and war propaganda, 68–69

Union of South Africa: controls media, 143; censorship in, 144, 242n82; and publishing radio news, 161; Constitution, 231n15; bans propaganda against people, 234n28; bans propaganda causing unrest, 237n48, 238n49; restricts doctrines, 239n52; and state secrets, 243n82; restricts disseminator, 245n92

Union of Soviet Socialist Republics: and protests, 7, 65, 175, 176–77, 178, 179, 249n9; begins foreign-language broadcasts, 7; and Communist propaganda, 8, 51, 175; and Western attitude toward, 20; and censorship, 46, 145; propaganda activities of, 46–54, 203; and book distribution, 47–48; and jamming, 47, 86, 87, 223n94; broadcasts of, 47; propaganda of diplomatic corps, 47; propaganda periodicals of, 48–52, 156, 187;

exchange programs of, 49; film distribution by, 49; and Western press, 51; peace propaganda of, 51; and satellite broadcasts, 53; nationalistic propaganda of, 53; propaganda evaluated, 54; and treaty responsibility, 66; and war propaganda, 71, 134, 179, 238n49; cultural treaties with satellites, 105; and freedom of speech, 117; and counterrevolutionary propaganda, 129, 135; protects its foreign security, 133; forbids assisting enemy, 137; controls media, 140, 241n65, 246n119; owns wire service, 141; registers radio sets, 142; access to information in, 146; and state secrets, 146; protests war propaganda, 179; institutes closed in Iran, 181; bans *British Ally*, 183; recognition of, 190, 191–95, 253n83, 254n99; founded, 192; attitude toward recognition, 195; and foreign correspondents, 196, 197; and treaties on propaganda, 200; Constitution, 231n15; protects state, 232n25; bans propaganda against people, 234n28; protects foreign states, 235n45; bans propaganda causing unrest, 238n49; restricts doctrines, 239n52; bans propaganda favoring foreign states, 240n53; and treason, 240n60; and state secrets, 243n82; controls radio, 246n119. *See also* RSFSR
—Armenian SSR, and treason, 240n60
—Azerbaijan SSR, and treason, 240n60
—Byelorussian SSR: bans propaganda against people, 234n28; and treason, 240n60
—Estonian SSR, and treason, 240n60
—Georgian SSR, and treason, 240n60
—Karelo-Finnish SSR, and treason, 240n60
—Kazakh SSR, and treason, 240n60
—Kirghiz SSR, and treason, 240n60
—Latvian SSR, and treason, 240n60
—Lithuanian SSR, and treason, 240n60
—Moldavian SSR, and treason, 240n60
—Tadjik SSR, and treason, 240n60
—Turkmen SSR, and treason, 240n60
—Ukrainian SSR: restricts doctrines, 239n52; and treason, 240n60
—Uzbek SSR, and treason, 240n60
—and Afghanistan: treaty of 1926 banning intervention, 225n112; treaty of 1931 banning intervention, 91; banning subversive propaganda, 225n129
—and Bulgaria: treaty of 1934 banning intervention, 91; treaty of 1948 banning intervention, 225n128; on cultural cooperation, 228n189
—and China: treaty of 1924 banning intervention, 224n112; treaty of 1945 banning intervention, 225n128; banning subversive propaganda, 225n129
—and China (Mukden), treaty of 1924 banning intervention, 224n112
—and Czechoslovakia, treaty of 1934 banning intervention, 91
—and Finland, treaty of 1948 banning intervention, 225n128
—and France, treaty of 1932 banning intervention, 91
—and Germany, notes of 1925 banning intervention, 225n112
—and Great Britain: notes of 1924 banning propaganda, 90; bans intervention, 193; notes of 1929 banning subversion, 91
—and Hungary: treaty of 1948 banning intervention, 225n128; on cultural cooperation, 228n189
—and Japan, treaty of 1925 banning subversion, 91
—and Norway, treaty of 1949 banning speech across border, 95
—and Persia, treaty of 1927 banning propaganda, 90–91, 225n129
—and Poland, treaty of 1945 of cooperation and nonintervention, 92
—and Romania: treaty of 1934 banning intervention, 91; treaty of 1948 banning intervention, 225n128; on cultural cooperation, 228n189
—and United States, notes of 1933 banning subversion, 91, 225–26n129
USSR Information Bulletin, ceases publication, 187
United Kingdom. *See* Great Britain
United Nations: Charter of, 17, 63–64, 71, 74, 172; and non-members, 63–64; Subcommission on Freedom of Information and the Press, 68, 86; and propaganda, 71, 201; condemns war propaganda, 71–72, 73, 200; condemns false news, 72, 73, 200; binding force of resolutions, 74; broadcasts jammed, 85; condemns jamming, 86; attacks censorship, 98–99; on freedom of information, 98, 99; on freedom of movement, 98, 99; advocates friendly propaganda, 99; and international disputes, 172; protests sent to, 178; and defini-

tion of propaganda, 200; and Nuremberg Trials, 206; mentioned, 34, 56, 189, 197. *See also* UNESCO

United Nations Educational, Scientific, and Cultural Organization (UNESCO): and Great Britain, 36; condemns war propaganda, 73; on freedom of information, 98; on cultural collaboration, 99; and Universal Declaration of Human Rights, 100

United Press: refuses to sell services to government, 26; mentioned, 20, 196

United States: propaganda expenditures of, 3; and protests, 7, 85, 175, 177, 178, 179, 186, 248n9; and recognition of USSR, 8, 190, 191, 194; begins international broadcasts, 9; radio reception in, 9; defines propaganda, 14; courts accept common definitions, 15; press attacked, 19; view of Japan, 19; cultural activities in Western Hemisphere, 22–23; propaganda activities of, 22–34; propaganda activities cut, 24; cultural exchanges of, 25–26; propaganda aims of, 25; private propaganda activities in, 26, 30–34; reorganizes information program, 27; and treaties, 65; and Tribunal of Honor, 68; condemns war propaganda and false news, 73, 219n34; rejects right of reply, 73; and Soviet jamming, 85; ignores wave-length allocations, 85; and freedom of speech, 115; bans propaganda against state, 121–22, 232n25; bans government propaganda at home, 124, 231n25; bans incitement to mutiny, 124; forbids incitement to murder, 124, 132; bans antireligious propaganda, 125; bans hatred propaganda, 125; protects foreign diplomats, 126; protects foreign states, 129, 236n45; and anarchists, 130, 136; and subversive organizations, 130, 135, 136, 239n52; bans belligerent propaganda, 130; bans revolutionaries, 130; ignores revolutionary propaganda against foreign states, 130; forbids breach of peace, 131–32; and crime through mails, 132; protects its international relations, 133; and Communists, 135, 153, 154, 169; and Nazi Bund, 136; and enemy propaganda, 138; and treason, 138, 167, 168, 240n60; controls media, 140, 143–44, 149, 241n68, 241n70, 246n119; controls radio, 140, 143–44, 149; licenses foreign broadcasts, 143; restricts aliens, 143–44, 149, 154, 170–71, 244n92; and film censorship, 144; and access to information, 145; and classified information, 146; and state secrets, 146, 243n82; and press offenses, 152; and radio offenses, 152–53; and press anonymity, 153; registers foreign agents, 154; excludes foreign publications, 156; and crimes abroad, 166; and jurisdiction, 166, 167, 168, 170–71; and foreign government employ, 169; and foreign travel, 169; accused of war propaganda, 179; information center closed, 181; and government propaganda abroad, 183–84; and relations with Bulgaria, 185; bans Polish center, 185; and recognition of Communist China, 190; and Comintern, 191–92; bars correspondents, 197; and use of Hungarian radio channel, 198, 223n94; on international law, 229n-7; Constitution, 231n15; protects officials, 233n26; bans propaganda against people, 234n28; bans propaganda causing unrest, 237n48, 238n49; re-examines Smith Act, 238n50; bans propaganda favoring foreign states, 240n53; controls disseminator, 244n92, 245n92

—and Germany, Federal Republic of, treaty of *1952* permitting U.S. radio propaganda, 107

—and Ireland: treaty of *1950* banning political activities, 95; on access to information, 106–7

—and Italy, treaty of *1948* on freedom of the press, 106

—and USSR, notes of *1933* banning subversion, 91, 225–26n*129*

United States Information Agency: established, 27–28; radio and television programs of, 28; documentary films of, 29; international press service of, 29; provides books, 29; incidents involving, 183–84, 187; Polish reprisals against, 197

United States Information and Education Act, 25

United States Information Service: and Berlin airlift, 18; activities of, 23; established, 23; investigated, 25; incidents in Yugoslavia, 181, 184; closed in Czechoslovakia, 184; closed in Poland, 184–85; closed in China, 185; closed in Romania, 185–86; closed in Hungary, 186

U.S. v. Bowman, 170
U.S. v. Burgman, 138, 240n53, 240n60
U.S. v. Davis, 247n10
U.S. v. Dennis, et al., 135, 232n25, 239n52
U.S. v. German-American Vocational League, Inc., 16, 213n13
U.S. v. Hautau, 12, 15–16
U.S. v. Pelley, 16, 213n13
U.S. v. Pink, 252n68
Universal Declaration of Human Rights, endorses freedom of expression, 97
Universality principle of jurisdiction, 164
Unrest, propaganda causing, 131–34
Upper Silesia, German and Polish propaganda in, 8
Uruguay: and freedom of speech, 116; bans propaganda by officials, 124; protects heads of state, 128; controls media, 143, 241n68; and jurisdiction, 171; and protests, 175; Constitution, 231n15; protects foreign states, 236n45; bans propaganda causing unrest, 238n49; bans war propaganda, 238n49; recognizes USSR, 254n99

Van Dyke, Vernon: on hostile propaganda, 57, 201; on responsibility for private propaganda, 60; on protection of diplomats, 126
Vatican City: and freedom of speech, 115; Constitution, 115, 231n15; protects heads of state, 128; controls news distributors, 143; protects foreign states, 236n45; controls media, 241n68
Vattel, Emer de: on subversive propaganda, 57; on responsibility for private propaganda, 58
Venezuela: and freedom of speech, 116; outlaws Communist party, 135; and censorship, 145; and foreign government employ, 169; Constitution, 231n15; bans propaganda causing unrest, 237n48; bans war propaganda, 238n49; and treason, 240n60; controls media, 241n65; controls disseminator, 245n92
—and Brazil, treaty of *1942* on cultural exchanges, 103
Verdross, A., 57, 60
Victory, 24
Viet Nam, Democratic Republic of: and freedom of speech, 115, 119; restricts aliens, 119; Constitution, 231n15
Viet Nam, Republic of, Constitution, 231n15

Vizetelly v. Mudie's Select Library, 243n-86, 244n92
Vogeler, Robert A., 182, 197–98
Voice of America: and Berlin airlift, 18; established, 23; activities of, 28; performance compared with BBC, 39–40; listening by Soviet satellites, 40, 160, 161; compared with Soviet broadcasts, 47; broadcasts protested, 86, 176, 184, 186; agreement with Germany, 107; broadcasts to China increased, 185; Hungarian incident involving, 198; mentioned, 30, 31
Voir, 24
VOKS: activities of, 49–50; institutes in Iran, 251n40
VOKS Bulletin, 48
Voorhis Act (U.S.), 154

War and the Working Classes, 48
War crimes, and treaties, 63. *See also* Nuremberg Trials
War mongering. *See* War propaganda
War propaganda: accusations, 65, 177, 178, 179; United Nations resolution on, 65, 200; condemned, 67–73, 219n34; forbidden under constitutions, 118; forbidden by municipal law, 132–34; in international law, 201
War Rights on Land, 203
"Waterfall" system of responsibility, 150
Wechsler, Herbert, on propaganda, 13
Wellington House (Great Britain), 34
West Rand Central Gold Mining Co., Ltd. v. The King, 229n5
Westlake, John, 57
White, Ralph K., 18
Whitton, John B., on hostile propaganda, 57, 201
Wilson, Elmo C., polls Hungarian listeners, 40
Wilson, Woodrow, 7
"Winds of Freedom," 33
Winterton, Earl, on British Council, 41
Wire services, controlled, 140–41
Women's Clubs, General Federation of, 31
Wong Wing v. U.S., 231n20
Woodward, J. L., 11
World Book Encyclopedia, 19
World Peace Congress, and war propaganda, 68
World Peace Council, 51
World Press Conference, on press and

international misunderstanding, 66–67, 96
World Publishing Co. v. Minahan, 243n85, 244n92
World War I, and beginning of systematic propaganda, 6
World-Wide Broadcasting System, Inc., 31
Wright, P. Quincy: defines propaganda, 10, 11; on hostile propaganda, 57
WRUL, 31

Yankee Network, In re, 241n70
Yeats, Steinberg, Stack, et al. v. U.S., 238n50
Yemen: and freedom of speech, 115; no constitution in, 231n15
—and Egypt, treaty of *1945* banning subversion, 94
Youmans v. Smith, 244n92
Young, Kimball, 11
Yugoslavia: Western attitude toward, 20; on false news, 71; on harmful propaganda, 71; protests jamming, 85–86; and freedom of speech, 117; protects convictions, 125; protects friendly nations, 129; bans alarmist reports, 131; forbids propaganda favoring enemy, 137, 240n53; owns wire service, 141; access to information in, 146; controls disseminator, 149, 245n92; restricts aliens, 149, 244n92; and foreign publications, 156–57, 158; and protests, 178;

expels correspondents, 180; bans USIS, 181, 184; USIS reopened in, 184; Constitution, 231n15; protects state, 232n25; bans subversion, 233n25; bans propaganda against people, 234n28; protects foreign states, 236n45; bans propaganda causing unrest, 237n48, 238n49; restricts doctrines, 239n52; controls media, 241n65, 241n70, 246n119; right of reply in, 243n82
—and Albania, treaty of *1947* on cultural exchanges, 105
—and Czechoslovakia, treaty of *1947* on cultural exchanges, 105, 228n186
—and Hungary: treaty of *1947* on cultural exchanges, 105; on friendly propaganda, 105
—and Italy, treaty of *1937* banning subversion, 92, 226n138
—and Poland, treaty of *1946* on cultural exchanges, 105
—and Romania: treaty of *1947* on cultural exchanges, 105; on friendly propaganda, 105

Z & F Assets Realization Corp. v. Howell, 252n68
Zellweger, Eduard, on responsibility for private propaganda, 59
Zinoviev, Grigori Evseevich: orders subversion in British army, 51–52; mentioned, 191, 193
Zollverein, The, 247n16